THE PERIPHERY OF THE EURO

Transition and Development

Series Editor: Professor Ken Morita
Faculty of Economics, Hiroshima University, Japan

The Transition and Development series aims to provide high quality research books that examine transitional and developing societies in a broad sense – including countries that have made a decisive break with central planning as well as those in which governments are introducing elements of a market approach to promote development. Books examining countries moving in the opposite direction will also be included. Titles in the series will encompass a range of social science disciplines. As a whole the series will add up to a truly global academic endeavour to grapple with the questions transitional and developing economies pose.

Also in the series:

The Periphery of the Euro
Monetary and Exchange Rate Policy in CIS Countries

Edited by

LÚCIO VINHAS DE SOUZA
European Commission, Belgium and the Kiel Institute for World Economics (IFW), Germany

and

PHILIPPE DE LOMBAERDE
United Nations University, Belgium

ASHGATE

Published by
Ashgate Publishing Ltd
Gower House
Croft Road
Aldershot
Hants GU11 3HR
England

Ashgate Publishing Company
Suite 420
101 Cherry Street
Burlington, VT 05401-4405
USA

Ashgate website: http://www.ashgate.com

British Library Cataloguing in Publication Data
The periphery of the Euro : monetary and exchange rate
    policy in CIS countries. - (Transition and development)
    1.Monetary unions - Former Soviet republics 2.Monetary
    policy - Russia (Federation) 3.Monetary policy - Belorussia
    4.Monetary policy - Ukraine 5.Euro area
    I.Souza, Lúcio Vinhas de II.Lombaerde, Philippe de
    332.4'947

Library of Congress Cataloging-in-Publication Data
The periphery of the euro : monetary and exchange rate policy in CIS countries /
[edited] by Lúcio Vinhas de Souza and Philippe De Lombaerde.
        p. cm. -- (Transition and development)
    Includes index.
    1. Monetary policy--Former Soviet republics. 2. Monetary unions--Former Soviet
republics. I. Lombaerde, Philippe de. II. Souza, Lúcio Vinhas de. III. Series.

    HG1072.P47 2005
    332.4'947--dc22

    ISBN-10: 0 7546 4517 7

2005026479

Printed and bound in Great Britain by Antony Rowe Ltd, Chippenham, Wiltshire.

Contents

List of Figures

List of Tables

Acknowledgements

This book arose from presentations made at the first meeting of the University Association for Contemporary European Studies (UACES) Study Group 'Monetary Policy in Selected CIS Countries', jointly organized by the Kiel Institute for World Economics (IFW) and the United Nations University – Comparative Regional Integration Studies (UNU-CRIS), and which took place at the UNU-CRIS premises at the College of Europe, in Bruges, Belgium, on July 12-13, 2004.

We would like to thank the UACES for the generous co-funding of this study group.

We are grateful to Eveline Snauwaert at UNU-CRIS for her outstanding job in co-organizing the workshop and preparing the camera-ready copy of the manuscript.

We are also indebted to Brendan George, Carolyn Court, Rosalind Ebdon and staff of Ashgate Publishing, and Luk Van Langenhove, Aurora Mordonu and Pascale Vantorre at UNU-CRIS.

Lúcio Vinhas de Souza
Philippe De Lombaerde

List of Authors

Bas van Aarle, Catholic University of Leuven, Belgium, and University of Nijmegen, Netherlands

Christian Bauer, University of Bayreuth, Germany

Olena Bilan, IERPC, Kyiv, Ukraine

Olga Butorina, Academy of Sciences, Moscow, Russian Federation

Vladimir Chaplygin, University of Kaliningrad, Russian Federation

Philippe De Lombaerde, United Nations University – Comparative Regional Integration Studies (UNU-CRIS), Bruges, Belgium

Akram Esanov, IFW, Kiel, Germany

Anne-Marie Gulde, International Monetary Fund, Washington D.C., United States

Bernhard Herz, University of Bayreuth, Germany

Etibar Jafarov, International Monetary Fund, Washington D.C., United States

Eelke de Jong, University of Nijmegen, Netherlands

Nina Leheyda, CDSEM, University of Mannheim, Germany

Christian Merkel, IFW, Kiel, Germany

Igor Pelipas, IPM, Minsk, Belarus

Vassili Prokopenko, International Monetary Fund, Washington D.C., United States

Gunther Schnabl, University of Tübigen and European Central Bank, Germany

Robert Sosoian, University of Nijmegen, Netherlands

Irina Tochitskaya, IPM, Minsk, Belarus and German Economic Team in Belarus, Minsk, Belarus

Ulvi Vaarja, Estonian Central Bank and Technical University of Tallinn, Estonia

Romain Veyrune, International Monetary Fund, Washington D.C., United States

Lúcio Vinhas de Souza, IFW, Germany, and European Commission, Brussels, Belgium

Chapter 1

The Periphery of the Euro:
An Introduction

Lúcio Vinhas de Souza and Philippe De Lombaerde

The aim of the studies collected here is to analyze a specific set of macroeconomic policies – namely, monetary and exchange rate policies – in selected Eastern European countries not covered (yet?) by the EU Enlargement process. Namely, the book has studies on the major CIS (Commonwealth of Independent States, the loose successor of the Soviet Union, bar the Baltic Republics) countries, but several of the studies use the new Eastern European EU member countries as a benchmark to study the CIS countries. Therefore, we analyze here current and prospective monetary and exchange rate policy options for them (for instance, the implications of the monetary (re)unification of Belarus and Russia, the viability of a floating cum inflation targeting in Russia and Ukraine). We also analyze the applicability of the EU monetary integration experience for them and, in an opposite direction, the prospects of a monetary (re)unification around the Russian Federation. To our knowledge, this is truly the first set of studies to formally deal with most of these questions.

Exchange rate policies in Eastern Europe since 1990

The debate concerning monetary integration in the European continent, both in Western and Eastern Europe, has been strongly influenced by the experience of the constitution of the euro area.[1] It is beyond the scope of this introduction to tell the story of the long and winding road towards the European Common Currency, the euro, from the 1970 'Werner Report', to the 1972 'Monetary Snake', to the 1979 'European Monetary System' and the Exchange Rate Mechanism (ERM) I (replaced by the ERM-II in 1993 after the series of speculative attacks experienced during 1992-93), to the 1989 'Delors Report', to the 'fixing' of the conversion rates in 1999 and the final physical introduction of the euro in January 2002.[2] Since

---

[1] Currently including Austria, Belgium, Finland, France, Germany, Greece, Ireland, Italy, Luxembourg, Netherlands, Spain and Portugal.

[2] See Vinhas de Souza and van Aarle (2004).

this date, the ECB – European Central Bank – has proven itself as a credible, effective central monetary authority, which is even more remarkable when one considers the many shocks experienced by the euro area during the brief period since 2002 (the deceleration of world economic growth in the beginning of the century, the oil price shock, the growing imbalances of the American economy and their effects on the euro-dollar bilateral exchange rate).

The expansion of the EU towards Eastern Europe, on 1 May, 2004 (when the Czech Republic, Estonia, Hungary, Latvia, Lithuania, Poland, Slovenia and Slovakia became EU members, with Bulgaria, Croatia and Romania expected to follow suit in 2007) has, in a rather real sense, 'brought the euro into Eastern Europe', as, with EU entry, the governors of the new member countries' central banks joined their western counterparts in the General Council of the ECB, a body that encompasses the central banks of all EU member-countries (who form the so-called 'European System of Central Banks' – ESCB – or 'Eurosystem'), regardless of their membership in the euro area. Beyond that, Estonia, Lithuania and Slovenia almost immediately after entry joined the ERM-II.

The path towards ERM-II and later euro memberships has not been homogenous for the new EU members: some chose hard currency regimes (currency boards), while others opted for floating exchange rate regimes, usually after an initial harder regime. In contrast to the founding member states of EMU, these new EU member states de jure do not have the right to opt out of the euro. As participation in ERM-II is a necessary precondition for the introduction of the euro and will take place only on request of the applicant country, they, however, *de facto* have discretion to decide when the introduction of the euro will happen. Participation in ERM-II with the exchange rate within the normal fluctuation bands for two years without tensions and devaluation is the key indicator in the assessment of exchange rate stability and constitutes one of the so-called Maastricht criteria, which have to be fulfilled before introduction of the euro. Unilateral adoption of the euro as a legal tender (euroization) is not acceptable from the standpoint of the Eurosystem and contradicts the 'spirit of the Treaty', which demands sufficient convergence in terms of nominal developments before the introduction of the euro.[3]

Given the lack of a clear EU membership perspective and the respective lack of a euro 'anchor', the experience of the non-Enlargement CIS countries with monetary independence is rather different. The dissolution of the Soviet Union at the end of 1991 did not immediately lead to the establishment of truly national monetary authorities capable of conducting an independent and effective monetary and exchange rate policy, as, until mid 1993, several of the former republics of the Soviet Union still used the rouble, the Russian national currency, and the central banks of those republics conducted their own policy simultaneously with the Bank of Russia. An interim period with the issuing of 'dirty floating' coupon currencies usually followed, which was more or less prolonged, depending on specific

---

[3]   See Schweickert, et al. (2004).

national circumstances (in the case of Ukraine, for instance, the new national currency, the hryvnia, was only introduced as late as 1996).

In practical terms, since 1995, when Russia introduced a sliding peg to the US dollar, all CIS countries, including the multiple pegs of Turkmenistan and Uzbekistan, seem to fix their exchange rates more or less tightly to the US dollar, either directly or via a targeting of the Russia rouble, which is itself targeting a nominal US dollar exchange rate (formally, from mid 1995 till August 1998, and informally, since 1999). This informal 'dollar zone' experienced a brief interruption caused by the Russian crisis of August 1998, which generated area-wide currency adjustments (effectively, devaluations of all the other CIS currencies towards the Russia rouble/US dollar), before a return to relative stability in 1999.

Therefore, in practical terms, the CIS may be characterized as a US dollar zone. There maybe structural reasons for that, as most CIS countries heavily depend on the export of commodities, which are still quoted in US dollars. Nevertheless, the euro has growing importance, due to the very strong trade and investment links of almost all CIS countries with the euro area, specially after the 2004 Enlargement. Additionally, the political changes in Ukraine opened the possibility of EU – and euro area – Enlargements towards some CIS countries themselves. Recent announcements by some CIS monetary authorities concerning the potential targeting of a euro/dollar basket as a way to introduce more exchange rate flexibility may also be seen as an indication of this.

The recent debate on regional monetary integration outside the EMU

The debate on monetary and exchange rate policies in the periphery of the euro-zone is connected to the new and worldwide debate on the adequacy (and optimality) of exchange rate regimes in transition and developing countries, triggered by the constitution of the EMU, on the one hand, and the Asian financial crisis at the end of the 1990s, on the other hand. The debate has also been stimulated by the 'rediscovery' of optimum currency area (OCA) theory and the progress that has been made in developing empirical tools to assess the OCA criteria.

According to the conventional view (based on de jure exchange rates) at least, exchange rates in the post-Bretton Woods period first moved in the direction of intermediate regimes, but 'moved back' to the two extremes of the policy spectrum (flexible exchange rates or hard pegs) since the 1990s. This phenomenon is known as the bi-polar view (Fischer, 2001). The bi-polar view is not only an empirical interpretation of recent monetary history but also a normative statement on the adequacy of exchange rate policies at the turn of the millennium in a world of more mobile capital. The intermediary systems are seen as being difficult to implement credibly and sustainably. Although this bi-polar view is shared by many analysts, there is no consensus however on the generality of the policy device. Bordo (2003), for example, defends the case for intermediate systems for transition countries that are lacking financial and institutional maturity to let their currency float freely. No consensus is reached either on the empirical facts or on their interpretation. On the basis of alternative classifications of de facto exchange rates, the bi-polar view seems less evident.[4]

Hard pegs and currency unions

Concentrating on the hard peg policy option, different countries have experimented with classical hard pegs, pegs to baskets, dollarization and monetary unions.

Currency unions outside Europe include the CFA zone (consisting of the West African Economic and Monetary Union – WAEMU – and the Central African zone), and the Eastern Caribbean Currency Union. Both currency areas have their roots in colonial times and institutions. The central banks of the CFA zone and the pound based currency board in the Caribbean were all established in the 1950s.[5] At the Lomé meeting of ECOWAS in 1999, heads of State proposed detailed plans for expanding the WAEMU integrating both francophone and anglophone states in West Africa. The idea of a Caribbean Monetary Union covering all CARICOM members was launched by the governors of the central banks in 1992.

To these experiences we should add the rand zone around South Africa, which is a combination of a currency board and regional cooperation between central banks, and a dollar zone in the Americas, now covering Panama (since 1904), Ecuador (since 2000) and El Salvador (since 2001).

All in all, regional monetary integration, even if we include the asymmetrical varieties, is thus (still) not that important. However, currency unions have been discussed in political and/or academic circles in ASEAN, SAARC, MERCOSUR, Andean Community, Central America, NAFTA, the East African Community Customs Union, and so on.

Ex post analyses

The experiences with monetary integration in Africa and the Caribbean have allowed for *ex post* type analyses that might have some relevance for other regions, especially where a combination of low incomes and weak economic institutions are found.[6]

The main findings of these studies can be summarized as follows.[7] As far as the incidence of monetary integration on growth is concerned, the result of simple methodologies (comparing growth performances of currency union members with

---

[4]   See, for example, Reinhart and Rogoff (2004).

[5]   In 1976, the Eastern Caribbean dollar was fixed in terms of the dollar, as a consequence of the devaluations of the pound and the uncertainties in the international financial system.

[6]   For a recent review of the CFA experience, see Fielding (2004).

[7]   See Cuyvers, et al. (2005).

those of control groups) are very much dependent on the choice of the control group. But if Sub-Saharan Africa is taken as a control group, CFA seems to show systematically higher growth rates than non-members. A similar result is obtained for the Eastern Caribbean Currency Union, taking CARICOM as a control group. With more sophisticated methodologies (explaining residuals from estimated growth models in terms of currency union membership) positive growth differentials are found but apparently are not significant.

There is empirical evidence that currency union membership significantly lowers inflationary expectations and inflation levels. Unilateral pegs work as nominal anchors but their effect on inflation appears to be lower than, for example, the effect of the CFA.

Ex ante OCA tests

As mentioned before, the methodological developments in OCA testing, triggered by the debate on the EMU and its optimal size, have spilled-over to policy research in other parts of the world. A (very) brief summary of this material reveals the following.[8]

Both CFA zone and Southern African rand zone show substantial amounts of heterogeneity and shock asymmetry, which suggests that alternative architectures should theoretically be considered. In the CFA zone, there is also evidence of endogeneity of the OCA criteria (Frankel and Rose, 1998), monetary integration causing more intensive intra-regional trade and higher correlation of shocks.

Work on monetary integration in the Americas generally finds that NAFTA, Mercosur and CARICOM are not OCAs.[9] Central America might be an exception as it shows higher levels of shock correlation. In this case, however, it is not necessarily clear whether a classical currency union would be superior to dollarization.

The work on East and Southeast Asia is not very conclusive but still different sub-groups with OCA properties have been identified. Many authors suggest gradual scenarios for monetary integration in that region but are doubtful of the political will to make this happen.

Monetary integration outside the EU: Research agenda

From the different policy experiences and prospects and the results of the academic work so far, a research agenda can be visualized.

First, more research should be directed towards the analysis of the effect of monetary integration on the quality and effectiveness of monetary policy, especially in countries with 'weak' monetary institutions (for example

---

[8]   See Cuyvers, et al. (2005) for more details.

[9]   Although sub-groups of for example MERCOSUR do have certain characteristics of OCAs.

quantification of gains of more independent regional central banks) and/or small countries (for example technical economies of scale in central bank operations and reserve pooling).

Second, research should be devoted to the different institutional and constitutional designs of monetary integration and their implications. Whereas in many countries fixing the exchange rate is the competence of the central bank, dollarization and the adoption of a different legal tender is a matter of the parliament. Decision-making processes in these two kinds of institutions are quite different.

Third, outside the EU, the external exchange rate of new currency unions becomes an issue. The cost-benefit evaluation of the currency union will depend on the choice of the external exchange rate, as for example in Central America or the Gulf Cooperation Council.

Fourth, more attention should go to the dynamic aspects of monetary integration and the Enlargement issue. Whereas OCA theory focuses basically on the evaluation of OCA characteristics for a given set of countries, for countries that are peripheral to existing monetary unions like the EMU, issues related to the entry-decision, the moment of entry, asymmetries, gradualism, the interaction between informal and formal money substitution (as in Latin America), chain effects and chaotic processes and so on, become more important. Because of the endogeneity of the OCA criteria (Frankel and Rose, 1998), the issue is not so much about whether a set of countries fulfills the OCA conditions *ex ante* but rather whether some minimum values (critical thresholds) for the relevant variables are reached *ex ante* so that the OCA conditions can be reached *ex post* through the endogeneity mechanisms. In evaluating the OCA conditions for countries in transition or development, one should also be aware of the fact that the application of OCA theory will not necessarily provide time-consistent results and policy prescriptions (De Lombaerde, 2004).

Finally, more research should be devoted to the role of political will, regional leadership/hegemony, regional political stability, institutions, regional linkage building and policy preference convergence (Cohen, 2003), and, in general, to the political economy of monetary integration.

Objectives and outline of the book

This book is structured as follows:

Part I of the book (EU Enlargement and Euroization) starts with the contribution by Gunther Schnabl (University of Tübingen and European Central Bank, Germany), where he compares the experience of CIS and East Asian countries, given that many of those countries, in spite of being classified as free floaters, *de facto* pursue dollar pegs. This chapter emphasizes the dollar denomination of short-term and long-term payment flows as reasons for exchange rate stabilization. Based on the analysis of 'competitive depreciations' and 'competitive appreciations' among the CIS and East Asian currencies it argues that the adherence to a common external anchor currency enhances macroeconomic stability. Finally, the potential of euro and rouble (CIS) as well as yen and yuan (East Asia) to challenge the dollar as anchor currencies in the respective regions is explored.

The following chapter, by Romain Veryune (International Monetary Fund, Washington DC, United States), highlights the importance of the trade off between credibility and flexibility, by studying currency boards in the new EU member states and remaining EU candidate countries, and their capacity to effectively bring down inflation to a low and stable level in a speedier manner than floating currencies.

In chapter 3, Ulvi Vaarja (Estonian Central Bank and Technical University of Tallinn, Estonia) studies how the collapse of the Soviet Union led to the creation of several newly independent countries, and the different choices in their monetary policy that laid the base for both the diversified outcomes one observes today and their future prospects. It concentrates the analysis in the comparison between the clear EU option made by the Baltic republics, as opposed to the Russia-centric policy of Belarus.

Part II of the book (Russia/CIS) starts with the contribution by Olga Butorina (Academy of Sciences, Moscow, Russian Federation), who examines the main principles, forms and tools of intergovernmental financial and monetary cooperation, in order to determine their applicability for the CIS.

In the following chapter, Christian Bauer and Bernhard Herz (University of Bayreuth, Germany), show that several CIS central banks have chosen the exchange rate as an intermediate policy target. Based on a microstructure model of the foreign exchange market with heterogeneous and technical traders, they classify *de facto* exchange rate regimes and derive a market based measure of the credibility of these regimes. Their results indicate that markets assign a relatively high degree of credibility to the exchange rate management of the CIS countries, albeit the paths to this credibility were quite different.

The final chapter of this part, by Christian Merkel, Akram Esanov (both IFW) and Lúcio Vinhas de Souza (IFW, Germany, and European Commission, Brussels, Belgium) reviews the recent conduct of monetary policy and the central bank's rule-based behaviour in Russia. Using different policy rules, they test whether the central bank in Russia reacts to changes in inflation, output gap and the exchange rate in a consistent and predictable manner. Their results indicate that during the period 1993-2002 the Bank of Russia has used monetary aggregates as a main policy instrument in conducting monetary policy.

Part III (Belarus) starts with the contribution by Igor Pelipas (IPM, Minsk, Belarus), who examines the influence of the different monetary aggregates on the consumer price index in Belarus during 1992-2002, evaluating the information content of these monetary aggregates and their usefulness in forecasting inflation and conducting monetary policy.

The following chapter, by Igor Pelipas (IPM, Minsk, Belarus) and Irina Tochitskaya (IPM, Minsk, Belarus and German Economic Team in Belarus, Minsk, Belarus), uses a time series framework to investigate the convergence of monetary policy indicators for Belarus and Russia, in the context of the potential creation of a monetary union between these two countries. Their results indicate that in 2001-2003 the coordination of monetary policy between the two countries in fact did not occur, raising additional doubts that Belarus is ready to introduce the Russian rouble as a legal tender.

In the same vein, the next chapter, by Anne-Marie Gulde, Etibar Jafarov, and Vassili Prokopenko (International Monetary Fund, Washington DC, United States) discusses the costs, benefits, and implementation challenges of a possible currency union between Belarus and Russia. It shows that Belarus and Russia are economically closely linked but nevertheless do not fulfil all 'optimal currency area' criteria, especially the macroeconomic symmetry condition. Furthermore, they argue that the different speeds of economic liberalization over the past decade have resulted in different economic structures, with Belarus still dependent on monetary financing of budgets and industries. However, they conclude that a final cost-benefit analysis also needs to consider that currency unification *may* bring substantial benefits from reduced transaction costs, an improved macroeconomic environment in Belarus, and by acting as a potential catalyst to advance structural reforms in Belarus.

Closing this part, the contribution by Vladimir Chaplygin (University of Kaliningrad, Russia) further discusses the probability of the creation of a monetary union between Russia and Belarus. He also discusses whether is it possible to launch the Russian rouble as a common currency for some of the regions and states in the CIS and what are the ways to do so.

The final part of the book (Ukraine), starts with the work by Bas van Aarle (Catholic University of Leuven, Belgium and University of Nijmegen, Netherlands), Eelke de Jong and Robert Sosoian (University of Nijmegen, Netherlands), who develop and estimate a dynamic open macro-econometric model of the Ukrainian economy, decomposing it into an official economy and its unofficial counterpart, and analyzing the adjustment process in both those parts of the economy.

In the following chapter, Nina Leheyda (CDSEM, University of Mannheim, Germany) investigates the determinants of inflation in Ukraine, applying cointegration analysis and error-correction modelling. It concludes that the exchange rate, wages and foreign prices have long-run effects upon inflation, while in the short-run inflation is determined by inertia, money supply, wages, exchange rate and real output as well as some exogenous shocks. The chapter concludes with policy implications.

Finally, in the last chapter of the book, Olena Bilan, (IERPC, Kyiv, Ukraine) discusses how the monetary and exchange rate policies have developed in Ukraine since the introduction of hryvnia in 1996. It gives a brief historical overview of the exchange rate arrangements, analyzes the current state of affairs in the realm of

The Periphery of the Euro: An Introduction9

monetary and exchange rate policy, and outlines implications for the medium-term future. She puts a particular emphasis on the specific features of monetary transmission mechanisms in Ukraine. The chapter concludes with an assessment of the viability of an inflation-targeting regime for Ukraine – a goal considered feasible over the medium-term by the local monetary authorities.

References

Bordo, M.D. (2003), 'Exchange Rate Regime Choice in Historical Perspective', *IMF Working Paper*, 160.
Cohen, B.J. (2003) 'Are Monetary Unions Inevitable?', *International Studies Perspectives*, 4, 3: 275-92.
Cuyvers, L., De Lombaerde, P., de Souza, E. and Fielding, D. (2005), 'Regional Monetary Cooperation and Integration', in M. Farrell, B. Hettne and L. Van Langenhove (eds), *Global Politics of Regionalism*, Pluto Books, London.
De Lombaerde, P. (2004), 'Optimum Currency Area Theory, Inter-Industry Labour Mobility and Industrial Development Paths', *Economia Internazionale*, LVII, 4: 429-39.
Fielding, D. (ed.) (2004), *The CFA Franc Zone 10 Years After Devaluation*, Special issue of *Journal of African Economies* (Oxford University Press), 13, 4.
Fischer, S. (2001) 'Exchange Rate Regimes: Is the Bipolar View Correct?', *Distinguished Lecture on Economics in Government*, American Economic Association, New Orleans, 6 January.
Frankel, J. and A. Rose (1998) 'The Endogeneity of the Optimum Currency Area Criteria', *The Economic Journal*, 108: 1009-25.
Reinhart, C.M. and Rogoff, K.S. (2004), 'The Modern History of Exchange Rate Arrangements: A Reinterpretation', *Quarterly Journal of Economics*, 119, 1: 1-48.
Schweickert, R., Gern, K.-J., Hammermann, F. and Vinhas de Souza, L. (2004) 'European Monetary Integration after the 2004 EU Enlargement', *Kiel Institute for World Economics Discussion Papers Series*, 431.
Vinhas de Souza, L. and van Aarle, B. (eds) (2004), *The Euroarea and the New EU Member States*, Palgrave-Macmillan Press, Basingstoke.

PART 1
EU ENLARGEMENT
AND EUROIZATION

Chapter 2

International Capital Markets and Exchange Rate Stabilization in the CIS and East Asia

Gunther Schnabl

Introduction

In 1997-98 a wave of financial and currency crises hit both East Asia and the Commonwealth of Independent States (CIS). Both regions suffered from the collapse of dollar pegs, toppling financial sectors and deep recessions. The following discussion about crisis prevention focused on more flexible exchange rate regimes to avoid misalignments and sharp adjustments of macroeconomic fundamentals (Fischer, 2001).

Despite the painful experiences of collapsing dollar pegs, exchange rate stabilization seems to have widely persisted. Calvo and Reinhart (2002) identify two reasons for this 'fear of floating'. When appreciation occurs, declining exports render governments unwilling to allow for exchange rate movements. In the face of depreciation liability dollarization endangers financial stability and therefore provides an incentive to stabilize exchange rates.

More recently, the discussion on the rationales for exchange rate stabilization has been extended to asset dollarization (McKinnon and Schnabl, 2004b) as the former East Asian crisis countries have become creditor countries. Similarly the CIS, Russia and more recently the Ukraine have run sustained current account surpluses, thereby accumulating increasing stocks of international dollar assets. Because foreign currency denominated assets imply a risk for domestic investors when the exchange rate fluctuates this may explain the persistence of exchange rate stabilization in both East Asia and the CIS.

Building upon the East Asian experience (McKinnon and Schnabl, 2004a; McKinnon and Schnabl, 2004b) this chapter tests for de facto exchange rate policies in the CIS and explores the rationale for exchange rate stabilization in both regions.

De jure versus *de facto* exchange rate stability in East Asia and the CIS

The current discussion about adequate exchange rate policies for developing countries and emerging markets is based on the 1990s wave of currency and financial crises in East Asia, Eastern Europe and Latin America. While the origins of the Russian crisis (1998) were to be found in country specific characteristics such as the economic structure, political failures in the transformation process, and fragile institutions, it had much in common with the previous Asian crisis (1997-98).

Like the East Asian countries, before the crisis Russia and its neighbouring (CIS) countries had pursued fixed exchange rate strategies against the US dollar. The soft pegs to the dollar in combination with high interest rate differentials against the US favoured speculative capital inflows and a deterioration of the current account position. These made the economies vulnerable to capital outflows and depreciation.

In both the CIS and East Asia, the reversal of short-term capital flows and the resulting collapse of the dollar pegs brought losses to the balance sheets of financial institutions with un-hedged currency exposures. Rising interest rates, which originated from attempts to stabilize the exchange rates, accelerated the wave of bankruptcies. Similarly to East Asia – where the collapse of several dollar pegs originated in Thailand – the sharp depreciation of the Russian rouble triggered a wave of depreciations in most of Russia's small neighbouring countries.

The case for exchange rate flexibility

The 1997-98 wave of speculative attacks against (soft) dollar pegs in the CIS, East Asia, and Latin America led to the conclusion that in emerging markets open to international capital flows soft pegs were prone to crisis. To avoid further turmoil the IMF recommended floating exchange rates to circumvent the gradual build-up of misalignments. Countries were recommended to either move towards flexible exchange rates or to pursue very hard pegs (currency boards or dollarization) (Fischer, 2001).

More specifically for the CIS, Keller and Richardson (2003: 11) have argued that 'excessively stable' nominal exchange rates may reinforce dollarization and thereby make it difficult to maintain control over monetary aggregates in the face of large capital inflows. The consequence would be a serious misalignment of exchange rates and an increasing risk of crisis.

As in East Asia (McKinnon and Schnabl, 2004a) and in Central and Eastern Europe (Schnabl, 2004), the IMF's bi-polar view of exchange rate arrangements is reflected in the CIS official exchange rate arrangements. Except for the hard peg of the Ukraine and the crawling peg of Belarus all CIS exchange rate arrangements are de jure classified as (managed or independently) floating.[1]

Pre- and post-crisis de facto exchange rate stability

The official IMF exchange rate arrangements have been criticized as inaccurate. Several studies – for instance by Calvo and Reinhart (2002) and Levy-Yeyati and Sturzenegger (2002) – have argued that countries continue to stabilize exchange rates while they are officially labeled free or managed floaters.

To assess de facto exchange rate stability in the CIS, pre-crisis and post-crisis exchange rate stabilization are compared here. Based on Calvo and Reinhart (2002), two criteria are used: monthly percentage exchange rate changes and monthly percentage changes of official foreign reserves.[2]

Nominal exchange rate volatility is a robust indicator for exchange rate stabilization. Within a world of free international goods and capital movements, exchange rate volatility – such as between the freely floating dollar and euro – is high. If, following Calvo and Reinhart (2002), the probability (P) is low (high) that monthly exchange rate changes fall outside an (arbitrary) band of, for instance, ±2.5 per cent, the currency can be rated as fixed (freely floating). Further, standard deviations (σ) of the nominal exchange rates indicate exchange rate stabilization if they are significantly lower than for the euro/dollar rate.

Governments stabilize exchange rates by intervening in foreign exchange markets. To prevent the domestic currency from appreciating (depreciating), the monetary authorities sell (buy) domestic currency in exchange for dollars, euros or yen. The stronger the efforts to stabilize the exchange rate, the higher is the probability (P) that monthly changes in official foreign reserves fall outside a predetermined band of – say – ±2.5 per cent.[3]

The results for the CIS countries are reported in Table 2.1 for the period before (January 1995 to July 1998) and after (January 2000 to December 2004) the Russian crisis. Similar to East Asia (except Japan)[4] the CIS countries pursued dollar pegging before the 1998 Russian crisis. While exchange rate volatility for some CIS countries is high, the indicator for the volatility of foreign reserves

---

[1] Turkmenistan and Uzbekistan have adopted multiple exchange rate systems with the dollar as a reference currency.

[2] Interest rates may serve as an additional tool for exchange rate stabilization, but they may be subject to considerable bias due to official interest rate controls.

[3] Official foreign exchange reserves not only change through foreign exchange intervention, but also for other reasons, such as government payments in foreign currency and interest receipts on foreign exchange reserves. Further, the dollar value of foreign exchange reserves is altered if the dollar exchange rate of third reserve currencies changes. Nevertheless high volatility of reserves is a clear indication for exchange rate stabilization.

[4] A detailed assessment of *de facto* exchange rate stability in East Asia has been conducted by McKinnon and Schnabl (2004a).

before the crisis gives a clear indication of exchange rate stabilization. The fluctuations of foreign reserves in all CIS countries are clearly higher than for the 'benchmark' free floaters US and euro area.

In addition, the volatilities of the nominal dollar exchange rates are significantly lower than for the euro/dollar exchange rate in Armenia, Azerbaijan, Georgia, Moldova and Russia. Higher exchange rate volatility in Belarus, Kazakhstan, the Kyrgyz Republic, Tajikistan and the Ukraine can be attributed to downward crawling pegs, since the volatility of reserves is high in these countries. Fully flexible rates would imply high exchange rate volatility in combination with low volatility of reserves.

During the Russian crisis – which started in August 1998 – all CIS currencies, with the exception of the Armenian dram and the Azerbaijan manat, suffered from sharp (but controlled) depreciations (Figure A.2.1). This is shown by a strong increase in the volatility of both nominal exchange rates and foreign reserves.[5]

There is evidence in favour of a return to dollar pegging in the CIS after the crisis. As shown in table 2.1, we observe less nominal exchange rate volatility than before the crisis for eight out of ten currencies: the Armenian dram, the Azerbaijan manat, the Belarusian rouble, the Kazakhstani tenge, the Kyrgyz som, the Russian rouble, the Tajik somoni and the Ukrainian hryvnia which has been tightly pegged to the dollar since late 2001.

Only the Moldovan lei and the Georgian lari exhibit more de facto exchange rate volatility after the Russian crisis than they did before the crisis, but much less volatility than the euro against the dollar. High volatility of foreign reserves in all countries is in line with this finding.

As all CIS countries, including the multiple pegs of Turkmenistan and Uzbekistan, fix their exchange rates more or less tightly to the dollar, the CIS seems to be on an informal dollar standard similar to East Asia before and after the Asian crisis.

Post-crisis the CIS dollar standard seems to be even more homogenous than the East Asian dollar standard, as in post-crisis East Asia exchange rate volatility against the dollar seems to have increased (Figure A.2.2). Some countries are reducing exchange rate fluctuations against the Japanese yen at lower frequencies while keeping their exchange rates fixed to the dollar at higher frequencies (McKinnon and Schnabl, 2004a). In contrast, in the CIS the dollar is the only anchor currency.

---

[5]   The estimation results are not reported for the sake of brevity.

Table 2.1   Pre- and post-crisis CIS exchange rate stabilization

| | Exchange Rate ($) | | | | Foreign Reserves ($) | | | |
| | P | | σ | | P | | σ | |
	Pre	Post	Pre	Post	Pre	Post	Pre	Post
Armenia	9.30%	3.85%	1.36%	0.97%	83.72%	34.69%	17.21%	3.48%
Azerbaijan	2.33%	0.00%	2.00%	0.21%	72.09%	61.22%	235.7%	8.12%
Belarus	42.86%	28.85%	4.59%	2.19%	86.05%	73.47%	17.23%	13.24%
Georgia	0.00%	5.77%	0.61%	1.26%	81.82%	63.27%	11.08%	6.59%
Kazakhstan	23.26%	1.92%	2.21%	0.72%	74.42%	81.63%	10.06%	5.65%
Kyrgyz Republic	18.60%	5.77%	2.95%	1.35%	82.86%	42.86%	19.87%	4.71%
Moldova	0.00%	7.69%	0.64%	1.37%	67.44%	57.14%	15.25%	5.06%
Russia	5.41%	0.00%	1.18%	0.78%	88.37%	75.51%	19.56%	5.36%
Tajikistan	55.81%	21.15%	15.18%	2.13%	77.78%	63.27%	20.16%	9.80%
Ukraine	23.26%	0.00%	3.37%	0.28%	76.74%	89.80%	21.33%	8.03%
US ($/€)	25.58%	32.69%	2.19%	2.59%	32.56%	30.61%	4.37%	2.43%
Euro Area (€/$)	25.58%	32.69%	2.19%	2.59%	n.a.	12.24%	n.a.	1.67%

Source: IMF, IFS. The indicators refer to percentage changes of monthly dollar exchange rates and foreign reserves. 'P' marks the probability that the respective criterion falls outside the predetermined band. 'σ' marks the standard deviation of the respective indicator. 'Pre' indicates the Russian pre-crisis period from January 1995 up to July 1998. 'Post' indicates the Russian post-crisis period from January 2000 up to June 2004. For Turkmenistan and Uzbekistan no data are available.

International Capital markets as rationale for informal dollar pegging in the CIS

McKinnon and Schnabl (2004a) provide the rationale for 'fear of floating' in East Asia. They argue that most developing countries and emerging markets are not able to choose their exchange rate regimes exogenously based on specific targets of economic policy making (such as reducing the risk of speculative crisis). Rather, the regime choice is interpreted as endogenous, determined by several interdependent factors inherent to developing countries and emerging markets: the need for macroeconomic stabilization, dollar invoicing of international trade, and dollar denomination of international capital flows.

Although macroeconomic stabilization and international goods markets have been traditionally regarded as the main driving forces of exchange rate stabilization, international capital flows have gained increasing importance as an explanatory variable for exchange rate policies (Eichengreen and Hausmann, 1999; McKinnon and Schnabl, 2004b).

Liability dollarization in debtor countries

As put forward by Eichengreen and Hausmann (1999), the rationale for exchange rate stabilization in emerging markets springs from underdeveloped capital markets ('original sin').

Due to a long tradition of inflation and depreciation, banks and enterprises in emerging markets and developing countries cannot use their currencies to borrow abroad or to borrow long-term, even domestically.[6] International creditors lend in dollars or euros and thereby shift the exchange rate risk of open positions in foreign debt to the debtor countries. The consequence is either a currency mismatch – projects that generate domestic currency are financed with foreign currency – or a maturity mismatch – long-term projects are financed with short-term loans.

Even emerging markets with a quite long record of price stability seem hardly to be able to borrow internationally in their domestic currencies. Instead, global investors typically denominate their claims in very few major international currencies – mostly dollar and euro and, to a lesser extent, yen, pound Sterling and Swiss franc. This dollar (or euro) liabilization creates an incentive for exchange rate stabilization at both high frequencies, that is, day-to-day or week-to-week exchange rate fluctuations, and low frequencies, that is, month-to-month or year-to-year exchange rate fluctuations.

---

[6]   Recently in the new Central and Eastern European EU member states a long-term bond market in domestic currencies has emerged. This can be attributed to the fact that the new EU members have the unique opportunity to import the reputation of the European Central Bank credibly by anticipating EMU membership.

Exchange rate stabilization at high frequencies Original sin affects exchange rate stabilization in emerging markets at high frequencies (McKinnon and Schnabl, 2004a). Most international short-term payment transactions of emerging markets and developing countries are denominated in US dollars or euros. The degree of dollarization of payment flows can be assumed to be even higher in dollarized economies such as the CIS.

Keller and Richardson (2003) and Mongardini and Mueller (1999) provide evidence for a high degree of dollarization in the Kyrgyz Republic and other CIS economies including Russia and the Ukraine. Keller and Richardson (2003) find evidence for ratchet effects (hysteresis): Once a country has achieved a high degree of dollarization, it may persist even if inflation returns to moderate levels. Oomes (2003) observes payment dollarization in Russia for large household transactions as well as for intra-CIS trade.

Because domestic capital markets are underdeveloped and shallow, an active forward market in foreign exchange against the dollar – or euro – is for the most part non-existent. If hedging instruments are available, individual owners of dollar liabilities see the cost of forward cover, that is the premium on buying dollars forward with the domestic currency, to be too high. The foreign exchange risk of short-term capital transactions typically remains un-hedged.

The government can provide an informal hedge for private short-term capital transactions by keeping the exchange rate stable at a daily or weekly (high frequency) basis. If short-term exchange rate fluctuations are minimized, private banks and enterprises can repay their short-term foreign currency (dollar or euro) liabilities with minimal exchange rate risk. This compensates for an underdeveloped private market in forward exchange.

As shown by McKinnon and Schnabl (2004a) for East Asia and by Schnabl (2004) for the Central and Eastern European countries governments tend to control exchange rate fluctuations of their currencies on a day-to-day basis. In order to assess high-frequency exchange rate volatility in the CIS, Figure A.2.3 plots the daily exchange rate fluctuations of the CIS currencies against the dollar. The euro/dollar exchange rate, which is widely acknowledged as a freely floating currency, is used as a benchmark. If day-to-day exchange rate fluctuations are significantly lower than for the euro/dollar rate it is taken as an indication of official exchange rate stabilization.

The individual currency plots in Figure A.2.3 show very clearly that since the crisis high frequency exchange rate volatility is significantly lower than for the euro/dollar rate in all CIS currencies. For Kazakhstan, Russia and the Ukraine where longer time series are available, the stabilization process after the Russian crisis can be observed.

Similarly, as shown in Figure A.2.4 the East Asian countries (except Japan) have tended to manage exchange rate fluctuations in their day-to-day operations. Exchange volatility against the dollar is significantly smaller for all East Asian countries (except Japan) than for the freely floating euro/dollar exchange rate.

Exchange rate stabilization at low frequencies From a low frequency perspective
the rationale for exchange rate stabilization in debtor countries originates in long-
term liability dollarization. If net debt is denominated in foreign currency, long-
term exchange rate stability is equivalent to reducing default risk on balance sheets
(Eichengreen, Hausmann and Panizza, 2003a, 2003b).

Exchange rate fluctuations affect the servicing and repayment costs of foreign
currency debt in terms of domestic currency. Specific, sharp depreciations put the
balance sheets at risk, possibly forcing indebted enterprises and financial
institutions into default. Even low-frequency exchange rate fluctuations around a
constant level incorporate a risk for the financial systems, as the increasing
uncertainty is likely to be reflected in higher risk premiums on domestic interest
rates.

Before the crisis in East Asia, the later crisis economies Indonesia, Korea,
Malaysia, Philippines, Thailand had – based on sustained current account deficits –
accumulated large stocks of foreign debt, denominated mostly in US dollars. When
the dollar pegs collapsed the foreign liabilities became inflated in terms of
domestic currency, leaving enterprises and financial institutions with high foreign
currency exposures bankrupt.

To shield domestic enterprises and financial institutions against volatile risk in
their balance sheets the government may control low-frequency exchange rate
fluctuations. Exchange rate stability enhances the stability of the domestic financial
system which contributes to macroeconomic stability, lower (real) interest rates
and thereby higher growth.

Empirical estimations by Eichengreen, Hausmann and Panizza (2003a) show
that liability dollarization is prevalent in most emerging markets and developing
countries which tend to be international net debtors. As shown in Table A.2.1 all
smaller CIS countries (except Russia and Ukraine) have run current account
deficits within the time period with data available. Rising international dollar
liabilities result from the fact that sustained current account deficits imply capital
imports.

In addition to dollarization of foreign assets, Keller and Richardson (2003: 19)
have observed liability dollarization in domestic CIS capital markets in the form of
dollar bank loans or mortgages. If a considerable part of domestic liabilities is
denominated in dollars, banks become even more vulnerable to exchange rate
fluctuations (Berg and Borensztein, 2000: 9).

Asset dollarization in creditor countries

While liability dollarization provides a rationale for exchange rate stabilization in
the smaller CIS debtor countries it cannot explain why Russia (and the Ukraine) –
which are becoming, based on sustained current account surpluses, increasingly
international creditors – are stabilizing the exchange rates of rouble and hryvnia
against the dollar. Similarly, although all East Asian countries are transforming
themselves into international creditors since their crisis, they have returned to

exchange rate stabilization. Even Japan, which has accumulated large international dollar assets since the early 1980s, has tempted to stabilize the yen against the dollar (Hillebrand and Schnabl, 2003).

McKinnon and Schnabl (2004b) explain the rationale for exchange rate stabilization in creditor countries which are not able to lend in their domestic currencies. Due to underdeveloped financial markets, capital controls or even simply the fact that dollar assets seem to be a more reliable store of value than the domestic currencies, private investors find dollar assets more attractive than claims on foreigners denominated in their home currencies. Even Japan, which has a highly developed capital market, holds its international assets mainly in US dollars.

Inversely, the United States as the largest debtor country by far is disinclined to hold debts denominated in foreign currencies. The position of the US dollar as the world's prominent international currency allows US private and public agents to borrow in domestic currency. The exchange rate risk of international lending is shifted to the creditors.

Exchange rate stabilization at high frequencies By fixing exchange rates at high frequencies the government can hedge the risk for private, short-term international lending. Potential market makers, such as banks, cannot easily cover transactions that involve buying the domestic currency forward for dollars because a convenient array of interest-bearing domestic bonds liquid at different terms to maturity is unavailable to hold.

The government can provide an overall hedge by minimizing exchange rate fluctuations on a daily or weekly basis. In specific for Russia and Kazakhstan, which are large exporters of raw materials and crude oil, these revenues are invoiced in US dollars. By minimizing exchange rate fluctuations on a daily basis as shown in Figure A.2.3, the governments provide a hedge for short-term income flows, even if the private sector is net creditor.

Exchange rate stabilization at low frequencies At low frequencies, the motivation for exchange rate stabilization by international creditor countries can be linked to the perception of risk by private and public holders of net foreign currency assets. For instance, as shown in Table A.2.1, Russia has run current account surpluses for most of the past decade that amount to roughly 200 billion US dollars. The current account surpluses are even more substantial in East Asia where all countries are running saving surpluses at least since the Asian crisis (Table A.2.2). The net international assets of Japan, which has run current surpluses since the early 1980s, are an estimated 1.5 trillion dollars. These stocks of international assets are overwhelmingly held in US dollars, for a considerable part in US government bonds.

In addition, and in contrast to East Asia, even Russia's domestic assets are partially held in US dollars. Keller and Richardson (2003: 19) distinguish asset dollarization in the form of dollar-denominated bank deposits (deposit dollarization) or holdings of dollar cash (currency dollarization). This makes Russia even more vulnerable to appreciations of the domestic currency.

If private Russian (Chinese or Japanese) investors accumulate their surplus current account earnings[7] in US dollars, they become anxious about appreciations of the domestic currency because their dollar assets would loose value in terms of domestic currency. This '*fear of appreciation*' may be compensated by higher interest rates in the debtor country as suggested by the open interest rate parity.[8] Yet with varying interest rates in the anchor country the perception of risk may change and runs into the domestic currency may occur. The depreciation pressure on the anchor currency may become sustained if inflation expectations in the anchor country rise.

Oomes (2003) argues for Russia and the Ukraine that in highly dollarized economies expected appreciation may cause runs into domestic currency and thereby de-dollarization. Once private investors decide to repatriate their international assets – or decide to convert domestic dollar assets into domestic rouble, yuan or yen assets – the governments may worry because the appreciation of the domestic currency will erode the competitiveness of the domestic export industry.

The upshot is that the governments in East Asia and the CIS may find it worthwhile to dampen appreciation pressure by foreign exchange intervention. Through the official dollar purchases private foreign assets are substituted by public foreign assets while the exchange rate is kept at levels which are perceived to be safe for domestic export enterprises and financial institutions.

As a result we observe a fast built-up of foreign reserves in both East Asia and the large CIS creditor countries Russia and the Ukraine (Figure A.2.5 and Figure A.2.6). In particular, since early 2002 when the dollar started its sustained depreciation against the euro, the foreign reserves have increased even faster.

Network externalities of common informal anchors

As shown above, liability and asset dollarization provide a strong incentive for any individual country in the CIS and East Asia to peg their exchange rate to the dollar. Driven by the increasing US demand for international goods and capital an increasing number of emerging markets are transforming themselves into international creditors. Hard or soft pegs to the dollar reduce the risk of short-term and long-term international lending thereby contributing to the macroeconomic stability of any individual creditor country.

Frankel (1999) has argued that no single currency regime is right for all countries at all times. Yet uncoordinated exchange rate strategies within a group of

---

[7]   The accumulation of liquid dollar assets can be accelerated by large FDI flows.

[8]   Such an interest rate differential in combination with yen appreciation has been observed between Japan and the US for more than two decades.

highly economically integrated countries or of countries competing in the same export markets may hinder intra-regional trade and disturb macroeconomic stability.

Intra-regional trade

Oomes (2003) attributes the persistence of dollarization in the CIS to domestic and international network externalities in the use of US dollars. As trade flows in all CIS countries are denominated in dollars, trade invoicing in dollars reduces the transaction costs for intra-regional trade.

McKinnon and Schnabl (2004a) argue that for East Asia the common adherence to the dollar has enhanced East Asian trade linkages by reducing transaction costs for intra-regional trade flows. Exchange rate stability against the dollar is argued to be more important for the intra-East Asian trade than for trade with the anchor country.

Figure 2.1 shows the regional composition of CIS exports in comparison to East Asian exports with focus on exports to the US, the EU25 and intra-CIS trade. For the CIS countries, much like in East Asia, the motivation for dollar pegging does not primarily arise from strong trade ties with the United States. Exports to the US as a percentage of overall exports range from close to 0 per cent for Tajikistan up to 8 per cent in Armenia.

In contrast, intra-regional exports account for about one third of total CIS exports and to about 50 per cent of East Asian exports. By jointly pegging their currencies to the dollar, the CIS and East Asian countries create a zone of intra-regional exchange rate stability which reduces transaction costs for intra-regional trade and thereby payment flows.

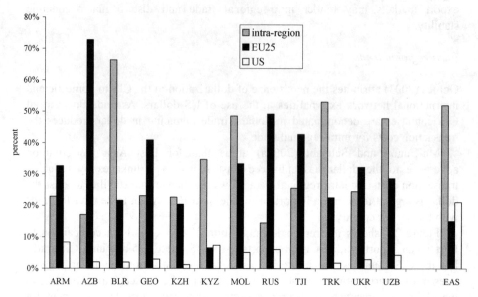

Figure 2.1   Exports by region of the CIS countries (2002)

Source: IMF: Direction of Trade Statistics. ARM = Armenia, AZB = Azerbaijan, BLR = Belarus, GEO = Georgia, KZH = Kazakhstan, KYZ = Kyrgyz Republic, MOL = Moldova, RUS = Russia, TJI = Tajikistan, TRK = Turkmenistan, UKR = Ukraine, UZB = Uzbekistan, EAS = East Asia (arithmetic average).

Macroeconomic stability

Due to the fact that both the CIS and East Asia are informal (and not institutionalized) dollar standards, they are far from having achieved maximum intra-regional exchange rate stability. While all CIS and East Asian countries stabilize exchange rates against the dollar, the individual countries have opted for different degrees of exchange rate stabilization (section two). The Ukraine, China, Hong Kong and Malaysia have chosen hard pegs to the dollar, Russia, Kazakhstan, Moldova, Korea, Taiwan and many other smaller CIS and East Asia countries have allowed for more flexible (soft) pegs. Small countries at the peripheries such as Belarus and Indonesia still allow considerable depreciations of their currencies.

Competitive depreciations
The choice of different degrees of exchange rate stability within economically integrated regions may interfere with the macroeconomic stability of the region, in particular if exchange rates of large countries fluctuate. Given close economic linkages and competition in third markets (such as the US for East Asia and the euro area for the CIS) secular depreciations of individual currencies cause deflation

in neighbouring countries. The incentive to let the currencies depreciate as well increases. If 'beggar-thy-neighbour depreciations' spread around a highly economically integrated region crisis may be the result.

This effect will be more pronounced the larger the countries which opt for depreciation, the larger the number of the depreciating currencies, and the more open the countries which are affected by depreciation. In pre-crisis East Asia the depreciation of the Japanese yen against the US dollar eroded the international competitiveness of Japan's small neighbouring countries (McKinnon and Schnabl, 2003), thereby contributing to the outbreak of the crisis and sharp depreciations of the Thai baht, the Korean won, the Indonesian rupiah, the Malaysian ringgit, and the Philippine peso (Figure A.2.2).

The depreciations of six East Asian currencies not only caused a deep recession in the crisis economies, but also in the neighbouring countries Hong Kong, Singapore and Taiwan which were able to sustain their dollar pegs. The outcome was an unprecedented recession for both the crisis and non-crisis economies (except China).

While in East Asia the depreciation originated in a smaller economy (Thailand) and spread to only some members of the East Asian dollar club, during the Russian crisis the competitive depreciations originated in the – by far – largest economy of the region. Not surprisingly, the collapse of the Russian rouble in August 1998 was followed by depreciations of most smaller CIS currencies including the Ukrainian hryvnia. Only Armenia and Azerbaijan, where trade is strongly focused on the euro area (Figure 2.1), were able to avoid the collapse of their dollar pegs.

To this end, the common adherence to one (external) peg will reduce the degree of competitive depreciations. Macroeconomic stability increases, the probability of crisis declines, and the growth potential is higher.[9] This insight can be seen as the main motivation for the creation of international currency arrangements such as the Bretton-Woods System in the 1940s or the European monetary integration process.

Competitive appreciations   While competitive depreciations originate within a setting of a stable anchor currency and macroeconomic instability at the periphery, the inverse case (competitive appreciations) may apply if monetary expansion in the anchor country accelerates.

Let's assume a scenario where money supply in the anchor country is growing faster than in the countries at the periphery of an informal dollar standard. The monetary expansion – even if it does not translate immediately into increasing consumer price inflation – may affect inflation expectations. If private investors adjust their international portfolios, the anchor currency gets under (sustained) depreciation pressure.

---

[9]   De Grauwe and Schnabl (2004) show for the Central and Eastern European economies that exchange rate stability against the euro can be associated with higher growth. This finding is even more robust if high inflation countries are included into the sample.

Appreciation pressure on the domestic currencies can induce different policy reactions at the periphery. The monetary authorities may show benign neglect and allow for the appreciation of the domestic currency. Prices for exports in foreign currency rise and dollarized international assets lose value. The appreciation of the domestic currency can be neglected more easily if exports (as per cent of GDP) are comparatively low and if international assets and liabilities can be issued in domestic currency.

Smaller, more open economies where growth depends strongly on exports may be concerned about the competitiveness of their export industries. Large international creditors such as Russia, China and Japan may become anxious about runs into the domestic currency, as sustained appreciation expectations may drive interest rates towards zero. The monetary authorities will be inclined to absorb (parts of) the domestic currency purchases (dollar sales) to prevent the domestic currency from appreciation.

During the 1990s, as shown in Figure A.2.5 and A.2.6, Russia and the Ukraine as well as all East Asian countries accumulated massive international reserves through foreign exchange intervention. The build-up of official dollar reserves has accelerated since early 2002 when the dollar came under sustained depreciation pressure.

Accelerating dollar purchases, as observed in the CIS and East Asia, induce inflationary pressure on the economy because the domestic money supply expands. Inflation may emerge in different sectors of the economy. At an earlier stage, stock and real estate markets may react sensibly to the monetary expansion. Asset price bubbles may be the consequence. Later on – as currently observed in China, Russia and the Ukraine – consumer price inflation is likely to increase.

Faced with the danger of inflation and overheating, the governments at the periphery have two options. If, as is currently the case in the Ukraine and China, the government is committed to a hard peg, the build-up of foreign reserves and the monetary expansion will be particularly fast. The only option to steer against overheating would be the sterilization of foreign exchange intervention.

To absorb the liquidity overhang, the monetary authorities may issue bonds and increase interest rates, providing the central bank has sufficient control over the banking sector. But inefficient banking sectors and underdeveloped financial markets may make it more difficult to tighten money supply. Because interest rate hikes will deteriorate growth prospects, the government may hesitate to slow down the economy.

In this environment it may be easier to let the currency appreciate in a controlled fashion on a monthly and yearly basis while keeping the exchange rate stable at high frequencies. The gradual adjustment of the exchange rate will slow down the growth of foreign reserves. The risk of inflation and overheating declines.

Once one country of the informal dollar standard has opted for appreciation the incentive for the others to follow increases. With the appreciation of, say, the Russian rouble the exports of the Ukraine to Russia and to third markets become more competitive. While the rising exports seem beneficial for the Ukraine initially, the additional growth stimulus may not be welcome in times of accelerating inflation.

Therefore, the Ukraine or China may decide to counteract inflation by letting its currency appreciate as well. This tendency may be enforced by mercantile pressure from trading partners, complaining about 'unfair' competition if the exchange rate is kept 'undervalued'. This mercantile pressure is likely to originate in the anchor country where imports from the periphery increase as countries prevent the appreciation of their currencies (McKinnon and Schnabl, 2004b).[10]

Patterns of competitive appreciations have recently emerged in both the CIS and East Asia. As shown in Figure A.2.1, since early 2002 the Russian rouble, the Georgian lari, the Kazakhstani tenge, the Kyrgyz som and the Tajik somoni have started to appreciate against the dollar. In contrast, the Ukraine has adhered to its hard dollar peg and therefore faces higher inflation.

In East Asia, Korea, Taiwan, Japan and Thailand have allowed controlled appreciations of their currencies against the dollar since early 2002. China, which has maintained its hard dollar peg, faces the danger of overheating, while Japan and the US exert pressure on the Chinese government to let its currency appreciate. China resists the revaluation of the yuan to avoid negative impacts on its export industry thereby risking a hard landing. The overhang in money supply is partially absorbed by sterilization efforts.

Outlook: Alternatives to the dollar as anchor currency in East Asia and the CIS

As shown in section two in both the CIS and East Asia, exchange rate stabilization against the dollar persists. An important rationale for stabilizing exchange rates originates in capital markets, that is, the inability to borrow or lend in domestic currencies (section three). Furthermore, as shown in section four, the common adherence to one external anchor currency enhances regional macroeconomic stability.

Liability and asset dollarization also explain why local currencies are unlikely to challenge the dollar as an anchor currency. As capital markets in both the CIS and East Asia (except Japan) remain underdeveloped, and will not become

---

[10] An exemplifying case study of such competitive appreciations is the collapse of the Bretton-Woods System in the early 1970s. The decision of the German central bank to abandon its parity against the dollar led to gradual appreciation of all central and northern European currencies. The joint appreciation of the European currencies which was institutionalized by the European (trade) integration process also included the Swiss franc which did not formally participate in the attempts to stabilize intra-EU exchange rates.

sufficiently developed in the near future, the chances for the Russian rouble and the Chinese yuan to emerge as local anchor currencies are currently low.

But what about the yen in East Asia or the euro in the CIS? To provide an international (anchor) currency the respective country has to fulfil both 'structural criteria' (large GDP, large trade volume and large capital markets) and 'political criteria' (low inflation, moderate government debt and a freely floating exchange rate). Although the Japanese yen presently seems to have a more important role as anchor currency in East Asia than the euro for the CIS (section two), the future prospects for the euro may be brighter.

Despite the large size of the Japanese domestic and export market and highly developed financial markets, Japan may currently not fulfill the political pre-conditions. The growth of money supply is high and volatile, while deflation persists. An unprecedented level of government debt among the OECD countries may signal higher inflation in the future. Japan seems unable to lend internationally in domestic currency. As Japanese monetary authorities have tended to stabilize the yen against the dollar, there is less need for the smaller East Asian countries to stabilize exchange rates against the yen.

In contrast, the euro fulfills both the structural and political pre-conditions for an anchor currency for the CIS. The Euro Area constitutes a large (closed) economy, with a large volume of international trade and with highly developed capital markets. Inflation is low and government debt in the Euro Area has been (on average) comparatively moderate. Euro Area enterprises and financial institutions are able to lend and to borrow internationally in domestic currency. The euro is floating freely without noteworthy foreign exchange intervention.

Although presently the CIS countries have few incentives to re-peg their currencies to the euro due to a high degree of dollarization, this may change in the future as appreciation pressure on the CIS currencies contributes to de-dollarization (Oomes 2003). The incentive to re-peg the CIS currencies to the euro springs from trade linkages which are particularly strong for Russia, as by far the largest economy of the region. If the rouble would be re-pegged to the euro, the smaller CIS countries would be obliged to follow in order to sustain the macroeconomic stability of their economies (see section four).

Appendix

Table A.2.1   CIS current accounts in comparison to the US (1990-2003)

	1990	1991	1992	1993	1994	1995	1996	1997	1998	1999	2000	2001	2002	2003
Per cent of GDP														
Armenia	-2.3%	0.0%	-61.6%	-7.6%	0.9%	-13.4%	-18.5%	-16.6%	-20.8%	-16.6%	-14.6%	-10.0%	-6.6%	-7.1%
Azerbaijan	1.6%	1.0%	-16.6%	-12.2%	-10.3%	-13.2%	-25.9%	-23.1%	-30.7%	-13.1%	-3.6%	-0.9%	-12.3%	-28.3%
Belarus	0.5%	0.8%	5.4%	-12.1%	-9.1%	-4.4%	-3.6%	-6.1%	-6.7%	-1.6%	-2.7%	-3.5%	-2.6%	-2.9%
Georgia	-0.8%	-0.5%	-2.4%	-40.3%	-33.8%	-14.8%	-10.8%	-10.5%	-10.2%	-7.8%	-4.4%	-6.5%	-6.0%	-7.5%
Kazakhstan	-22.9%	-7.1%	-51.6%	-8.6%	-7.8%	-3.2%	-3.6%	-3.5%	-5.4%	-0.1%	4.2%	-4.0%	-3.5%	-0.2%
Kyrgyz Rep.	-4.2%	8.2%	-5.7%	-15.7%	-10.8%	-16.0%	-23.2%	-8.3%	-22.9%	-15.7%	-5.3%	-2.0%	-2.2%	-2.3%
Moldova	-0.6%	0.5%	-4.5%	-13.4%	-6.8%	-7.9%	-11.1%	-14.2%	-17.3%	-6.0%	-9.0%	-4.9%	-6.0%	-9.3%
Russia	-0.5%	0.5%	-1.4%	1.4%	1.9%	1.4%	2.1%	-0.6%	-0.8%	11.3%	17.2%	10.9%	8.9%	8.3%
Tajikistan	-10.8%	3.7%	-16.8%	-27.5%	-17.3%	-17.0%	-6.7%	-5.0%	-8.3%	-3.4%	-6.3%	-7.1%	-2.7%	-1.3%
Turkmenistan				13.2%	16.2%	-0.3%	0.1%	-21.6%	-32.7%	-14.8%	8.4%	1.7%	6.5%	4.6%
Ukraine	-0.4%	-1.7%	-3.0%	-6.1%	-5.9%	-5.2%	-2.7%	-3.0%	-3.1%	2.6%	4.7%	3.7%	7.5%	5.8%
Uzbekistan	-2.5%	14.4%	-6.6%	-7.8%	1.8%	-0.2%	-8.8%	-4.0%	-0.8%	-0.8%	1.6%	-1.0%	1.2%	8.9%
Billions of Dollars														
Total CIS	-15.85	1.54	-3.24	0.13	2.51	0.26	2.49	-8.91	-9.56	20.70	46.32	32.84	32.25	36.63
Total US	-78.97	3.75	-48.01	-81.99	-117.68	-105.22	-117.20	-135.98	-209.56	-296.82	-413.45	-385.70	-473.94	-530.67

Source: IMF, World Economic Outlook. Shaded areas indicate current account surpluses.

Table A.2.2   East Asian current accounts in comparison to the US, 1990-2003

	1990	1991	1992	1993	1994	1995	1996	1997	1998	1999	2000	2001	2002	2003
							Per cent of GDP							
Japan	1.45	1.96	2.97	3.02	2.72	2.10	1.40	2.25	3.02	2.57	2.52	2.11	2.83	3.2
Singapore	8.45	11.32	11.87	7.24	16.17	17.67	15.16	15.58	22.59	18.60	14.48	19.00	21.50	30.9
Taiwan	6.96	7.11	4.14	3.14	2.66	2.07	3.91	2.43	1.29	2.78	2.86	6.36	9.09	10.0
Indonesia	-2.61	-3.32	-2.00	-1.33	-1.58	-3.18	-3.37	-2.27	4.29	4.13	5.32	4.88	4.52	3.9
Korea	-0.79	-2.82	-1.25	0.29	-0.96	-1.74	-4.42	-1.71	12.73	6.03	2.65	1.93	1.28	2.0
Malaysia	-1.97	-8.51	-3.67	-4.46	-6.06	-9.71	-4.43	-5.92	13.19	15.92	9.41	8.28	7.58	11.1
Philippines	-6.08	-2.28	-1.89	-5.55	-4.60	-2.67	-4.77	-5.28	2.37	9.48	8.24	1.84	5.38	2.1
Thailand	-8.53	-7.71	-5.66	-5.09	-5.60	-8.07	-8.07	-2.00	12.73	10.13	7.60	5.40	6.05	5.6
China	3.13	3.32	1.36	-1.94	1.28	0.23	0.88	4.09	3.30	2.11	1.90	1.46	2.86	2.1
Hong Kong									1.53	6.40	4.28	6.11	8.50	11.0
United States	-1.36	0.06	-0.76	-1.23	-1.66	-1.42	-1.50	-1.54	-2.34	-3.14	-4.19	-3.90	-4.59	-4.9
							Billions of US Dollars							
Total East Asia	54.51	73.75	117.48	117.80	132.85	93.83	44.17	129.37	244.51	231.69	213.68	179.14	238.88	255.19
Total US	-78.96	3.69	-48.03	-81.95	-117.71	-105.19	-117.16	-127.68	-204.67	-290.87	-411.46	-393.74	-480.86	-541.80

Source: IMF, World Economic Outlook. Shaded areas indicate current account surpluses.

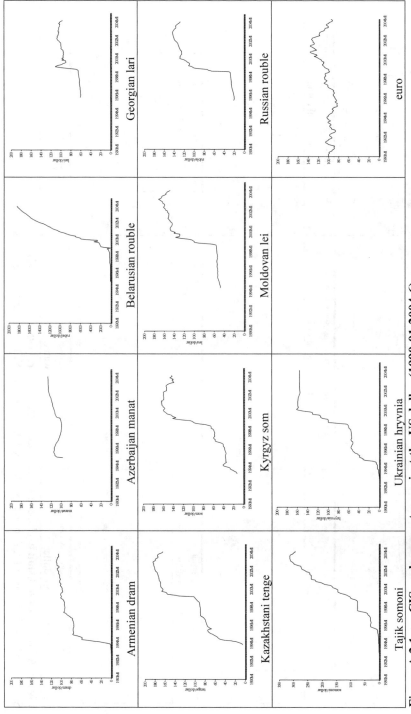

Figure A.2.1   CIS exchange rates against the US dollar (1990:01-2004:6)
Source: IMF, IFS. Index 1998:01 = 100. Note different scales for the Belarusian rouble and the Tajik somoni.

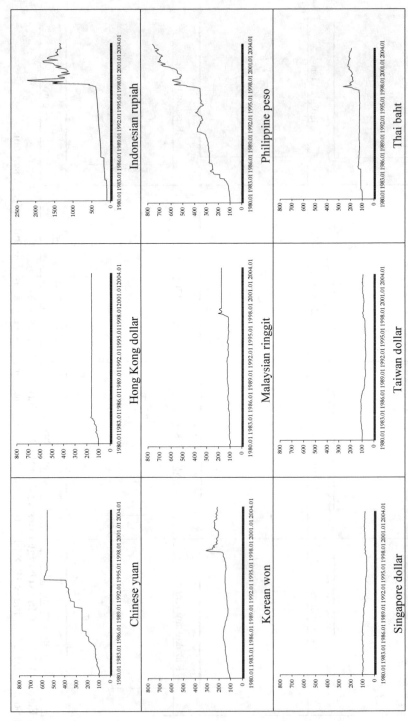

Figure A.2.2   East Asian exchange rates against the dollar, (1980:01-2004:04)
Source: IMF, IFS, Central Bank of China. Index 1980:01=100. Note different scale for Indonesia.

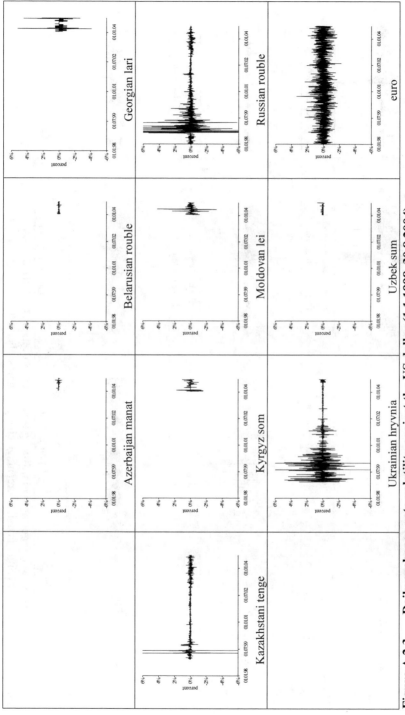

Figure A.2.3   Daily exchange rate volatility against the US dollar (1.1.1998–30.8.2004)
Source: Datastream. Volatility is daily percentage changes against the dollar.

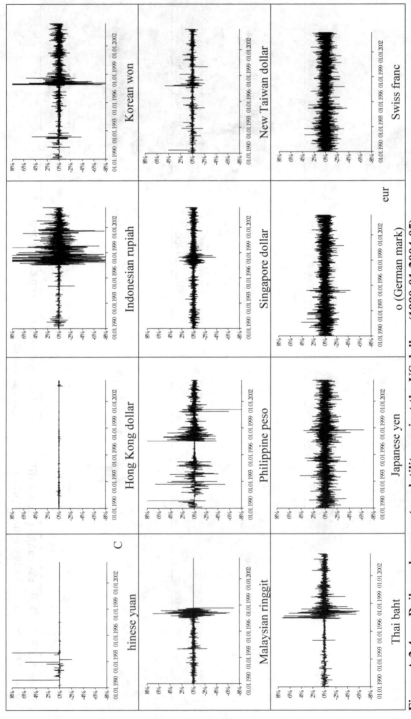

Figure A.2.4　Daily exchange rate volatility against the US dollar, (1990:01-2004:05)
Source: Datastream. Volatility is daily percentage changes against the dollar.

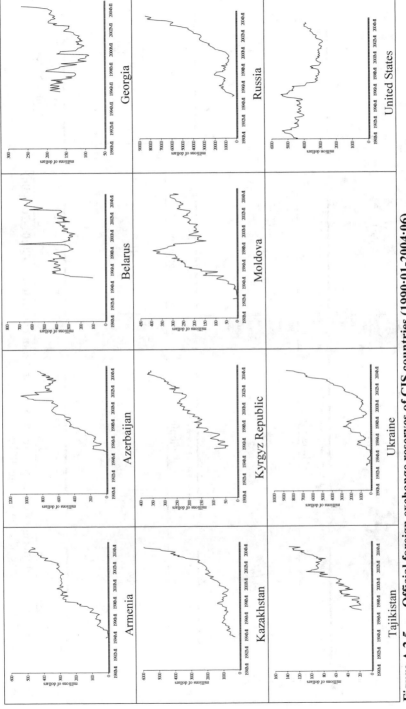

Figure A.2.5   Official foreign exchange reserves of CIS countries (1990:01-2004:06)
Source: IMF, IFS. Millions of dollars. Note different scales.

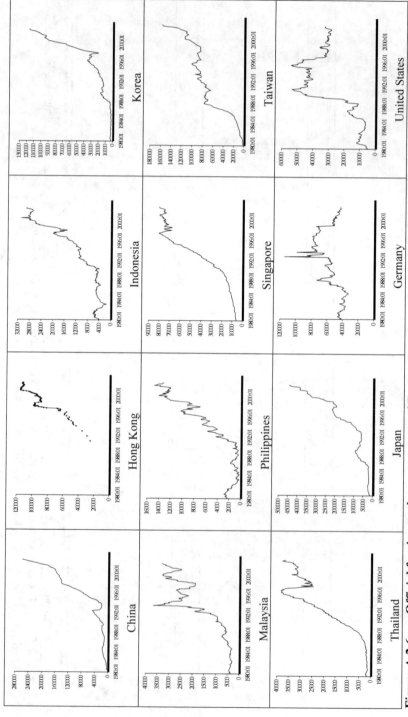

Figure A.2.6   Official foreign exchange reserves of East Asian countries, (1980:01-2004:06)
Source: IMF, IFS. Millions of dollars. Note different scales.

References

Berg, A. and Borensztein, E. (2000), 'The Choice of Exchange Rate Regime and Monetary Target in Highly Dollarized Economies', *IMF Working Paper*, 00/29.

Calvo, G. and Reinhart, C. (2002), 'Fear of Floating', *Quarterly Journal of Economics*, 117: 379-408.

De Grauwe, P. and Schnabl, G. (2004), 'Exchange Rate Regime and Macroeconomic Stability in Central and Eastern Europe', *CESIfo Working Paper*, 1182.

Eichengreen, B., and Hausmann, R. (1999), 'Exchange Rates and Financial Fragility', *NBER Working Paper*, 7418.

Eichengreen, B., Hausmann, R. and Panizza, U. (2003a), *The Pain of Original Sin*, Mimeo.

Eichengreen, B., Hausmann, R. and Panizza, U. (2003b), *The Mystery of Original Sin*, Mimeo.

Fischer, S. (2001), 'Exchange Rate Regimes: Is the Bipolar View Correct?', *Journal of Economic Perspectives*, 15: 3-24.

Frankel, J. (1999), 'No Single Currency Regime is Right for All Countries or at All Times', *Princeton Essays in International Finance*, 215.

Hillebrand, E. and Schnabl, G. (2003), 'The Effects of Japanese Foreign Exchange Intervention: GARCH Estimation and Change Point Detection', *JBICI Discussion Paper*, 6.

International Monetary Fund, *Annual Report on Exchange Rate Arrangements and Exchange Restrictions*, Washington DC: IMF (various issues).

Keller, P. and Richardson, T. (2003), 'Nominal Anchors in the CIS', *IMF Working Paper*, 03/179.

Levy-Yeyati, E. and Sturzenegger, F. (2002), *Classifying Exchange Rate Regimes: Deeds vs. Words*, Mimeo.

McKinnon, R. and Schnabl, G. (2003), 'Synchronized Business Cycles in East Asia and Fluctuations in the Yen/Dollar Exchange Rate', *The World Economy*, 26, 8: 1067-88.

McKinnon, R. and Schnabl, G. (2004a), 'The East Asian Dollar Standard, Fear of Floating, and Original Sin', *Review of Development Economics*, 8: 331-60.

McKinnon, R. and Schnabl, G. (2004b), 'The Return to Soft Dollar Pegging in East Asia: Mitigating Conflicted Virtue', Forthcoming in *International Finance*.

Mongardini, J. and Mueller, J. (1999), 'Ratchet Effects in Currency Substitution: An Application to the Kyrgyz Republic', *IMF Working Paper*, 99/102.

Oomes, N. (2003), 'Network Externalities and Dollarization Hysteresis: The Case of Russia', *IMF Working Paper*, 03/96.

Schnabl, G. (2004), 'De Jure Versus De Facto Exchange Rate Stabilization in Central and Eastern Europe', *Aussenwirtschaft*, 59, 2: 171-90.

Chapter 3

From the Planned Economy to Independent Monetary Policy: A Study of the Baltic Countries' Decisions and Developments

Ulvi Vaarja

Introduction

The collapse of the Soviet Union led to a creation of numerous independent countries that began the transition from a centrally planned to a market economy. In the process they came to make radically different choices in their monetary policy that laid the base for the diversified outcomes of today and prospects for the future.

The chapter aims to analyse the decisions taken in the Baltic countries for breaking away from the rouble-system and using tight monetary policy to curb inflation. Estonia and Lithuania used the most radical method – the peg to a foreign currency under the currency board arrangement, and Latvian currency is fixed to the IMF's accounting unit the SDR.

The chapter compares the decisions taken with the ones that have kept their close neighbour Belarus tightly connected to Russia and intending to form a monetary union with it.

Since all the countries looked at in the chapter had or have close relations with the International Monetary Fund via assistance from the organization in their first years of regained independence, the chapter briefly looks at the influence of the IMF on the decisions taken by the countries.

The second section of the chapter gives an overview of the theoretical background of the decisions taken by the countries and elaborates on the implications of these theories.

The third section is on the introduction of the independent monetary policy and local currency in the three Baltic countries giving the background for the decisions made and a chronology of them.

The fourth section discusses the developments since the introduction of the pegs giving an overview and chronology, but also the inflationary and economic growth outcomes in the Baltics

The fifth section gives a short insight into the situation of the financial sector in the respective countries.

The sixth section gives an overview of the developments in Belarus contrasting the clear cut break-away from the Soviet system by the Baltic countries with the radically different direction taken by their close neighbour.

Theoretical basis for the decisions taken by the Baltic countries

The theoretical basis for the monetary policy decisions taken by the Baltic countries lies in the theories of pegged exchange rate regimes having a strong curbing impact on inflation and via that enhancing overall economic growth. The idea of using an exchange rate based stabilization lies in choosing an exchange rate system that determines the rate at which foreign exchange transactions take place and the accompanying institutional arrangements and policies have to be consistent with it.

Some of the theoretical background in both the Baltics and Belarus cases is also given in the theory of optimum currency areas, which suggests that countries benefit from adopting the same anchor as trade partners, since this reduces their bilateral exchange rate variability. Meissner and Oomes find that, after controlling for other factors (such as country size, openness, and colonial history), the probability of choosing a particular anchor currency increases with the amount of trade with other countries that use this same anchor.

The behaviour of transition economies during the nineties is illustrative of the dynamics of anchor currency choice. Following the break-up of the Soviet Union in the early nineties, most transition economies initially fell in the 'freely falling' category for several years, and then increasingly started tying their currencies to the deutschmark and the US dollar. Interestingly, the choice of anchor was almost perfectly divided among regional lines: while Central and Eastern European countries chose to anchor to the deutschmark (later the euro), most former Soviet Union republics chose the US dollar as their anchor (with the exception of Estonia, which adopted a currency board arrangement with the deutschmark; and Latvia, which chose the SDR) (Rogoff et al., 2003).

According to theory the choice of the exchange rate regime depends on:

1. Initial conditions
   a. Macroeconomic conditions
   b. Institutional set-up
   c. Availability of foreign reserves, and so on
2. Structural characteristics
   a. Fiscal stability (as the Argentina case clearly demonstrated the choice of a hard peg doesn't solve the underlying problems by itself)
   b. Openness

    i. Smaller, more open and actively trading countries tend to have more fixed exchange rates

  c. Labour market flexibility

3. Type of shocks affecting the economy (external or domestic, real or nominal and symmetric or asymmetric)
4. Policymakers' credibility
5. Economic objectives (disinflation, external adjustment, output stabilization).

An important aspect is that all the pegged rates can be chosen unilaterally and the responsibilities for making the system work lie on the country declaring and using the fixed exchange rate only.

The fixed exchange rate regimes have numerous advantages amongst which the more important ones are:

1. Reduces exchange rate volatility and uncertainty that could adversely affect trade and financial system
2. Anchor for nominal prices that acts to dampen inflationary pressures
3. Promotes prudence and credibility – authorities' hands are 'tied' to keep the fix, so they cannot engage in adverse economic policies.

The argument of a pegged exchange rate promoting a pre-commitment to anchor inflationary expectations was used extensively in the eighties for the ERM and in the nineties for currency boards and other hard pegs in transition and emerging countries (Bordo, 2003). However we also have to take notice of the important drawbacks including:

1. Constraints on economic policy meaning that policy flexibility to deal with domestic or external shocks and volatile capital flows is lost.
2. Tendency of the real exchange rate to appreciate:
   a. Occurs when the inflation differentials are still high, so also causes tension between disinflation and competitiveness objectives. Also occurs if the peg currency is chosen incorrectly (doesn't reflect trade partners).
3. Level of the peg – whilst setting it the authorities need to have a notion of what the possible fundamental equilibrium rate could be and try to set an appropriate rate according to that. There usually is a need to allow some room for accommodation of the possible appreciation.
4. Level of the adequate reserves – should the case of having to defend the peg in a speculative attack occur.
5. Risk of perception of implicit exchange rate guarantees that encourages excessive unhedged foreign exchange risk taking; short-term capital inflows that can be reversed easily and discourages foreign exchange market development.

According to the International Monetary Fund's de facto classification, the currency board arrangement (CBA) is the harshest exchange rate system of pegging a country's currency to another one's. The only stricter version of monetary policy indiscretion would be having no separate legal tender (dollarization or euroization).

As the currency board theory states that the national currency of the country in question needs to be backed with foreign reserves, then whilst taking the decision of introducing the currency board system, the following questions need to be answered:

1. What to back the national currency with
2. What to peg it to
3. Which liabilities should the currency board back.

Single versus basket peg is a matter of inflation versus competitiveness. The easiest way would be to choose a single low inflation trade partner, because if the peg is not made to the main trade partner, the movements of the pegged currency against the trading partners' currencies would affect competitiveness. For example, Lithuania had a currency board system with a fixed peg to US dollar (USD), however trade was mainly with Germany and other European countries, so when the USD appreciated versus these currencies, so did the litas and Lithuanian competitiveness fell.

Choosing the parity of the peg, the following matters arise:

1. Estimation of the fundamental equilibrium rate (real exchange rate to achieve a desirable and sustainable target for the medium term current account at full employment level) and choice of a parity realistic enough and close to it.
2. Risk of over-appreciated or over-depreciated peg: the first diminishes competitiveness quickly, the other slows down disinflation. It might be more desirable to start with an over-depreciated level in order to provide a cushion for subsequent inflation differentials and compliment the peg with additional anchors (for example income policy, structural reforms).
3. In choosing the form of the peg, the credibility of the authorities and the macroeconomic conditions in the country are the prerequisites for success. If a crawl is introduced, the rate and slope of it needs to be decided upon. If crawling bands are used, then the question of the band width and intervention rules (at margins or intra-marginal) arise.

The advantages and drawbacks of a CBA are those of fixed regime in a more extreme form. They enhance the credibility of a fixed regime due to the long-term commitment to stick to rigid exchange and backing rules (in many cases set in the central bank law) and the higher cost of abandoning fixed parity (IMF, 2001). They also imply a far-reaching surrender of monetary policy. After a shock the adjustment has to come by wage and price adjustment (instead of interest or exchange rate one), very short-term interest rate volatility cannot be smoothed and the lender of the last resort function is eliminated.

Both in the Baltics' most recent developments (joining the European Union and eventually the unified currency – the euro) and the Belarus-Russia monetary union cases the arguments for giving up the national currency apply. An emerging country that completely gives up its national currency stands to make several gains:

1. The devaluation risk will be greatly reduced.
2. Information costs will decline that should translate into better informed investors and reduced vulnerability to herd behaviour.
3. Increase in the demand elasticity for emerging markets equity of foreign traders
4. Financial assets and liabilities will be matched in terms of currency denomination.
5. Reduced information frictions and enhanced credibility will result in better access to international capital markets (Mendoza, 1989).

Already currently the financial systems of the Baltic countries are quite highly dollarized in the sense that their assets and liabilities are up to a large extent denominated in foreign currencies. Also according to theory higher dollarization appears to be associated with less flexible exchange rate regimes among emerging markets, consistent with 'fear of floating' (Calvo and Reinhart, 2000).

Fear of floating appears to be strongest in highly dollarized emerging markets, where pegged regimes are more prevalent than in less dollarized countries in the group. However, fear of floating does not explain why other developing countries with high dollarization ratios appear to prefer regimes with limited flexibility to pegs. A possible explanation for this could be that many of these countries became highly dollarized following a 'freely falling' episode, and lacked the credibility necessary to defend a peg.

Privatization has been extremely important in the transition from plan to market. It has been the way of imposing hard budget constraints and promoting restructuring. It has also helped to create the institutions for corporate governance and increase demand for stronger property rights. Empirics prove that:

1. Privatization to concentrated outsider owners (investment funds, foreigners, and blockholders) has benefited restructuring
2. Privatization to diffuse owners and to enterprise workers and managers (insiders) has not been beneficial (it has been worse than state ownership) (Djankov and Murrell, 2000).

If the rapid privatization scheme (like in the Baltics) is used, strengthening and enforcing the regulatory and supervisory framework are crucial to enhance the accountability of corporate boards and managers, protect the rights of minority shareholders and promote disclosure. It also requires openness to foreign investors who can buy large blocks of shares relatively quickly, comply with all the capital market regulations and facilitate the concentration of ownership (World Bank, 2002). The Baltic countries' governments (especially that of Estonia) were ready to take the bold step of opening the full privatization program to foreigners.

According to all the reasoning given above and probably some more with some country and situation-specific modifications, the decisions on the monetary policy and financial sector development were taken in the Baltic countries of Estonia, Latvia and Lithuania as given in the next paragraph.

The course of 'action': Introduction of the pegs

The economic situation in the Baltic countries began to worsen in the 1980s. The causes were the problems arising from the beginning of the breakdown of the Soviet Union: the administratively regulated prices caused excess demand/supply of certain goods, price differences between goods in private and state shops were 100-500 per cent and the GDP fell by a few per cent. The problems deepened with the collapse of the Soviet planning system that caused large disruptions in both trade and financial channels and brought along a systemic shock.

In 1989, a law on economic independence in the Soviet Union was adopted that granted the Baltic states with a degree of autonomy that provided an opening that Estonia used to re-establish the Bank of Estonia on 1 January 1990. The Bank of Estonia was originally founded in February 1919 when Estonia first gained independence, but was closed in June 1940 following Estonia's annexation by the Soviet Union.[1] However most financial operations remained centralized in the Tallinn branch of the Soviet State Bank (Gosbank) and the Bank of Estonia activities were largely confined to developing a strategy for achieving greater economic autonomy for Estonia within the Soviet Union. It shortly also took over the Tallinn branch of the Foreign Trade Bank of the Soviet Union. This bank's responsibilities were largely commercial, but they provided the bank staff with important experience in managing foreign assets.

The idea of creating a separate monetary system to stabilize the economy started to evolve. There was some initial discussion on whether the monetary reform should lead directly to an introduction of a local independent currency or whether a transition period with the use of vouchers would be of use.

Growing political tension between Estonia and the Soviet Union led to the retraction by Moscow of some measures of economic activity, but the commitment of Estonia to currency reform remained strong and found expression in the formation of the Monetary Reform Committee in March 1991 (Knöbl et al., 2002). It was tasked with framing the general principles of monetary and currency reform and also given extensive powers to promulgate legislation related to these reforms.

In late 1991 a decision was taken by the Bank of Estonia that the preferred route would be moving directly to independent currency, because vouchers would

---

[1]   Bank of Estonia website (www.eestipank.info) on the history of the bank.

not help with the problem of a high level of inflation. It was feared that if a rapid reduction in inflation did not accompany the introduction of the new currency, the scarce foreign exchange reserves might be depleted in defending an unrealistic exchange rate. In recognition that additional foreign exchange would be needed to support the new currency, the Bank of Estonia suggested initiating discussions on a foreign financed stabilization fund or by pledging Estonia's state-owned forests.

Initially Estonia turned to the IMF in October 1991, but the organization said that Estonia needed to be a member first and implement credible policies to get support from the IMF. In January 1992 150,000 cubic meters of forests (valued at 150 million USD) ready for felling were committed to the Bank of Estonia balance sheet. They were removed finally in June 1997.

However the economic situation kept deteriorating. As Russia moved to the world market prices for energy and raw material exports to the Baltic countries, the countries faced a severe terms of trade shock in 1992 (TOT deteriorated by more than 20 per cent of GDP). As a result, industrial production, employment and output fell rapidly, annual inflation reached triple and even quadruple (for example year-on-year inflation in Estonia in June 1992 was 1080 per cent) digit levels and real income deteriorated (for example in the first quarter of 1992 real wages in Estonia fell by 52 per cent).

To stabilize the economies in crisis, lower the hyperinflation and restore GDP growth, all the Baltic countries came to the conclusion that under the circumstances there was no choice but to use 'shock therapy', that is adjust rapidly.

The main aim was to achieve economic stabilization with the help of tight monetary and fiscal policies, accompanied by strong packages of structural measures for institution building and creation of the favourable conditions for business development. As the new (endogenous) growth theories state that one important reason for differences in economic growth in countries is inflation and empirical analysis suggests that the growth rate increases most when the stabilization includes bringing its level down to about 20 per cent a year, the countries concentrated on tight anti-inflationary monetary policies (Olson et al., 1997; Bruno, 1995).

The economic environment was worsening quickly and the fear that Estonia would be flooded with roubles because of some coupon systems possibly introduced in the other republics served to underscore the urgency of implementing a coherent reform strategy. So the meeting of the Monetary Reform Committee was called in January 1992.

Initially the Governor of the Bank of Estonia preferred the ideas of introducing the gold standard, but as they did not turn out to be viable, after the visit of Jeffrey Sachs to Estonia in April 1994, when he proposed to Siim Kallas (Governor of the Bank of Estonia at that time) that Estonia should adopt a currency board, a decision on the currency board arrangement was taken soon enough. Relevant legislation was drafted in early May 1992, partly with the help from an IMF technical advice (Estonia had become a member in May 1992).

As a result of the decision, Estonia became the first country to leave the rouble area and, by doing so, to try to insulate its economy from the inflationary impulses from the Former Soviet Union, in June 1992. Despite opposition from the IMF[2], the decision to use the most radical method of fixing the exchange rate of the local currency versus some other, the currency board system was taken, since the theoretical knowledge is that fixed exchange rates help lower inflation and interest rates. The local currency (kroon) was fixed to the German mark at the rate of one DEM (mark) to eight EEK (kroon).

Concerning the backing of the CBA, the Bank of Estonia and Sachs first supported the coverage of broad money with foreign exchange reserves (that would have been the monetary liabilities of both the central and commercial banks). Foreign exchange in the amount of 200-300 million USD would initially have been needed for that. Another option would have been the Hong Kong model of backing the currency notes only. An intermediate decision was reached by which only Bank of Estonia liabilities would be covered by foreign exchange. Covering broad money would have been impracticable because it would have constrained the banking sector unnecessarily and because foreign exchange reserves were insufficient. The system of bank reserves was maintained partly because there was no effective interbank clearing system outside the Bank of Estonia and also to ensure that banks held precautionary balances against unexpected outflows. The deposits also had to be covered with foreign exchange.

As Estonia hoped to ultimately join the European Union and to have its main trade relations in the future with it, initially a peg to the ECU was considered. However since such a peg would not have been as transparent as a link to a single well-known currency, the choice was made to peg the kroon to DEM. For simplicity, the exchange rate was fixed at the nearest whole DEM multiple to the prevailing rouble/USD market rate.

On what to back the CBA with, there was no choice to make, since there were practically no foreign reserves available, except for the gold that had been restituted from the United Kingdom – gold held as foreign exchange reserves by the Republic of Estonia prior to the annexation by the Soviet Union in 1940. After Estonia regained independence selected depositories recognized the claims and returned Estonian gold, however at the time of the currency reform, only the gold from the Bank of England was available (about USD 52 mill). Thus the currency board arrangement started with a backing of only 90 per cent of the liabilities of the Bank of Estonia with full backing realized following the further gold restitution from Sweden and the Bank for International Settlements in the amount of USD 45 mill in July. The total required to cover the liabilities was initially USD 63 mill.

To enhance credibility in the local money and the exchange rate system both among local and foreign economic agents, an exchange window where individuals and enterprises could come and exchange unlimited quantities of kroons into DEM was introduced.

---

[2]   To enhance flexibility, the IMF usually suggests floating exchange rate regimes.

A framework for fiscal policy was created by the currency board arrangement, since any budget deficit had to be constrained to what could be financed in the domestic financial market outside the Bank of Estonia or abroad. The probability for that at the time was close to zero implying that the budget needed to be roughly balanced.

As a measure of an unconventional CBA, the lender of last resort function was de facto retained, but it could only be carried out within strict limits of excess foreign exchange cover of base money.

The introduction of the kroon went relatively smoothly, the only miscalculation was the underestimation of the demand for the new notes over the first weekend of its introduction, but the shortage was quickly rectified.

Latvia left the rouble area a month later than Estonia did, and introduced the Latvian rouble (with an initial rate of 1:1 with the Russian one) that was eventually replaced with the local currency existent today – the lats. It was initially allowed to float and in February 1994 was informally pegged to the IMF's accounting unit SDR.

Lithuania was the last of the three to exit the rouble zone in October 1992 when the talonas (their interim currency) was taken into use. Because of weak monetary discipline, limited independence of the central bank and political pressure to extend credit being high, the talonas depreciated a lot. The monetary policy was tightened in May 1993 with the preparations for adopting the currency board system and introducing the litas.

The idea of introducing a currency board arrangement in Lithuania was originally the government's and the Bank of Lithuania opposed it. After quite strong debates on the issue, the parliament passed the necessary legislation providing the legal basis for setting up the CBA and giving the government the right to fix the exchange rate in consultation with the Bank of Lithuania. The CBA was set up on 1 April 1994 when the national currency litas was pegged to the USD at 1 USD = 4 LTL.

The decision of using the dollar as the anchor currency was made because:

1. Most foreign currency denominated assets were in dollars
2. Most transactions were carried out in dollars because of high domestic inflation
3. Ninety per cent of trade was denominated in dollars (Alonso-Gamo et al., 2002).

As was the case in Estonia, the CBA was somewhat unorthodox in the sense that the Bank of Lithuania retained many functions of the central bank (lender of last resort up to the limit of excess coverage of reserve money, some money market instruments to be used to influence liquidity).

Structural reforms, price and trade liberalization and introduction of a two tier banking system (Central Bank and commercial banks) supported the financial measures in all the Baltic countries.

Developments after introducing the hard pegs

The first phase of the transition involved a banking crisis in Estonia (in 1992-93) and in the next phase the crises emerged also in Latvia (1995) and Lithuania (1995-96). Early stages of these crises involved government intervention in support of problem banks, a central bank moratorium on some of them and subsequent closure or liquidation of a number of large ones. About a third of the broad money stock was destroyed during these banking crises. But even the failure of the larger banks had limited systemic effects. The short-term reaction to the problems with the banking sector was strengthening supervision and legislation governing the banking industry.

Part of the crises can be attributed to the authorities' wish to create a functioning financial sector, and for facilitating the process, giving the banking licenses fairly easily. As the economies were still at the very beginning of the transition period, the management and staff of some of the banks were not experienced enough to run the system adequately, so the institutions started to face problems and ended up in crisis.

Initial stabilization was achieved starting from 1995. The main elements were the continuation of financial stabilization through tight financial policies and a speedup in further structural reform. The key achievements of this period were a remarkable decrease in inflation (it came down to single digits) and rapid economic growth (double digits in Estonia in 1997) (Figure 3.1 and 3.2). The drawback of the fast recovery was the large current account deficits in all three countries.

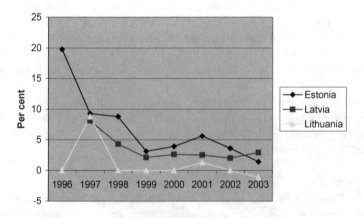

Figure 3.1   Inflation in the Baltic countries

Source: Central Banks and Statistics Departments.

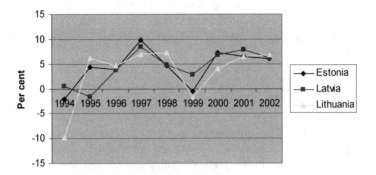

Figure 3.2   Growth in the Baltics

Source: Respective Central Banks and Statistics Departments.

In the period between 1994 and 1997, the recovery of GDP growth helped to sustain the CBA in Lithuania. However the Bank of Lithuania violated the idea of the CBA in 1994-95 by letting one of the banks withdraw required reserves to lend to a utility, and government pledged some foreign reserves to borrow from abroad. The overall fiscal stance was also expansionary and helped undermine the CBA.

Some banking restructuring took place in Lithuania in 1996, but the government taking responsibility for the financial burden associated with it and overall tightening of the fiscal stance contributed to sustaining the CBA.

In 1997, the Estonian economy showed signs of overheating caused by significant foreign capital inflows and resulting in large domestic credit expansion and the stock prices high up in the sky. As a result, the central bank of Estonia in close co-operation with the IMF worked out a long list of measures curbing the credit expansion and making the control over the banking system more efficient. Among others the measures included raising the levels of capital adequacy and minimum capital of the banks, increasing required reserves and amending legislation on the banking industry. It resulted in the closure of some more banks and a slowdown of the economy. The stock market crash in late 1997 boosted the slowdown even more. At the same time period an exit strategy from the CBA was worked out in Lithuania.

Then in 1998 the Russian crisis hit. Even though a lot of effort had been made in reorienting the external trade of the Baltic countries to the West, trade relations with Russia were still remarkable. Export shares of Russia and the CIS were respectively 15 per cent and 20 per cent for Estonia, 20 per cent and 30 per cent for Latvia and 25 per cent and 45 per cent for Lithuania (Knöbl and Haas, 2003). As exports fell, output declined and the economies went into recession. The problems in Estonia deepened and Latvia faced a similar crisis where heavy strains emerged on the banking sector and some banks went down. In Lithuania the response was a loosening of fiscal policy and the budget deficit rose from 3.5 per cent in 1991 to

8.5 per cent in 1999. In order to have a nominal anchor in the 'tough times', a decision was taken to abandon the exit strategy, so monetary policy remained tight in all the countries with no changes to the currency boards in Estonia and Lithuania or the exchange rate peg in Latvia.

Because of the recession at the time and after the Russian crisis that also brought along quite large currency substitution, the Lithuanian CBA was almost to collapse in 1999. The fiscal position deteriorated substantially and currency substitution intensified as both domestic and foreign agents shifted into dollar deposits and cash. The government took some corrective measures including bringing the deficit down and it helped to prevent a banking crisis from occurring.

Thanks to serious efforts taken, the Baltics recovered from the effects of the Russian crisis quite rapidly. Exports to the West (mainly to the European Union countries) rose quickly from 1999 (Figure 3.3) and the attention of the countries was turned to preparations for European Union accession. As a matter of fact the negotiations with the EU became the most important policy issue and the possible upcoming membership enhanced further structural reforms (especially in Latvia and Lithuania).

As the trade with the European Union countries intensified (the share of exports to the EU had increased to almost half of the total), the dollar peg was not serving the economy well enough any more (Figure 3.4). Because of the EUR/USD volatility in 1999 the Lithuanian exporters became affected by the appreciation of the dollar, so the government and the Bank of Lithuania decided to re-peg the currency to the euro.

The announcement on the issue was made without further comments on the dates and modalities that generated some uncertainty in the system and gave rise to speculations about possible devaluation associated with the re-peg. It caused the authorities to enhance transparency and choose for the option of announcing the next steps well in advance.

As the level of dollarization in the economy was high and it was assumed that at least half a year would be needed for the agents to rearrange their financial arrangements in order to reduce the balance-sheet effects, the announcement that re-pegging would take place on 2 February 2002 was made seven months in advance.

The re-pegging took place smoothly, the Bank of Lithuania managed to convert its official reserves into euro-denominated assets, and the economy adapted to the announcement so well that the fears of devaluation disappeared almost immediately.

As also shown in the earlier empirics by Ghosh, Gulde and Wolf (1998) the CBAs and hard pegs perform well on both inflation and economic growth.

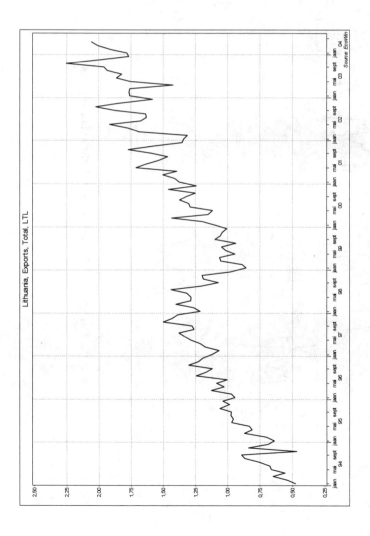

Figure 3.3   Lithuanian exports, LTL

Source: Ecowin.

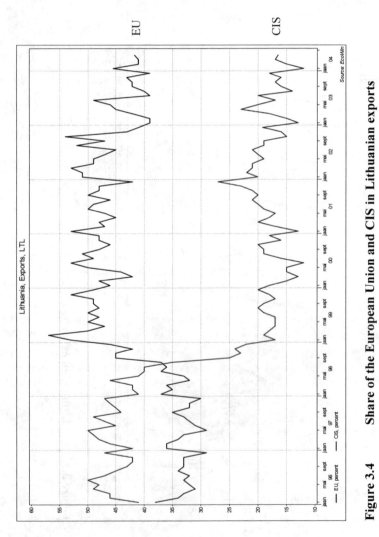

Figure 3.4   Share of the European Union and CIS in Lithuanian exports

Source: Ecowin.

The current situation in the Baltic countries has proved it once again, being flourishing: all the countries are experiencing rapid economic growth and low levels of inflation. The fiscal positions of the countries are in all cases almost balanced and levels of government debt are relatively low compared to those of the other European Union member countries (Table 3.1).

Table 3.1   Selected macroeconomic indicators in the Baltic countries

	HICP inflation		GDP growth		Fiscal deficit (% of GDP)		Public sector debt (% of GDP)	
	2002	2003	2002	2003	2002	2003	2002	2003
Estonia	3.6	1.4	6.0	4.8	0.9	2.6	5.7	5.8
Latvia	2.0	2.9	6.1	6.7	-3.0	-1.8	15.2	15.6
Lithuania	0.4	-1.1	6.8	9.0	-1.4	-1.7	22.8	21.9

HIPC - period average.
Source: ECB, Eurostat, Central Banks and Departments of Statistics.

Situation of the financial sector in the respective countries

Although a CBA may help stabilize inflation and interest rates over the medium to long term, banks operating in CBA countries are likely to face high day-to-day interest rate volatility because interest rates play a major role in the CBA adjustment mechanism and monetary operations are constrained by the backing rule. So banks in the CBA countries have to accept the burden of adjustment. Interest rates may also increase to defend the fixed exchange rate in a country that faces systemic capital outflows. So small and undercapitalized banks may become insolvent (Santiprahob, 1997).

In most CBA countries, banks play the most important role in interest rate arbitrage. Since unsound banks tend to take higher risks, depositors demand higher premiums on their deposit rates. A part of the spread between German and Estonian deposit rates in 1993 is attributable to the banking crisis of 1992-93. The same type of explanation of a weak banking system (of many banks being initially undercapitalized and their assets being inflated by the high level of inflation) can be used in the Lithuanian case at the time of the introduction of the CBA. In both currency board countries the banking sector problems also led to sharp increases in the currency to broad money ratios.

After regaining independence, the mono-bank system of the Soviet times was broken up into a two-tier banking system. The initial strategy of the authorities was to increase competition and bring down interest rates, so they granted licenses fairly liberally with little regard to prudential requirements and regulation (Berglöf and Bolton, 2003).

Bank ownership and the ownership structure of their clients in the initial period of transition was largely the state, however after large restructuring of the system, the foreign ownership has increased substantially (for example, in Estonia more than 80 per cent, and in Latvia over 50 per cent is foreign owned). Foreign owners have not only brought in capital, but also know-how and corporate governance practices.

Nowadays the financial system in the Baltic States is heavily bank-based and closely resembles the Western European model of universal banks that offers a broad range of services.

There are seven banks currently operating in the Estonian banking market, however after joining the European Union some increased foreign interest in setting up local branches has been observed. All seven banks are profitable and the total profits have been increasing steadily (16 per cent y-o-y in 2003). Total assets of the banking sector in 2003 made 6.3 bill EUR (Figure 3.5).

For the first time in the regained independence history, the loans given by the Estonian banking sector exceeded deposits taken in 2003, so the banks became dependent on external financing. As foreign investors own approximately 85 per cent of the total assets of the banking sector, most of the extra financing needed came from the parent banks in Scandinavia. Some of it was, however, acquired from the market too as the margins over the European Union interest rates are almost negligible.

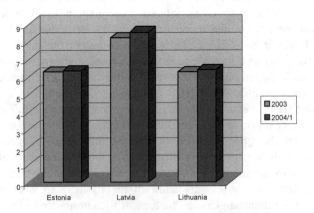

Figure 3.5   Assets of the Baltic banking sector, billion EUR

The securities market is relatively unimportant in Estonia: both primary and secondary market volumes decreased over the course of 2003. Emissions of securities have decreased, and as most of the securities acquired are purchased with the intention to be kept until maturity, the secondary market trade in them is small. Turnovers on the Estonian equities market are also small and only the shares of a fixed number of companies are traded.

The Latvian banking system differs somewhat from the Estonian and Lithuanian ones in the sense that the number of operating banks is larger. Since Latvia has a larger minority population of Russians and closer ties to the Russian economy, the past banking problems in Russia and the rest of the CIS have facilitated the evolution of a segmented banking system: resident business, nonresident business, and a combination of the two. So only a few banks focus exclusively on servicing the domestic market (IMF, 2003).

The share capital of the Latvian banking sector increased by 8.5 per cent in 2003 to a total of 200 million EUR. The share of foreign ownership was 53.9 per cent and the state still owned 6.5 per cent of the shares of the banking sector retaining the ownership of one smaller bank and a minor share in another one. The total assets of the sector increased by 29.3 per cent in 2003 and totalled to 8.24 billion EUR.

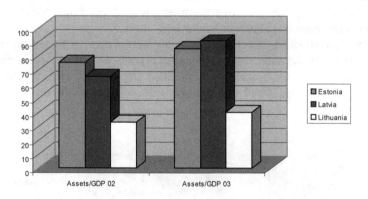

Figure 3.6   Assets of the Baltic banks, % of their respective GDP

The share of the total assets of the Latvian banking sector in the total assets of all the Baltic countries' ones decreased slightly to 40.1 per cent. The total assets of the Latvian banking system are about 30 per cent larger than those of Estonian and Lithuanian respective sectors. All the banks were profitable last year and the total profits of the sector increased by 27 per cent.

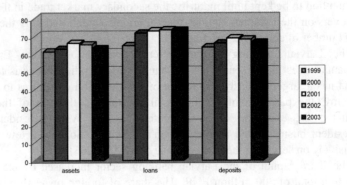

Figure 3.7   Market share of the five largest banks in Latvia

For the first time in the period after regaining independence, loans became the most important assets in 2003 totalling to 52.5 per cent of the total assets of the sector. On the liabilities side 65.3 per cent of the total were deposits of which the non-resident deposits increased the most (by 23.5 per cent). Ninety per cent of those were made by the private enterprises.

Six investment brokers and 20 banks were active in the securities market. Almost ⅔ of the total trading took place with the government securities, the amount of these deals doubled within 2003 (figure 3.8). Trading with corporate bonds went up by 28 per cent and made 23 per cent of the total trading in the securities market.

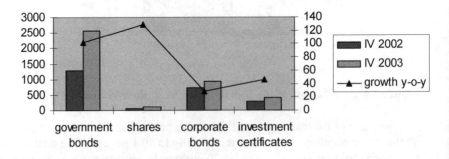

Figure 3.8   Turnover of the Latvian securities market (million LVL)

The total assets of the banking sector in Lithuania increased by 27.8 per cent in 2003 and totalled approximately 6.3 billion EUR. From the 13 banks in the market ten domestic and one foreign bank's branch were profitable (y-o-y growth in total profits of the sector was 63 per cent). Two branches of foreign banks accumulated losses.

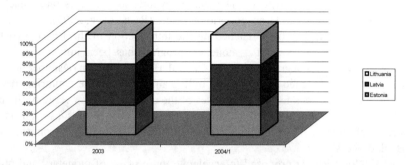

Figure 3.9   Share of the countries' banking sectors in the total of the Baltics

As is also the case in Latvia, the credit growth in 2003 was rapid (52.5 per cent y-o-y). 75 per cent of the whole loan portfolio were loans taken by the corporate sector.

70 per cent of the turnover of the securities market was trade in government securities. A total of 18 brokers and 9 commercial banks were participating in the trade.

The situation in Belarus

The exchange rate regime of Belarus is a crawling band in the terms of the rouble, given the monetary union arrangement with Russia. The country has maintained close economic relations after the break-up of the Soviet Union with neighbouring Russia and is intending to create an economic and monetary union with it.

Inflationary pressures have eased since mid-2000 with liberalization of the foreign exchange market. The resulting inflows of foreign currency have helped curb pressures on the exchange rate and increased confidence in the currency. The short-term dynamics of inflation are strongly influenced by non-monetary factors (like sudden and large changes in the prices of food and energy). The weight component of food items in the consumption basket is high (circa 64 per cent) which exacerbates the seasonal component of the CPI (Somner, 2003). Supply shocks have had a large impact on inflation in recent years (for example, in 2002 the annual inflation rate was 35 per cent of which 12 per cent was attributed to various shocks). The tendency is that the share of monthly inflation volatility explained by these shocks has increased as the monthly rate has gone down (Figure 3.10).

The discussions on a union of Belarus and Russia began in 1994 and reached an important stage in 1999 when an agreement was reached, since the economies are closely integrated. Over 60 per cent of Belarus's trade turnover is with Russia. Russian exports to Belarus being dominated by oil and gas (a lot of which is being produced to be re-exported to Central and Western Europe) through the pipelines on the Belarusian territory. The main exports of Belarus are machinery, agricultural products and transportation services (Richardson, 2003).

An agreement has been reached on the introduction of the Russian rouble in Belarus and in this context a monetary program has been implemented by the Belarus authorities, agreed with the Central Bank of Russia. Another important agreement was reached in June 2002 by the authorities of the countries. It was to assure fair conditions for the enterprises of the countries on the verge of the union. The program contained various monetary and fiscal measures as well as some structural reforms. The program also included a stabilization loan from the Central Bank of Russia.

Mid-2002 Russia proposed to accelerate the process of monetary and political unification by advancing the introduction of the Russian rouble in Belarus to 1 January 2004 and being followed by a referendum in both countries on further political integration. However the Belarusian authorities rejected the offer and stuck to the present situation of an eventual creation of a Union State.

The advantages of the monetary union for Belarus are that it would import the economic policy of Russia and if the credibility of the union is not questioned, it should increase positive investor sentiment towards the country. Anecdotal evidence from some foreign investors having done business in the country supports the view that they are currently reluctant to inject money into the economy on the basis of fears of their enterprises being renationalized.

Another huge advantage is that inflation would immediately fall to less than half of the current levels and it should contribute to growth in the country via increases in private sector investment and better access to the international markets. The next potential advantage of the union could be the stimulus it might provide for the trade with Russia via reduced transaction costs (Frankel and Rose, 2000). The union would probably also help to increase the pace of structural reforms in Belarus.

However, from the perspective of optimal currency area theory (Mundell, 1961), the two countries might not form an OCA, since external shocks tend to affect them asymmetrically as oil and gas price rises improve the Russian external position opposed to that of Belarus. Adverse weather tends to affect Belarus more.

Another potential drawback of the union could be that the Russian rouble might appreciate significantly against the major currencies over the medium term as the capital inflows continue. In the union, Belarus would automatically import that appreciation. Capital inflows to Russia have been very pronounced for some time, and these have put significant upward pressure on the exchange rate. Until recently, the Russian authorities seemed to prefer to accept some excess inflation, rather than risk any adverse impact on exports and industry of a significant appreciation. However, in 2003 significant real appreciation of the Russian rouble took place, and – if oil prices stay high and Russia continues to be an attractive destination for investment – there is a chance that the real appreciation will continue.

If it does, once Belarus has joined a currency union with Russia, Belarusian industry will face increasing competitive pressure stemming from the higher value of the currency (a problem known as the 'Dutch disease'). While this need not be a major problem – indeed, it has been argued that the competitive pressure will eventually prove to be salutary for Russian industry – it could be very painful in Belarus. Further, while those regions of Russia that are hit hardest by a loss of competitiveness would in principle have access to the Russian system of fiscal federalism, Belarus would not (Odling-Smee, 2003).

A huge risk from the union stems from the financial sector of Belarus. The sector, still largely being state owned, is being instructed by the state to lend to some specific sectors or enterprises (often at subsidized interest rates). This is likely to have eroded the quality of the banks' loan portfolio. It implies that some day there would be a need for the financial sector reform that might be more difficult to carry out under the currency union system as it would bear huge costs. The National Bank of Belarus might not be able to carry out the lender of last resort function under the arrangement either, as it would have lost its independence.

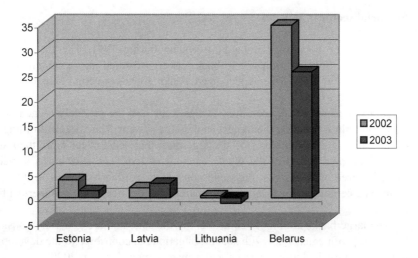

Figure 3.10   Inflation in the Baltics and Belarus

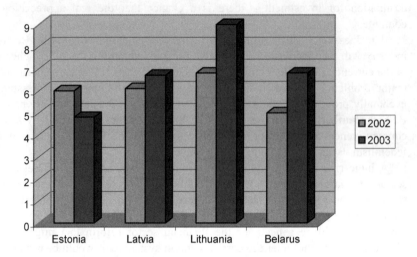

Figure 3.11   Economic growth in the Baltics and Belarus

Financial sector in Belarus

Belarus moved to a two-tier banking system during 1991. The former Belarus branch of the Soviet Union's state bank was transformed into a central bank and the branches of the former specialized banks were converted into commercial banks.

In 1996 a merger between the Savings Bank and the privately owned Belarus Bank took place, creating the largest bank in the system. The 'system-forming' part of the banking sector consists of six large ones that account for more than 80 per cent of the total assets of the whole banking system. The state owns a majority share in three of the largest ones and considerable minority shares in the rest of them. The central bank of Belarus has shares in a number of the commercial banks too.

The large banks are highly controlled by the state and are generally considered to be non-profit enterprises with social obligations to contribute to the development of the economy, including by their senior management (Taylor, 2000).

In addition to the aforementioned, there is a number of locally owned banks and some joint ventures. The former ones tend to belong to state-owned enterprises like, for instance, the national gas company.

Some progress has been made in improving the capitalization of the banking system and in provisioning for non-performing loans. However, while equity in the banking system has increased in real terms, lending by the banks increased more rapidly during the same period.

Financial markets in Belarus are underdeveloped and the financial intermediation is weak. The economy (including the banking sector) is dominated by the state and equity markets are almost non-existent. The main options for savers are cash, bank deposits, government bonds and precious metals.

The leading banks are required to make loans to specific sectors and enterprises (the state-owned ones remain the primary borrowers from the system). The sector getting the most out of the banking system is agriculture in support of which large sums are being spent according to government instructions.

Part of the banking system assets are subject to government guarantees, especially in the case of the loans to the agricultural sector. The extent of the guarantees might mean that the government will have difficulty in meeting its obligations should it ever be called to do so.

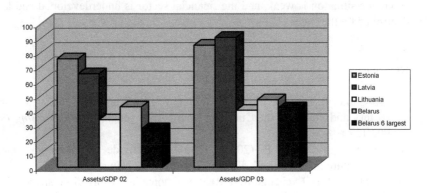

Figure 3.12   Assets of the banking sector as % of GDP

In addition to that, the Belarus economy is highly dollarized, because of both a poor macroeconomic environment with high and variable interest rates and an institutional setting that has encouraged the use of foreign currency rather than Belarusian roubles.

Conclusions

The collapse of the Soviet Union led to the creation of numerous independent countries that began the transition from a centrally planned to a market economy. In the process, they made radically different choices in their monetary policy that laid the base for the diversified outcomes of today and prospects for the future.

The analysis done in the chapter, leads to the conclusion that the monetary policy choices of the Baltic countries in curbing their inflation with the help of the most extreme choices of pegged exchange rates have been very efficient. The inflation rates in the respective countries have come down to levels lower than that of the European Union average (in the Estonian and Lithuanian cases) and are relatively low in Latvia too.

The stabilization steps have also paved the way for achieving high and sustained levels of economic growth for a number of years already and enhanced both nominal and real convergence with the rest of the European Union which the countries joined on 1 May 2004.

The clear cut-away has also facilitated financial sector development, so that the banking sector of the Baltic countries has been almost totally privatized and is profitable and sound.

As opposed to the Baltic countries, it seems that Belarusian reliance on close relations with Russia has hampered the structural reforms necessary for ensuring sustainable growth. Inflation rates have remained relatively high, the overall economic situation is weak, and the financial sector is underdeveloped and largely controlled by the state.

References

Alonso-Gamo, P. Fabrizio, S., Kramarenko, V. and Wang, Q. (2002), 'Lithuania: History and Future of the Currency Board Arrangement', *IMF Working Paper*, P02/127.

Berglöf, E. and Bolton, P. (2003), 'The Great Divide and Beyond: Financial Architecture in Transition', *William Davidson Working Paper*, 414.

Bordo, M. (2003), 'Exchange Rate Regime Choice in Historical Perspective', *IMF Working Paper*, 03/160.

Bruno, M. (1995), 'Does Inflation Really Lower Growth?', *Finance and Development*, 32, pp.35-38.

Calvo, G. and Reinhart, C. (2000), 'Fear of Floating', *Quarterly Journal of Economics*, 117, 2.

Djankov, S. and Murrell, P. (2000), *The Determinants of Enterprise Restructuring in Transition: An Assessment of Evidence*, World Bank.

Enoch, C. and Gulde, A.-M. (1997), *Making a Currency Board Operational*, IMF PPAA/97/10.

Frankel, J. and Rose, A. (2000), 'Estimating the Effects of Currency Unions on Trade and Output', *NBER Working Paper*, 7857.

Ghosh, A., Gulde, A.-M. and Wolf, H. (1998), 'Currency Boards: The Ultimate Fix', *IMF Working Paper*, 98/8.

IMF (2003), 'Capital Markets and Financial Intermediation in the Baltic States', *IMF Country Report*, 03/115.

IMF (2001), *Monetary and Exchange Rate Regimes in the Central European Economies on the Road to EU Accession and Monetary Union*, IMF.

Knöbl, A. and Haas, R. (2003), 'IMF and the Baltics: A Decade of Cooperation', *IMF Working Paper*, 03/241.

Knöbl, A., Sutt, A. and Zavoico, B. (2002), 'The Estonian Currency Board: Its Introduction and Role in the Early Success of Estonia's Transition to a Market Economy', *IMF Working Paper*, 02/96.

Meissner, C. and Oomes, N. (2004), 'Why Countries Fix the Way They Fix', *IMF Working Paper*.

Mendoza, E. (1989), 'Why Should Emerging Economies Give Up National Currencies: A Case for "Institutions Substitution"', *NBER Working Paper*, W8950.

Mundell, R. (1961), 'The Theory of Optimum Currency Areas', *American Economic Review*, 51, 4.

Odling-Smee, J. (2003), *Monetary Union Between Belarus and Russia: An IMF Perspective*, IMF.

Olson, M., Sarna, N. and Swamy, A. (1997), *Governance and Growth: A Simple Hypothesis Explaining Cross-Country Differences in Productivity Growth*, Center for Institutional Reform and the Informal Sector, University of Maryland.

Richardson, T. (2003), 'Belarus-Russia Union: Progress Report', *IMF Country Report*, 03/119.

Rogoff, K., Husain, A., Mody, A., Brooks, R. and Oomes, N. (2003), 'Evolution and Performance of Exchange Rate Regimes', *IMF Working Paper*, 03/243.

Santiprahob, V. (1997), *Bank Soundness and Currency Board Arrangements: Issues and Experiences*, IMF PPAA/97/11.

Schipke, A. (2002), 'Belarus-Russia Monetary Union', Chapter V of Republic of Belarus: Selected Issues, *IMF Country Report*, 02/22.

Somner, M. (2003), 'Core Inflation in Belarus', *IMF Country Report*, 03/119.

Taylor, M. (2000), 'An Assessment of Banking Sector Vulnerabilities', *IMF Staff Country Report*, 00/153.

World Bank (2002), *Transition: The First Ten Years*, Washington: World Bank.

Chapter 4

The Credibility Problem of Euro Candidates

Romain Veyrune

Introduction

This chapter deals with the new member states that entered the EU in 2004, with the exception of Malta and Cyprus, the countries probably entering in 2007 (Bulgaria, Croatia and Romania), and Turkey. All of them (except Turkey) are transitional countries of Central and Eastern Europe. With the transition, new institutions with a low level of experience became responsible for issuing a new currency. These countries have experienced high inflation periods due to the liberalization of prices. In addition, the monetary authorities are not credible as they do not benefit from an established reputation.

Early in the nineties, these countries wished to apply for membership to the European Union. This integration became a reality on 1 May, 2004. At that time, the integration concerned only the Economic Union and not the Monetary Union; however, it opened wide perspectives for euro integration. In fact, the Copenhagen Treaty foresees that the new members acquire all the communal *acquis* to which the euro belongs. They do not have special derogations comparable to those given to Great Britain, Denmark and Sweden. The referendum poll for the adhesion implicitly encloses the commitment to integrate the euro zone in the near future. The criteria for euro integration are based on the Maastricht treaty: the exchange rate should be stable inside the ERM II for at least two years; the fiscal deficit should not exceed three per cent and the debt 60 per cent of GDP. These criteria aim at enhancing the credibility of monetary policy before integration. Hence, the authorities have to achieve a 'jump' in terms of credibility.

We focus on currency boards. They are a monetary and exchange rate regime which, on the one hand, institutionally fixes the exchange rate and, on the other hand, regulates (limits) the base money backing. This regime imposes constraints which could ease the achievement of the convergence criteria.[1] The aim of this chapter is to compare the results in terms of credibility of currency boards and of other exchange regimes for the eleven candidates in our sample.

The first part of the chapter considers the impact of currency boards on credibility in the light of the literature. The second part gives some empirical insights of this impact using tests based on Kalman filter estimation. We use a sample of eleven candidate countries over the period 1990-2004. Among them, three have adopted a currency board (Bulgaria, Estonia and Lithuania).

Credibility and currency boards

Kydland and Prescott (1977), Barro and Gordon (1983) and Backus and Drifill (1985) have developed important theoretical support for the dominance of rules over discretion. These authors construct games based on the interaction between the central banker and the public. They use a representation of the trade off between inflation and growth consistent with an expectations augmented Phillips curve.

They conclude that the optimal (disinflation) plans are inconsistent when the monetary policy is discretionary. Indeed, if the monetary authorities are free from constraint, they have strong incentives to deviate from their commitments. This temporal inconsistency appears because once the disinflation policy is believed, the government can benefit from a strong gain in terms of growth if it produces some excess inflation not expected by the public. Aware of these strong incentives, the public chooses the rate of growth of nominal wages independently of the commitment of the government. Hence, if the government respects its commitment and opposes the expectations of people, it would undergo a severe recession. Finally, the government would tend to validate the expectations of the public. Hence, the temporal inconsistency is based on the fact that the optimal plans *ex ante* are no more optimal *ex post*. The solution for suppressing the inflationary bias due to the inconsistency is to replace discretion by 'simple rules' established *ex ante*. A rule is called simple if it is easily verifiable and not conditional. Indeed, the commitment could be legitimately believed and the optimal plans, that is the disinflation, is achieved at a null cost. The legal (institutional) fixing of the exchange rate in the framework of a currency board is consistent with these rules.

Rogoff (1985) contests the relevance of rule dominance. He introduces the occurrence of shocks independent from the authorities[2], which affect the domestic

---

[1] Currency boards achieve sharp disinflation, stabilize the exchange rate, ease the convergence of prices and interest rates towards the anchor standards represented by Germany in the period 1990-2004 and reduce public debt.

product and which could be accommodated by the exchange rate (devaluation) and/or by monetary policy (growth of base money supply). The independent shocks could be accommodated because the government benefits from private information on shocks which allows it to produce inflation not expected by the public.[3] There is thus a trade off between credibility and flexibility. In this case, the two solutions formerly investigated (rule and discretion) become corner solutions, equally expensive in terms of social welfare because of an inadequate accommodation of independent shocks or because of a rate of inflation which is permanently too high.

Rogoff (1985) proposes an alternative which is more beneficial for social welfare. It is enough to give the monetary power to an independent institution well known for having conservative preferences. These institutions have a higher aversion for inflation compared to the government, but the design of the monetary policy is completely discretionary. The conservative central banker tries to minimize inflation but is able to dampen the consequences of independent shocks. If the reputation and the independence of the banker are well established with the public, the cost of disinflation is reduced without completely abandoning the flexibility of the monetary policy.

An illustration of the inclusion of independent shocks can be found in the model of Persson and Tabellini (1999).[4] They depict the trade-off between inflation and growth as an expectations augmented Phillips curve. In order to include the shocks and the preferences for inflation and growth, we add a loss function of the authorities such as:

$$L = (x - x^*)^2 + (1/k)\pi^2 \tag{1}$$

k is the share of the shocks accommodated by the authorities. These shocks, if they are not accommodated, that is, if there is no modification of the exchange rate or of the base money growth, do not lead to more inflation but to a decrease in the output. By contrast, the accommodation of shocks neutralizes their impact on the output in the short run but raises inflation. Hence, $(1/k)$ stands for the inflation aversion. The authorities more opposed to inflation are likely to afford more costs from shocks and to accommodate shocks less. Hence, the lower the accommodation (k) of shock, the higher the coefficient of inflation aversion.

---

[2] We distinguish between shocks due to the authorities and shocks independent from the authorities.

[3] If private agents benefit from complete information the room for discretionary policy becomes null and the dominance of the rule could not been contested.

[4] The model of Persson and Tabellini (1999) is presented in Appendix A.4. 1.

The term π stands for the inflation rate. This depends on the one hand, on accommodated independent shocks and, on the other hand, on shocks due to the government and unexpected by the public in order to reach the desired level of output (x^*). The term (x) stands for the actual product. Minimizing this loss function leads to an inflation equation depending on independent shocks as highlighted by Lohmann (1992):

$$\pi_d = -\varepsilon(k) + (x^* - 6)(k) \tag{2}$$

The first part of the equation shows the accommodation of independent shocks. The second part, in which 6 stands for the long run real income, represents the inflationary bias, that is, the inflation inertia. We can thus draw the inflation reaction function as follows:

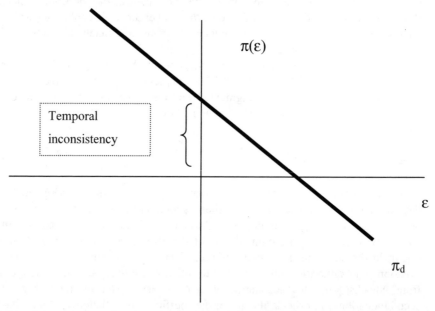

Figure 4.1   Reaction function in a purely discretionary regime

Figure 4.1 highlights the inflationary bias of the discretionary policies. The authorities accommodate completely the shocks, that is $k>=1$. Monetary policy has an inflationary impact to which we should add the bias towards more inflation due to the temporal inconsistency. This bias is shown in Figure 4.1 by the intercept $(x^* - 6)(k)$.

The only objective of the 'optimal' policy would be to accommodate completely the independent shocks, $k = 1$, and the inflationary bias, that is, the temporal inconsistency, would be null. The optimal reaction function (π_i) would depend only on shocks and could be written in the following way:

$$\pi_i = -\varepsilon \qquad (3)$$

This reaction function can be easily drawn as:

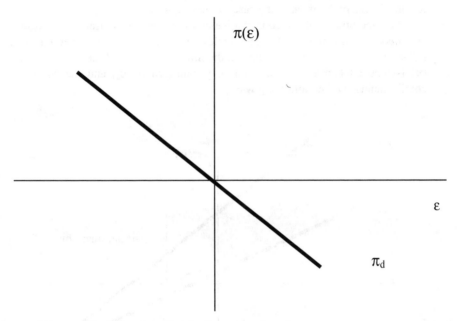

Figure 4.2   Reaction function in the optimal regime

The inflation is only due to the occurrence of shocks. We assume that the authorities influence real variables because they benefit from an advantage in terms of information. Indeed, these shocks are part of the private information of the monetary authorities, thus they are not verifiable by the public. Hence, the inflation due to the accommodation is not expected by the public, which explains why it can be used in order to reduce the real effects of shocks.

However, a simple rule is not defined in the same way. As an illustration, a simple rule could be to take a firm commitment not to accommodate any shocks as k tends to 0. The reaction function becomes thus a very simple rule:

$$\pi_{ir} = 0 \qquad (4)$$

The inflation fully disappears (by simplification we assume a rule that fixes the inflation rate at 0), however, no independent shocks whatever their size are accommodated. This regime is viable only if the independent shocks are very low. By contrast, it could be dismissed if the independent shocks are big and frequent; hence the rule is not really viable. The doubt about the viability of this kind of simple rule lowers their credibility.

The solution according to Rogoff (1985) is thus to find an institution with growth preferences that are lower than the ones of the government and the public in order to benefit from a credibility gain, but strictly superior to 0 in order to avoid the drawbacks highlighted in the case of the simple rule.

The appointment of the conservative and independent central banker results in an important lowering of k, that is, the banker has a higher aversion against inflation than the government. Indeed, the inflationary bias of the reaction function (π) is reduced between the discretionary equilibrium (π_d) and the conservative equilibrium (π_c) in the following way:

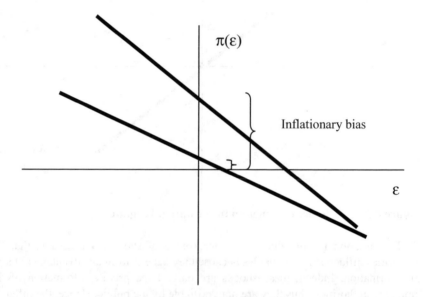

Figure 4.3   The independent and conservative central banker

The inflationary bias is significantly reduced and the ability to compensate the shocks is preserved. The bias does not disappear completely because of the conservation of some discretion. This strategy assumes that the authorities are able to convince the public, without costs or mistakes, of the independence and the degree of conservatism of the banker. These conditions are far from obvious, in particular for countries coping with important problems of credibility as it is the case in countries in transition or development. They are hardly met because of the presence of private information (Canzoneri, 1985) which gives an *ex post* incentive for the government to cheat, that is, to mislead the expectations of the public.

However, from a theoretical point of view, the regimes based on rules are not necessarily sentenced. Persson and Tabellini (1990) establish the kind of rule that could be an answer to Rogoff's criticism. This rule is called 'conditional rule' and is different from the 'simple rule'. The simple rule is a mechanic principle which regulates monetary policy whatever the state of the nature. The contingent rule is restrictive in normal times, but could be loosened in exceptional times, that is, the rule becomes conditional on the state of the nature.

The rule is applied in normal times, but can be temporarily abandoned in case of shocks passing some admitted limits. The cases for temporarily abandoning the rule are clearly regulated and *ex ante* announced to the public with some verifiable evidences. The authors (Persson and Tabellini, 1990; Giovanini, 1993) illustrate this with the fixed exchange rate of the international monetary system of Bretton Woods or the exchange rates in the European Monetary System. The examples reveal some difficulties in the implementation of conditional rules. In many cases, the residual discretion brings back enough temporal inconsistency so as to jeopardize the credibility on which the rule is based.

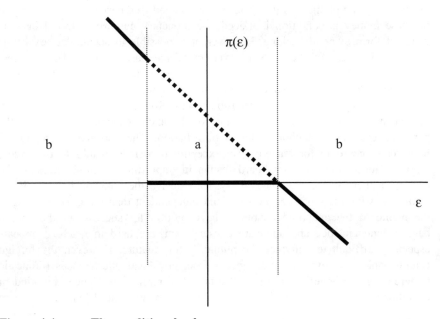

Figure 4.4   The conditional rule

This kind of conditional rule is similar to a rule with several states; if the shocks are under a certain limit (a), the simple rule is applied, however, if the shocks are beyond the limit (b), the rule is temporarily abandoned for discretion with the claim to return quickly to the rule.

Are currency boards based on a conditional rule?

In order to eliminate the temporal inconsistency, the commitment to fix the exchange rate should be restrictive enough in order to remove the rate from the discretion of the government. The most used method consists of giving an institutional aspect to the fixation. Currency boards achieve this institutionalization by introducing a determined rate with only one currency in the law or the constitution. Indeed, the alteration of the rate supposes a legal process which is assumed long and open.

An additional constraint on monetary policy is necessary to achieve the credibility of the exchange rate fixation. In the case of currency boards, it is another rule: the impossibility to use domestic assets to back the base money. The viability of the fixation is propped up by an automatic adjustment of the overall balance. The credibility of the system is based on the automatic and implacable appearance of the external adjustment.

The first rule, the exchange rate fixity, is a simple rule, easily and at all times verifiable by the public. On the contrary, the second rule based on the backing of the base money is conditional. Indeed, the monetary authorities forbid backing different form external backing. However, it is possible to accumulate exchange reserves in excess of the perfect coverage of the base money.[5] These excess reserves could be used in crisis periods to allow some discretionary policy, that is, to accommodate part of the shocks without breaking the coverage rule.

The currency board rules are also robust to the Rogoff (1985) criticism. Indeed, the second rule obliges monetary policy of the anchored country to mimic the performances of the anchor in terms of inflation. The currency board admits however some room for maneuver in exceptional periods, thanks to the excess reserve. Hence, the currency board results in importing the preferences of the central banker of the anchor country. Obviously, the 'anchor banker' is an institution which is more conservative and independent than the government and the public of the anchored country. The condition for success for the central banker, independence and adequate conservatism, are hard to reach, it appears especially difficult to convince the public of this feature. However, the foreign central banker is obviously independent from any local interferences (domestic preferences) and benefits from a well established reputation. Hence, this kind of conditional rule seems as efficient as the conservative central banker but more

---

[5]   The historical cases of currency boards impose a strict coverage (100 per cent) admitting only small excess reserve in order to deal with the revaluation of the backing currency.

easily tractable. The currency boards import thus the credibility of the anchor that would lower the inflationary bias of the monetary policy towards the inertia level of the anchor, as in the 'conservative' equilibrium depicted in Figure 4.3.

Among the candidates, Bulgaria, Estonia and Lithuania have adopted a currency board, respectively in 1997, 1992 and 1994. They are small open and transitional countries. Bulgaria and Estonia have fixed their exchange rate in terms of the Deutsch Mark and then the euro. Lithuania anchored its currency to the dollar until 2002, then to the euro.

The following table presents data for the countries of the sample on population and GDP as a share of the corresponding data for Germany. This relative GDP is the median product over the period in SDR divided by the same variable for Germany. The relative population is the population in million divided by the same variable for Germany. We also include the historical record of the exchange rate regimes over the period, as determined by Reinhart and Rogoff (2004) (Table 4.1).

Table 4.1   Population, GDP and exchange rate regimes in the sample countries

Country	POP/POP (Ger) %	GDP/GDP (Ger)%	Exchange rate regime
		Currency boards	
Bulgaria	9.9	0.6	1990-97: free floating
			1997-99: currency board (01/07/04), Deutsch mark anchor (DM)
			1999-2004: currency board, euro anchor
Estonia	1.68	0.25	1992- 99 currency board, DM anchor
			1999-2004: currency board, euro anchor
Lithuania	4.27	0.52	1992-94: free floating
			1994-2001: currency board, dollar anchor
			2001-04: currency board, euro anchor
		Quasi-currency boards	
Latvia	2.9	0.3	1992-94: free floating
			1994-04: anchorage SDR (quasi Currency Board)
Croatia	5.4	0.9	1992-94: free floating
			1994-99: anchorage (DM) +/- 2% (quasi CB)
			1999-2004: anchorage (euro) +/- 2% (quasi CB)
		Reference	
Germany			

			Other candidates
Czech Republic	12.5	2.7	1990-96: de facto crawling bands around the DM (+/- 2%) 1996-97: de facto crawling bands DM (+/- 5%) 1997-2004: managed floating
Hungary	12.2	2.1	1990-92: crawling bands DM (multiple rates). 1992-94: crawling bands DM (+/- 5%) 1994-99: crawling bands ECU (+/- 2). 1999-2004: crawling bands (pre-announced rates)
Poland	47	7.4	1990-91: anchorage dollar 1990-93: crawling peg dollar (pre-announced) 1993-98: crawling band with the dollar and the DM widening of the band of 5 to 10% 1998-99: crawling band euro 5% 1999-2004 managed floating
Romania	27	1.53	1990-2001: free and managed floating 2001-04: crawling band euro 5%
Slovakia	6.5	1	1993-97: crawling bands DM (2%) 1997-98: crawling band DM (5%) 1998-2004: managed floating at less than 5% DM/euro
Slovenia	2.4	0.91	1992-99: de facto crawling bands DM (2%) 1999-2004: de facto crawling bands euro (2%)
Turkey	81	7	1990-99: free floating 1999-2001: crawling bands euro (5%)

The candidates are classified by categories. The first two, currency boards and quasi-currency boards, stand for the countries which chose a non-conditional fixation of exchange rate for most of the period. The category quasi-currency board gathers the countries pursing a policy which is similar to that of a currency board but without institutional commitment. They are the relevant counterfactual for currency boards because only the de jure commitment distinguishes them. In addition, they are also countries quite close to the currency boards in terms of size and localization. Indeed, the Latvian Republic could be compared with its Baltic colleagues and Croatia is a Balkan country similar to Bulgaria.

The remainder of the counterfactual is composed of the other candidates which have chosen more flexible exchange rate regimes as 'adjustable pegs', that is, crawling pegs or crawling bands. Their size is relatively more important but they are still small in absolute figures. The biggest countries, Poland (47 per cent of the German population) and Turkey (81 per cent), have a median GDP below eight per cent of the German GDP. The candidates all belong to the same geographical region; they make-up an extensive geographic block, and, to our knowledge, there is no major remoteness phenomenon. Hence, they have the ability to be well integrated to the European Union in terms of trade and finance; a low level of integration should be attributed rather to political than to structural factors.

Empirical analysis of the currency board credibility for candidates from Central and Eastern Europe

The empirical method is based on a panel of monthly inflation data for the candidates to the European Union (except Malta and Cyprus) for the period 01:1990-12:2004. In particular, we are interested in the countries that had chosen a currency board as their exchange rate regime (Bulgaria, Estonia and Lithuania). The results for the other candidates are used as counterfactual. As a reference for the entire group, we use the estimation for Germany.

If the monetary authorities decide to import the preferences of a foreign central banker, they would mimic the performances in terms of inflation of the anchor. A successful achievement of this policy would be reflected in the data by the co-integration of the inflation rate of the anchor and the anchored. The relation could be written in the following way:

$$\pi_t = \pi_g + e_t \tag{5}$$

The domestic inflation rate π_t is equivalent to the reference inflation rate π_g (with g for Germany) and random shocks e_t independent from the authorities. This equation does not include a constant and stochastic or deterministic trends, which could reveal deviations in performances. The equation (5) is equivalent to the test of integration of inflation rates. We restrain the coefficient to be equal to 1 in order to be consistent with the mimicking strategy. Factors different from political willingness could influence the relation as the size and the degree of integration in the European Union.

One of the ways to test the inflation integration is to estimate the tendencies held in e_t which is computed as the differences between the domestic inflation rate and the German inflation rate.

Table 4.2   **Monetary integration of the candidates**

Country	RU t/critical value (number of observations)	Exchange rate regime
Currency boards		
Bulgaria 1991-2004	-2.49/-2.58 (82)	1990-97: free floating 1997-99: currency board (01/07/04), Deutsch mark anchor (DM) 1999-2004: currency board, euro anchor
Bulgaria 1997-2004	-11/-2.59 (135)	1990-97: free floating 1997-99: currency board (01/07/04), DM anchor 1999-2004: currency board, euro anchor
Estonia	-14.85/-2.59 (135)	1992-99: currency board, DM anchor 1999-2004: currency board, euro anchor
Lithuania	-7.6/-2.58 (135)	1992-94: free floating 1994-2001: currency board, dollar anchor. 2001-04: currency board, euro anchor
Quasi-currency boards		
Latvia	-13/-2.58 (135)	1992-94: free floating 1994-2004: anchorage SDR (quasi Currency Board)
Croatia	-4.1/-2.58 (135)	1992-94: free floating 1994-99: anchorage (DM) +/- 2% (quasi CB) 1999-2004: anchorage (euro) +/- 2% (quasi CB)
Reference		
Germany		
Other candidates		
Czech republic	-1.39/-2.58 (135)	1990-96: de facto crawling bands around the DM (+/- 2%) 1996-97: de facto crawling bands around the DM (+/- 5%) 1997-2004: managed floating
Hungary	-1.4/-2.58 (135)	1990-92: crawling bands DM (taux multiple). 1992-94: crawling bands DM (+/- 5%) 1994-99: crawling bands ECU (+/- 2) 1999-2004: crawling bands (pre-announced rates)
Poland	-1.57/-2.58 (135)	1990-91: anchorage dollar 1990-93: crawling peg dollar (pre-announced) 1993-98: crawling band with the dollar et lè DM widening of the band of 5 to 10% 1998-99: crawling band euro 5% 1999-2004 managed floating

Romania	-1.7/-2.58 (135)	1990-2001: free and managed floating
		2001-04: crawling band euro 5%
Slovakia	-1.53/-2.58 (135)	1993-97: crawling bands DM (2%)
		1997-98: crawling band DM (5%)
		1998-2004: managed floating at less than 5%
		DM/euro
Slovenia	-7/-2.58 (135)	1992-99: de facto crawling bands DM (2%)
		1999-04: de facto crawling bands euro (2%)
Turkey	-0.82/-2.58 (135)	1990-99: free floating
		1999-2001: crawling bands euro (5%)

The countries that apply unconditional fixation (not adjustable), the currency boards and the quasi-currency boards, benefit from inflation integration as defined in equation (5). Slovenia, which has implemented an adjustable peg, in fact a crawling band (-/+ two per cent), is the exception. In the case of Bulgaria, we notice the disappearance of trends with the implementation of the currency board. Most of these countries are small, which eases their inflation integration and stimulates them to fix their exchange rate. The rate is fixed with the euro (previously with the DM) or a currency basket where the euro has an important weight, except for Lithuania which uses the dollar as anchor. Despite the anchorage of the Litas on the dollar between 1994 and 2002, the Lithuanian inflation is nevertheless integrated with German inflation mainly because of strong commercial and financial links. The same explanation could be used for integration of the Slovenian inflation in the framework of an adjustable peg. In addition, it is likely that the adjustment possibility of the regime has not been used because of the external constraint which restrains monetary policies in small countries. Hence, the regime is adjustable de jure but not de facto.

The inflation integration is the result of the size of countries and the willingness of the monetary authorities to fix the exchange rate lastingly, that is, to import the preferences of the anchor. The other candidates are both countries of small size, as Hungary, the Czech Republic or Slovakia, and bigger countries, as Poland and Turkey. However, their size is still small in comparison to the European Union and their integration in the Union is quite high. This integration was also increased by the integration process. In these cases, important divergence is noticed between the local inflation rate and the German inflation, they could be explained by different choices in terms of exchange rate strategies. All of the diverging countries have chosen adjustable pegs as crawling pegs and crawling bands.

In conclusion, we actually notice a mimicking strategy which reveals the importation of foreign preference/aversion for inflation in countries using unconditional pegs as currency boards and quasi currency boards.

One way to measure the inflationary bias is to estimate the level of inflation inertia. If inflation is inert, this reveals that people do not believe in a modification (lowering) of the inflation pace, that is, disinflation; the temporal inconsistency is thus high. The inertia of inflation tends to lower with credible disinflation plans and with hyperinflation episodes, in this last case, the variations of the estimated coefficient are very important.

The countries of the region implemented stabilization plans in the 1990s in order to stop monetary confusion due to the transition (except in Turkey). These stabilization plans are close to disinflation plans; the goal is to interrupt hyperinflation or chronic inflation episodes. Hyperinflation is not a viable phenomenon; it could thus be stopped quickly and without cost (Cagan, 1956) by a credible plan. On the contrary, the low level of credibility of monetary authorities could lead to chronic inflation, that is, a lasting high inflation pace. This inflation regime is characterized by high inertia and temporal inconsistency of monetary policy. Indeed, as people do not believe in the reduction of inflation, the pace remains steady or accelerates. The enhancement of monetary policy credibility contributes to break the inertia.

A low level of inflation inertia means that people do not consider inflation as a strategic variable anymore and are confident of the decisions of the monetary authorities to maintain low inflation. In particular, inflation is not likely to follow a random walk, typical of chronic inflation but a random process due to the accommodation of random shocks, independent from the authorities. However, in the facts, we notice a high inertia in regimes of low inflation. Indeed, the inertia varies during the modification of the inflation pace. It lowers mainly when people change their expectations but increases anew when they expect stable and low inflation.

In order to assess the levels of inertia we use a kalman filter. This kind of estimation is based on recursive OLS which allows for the estimation of time varying coefficients. The inertia of inflation which is interpreted as temporal variability is not directly observable but could be estimated thanks to the measurement equation (6):

$$\pi_t = \alpha_t \pi_{t-1} + e_t \tag{6}$$
$$\alpha_t = \alpha_{t-1} \tag{7}$$

α_t shows inertia, the variable that could not be directly observed, that is, the state variable ((7) is the state equation). The measurement equation (6) is a simple autoregressive process on inflation. The frequency is monthly; the inertia is thus evaluated in the short run. The following table gives the average value of the state variable, the moment when inertia drops the most (see graphs in Appendix A.4.2) and we remember the historical record of the exchange rate regime for each countries over the period. The column 'break' shows the most important variation of inertia and in parentheses the date when this break occurs. The column 'change in inflation pace' gives the median monthly inflation rate (on yearly basis) before and after the break date of inertia.

The non conditional exchange rate regimes, currency boards and quasi currency boards have an average level of inertia smaller and closer to the rate of Germany than the remainder of the sample. There is one important exception: Lithuania has a high level of inertia that could be explained by domestic political conflict about the exchange rate regime (Blanc and Ponsot, 2004) and by an inappropriate anchorage on the dollar which could lead to a pass-through contributing to strengthening the inflation inertia. However, this fact does not compromise the performances in terms of inflation. To the opposite, the inertia drops with the implementation of the currency board in 1994, then increases to a high level. After this break, the inflationary regime lowers in a dramatic way.

Table 4.3   Inertia and pace of inflation in the candidate countries

Country (period)	α	Break	Change in inflation pace	Exchange rate (Reinhart and Rogoff 2004)
Currency boards				
Bulgaria (1991:01/ 2004:04)	0.44	-0.13 (1997:04)	87/6.63	1990-97: free floating 1997-99: currency board (1997:07), Deutsch mark anchor (DM) 1999-2004: currency board, euro anchor
Estonia (1992:01/ 2004:04)	0.56	-0.16 (1992:05)	290/6.5	1992-99: currency board, DM anchor (1992:05) 1999-2004: currency board, euro anchor
Lithuania (1992:05/ 2004:04)	0.85	-0.03 (1993:08)	660/2.75	1992-94: free floating 1994-2001: currency board, dollar anchor (1994:03). 2001-04: currency board, euro anchor
Quasi-currency boards				
Latvia (1992:05/ 2004:04)	0.44	-0.202 (1992:08)	286/5.4	1992-94: free floating 1994-2004: anchorage SDR (quasi Currency Board)
Croatia (1989:12/ 2004:04)	0.48	-0.55 (1992:09)	449/4.35	1992-94: free floating 1994-99: anchorage (DM) +/- 2% (quasi CB) 1999-2004: anchorage (euro) +/- 2% (quasi CB)
Reference				
Germany	0.31			..

		Other candidates		
Czech Republic (1993:01/ 2004:04)	0.49	-0.25 (1994:03)	9.7/5.25	1990-96: de facto crawling bands around the DM (+/- 2%)
		-0.14 (1997:06)	9.1/3.75	1996-97: de facto crawling bands around the DM (+/- 5%)
				1997-2004: managed floating
Hungary (1989:01/ 2004:04)	0.64	-0.045 (1991:09)	27/17	1990-92: crawling bands DM (taux multiple).
				1992-94: crawling bands DM (+/- 5%)
		-0.036 (1993:03)	24.7/14.6	1994-99: crawling bands ECU (+/- 2).
				1999-2004: crawling bands (pre-announced rates).
Poland (1989:01/ 2004:04)	0.97	-0.19 (1990:03)	226/16.15	1990-91: anchorage dollar
				1990-93: crawling peg dollar (pre-announced)
				1993-98: crawling band with the dollar and the DM widening of the band of 5 to 10%
				1998-99: crawling band euro 5%
				1999-2004 managed floating
Romania (1991:01/ 2004:04)	0.80	-0.2 (1991:06)	230/48	1990-2001: free and managed floating
		-0.101 (1993:07)	227/42	2001-04: crawling band euro 5%
		-0.06 (1997:05)	178/40	
Slovakia (1994:01/ 2004:04)	0.48	-0.21 (1999:09)	7/8	1993-97: crawling bands DM (2%)
				1997-98: crawling band DM (5%)
				1998-2004: managed floating at less than 5% DM/euro
Slovenia (1992:12/ 2004:04)	0.79	-0.07 (1992:05)	71/9.03	1992-99: de facto crawling bands DM (2%)
				1999-2004: de facto crawling bands euro (2%)
Turkey (1989:01/ 2004:04)	0.99	-0.01 (1989:10)	62/67	1990-99: free floating
				1999-2001: crawling bands euro (5%)

Some countries have a stable coefficient of inflation inertia. The Baltic states implemented early and efficient stabilization plans at the beginning of the transition (1992-93). These plans are based on an unconditional exchange rate fixation. They permit to break the inflationary expectations quickly and to install a low inflationary pace for stable inertia. The success of these plans is due to their early implementation and to the radical changes imposed by the regime. They occur after very high inflation episodes, typical of the beginning of the transition, which contribute to the reduction of inflation inertia.

The other regimes classified as unconditional pegs have a different history. The reforms are undertaken later during the transition and are consecutive to high inflation periods, especially for Bulgaria that went through a period of chronic inflation during the years 1991 to 1995. Unfortunately, the reforms take place only after the appearance of hyperinflation which contributes to breaking the inertia and hence eases the success of the regime. Following the implementation of the regime, the inflation rate stays low.

There are no striking differences between currency boards and quasi-currency boards. We notice however that the lower inertia coincides (Estonia) or precedes by a few months (Lithuania and Bulgaria) the implementation of the currency board. In the case of quasi-currency boards, the drop of inertia follows the end of hyperinflation and precedes largely the fixation of the exchange rate. We infer from this evidence that both regimes have the same effects in the long run but that the currency boards have a more rapid and deeper impact on expectations.

In the other cases, the first month of the transition is often omitted; the data are not available in the Czech Republic and Slovakia before 1993-94 because of the secession. Hence, there is less hyperinflation recorded (except in Poland). Romania and Turkey undergo chronic inflation without significant inflection of the pace; it lowers in Romania but stays at a high level (between 50 per cent and 40 per cent). In the cases of Czech Republic, Hungary and Slovakia, the break in the inertia coefficient indicates a lowering of the inflation pace but less pronounced than under an unconditional peg; the pace after the rupture stays also higher. Poland undergoes hyperinflation episodes during the years 1990-91, then the median rate stabilizes and lowers but stays higher than the rate of unconditional pegs.

In conclusion, the implementation of the currency boards produces a sharp reduction of the inertia (except in Lithuania). In all cases, the implementation of the regime reduces the inflation pace. The coincidence between the reduction of inertia (temporal inconsistency) and the lowering of inflation permits us to deduct a positive effect of the regime on credibility. The Lithuanian anomaly could be explained by political disagreement on the choice of the exchange rate regime and a non relevant choice of the anchor.

The counterfactual given by the quasi-currency boards, Latvia for the Baltic countries and Croatia for Bulgaria do not allow to show different effects between *de jure* and *de facto* currency boards. However, the quasi-currency boards pursue a lasting exchange rate fixation and preference importation which are the conditions for credibility enhancement in our model.

The counterfactual given by the other candidates strongly supports the unconditional fixation. The stabilization is less rapid, the inertia level stays high and the lowering in inflation is small or null for the country implementing flexible or adjustable fixations.

Conclusion

The currency boards in the transition are a very good illustration of a firm commitment to exchange rate and base money rules in order to enhance the credibility of monetary policy. We support the idea that by importing the preferences of the anchor and preserving some discretionary room, the monetary authorities are in a position equivalent to the one of an independent and conservative central banker without having to establish their reputation, which might be quite costly.

The empirical test corroborates the reduction of inflation inertia by the currency boards and the convergence of the inertia towards the anchor level. The efficiency of the regime is conditional on the choice of the relevant exchange rate anchor and the strong support of the government to the chosen rule, even if it looks well established (cf. the case of Lithuania).

Appendix A.4.1 Equations of the Persson and Tabellini model

Persson and Tabellini (1999) synthesized in a model the main results of the literature on credibility. Their model is based on a set of equations describing the economy, on the demand side:

$$\pi = m + v \tag{A1}$$

The inflation level (π) is determined by the money supply m which stands for the growth of the base money, and the money demand shocks v standing for the variation of the circulation speed.

On the supply side:

$$w = W + \pi^e \tag{A2}$$

The public has an objective of real wages W. Hence, they include the rationally expected inflation rate (π^e) in the demanded nominal wage (w).

The production (x) is defined as an expectations augmented Phillips relation:

$$x = \gamma - (w - \pi) - \varepsilon \tag{A3}$$

γ is a parameter which stands for the absolute rate of growth, ε stands for the supply shocks and the expression (w-π) gives the Phillips relation. Using equations A2 and A3, we obtain the expectations augmented Philips relation.

$$x = \theta + (\pi - \pi^e) - \varepsilon \tag{A4}$$

θ is equal to γW; it could be interpreted as the activity level for a given real wage, that is, the natural rate of activity. With the economy described in this way, two kinds of behaviour can be considered: the authorities follow a rule (exchange rate union) or they keep their discretionary capacities (the ability to accommodate shocks).

Appendix A.4.2

Figure A.4.1   Inflation and inflation inertia

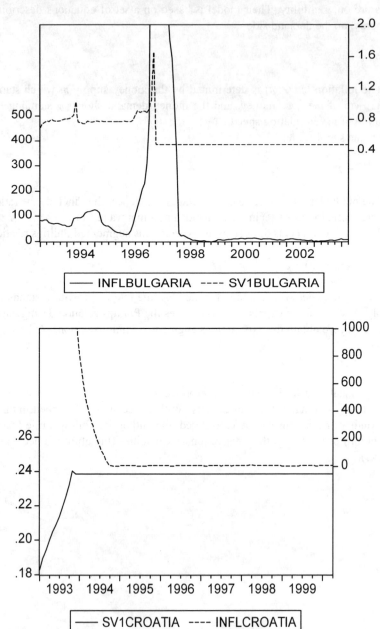

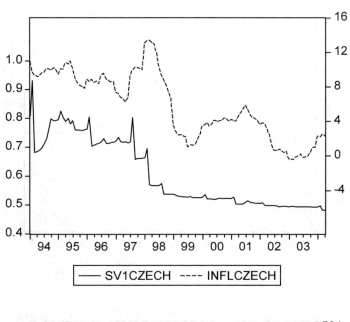

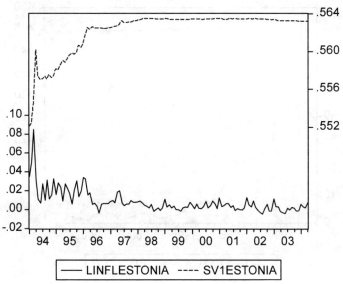

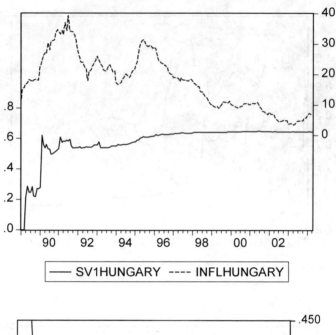

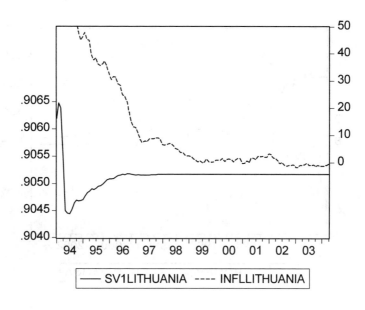

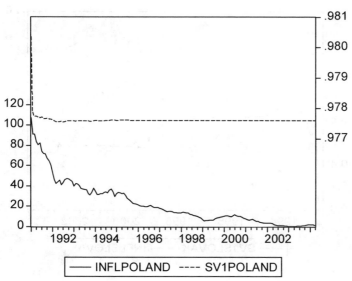

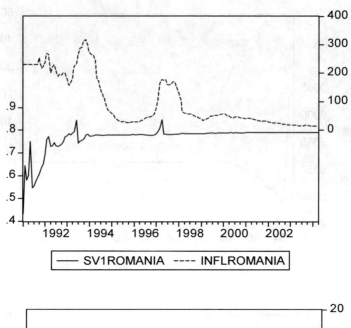

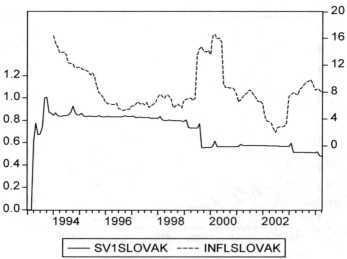

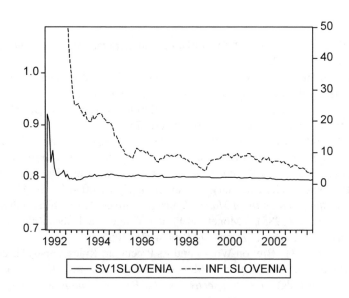

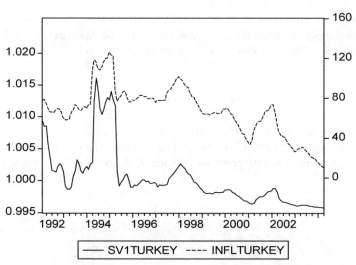

References

Backus, D. and Drifill, J. (1985), 'Inflation and Reputation', *American Economic Review*, 75: 530-38.

Barro, R. and Gordon, D.B. (1983), 'Rules Discretion and Reputation in a Model of Monetary Policy', *Journal of Monetary Economics*, 12: 101-21.

Blanc, J. and Ponsot, J.-F. (2004), 'Crédibilité et Currency Board: Le Cas Lithuanien', *Revue d'Economie Financiére*, 75.

Bordo, M. and Kydland, F. (1996), 'The Gold Standard as a Commitment Mechanism', in T. Bayoumi, B. Eichengreen and M. Taylor (eds), *Modern Perspectives on the Gold Standard*, Cambridge: Cambridge University Press.

Cagan, P. (1956), 'The Monetary Dynamics of Hyperinflation', in M. Friedman (ed.) *Studies in Quantity of Money*, Chicago: University of Chicago Press.

Canzoneri, M.B. (1985), 'Monetary Policy Games and the Role of Private Information', *American Economic Review*, 75: 1056-70.

Giovanni, A. (1993), 'Bretton Woods and Its Precursor: Rules Versus Discretion in the History of International Monetary Regimes', in M. Bordo and B. Eichengreen (eds), *A Retrospective of the Bretton Woods Monetary System: Lessons for International Monetary Reform*, NBER.

Kydland, F.E. and Prescott, E.C. (1977), 'Rules Rather than Discretion: The Inconsistency of Optimal Plans', *Journal of Political Economy*, 85: 473-90.

Lohmann, S. (1992), 'Optimal Commitment in Monetary Policy: Credibility Versus Flexibility', *American Economic Review*, 82: 273-86.

Persson, T. and Tabellini, G. (1990), *Macro-economic Policy, Credibility and Politics*, Chur: Harwood Academic Publishers.

Rogoff, K. (1985), 'The Optimal Degree of Commitment to an Intermediate Monetary Target', *Quarterly Journal of Economics*, 100: 1169-90.

Rogoff, K. and Reinhart, C. (2004), 'The Modern History of Exchange Rate Arrangements: A Reinterpretation', *Quarterly Jourrnal of Economics*, 119/1.

PART 2
RUSSIA AND CIS

Chapter 5

Principles of Monetary Integration and Their Relevance for the CIS

Olga Butorina

Forms of financial integration

Currency zones are the first and the most obvious form of monetary integration. The simplest monetary unions were formed very soon after money as such had appeared. While the first coins were minted in the seventh century B.C. in Lydia (Asia Minor) policies of Ancient Greece already agreed on mutual circulation of their coins in the sixth century B.C. Such a union, for example, was founded by cities of Boeotia in Central Greece. During Caesar's rule (middle of the first century B.C.) the western part of the Roman empire actually became a zone of the Roman Denari. The subsequent history of monetary unions can be traced from the Hanseatic monetary union of the fourteenth century, to Latin and Scandinavian unions of the second half of the nineteenth century and to the modern Economic and Monetary Union of the EU.

Currency zones may be built on two different foundations. The first implies that member-states have equal (or nearly equal) rights, and the currency zone is their joint venture. Its rules and mechanisms are developed collectively. However, it also happens that countries with weak monetary systems group around a state with a strong international currency. Therefore, it is the latter who lays the grounds of the monetary zone and makes minor participants obey the rules. All the main functions such as emission, liquidity management, interest rate policy and foreign exchange operations are in the hands of the main state. This was true for post-war currency zones of the pound sterling and the US dollar (founded on the basis of corresponding pre-war blocks), as well as for the zones of the French franc, the Portuguese escudo and the Dutch guilder. To be sure, dollarization is an extreme version of this relationship.

Exchange rate stabilization is another widespread form of monetary integration. The crash of the Bretton-Woods system of fixed rates raised the question of limiting chaotic movements of exchange rates. It was especially important for West European countries because of intensive intra-regional trade and investment flows. In 1972, the European Economic Community set up the Exchange Rate Mechanism, often referred to as the 'snake' in the 'tunnel'. It introduced a simple band, or a target zone. To keep exchange rates within the margins market interventions were launched. If a currency was losing market value, the national central bank had to buy national currency against the strongest (intervention) currency and vice versa in case of appreciation. This mechanism still exists: at the advent of the euro the ERM-2 was designed for the euro-zone outsiders. At present, four currencies: the Danish krone, the Estonian kroon, the Lithuanian lit and the Slovenian tolar participate in the system.

The European Monetary System (that linked the ERM with the new European Currency Unit – ECU) was founded in 1979. The already existing exchange rate stabilization tools were improved and some new ones were put into place. The powers of the European Monetary Cooperation Fund (established in 1972) were expanded and the member-states transferred 20 per cent of their national reserves of gold and foreign currencies to it. The fluctuation margins were widened, bilateral (symmetrical) interventions were introduced instead of unilateral. The agreement concluded between the central banks stipulated that if a currency diverged from the ECU central rate by 75 per cent of the maximum limit, intramarginal interventions started to prevent exchange rate tensions.

Common measures aimed at exchange rate stabilization, may be taken not only within integration unions. For example, in 1985 the G5 (USA, Great Britain, France, Germany and Japan) concluded the Plaza Agreement providing joint actions for reducing the market rate of the US dollar that was overvalued at that time. This multilateral dialogue led to the Louvre Accord, signed by the G7 in February 1987. The agreement established two fluctuation bands: a narrow (+/-2.5 per cent) band and a wide (+/-5 per cent) band. When the rate approached the first margin, voluntary interventions may begin and at the second margin obligatory interventions had to be started (Funabashi, 1988; Alogoskoufis and Portes, 1997; Eichengreen, 1997).

At the end of the 1990s, in view of the introduction of the single European currency, the USA, the EU and Japan discussed the idea of pegging the main world currencies. Though the initiative was considered unfeasible, the problem of managing the exchange rates of the major world currencies still persists. Because of sharp fluctuations of the euro-dollar exchange rate and, especially, the strong depreciation of the dollar during 2002-2004, the issue was constantly raised at the G7 summits and ministerial meetings. Representatives of China were invited to the one that took place in London in February 2005. The Western countries tried to persuade China to abandon the tight peg of the yuan to the US dollar; they hoped that this would make life easier for other trading nations including the European Union. However, China was too cautious to take any obligations.

Countries of Southeast Asia provide another example of similar practice. After the regional financial crises of 1997, Indonesia, Malaysia, Philippines, Singapore and Thailand concluded the ASEAN Swap Arrangement under which liquidity is submitted to a country for carrying out market intervention to prevent its currency from sharp depreciation. Credits are lent for a period from 90 days to two years at certain interests, while government bonds serve as collateral. A meeting in Thailand in May 2000 extended this agreement to a system of swap arrangements within ASEAN+3 (China, Japan and South Korea) which is called the Chiang Mai Initiative (CMI). It covers the basic principles and operational procedures for bilateral swap transactions designed to provide liquidity support for member countries that experience short-run balance of payments deficits in order to avoid a crisis and to stop a possible regional contagion. At the beginning of 2004, the total amount of bilateral swap arrangements covering all 13 countries was estimated at around $35 billion. The maximum amount of money any individual country could draw ranged from $1billion to $3.5 billion (UN, 2004).

In fact, the CMI looks like the European currency snake without a tunnel: swap credit lines exist just by themselves. Obviously, officially declared margins would impose too rigid obligations over the member states as they would clearly define targets to the speculators and, thus, increase the vulnerability of the whole mechanism.

Trans-border settlement systems exist in two basic forms: netting systems (multilateral clearing) and gross settlement systems. The first one requires a clearinghouse that regularly offsets bilateral requirements and calculates a cumulative balance (active or passive) for each participant. The participants settle their payments only with the clearinghouse and not with each other. On the contrary, gross settlement systems are based on bilateral links. Payments are effected between commercial banks of different countries through participants of the system – the central banks, major commercial banks or their associations. To minimize operational risks, net credit and debit limits are used in netting systems and collateral requirements for opening long positions in gross settlement systems.

In 1950, seventeen countries of the Organization of European Economic Cooperation organized the European Payments Union that established a multilateral clearing system. It was aimed to restore the convertibility of the West European currencies and to get rid of the bilateral barter in the post-war intra-European trade. The Bank for International Settlements (BIS) in Basle served as a clearing house and it managed the resources of the EPU. By 1959, the union had successfully fulfilled its tasks, and the system of multilateral payments was re-established.

In 1985, the largest commercial banks of Europe founded the Euro Banking Association that presents another example of a multilateral clearing system. Originally, it operated in ECU and the BIS was its clearing house. In 1999, payments were switched into euros and the European Central Bank undertook the clearing functions. The daily balances are now settled through the Trans-European Automated Real-Time Gross Settlement Express Transfer system (TARGET) – payment mechanism of the European System of Central Banks (ESCB). Consequently, this purely commercial initiative acquired a supranational component and was involved in the process of intergovernmental integration.

Initially, TARGET was designed as a tool within the European Monetary Union mainly meant to provide cross-border transfers between national central banks of the euro zone, and then it was also decided to use it for commercial settlements. The system consists of three elements: 1) one real-time gross settlement (RTGS) system in each of the EU Member states, 2) the ECB payment mechanism, and 3) a system of common procedures (interlinking) that allow cross-border transfers throughout the EU to move from one system to another. Trans-border payments (with a daily volume of up to 500 billion euro) are effected on a decentralized basis - through national central banks and without ECB involvement. The TARGET2 system is now in the preparation stage; according to the existing plan, it will start operations on 2 January 2007. The new system is meant to provide a harmonized service level, to apply a single price structure and to guarantee cost-effectiveness (ECB, 2004).

In September 2002, the Continuous Linked Settlement Bank (CLSB) was established in New York by the largest world's commercial banks in cooperation with the national central banks and monetary authorities of their countries. The CLSB allows to minimize risks connected with the trans-border payments and arising from a potential opportunity not to receive the bought currency after delivering the sold currency. In December 2004, 58 commercial banks were participants of the system with a daily turnover of 170,000 payments amounting to $1.9 trillion. Having started with seven currencies, CLSB now operates in 15 currencies: the US dollar, the euro, the Japanese yen, the pound sterling, the Swiss franc, the Danish krone, the Norwegian krone, the Swedish krona, the Canadian dollar, the Australian dollar, the Hong Kong dollar, the won of the Republic of Korea, the New Zealand dollar, the Singapore dollar and the South African rand. All operations are carried out through the central banks or monetary and credit authorities of the countries that issue the mentioned currencies. This system as well as the Euro Banking Association and the TARGET combine multinational business with certain elements of intergovernmental integration.

Consolidation of financial markets includes various measures that may be divided into three types. The first implies elimination of foreign exchange controls and barriers in the way of capital movements. This trend has become worldwide since the 1980s both at regional and global level. Whereas in 1976, just 41 countries observed the undertakings set out in Article VIII of the IMF Articles of Agreement (which bans restrictions on current payments, discriminatory exchange practices, and barriers in the way of funds repatriated by foreign investors), in 2004, their number rose to 158. In post-war Europe the most rigid foreign exchange restrictions were removed by the EPU in order to restore convertibility of the European currencies. Nevertheless, many of them were preserved. England, until the mid-1970s, for example, prohibited residents from buying foreign cash in excess of a very low limit, while France in 1983 imposed some very stringent rules on repatriating export earnings, buying foreign currency to pay for imports, covering foreign exchange futures, and making investments abroad. The movement of capitals was liberalized in the EU only in 1992, according to the Single European Act that proclaimed a program of creating a single internal market.

The second direction is mutual opening and consolidation of markets for financial services. In 1998, the EU adopted the Financial Services Action Plan that was aimed at creating the single stock market in 2003 and the single financial market in 2005. For this purpose, new legislative acts – the Council's regulations and directives – were adopted. They harmonize rules covering accounting practices and standards, insurance intermediaries, collateral, market abuse, distance marketing of financial services, activities of financial conglomerates and pension funds, and so on.

The ASEAN Framework Agreement on Services was signed in 1995, and in 2002, it was developed by the Protocol to Implement the Second Package of Commitments on Financial Services. Member countries agreed to enhance cooperation, to open service sectors, including financial services. The Protocol ensures that ASEAN member states that are non-WTO members are accorded the same treatment as other ASEAN members. The purpose is to elaborate a road map towards a free flow of financial services by 2020 (UN, 2004).

The third direction is the development of the market infrastructure. It embraces such actions as mutual access to stock exchanges, prospectus of emission, concerted release of government bonds, assistance in issuing securities denominated in national currencies, joint attraction of foreign investments, monitoring of financial markets, exchange of information between monetary authorities, providing technical assistance, training of experts, and so on.

Types of monetary zones

The history of monetary cooperation enables us to define five basic types of monetary zones:

1. A mutual agreement between independent states on the simultaneous circulation of their national monetary units as legal tender within the territories of the member states.
2. A mutual agreement between independent states on a collective switch to a monetary unit of one of them.
3. A union with a collective unit of account which exists along with national currencies and is used for specific purposes, money for trans-border intra-regional payments.
4. An economic and monetary union with a single currency which replaces national money of member states.
5. A unilateral switch to a foreign currency that replaces national money (Figure 5.1).

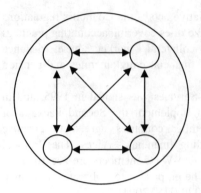

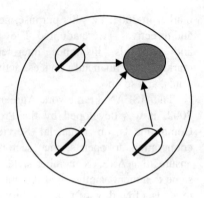

| Type 1 | Simultaneous circulation of national monetary units. | Type 2 | A collective switch to the strongest national currency. |

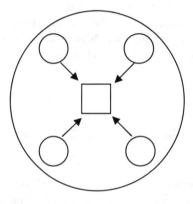

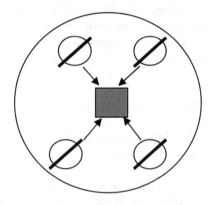

| Type 3 | Introduction of a collective unit of account which exists along with national currencies. | Type 4 | A collective switch to the single currency. |

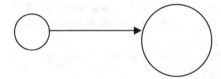

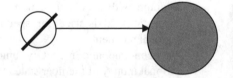

Type 5   A unilateral switch to a foreign currency (preserving a national currency or withdawing it).

Key: ( ) a national currency ;   ☐ a new monetary unit;

Monetary units that replace previous ones are marked with dark colour. A circle around a scheme means a multilateral agreement.

Figure 5.1   Types of monetary zones

Simultaneous circulation of national currencies was the first form of monetary cooperation in the history of mankind and was invented by the ancient Greeks. The same recipe was used in monetary unions that emerged in the second half of the nineteenth century. In 1865, in order to expand its economic influence, France initiated the Latin monetary union that was joined also by Belgium, Italy, Switzerland and Greece. Coins of five states (all of them practiced bimetallism) freely circulated and were the official means of payment within the whole union.

In 1872, Sweden, Norway and Denmark formed the Scandinavian monetary union. All three countries had the silver standard whereas their nearest neighbours — Great Britain and Germany — had already switched to the gold standard. This evoked extra risks for the Scandinavian foreign trade and, generally, for their economic power. Therefore, it was decided to form a common monetary area and to switch together to the gold standard by minting a common coin — the golden krone. Coins of each country were accepted in the two others, and the mintage of change money from silver and bronze was not limited. However, the central banks were obliged to repatriate the change money at first request and/or to exchange it for gold at face value. The agreement also regulated emission and circulation of paper money.

The monetary union of Belgium and Luxembourg that was a part of their economic union concluded in 1921 presents one of the few recent experiences of an official parallel circulation of national currencies. The Luxembourg franc and the Belgian franc were given equal values and their parity was fixed. The Belgian banknotes were legal tender in Luxembourg while the Luxembourg money was not accepted in Belgium (though it was easily exchanged for the local currency). This union existed till 1999 when the two countries entered the euro zone. Interestingly, Luxembourg did not have a central bank before the EMU was established. The National Bank of Belgium was in charge of the emission, and the foreign exchange control was enacted by the joint authority. This particular fact indicates that there was a real bilateral arrangement and not just a de-facto dollarization process.

In fact, parallel circulation of national money was typical for an epoch of full-bodied money. After fiat money dismissed real silver and gold coins throughout the world and especially after the crash of the gold standard this tool of monetary cooperation lost efficiency and thus popularity. It is worth noting that during a three-year transition period (from 1 January 1999 to 28 February 2001) when the euro existed in an invisible form and national currencies of the EMU member-states circulated as sub-units of the euro with fixed parities between them, there was no parallel circulation of the latter within the euro-zone. In fact, one could not pay for goods purchased in Germany with French francs or Italian liras. Moreover, the period of parallel circulation of the euro coins and banknotes with the national coins and banknotes was shortened to a mere two months (from 1 January 2001 to 28 February 2001) instead of the previously planned six months.

Therefore, parallel circulation of currencies of CIS countries is not considered as a probable scenario. However, in the event of a potential Russia-Belarus union, it will be necessary to fix irrevocably the exchange rates (preferably 1:1 for the convenience of calculation), to introduce a single control over the monetary growth, to start close coordination of budgetary policies and the issuance of government bonds.

A concerted switch to the strongest national currency is a rare tool of monetary integration. It is interesting to look at the processes of economic consolidation in Germany before its unification in 1871. In 1833, numerous German lands founded a customs union and, in 1837, the Southern lands agreed to switch altogether to the currency of the strongest state – the Bavarian guilder, or florin. A year later, a similar agreement was concluded by the Northern lands, and the Prussian thaler became their collective currency. At the same time, both unions signed the Dresden monetary convention, under which the rates of the thaler and the guilder were irrevocably fixed. Both currencies circulated within the two unions under the same severe rules of emission. Rules controlling emission of the change money, first introduced in the guilder zone were expanded over the thaler zone.

The Dresden convention also envisaged the creation of a new collective currency – *vereinsmünze*. When Austria joined the German customs union in 1857, they all signed the Viennese monetary convention, which gave life to another collective monetary unit – *vereinsthaler* (Janssen, 1911; Tafunell, 1998).

As we can see, during the unification of German monetary systems different tools were used: concerted transition to a currency of the strongest state, parallel circulation of national coins and banknotes, and introduction of new monetary units.

The twentieth century saw the emergence of several monetary blocks that united the present or former metropolis with their dependent territories, like, for instance, the sterling block or the French franc zone. Countries with fragile monetary systems used the currencies of the strongest state, but these formations could not be regarded as integration because relations between partners were not equal. Cases of a coordinated switch of several countries to a currency of one of them are unknown to the author. With certain reservations, such unions like the former union between Belgium and Luxembourg may be attributed to this form: in the given case, a small state switched to a stronger currency retaining its own monetary unit. The same principle was put into the basis of the South African rand zone created in 1974-1980 by the South African Republic, Lesotho and Swaziland. However, there the process went the other way round: two tiny countries introduced their own money (without squeezing the currency of the dominating state that circulated within their territories earlier).

This form of monetary cooperation also does not represent any interest for the CIS.

Introduction of a collective monetary unit with the preservation of national currencies has been known in Europe since fourteenth century. In 1392, cities of the German Hanse formed a monetary union and started to mint coins of a uniform sample that became widespread in Lubeck, Hamburg, Rostock, Cologne and some other cities. The agreement expanded the financial space of Hanse and helped to solve problems arising from the large number of emitters (in fact, every small princedom or duchy minted its own money). The introduction of common coins made it possible to decrease costs of transactions (converting), to increase their velocity, and also to improve acceptability of the money. Collective monetary units circulating alongside national money existed, as we remember, also in the Scandinavian monetary union and in the union of Bavaria and Prussia.

They became particularly popular after World War II. The European Payments Union had its own units of account, each unit was equal to the gold content of one US dollar at the par value of each currency to the dollar. In 1972, member states of the European Economic Community founded the European Monetary Cooperation Fund (EMCF) which was responsible for settlements and processing very short-term and short-term credits inside the 'snake'. The EMCF got its unit – the European Monetary Unit of Account – EMUA, which was equal to 0.8867088g fine gold, corresponding to the value of the dollar up to 1971. Later, the initiative was taken to redefine the EMUA as a basket of currencies, but it was rejected (Bernholz, 1999). The European Currency Unit, ECU, appeared in 1979 as an element of the European Monetary System. It was a basket currency, and the weights of national currencies in it could be reconsidered from time to time (once in several years) since tensions inside the EMS were relieved by parity alignments. EMU substantially facilitated settlements between the member states of the Community, and played an important role in stabilization of the exchange rates in Western Europe. Official reserves of EEC member states were denominated in ECU and the private use of ECU started in the 1980s. ECU successfully existed until the advent of the euro in 1999.

On 1 January 1970 the International Monetary Fund issued its unit of account – Special Drawing Rights (SDR). At first, the rate of the SDR was strictly fixed to the US dollar, and from 1974, the SDR was converted into a basket of 16 currencies. In 1981 their number was reduced to five: the US dollar, the Deutsche Mark, the Japanese yen, the French franc and the pound sterling. As of 1999, the basket consists of the following shares: 45 per cent – the US dollar; 29 per cent – the euro; 15 per cent – the Japanese yen; 11 per cent - the pound sterling.

The former Council for Mutual Economic Assistance (Comecon) – a regional integration union of socialist countries – also had its unit of account – the transferable rouble. As in the EPU, it was introduced to facilitate payments among member states and to switch from bilateral settlements to multilateral settlements. Originally, it was equal to the official gold content of the USSR rouble, and then its exchange rate was defined on the basis of a basket with regard to the main convertible currencies of the world as well as to some non-convertible currencies like the Indian rupee, the Egyptian pound, the Turkish lira and some others. This unit was meant only for international transactions – it was used as an invoice currency in foreign trade contracts between member states, as a means of payment and a currency for intra-zone credits and investments. The transferable rouble existed from 1964 to 1990. During that period the overall value of deals effected in it amounted to 4.5 trillion transferable roubles, or \$25 trillion (Borisov, 1997).

Different regional groupings of Asia, Africa and Latin America created more than a dozen of various units of account. However, most of them had little significance and short histories.

As we can see, the creation of a unit of account does not require that member states fulfill any stringent economic preconditions. Methods of their formation are so diverse and flexible that they are applicable for nearly any particular situation. Therefore, a collective unit of account could have been successfully introduced in the CIS or in other post-USSR regional unions (like the Eurasian Economic Community (EURASEC), founded in October 2000 by Belarus, Kazakhstan, Kirghizia, Russia and Tajikistan) several years ago. And now it is feasible to do it in a short-time perspective. The advent of such a unit would allow member states to decrease considerably the share of foreign currencies in their foreign trade settlements (at present up to 90 per cent of intra-CIS transactions are invoiced in US dollars). Consequently, it would promote regional trade and reduce the exposure to external shocks, including sharp fluctuations of the world's main currencies. All that is necessary to introduce the CIS unit of account is strong political will and a highly qualified preparation of the project.

Introduction of a single currency, on the contrary, requires immense efforts. The European Union is the only regional grouping that has achieved this result and no other regional organizations are capable of doing it in the foreseeable future.

Are the CIS countries, even in long-term prospect, capable of forming an economic and monetary union and switching to a single currency, similar to the euro? The history of European integration tells us that a monetary union is possible only if it is coupled with an economic union. This means that member states should not simply coordinate their economic policies, but also introduce a common economic policy (like Broad Economic Policy Guidelines, national stability/convergence programs and convergence criteria in the EU). Moreover, before moving to the EMU, a regional grouping should pass through previous stages of integration: a free trade area, a customs union and a single (or common) market providing full freedom of movement of the goods, services, capitals and people. Such a procedure is a stringent law of integration that could not be flouted even by the Europeans: the Werner Plan of 1970 that envisaged that the EEC would form a monetary union by 1980 failed not only because of external shocks (the crash of the Bretton-Woods system and oil crises) but also because member states had no real economic coordination and had not yet proceeded to the single internal market.

But in the CIS, even a customs union has not yet been achieved, and at present, there are few preconditions for the creation of a single internal market. In fact, many factors would impede moving to the highest stages of economic integration, like weak industrial potential, different social and economic structures (some countries have a market economy, others have a planned economy, while still others combine these two with feudal traditions and natural economy), similar commodity structures of exports, and high shares of third countries in foreign trade. Thus, an attempt to observe Maastricht criteria would require enormous effort on the part of CIS countries and – what is most important – would be completely useless. Hypothetically, even if all or some countries of the Commonwealth decided to go over to a monetary union and to achieve a high degree of economic convergence, first, this would require special criteria that would imply specific features of transition economy (so, they should be Alma-Ati or Gomel criteria rather than Maastricht), and, second, member states would need a certain stability pact. Being aware of the difficulties the EU faces in implementation of its Stability and Growth Pact, one could hardly recommend it to the present-day CIS.

It is noteworthy that many regional groupings use the simplest models of integration and have no desire to establish a full customs union or a single internal market. For instance, NAFTA is a free trade zone and ASEAN is just creating it. This fact, however, does not devalue the importance of integration for the countries of the region or lower the effectiveness of its mechanisms.

Unilateral switch to a foreign currency allows a country to quickly restore trust toward local money (which, in fact, ceases to be national), and to get rid, once and for all, of problems concerning inflation, exchange rates, interest rates and many others. All these functions are transferred to the monetary authorities of a country whose currency is introduced instead of the national. Such a way of stabilization is widely practiced by former colonies, protectorates, small islands and tiny states. They pragmatically change monetary independence for the right to use the currency trusted and accepted all over the world.

Panama, from its very foundation in 1904, accepted the US dollar as national currency. The severe economic and political crisis in Ecuador resulted in its full dollarization: in 2000 the national currency – *sucre* – was replaced by the US dollar. From 2001, El Salvador allowed US dollars to circulate in the country alongside the local *colon* (the latter now accounts for a mere 30 per cent of the currency in circulation). In Guatemala, the local *quetzal* is used together with the US dollar. The Swiss franc is legal tender in Liechtenstein. From 2002, Monaco, Andorra, the Vatican and San Marino switched to the euro, whereas they earlier used the French franc, the Spanish peseta, and the Italian lira. Montenegro has unilaterally replaced the former Yugoslavian dinar with the euro.

Such a scenario has nothing to do with financial integration in the CIS. After the first decade of structural reforms, they have all managed to achieve a certain degree of monetary and financial stabilization and are now taking action to widen the functions of national currencies, to develop home financial markets and to withdraw foreign money from internal circulation.

Tools of monetary integration

The given review shows that every particular monetary grouping has its specific structure. Even those unions that were formed at the same time (for instance, Latin and Scandinavian unions) differed from each other in their purposes, instruments and policies. Pure forms of integration that exist in theory are not relevant for real life. For example, the EMU, being a pioneer of a single currency, nonetheless includes some elements that are not obligatory attributes of such a monetary zone from the theoretical point of view. These are: gross settlements system (TARGET), Financial Services Action Plan and ERM-2 for the outsiders of the euro zone.

Therefore, the primary task of the CIS is to elaborate a tailored strategy of financial cooperation, or to opt for its own integration menu. For this purpose, it is useful to break down known monetary groupings up to primary components and to find out whether each of them could be applicable to the present situation in the CIS (Table 5.1).

As it has been proven, *a single currency* (that also requires a common economic policy and a single monetary policy) is not relevant for the CIS, it may be neither feasible nor efficient for them. This assessment will remain true, at least within the next 20 years.

A target zone will not bring sufficient benefits to the CIS in the coming 10-15 years. First, the CIS trade is mainly bilateral and not multilateral as within the EU. For nearly all CIS members, Russia is the number one trading partner and accounts for 40-80 per cent of their intra-regional trade flows. Therefore, multilateral coordination of exchange rates will not be very efficient. Second, expenses for maintenance of a target zone would be really huge. Given different economic structures and policies, comparatively weak currencies and high mobility of capitals, enormous funds will be needed for market intervention. During 11 months of the EMS crisis in 1992-93, the central banks of Great Britain, France, Italy, Spain and Sweden spent $100 billion on intervention (Mishkin, 1995). The Bundesbank alone spent DM 145 billion that stood for about $90 billion (Bernholz, 1999). At present, only Russia among the CIS member states has large official reserves, at the end of 2004 they amounted to $125 billion. The reserves for Ukraine were about $10 billion and for Kazakhstan, $9 billion. Other countries' reserves were much smaller. For example, in Belarus and Kyrgyz Republic they were less than $1 billion. In the case of a target zone, currencies with insufficient backing will fall easy prey to speculations. Thirdly, for sustainable coordination of exchange rates the national central banks would need, if not identical, then very close interest rates that are impossible without real economic convergence.

Table 5.1   **Some monetary and financial unions and their main tools**

	European Payments Union	European currency snake	European Monetary System	Economic and Monetary Union	ERM-II	Chiang Mai Initiative	Applicability for the CIS
1. Single currency + single monetary policy	--	--	--	+	--	--	--
2. Target zone	--	+	+	--	+	--	--
3. Unilateral interventions	--	+	--	--	--	+	+
4. Pooling of official reserves	--	+	+	+	--	--	-- +
5. Concerted interventions	--	--	+	--	+	--	--
6. Swap credits for market interventions	--	+	+	--	--	+	+
7. Collective unit of account	+	--	+	--	--	--	+
8. Trans-border multilateral clearing	+	--	--	--	--	--	+
9. Trans-border gross settlements	--	--	--	+	--	--	+
10. Removal of foreign exchange controls	+	--	--	--	--	--	+
11. Financial markets integration	--	--	--	+	--	--	+

Note: ERM-II is a part of the EMU, and here it is shown separately for the convenience of the analysis. Within the ERM-II short-term credit facilities (up to three months) are available for market intervention. At the time of writing, they amount to EUR 300 million for Estonia, to EUR 350 for Slovenia, to EUR 390 million for Lithuania, to EUR 730 million for Denmark.

Fourthly, at the beginning of the 1990s, the turnover of the world financial markets increased dramatically. While in 1989, its daily value was near $600 billion, in 1995, it grew to $1,200 billion and in 2004, it climbed to $1,900 billion

(BIS, 2004). Consequently, methods of regional exchange rate stabilization that had been used previously lost their efficiency. Regimes of pegged but adjustable rates like the EMS of the 1980s in which governments attempted to hold exchange rates within narrow bands were no longer viable (Eichengreen, 1994).

Unilateral interventions that were used in the European currency snake and are now a part of the CMI, can also be taken on board by the CIS. Their main purpose is to prevent a currency from a sharp depreciation in case of an endogenous shock or an organized attack. It should be added that due to the overall weakening of the international position of the US dollar and a growing twin deficit (fiscal and current account) there may emerge a tricky situation when the CIS members would have to keep their currencies from an undesirable strengthening.

As for *concerted, or symmetrical interventions*, this tool will not be adequate for the CIS. First, the Commonwealth does not have and never will have a polycentric structure like the European Union where there are at least four big countries. On the contrary, Russia accounts for two thirds of the population and the GDP of the CIS. Not surprisingly, it is the greatest holder of foreign exchange reserves. This means that intervention in support of all other currencies, besides the Russian rouble, and partly, the Ukrainian hryvnia and the Kazakhstan tenge, would lie on the Bank of Russia.

Second, the central rates of the European currencies within the EMS were stipulated against the ECU and to other currencies of member-states. Thus, joint action was normally effected in two intervention currencies – a depreciating national currency and the Deutsche Mark. In all CIS countries, exchange rates are oriented towards external currencies, mainly, the US dollar. Therefore, the second intervention currency will be the dollar rather than the Russian rouble. In other words, bilateral interventions may exist if currencies of the CIS member states are pegged to each other or to a collective unit of account, for example, to a basket currency compiled of the national currencies. Should this take place, the national central banks will keep part of their official holdings in the CIS unit of account, as well as in Russian roubles, the Kazakhstan tenges, the Ukrainian hryvnias, and so on.

A collective unit of account, as it was pointed out above, can be created in the CIS without any serious difficulty. Its basket may include both foreign currencies, and national. The latter would, of course, be the most appropriate, since it would stimulate the usage of national currencies. At present, none of them enjoys more than a negligible share in domestic foreign trade, let alone in the international investment operations.

Pooling of official reserves is, in general, possible inside the CIS. However, because of the great asymmetry in the volumes Russia and other member states hold, this measure does not seem very useful, at least at present. Probably, after a collective unit of account is subsequently created, such a step will be more justified.

Bilateral swap credits would be extremely useful for the CIS member states, as they add a lot to the foreign exchange stability and need nearly nothing, except for competent professional elaboration of agreements. In ASEAN the first agreement of this type was signed in 1977, and at the end of the 1980s it got its second breath by drawing up the Chiang Mai Initiative. The number of bilateral credit lines within CMI is constantly growing. In 2001, there were five, in 2002, six more appeared, and in 2003 they increased by another five. In most cases, countries with large foreign exchange reserves – Japan, China and South Korea offer their partners (among them also Thailand, Philippines, Malaysia, Indonesia and Singapore) loans in dollars. However, three credit lines created by China envisage that Japanese yens, South-Korean wons and the Philippine peso are exchanged for yuans. In January 2005, Thailand and Japan reformed the existing agreement of 2001 under which Japan was ready to sell dollars for bahts. Now the arrangement has become bilateral – in case of emergency each country will sell dollars in exchange for the national currency of a borrower.

A similar framework can be well implemented in the CIS. The Bank of Russia and also, probably, the central banks of Kazakhstan and Ukraine could open credit lines for other member states. These measures would considerably reduce the risk of an abrupt depreciation of the national currencies. Even if the amount of resources under the agreements is not really that big, it will give an important signal to the markets because the central banks involved will gain extra possibilities to counter speculative attacks without enlarging their reserves. It is also important that the funds will be available on first call, compared with IMF financial assistance which is always very late and often entail heavy moral pressure, macroeconomic constraints and an abrupt capital outflow.

By the way, special criteria would be quite appropriate in this framework. Their main purpose would be not to reach economic convergence but to maintain strong fiscal discipline. The size of available credits may depend on budget consolidation.

Trans-border multilateral clearing is also possible in the CIS. It is important that all the tools of such systems are well-known and well-tested. A multilateral clearing normally needs a single unit of account and a clearing house that could be the Interstate Bank of the CIS or another financial institute. If multilateral clearing will not be supported at once, it is useful to begin, at least, with bilateral clearing. Anyhow, it would be a good starting point and could diminish the demand for US dollars in intra-regional trade. One may recollect that during the Soviet era settlements between the USSR and Finland were made in a special bilateral unit – a clearing rouble, and both parties benefited from the system.

To organize a trans-border gross settlement system, like TARGET, member states need to have national real-time gross settlement systems (RTGS). In June 2004, the Bank of Russia and SWIFT signed an agreement on building such a system in this country. Afterwards, similar systems will probably emerge in other member states. When they are launched, at least in several countries, it will be possible to connect them in a joint circle.

Any group of countries can agree on *easing of foreign exchange controls*, especially, if their financial markets are approximately at the same level of development, that is quite fair for the CIS. The majority of member states have signed under Article VIII of the IMF Articles of Agreement and their currencies are *de jure* convertible. Now it is necessary to achieve the highest reasonable level of convertibility and to introduce every-day bilateral market quotations of national currencies of the CIS countries. This task is clearly specified in the Concepts of Cooperation and Coordination of Activities of CIS Member States in the Monetary Sphere adopted by the Council of Heads of Governments of the CIS countries on 15 September 2004.

Consolidation of financial markets is also a feasible and appropriate task for the CIS. The first step in this direction was taken by the International Association of Currency Exchanges of the CIS countries founded in 2000 by the 16 exchanges from eight member states. Its main goal is to create a common currency exchange area and to improve positions of CIS exchanges in their cooperation with the European platforms. Besides, the parties agreed to exchange information and to monitor developments in the financial markets of the CIS, to promote the admission of non-residents to the exchange operations, to facilitate capital flows in national currencies and to enhance introduction of the international standards of stock market operations. In the mentioned concepts of monetary cooperation of the CIS countries it is said that member states shall grant each other the most favoured nation regime in the sphere of financial services, and shall adopt a single list of restrictions on the access to the markets of financial services. Hopefully, this will allow them to pool the efforts of the member states and the private sector in the process of creating a deep and liquid common financial market of the CIS.

References

Alogoskoufis, G. and Portes, R. (1997), 'The Euro, the Dollar, and the International Monetary System', in P.R. Masson, T.H. Krueger and B.G. Turtelboom (eds), *EMU and the International Monetary System*, Washington: IMF.

Bank for International Settlements (2004), *Triennial Central Bank Survey of Foreign Exchange and Derivatives Market Activity in April 2004*, Basle: BIS.

Bernholz, P. (1999), 'The Bundesbank and the Process of European Monetary Integration', in Deutsche Bundesbank, *Fifty Years of the Deutsche Mark: Central Bank and the Currency in Germany since 1948*, Oxford, New York: Oxford University Press.

Borisov, S. (1997), *Rubl: zolotoy, chervonny, sovetsky, rossiisky. Problema konvertiruemosti*, Moscow: Infra-M.

Eichengreen, B. (1994), *International Monetary Arrangements for the 21st Century*, Washington: Brookings Institution.

European Central Bank (2004), *Annual Report – 2003*, Frankfurt-am-Main: ECB.

Funabashi, Y. (1988), *Managing the Dollar: From the Plaza to the Louvre*, Washington: Institute for International Economics.

Janssen, A.E (1911), *Les conventions monétaires*, Paris: F.Alcan and R.Lisbone.

Mishkin, F. (1995), *The Economics of Money, Banking and Financial Markets*, HarperCollins College Publishers.

Tafunell, X. (1998), 'La UEM y las lecciones de la historia: las uniones monetarias en Europa durante el siglo XIX', in A. Anchuelo (ed.), *Consecuencias ecónomicas del euro*, Madrid: Editoral Civitas.

United Nations (2004), *Meeting the Challenges in an Era of Globalization by Strengthening Regional Development Cooperation*, New York: U.N. Economic and Social Commission for Asia and the Pacific.

Chapter 6

The Credibility of CIS Exchange
Rate Policies

Christian Bauer and Bernhard Herz

Introduction

Several CIS central banks have chosen the exchange rate as an intermediate policy target. By pegging their exchange rate governments typically want to promote trade and/or improve the credibility of their monetary policy. Thus an exchange rate anchor is considered to be a straightforward way to improve the transparency and accountability of monetary policy as the exchange rate is a simple, easily understandable and measurable indicator.

After the contagion effects of the 1998 Russian rouble had abated, the CIS countries chose different paths to regain monetary stability (see Keller and Richardson, 2003). Belarus, Kazakhstan, Russia, and Ukraine have reduced inflation considerably by managing their (US dollar) exchange rates. The crawling band of the Belarus rouble to the US dollar and/or the Russian rouble, however, still implies high two digit inflation levels, while the de facto bands of Kazakhstan, Russia, and Ukraine lowered inflation below 12 per cent. The Ukraine in 2002 even experienced a slight deflation. The main objective of monetary policy in the CIS is price stability, accompanied by exchange rate stability (Belarus and Ukraine) or prevention/limitation of a real appreciation (Kazakhstan and Russia). The central banks in Russia and Ukraine have de facto operational independence. The central banks in Belarus and Kazakhstan, on the other hand, are neither de jure nor de facto independent.

Having experienced the 1998 Russian rouble crisis and the 2001 crisis of the neighbouring Turkish lira, investors as well as long term trade contractors are particularly wary in their assessments of the economic situation and policies of the CIS. Therefore, markets' assessments of the CIS monetary policy might serve as a valuable indicator of the (future) economic stability in this region.

We analyze the exchange rate behaviour and the credibility of the exchange policy in a micro-structure model of the foreign exchange market. This approach is based on market sentiments and has the major advantage that the empirical analysis relies on exchange rate data only. In particular, it does not need any macroeconomic data nor any data on the market micro-structure, both potential sources of data problems.[1] Our approach is based on Jeanne and Rose (2002) which we extend by taking into account the macroeconomic environment. The market micro-structure is based on the interplay of fundamental and technical traders. As in De Long, Shleifer, Summers, and Waldmann (1990), technical traders react to trend signals and create excess volatility through their actions (see also De Grauwe, Dewachter, and Embrechts, 1993; Frenkel, 1997; and Hung, 1997). Strong signals, for example steep or rampant trends, induce technical traders to enter the market thereby increasing the exchange rate volatility. This yields a U shaped relation between the observed exchange rate trend and volatility, that is, observed exchange rate volatility 'smiles'.

Monetary policy influences the volatility of the exchange rate via two channels, fundamental exchange rate volatility and, via the credibility channel, excess volatility. In the case of a managed exchange rate the conditional volatility of the exchange rate is low either due to currency market interventions and/or an exchange rate orientated interest rate policy. In contrast, exchange rate volatility is high in the case of a floating rate regime. If the exchange rate management is credible, excess volatility is low as technical traders will react more reluctantly to trend signals, since they expect trend breaking interventions. Obviously excess volatility is high, if the credibility of the exchange rate regime is low.

Combining these results we can identify four sectors corresponding to four types of exchange rate regimes in the fundamental volatility-excess volatility plane:

1. Credibly managed exchange rate regimes with low base and low excess volatility
2. Non-credibly managed exchange rate regimes with low base and high excess volatility
3. Floats of large currencies with high base and low excess volatility
4. Floats of small currencies with high base and high excess volatility.

Tight pegs with virtually no exchange rate volatility and currency crises with extremely high volatility are the border cases.

In our empirical analysis we compare the exchange rate policies of Belarus, Kazakhstan, Russia and Ukraine as the four largest and economically stable CIS countries with the benchmark of three potential candidates for an EU accession, namely Bulgaria, Romania and Turkey. In doing so we focus on:

1. The official exchange rate regime
2. The de facto exchange rate behaviour
3. The markets' assessments of the exchange rate policies, that is the credibility of the central banks'' announcements and actions.

---

[1]   See Keller and Richardson (2003) for the severe problems of obtaining consistent economic data for several CIS countries.

We empirically determine the development of de facto exchange rate regimes of these countries and test their credibility as assessed by the market participants. In contrast to classification schemes in von Hagen and Zhou (2002), Levy-Yeyati and Sturzenegger (2004), or Reinhart and Rogoff (2004), we explicitly differentiate between exchange rate regimes with high and low credibility. Concerning the choice of the nominal anchor the high level of dollarization in the CIS[2] has made the US dollar the natural choice. However, the degree of dollarization is currently declining in some of these countries. Therefore monetary policy in the CIS might be re-orientated in the long run. The growing importance of the euro area trade might suggest the euro or an euro-US-dollar currency basket as a nominal anchor (see Keller and Richardson, 2003). Therefore we analyze both the euro and the US dollar exchange rates of the CIS countries.

In a first step we analyze the measured exchange rate trend and volatility relation with OLS regressions. Our empirical results confirm the model prediction of an U shaped relation between observed exchange rate trend and volatility. Using a parametric regression on separate windows we then analyze the evolution of monetary policies and their credibility throughout the sample period.

We find that in the case of all four CIS countries the markets assign a relatively high degree of credibility to the exchange rate management. The paths to credibility, however, were quite different. Russia had reached some stability and credibility as early as 1995. The Ukraine and Kazakhstan gained stability for the first time in 1996 and 1997 respectively, while Belarus had considerable credibility problems until 2000. The 1998 Russian rouble crisis disrupted the exchange rate policies in all of these countries and each country went its own way to recover.

Belarus, like Romania, manages the exchange rate as a crawling peg. Romania pegs its exchange rate to the euro, while Belarus has chosen the USD as nominal anchor. Markets assign a certain degree of credibility to both crawling pegs. The relatively constant rates of depreciation appear to have only nominal effects. Taken together all four CIS countries have reached relatively high levels of stability and credibility compared to the benchmark of the potential EU accession countries.

The growing importance of the euro area trade also seems to affect the exchange rate policy. The stabilization of the USD exchange rates also includes the smoothing of the euro rates, however to a somewhat lower degree.

The remainder of the chapter is organized as follows. In section 1 the choice of the nominal anchor for an exchange rate regime is discussed. We shortly describe the phenomenon of de-dollarization based on the empirical evidence for the newly gained credibility. In section 2 the theoretical model is developed while section 3 presents the empirical evidence. Section 4 concludes.

---

[2]   Ohnsorge and Oomes (2004) estimate that at the beginning of 2003 about 40 per cent of the effective broad money aggregate in Russia consisted of foreign currency deposits and foreign currency in circulation.

Exchange rate volatility and nominal anchor

When deciding on its exchange rate policy a government has to determine two key features:

1. The degree of exchange rate stabilization
2. The nominal anchor, that is the exchange rate which is to be stabilized.

In the case of the CIS there have been strong incentives for exchange rate stabilization as these countries have developed into open economies which do not have a long history of macroeconomic stability. Concerning the nominal anchor the USD has been a natural choice because of its central role as an international currency. The CIS and especially Russia heavily depend on the export of commodities which are quoted in US dollars. Also the high degree of dollarization in the CIS (see Table 6.1) might have been an argument for the US dollar as the nominal anchor. Another possible anchor is the euro because of the growing importance of the trade with the euro area. Also, the CIS have traditionally strong trade relations with some of the new EU members which are on their way to join the European exchange rate mechanism (ERM2) and subsequently the European Monetary Union (EMU).[3] Last but not least there is a considerable inflow of foreign capital from the euro zone into the CIS. In order to further improve trade and investment relations a stronger orientation of the exchange rate policy towards a euro anchor could thus become appropriate.

Formally, the exchange rate policy implies choosing the feedback parameters α and λ from $(0,1)$.

$$m = \frac{1-\lambda}{\lambda}\left[(1-\alpha)\left(e_{euro} - \bar{e}_{euro}\right) + \alpha\left(e_{dollar} - \bar{e}_{dollar}\right)\right]$$

---

[3]   Slovenia, Estonia and Lithuania joined the ERM2 on the June 28, 2004.

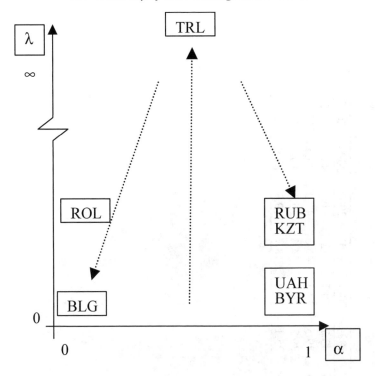

Figure 6.1   Stylized presentation of the exchange rate regimes of CIS and potential EU accession countries

e denotes the exchange rate, and m is a policy instrument, for example money supply or an interest rate. The feedback parameter λ describes to what degree a central bank stabilizes its exchange rate, while parameter α determines the relative weight of the Deutschmark/euro and the US dollar as nominal anchors. e denotes the respective exchange rate target. Low values of λ imply a strong reaction of the central bank to exchange rate movements, that is a fixed exchange rate regime. $\alpha = 0$ indicates a euro peg and $\alpha = 1$ a dollar peg (see Figure 6.1).

We now want to analyze the role of the dollarization level for the choice of the nominal anchor more closely and the (future) orientation of the monetary policy in the CIS countries. The dollarization ratios (see Table 6.1) sharply increased in the aftermath of the rouble crisis of 1998 (Kazakhstan, 1999). In 2003 Kazakhstan and Russia, and Belarus since 2001, show significant signs of de-dollarization. This tendency continues in 2004. The Ukrainian dollarization ratio increases from 2001 to 2003 and begins to slightly decrease in 2004.

Table 6.1   **Dollarization ratios**

	1993	1994	1995	1996	1997	1998	1999	2000	2001	2002	2003	2004
Belarus	37.7	56.5	23.5	24.2	27.3	55.6	43.7	58.7	52	49	44.2	42.5
Kazakhstan	54.6	26.2	24.3	20.5	10.5	10.4	29.5	37.4	46.6	47,3	35.5	33.7
Russia	29.5	28.8	20	19.4	18.5	29.9	29.2	26.9	24.5	25.4	18.9	17.3
Ukraine	19.4	32	22.8	18.3	13.3	21.3	25.1	23.2	18.7	19.3	21.9	21

Source: IMF European II department database.

In all countries the dollarization ratio was very high when the de facto management vis-à-vis the US dollar was introduced in 1999 or 2000.[4] The increase of the dollarization ratio is a direct consequence of the low credibility of the monetary policy of that period. The 1998 crisis greatly damaged the credibility of the rouble and the Russian banking system. Situations were similar in the other CIS countries. Rebuilding credibility after 1998, the Russian central bank faced severe challenges. The new intermediate policy target had to ensure monetary stability to give the economy a reliable basis for growth. This target had to be simple and transparent to help rebuild credibility. Given the high level of dollarization the choice of the US dollar exchange rate as nominal anchor was the most efficient if not the only way to rebuild credibility of the monetary policy in this situation.

In the empirical section 3 we show that the CIS countries have managed to rebuild credibility of their monetary policies.[5] Since 2003 the degree of dollarization in Russia is in decline due to the improved credibility of the banking system as well as increased internal and external monetary stability.[6] A further de-dollarization could offer new options for CIS monetary policy makers. If the level of dollarization is sufficiently low, alternative intermediate targets become practical. The challenge then is to switch to another more appropriate target without losing the credibility gained via the US dollar peg.

What are the alternative targets the Russian central bank could use? In principle monetary policy can choose between two types of intermediate targets with each type bearing characteristic challenges for sustaining credibility through the change of the policy target. Typically, transferring credibility should be the easier the fewer changes there are in the policy framework. The first approach is to continue the peg but switching to a new exchange rate anchor, for example the euro or a currency basket.[7] In this case it should be relatively easy for monetary policy to sustain credibility because it has already established a record of a credible policy within an exchange rate framework. In the second case, the choice of an internal anchor like inflation or nominal GDP targeting, maintaining credibility might be more difficult. Monetary policy in the CIS has not established a positive record for this class of targets so that the uncertainty associated with this type of targets might be considerable.

---

[4] The increase of the dollarization ration in Kazakhstan goes along with the strong depreciation of the Tenge in 1999.

[5] The theoretical model does not explicitly include the level of dollarization within a country. It merely yields tools to analyze the credibility of a country's monetary policy assigned by the market.

[6] Ohnsorge and Oomes (2004) convincingly argue that a number of particularities – like the missing inflation puzzle – Russia's monetary policy has been characterized by in the past years are directly linked to the high level of dollarization and the de-dollarization.

[7] For example the switch of the nominal anchor in the Eastern Caribbean in 1976 from pound Sterling to US dollar.

While the process of de-dollarization and currency appreciation is best understood in the case of Russia, the situation is very similar in other CIS countries.

They too have regained credibility and stability of the exchange rate. In the case of Kazakhstan the currency has appreciated vis-à-vis the US dollar in step with the Russian rouble and monetary policy has regained credibility (see below for a detailed analysis). The crawling peg of the Belarus rouble is credible and stronger orientation of Belarus towards Russia, which could even lead to the proposed currency union, goes hand in hand with a more stable exchange rate. Finally, while the Ukraine hryvna did not appreciate, its US dollar exchange rate has remained nearly stable since 2002. In 2003 the credibility of the hryvnia was lower than that of the other three CIS exchange rates (see below), which might be one reason for the late tendency of de-dollarization.

Taken together, the process of de-dollarization might evoke similar policy opportunities in these CIS countries as has been discussed for the case of Russia.

Market assessments of the exchange rate regime

The basic model

Market assessments of the underlying exchange rate and monetary policy crucially affect the viability and the economic consequences of an exchange rate regime. The second generation currency crises models for example show how self-fulfilling expectations of market participants can trigger currency crises (see, for example, Obstfeld, 1994; and Jeanne, 2000). Adoptions of the Barro-Gordon model to exchange rate regimes analyze the role of credibility for the effects of monetary policy (for example, Melitz, 1988; Andersen, 1994; or Bensaid and Jeanne, 2000). If decisions on exchange rate policy are discretionary rather than rule based, low credibility and self-fulfilling expectations lead to a suboptimal policy output. Such a rule should be an explicitly stated and verifiable policy including the choice of the nominal anchor and target exchange rate.

We base our empirical analysis of exchange rate behaviour and the role of market sentiments on a micro-structure model of the foreign exchange market which also takes into account the macroeconomic environment. In particular we are interested in the role of technical trading in currency markets. The impact of technical trading on asset volatility has been analyzed by Bertola and Caballero (1992) for exchange rates and has been generalized for other assets by Balduzzi, Foresi, and Hait (1997). Our model generalizes the approach of Jeanne and Rose (2002) by introducing technical trading and non IID macroeconomic variables.[8]

The macroeconomic aspects of the model are captured by a conventional two country monetary model of the exchange rate with freely mobile capital. In money

---

[8]   For a more detailed discussion of the theoretical model, see Bauer and Herz (2005b).

market equilibrium, money supply m_t equals the interest elastic money demand in both countries. The exchange rate is given by:

$$e_t = m_t - m_t^* + \alpha\left(i_t - i_t^*\right) + q_t,$$ (1)

where p denotes the price level, i the interest rate, and q the real exchange rate.[9] Foreign is a large country that remains in the long run equilibrium, that is foreign macroeconomic variables are normalized to:

$$m_t^* = p_t^* = i_t^* = 0,$$ (2)

so that the exchange rate equation (1) simplifies to:

$$e_t = m_t + \alpha i_t + q_t.$$ (3)

The micro-economic aspects of the model build on an overlapping generations model with risk averse heterogeneous traders. The foreign country is large relative to the home country so that the market processes are driven by the foreign traders' investment decisions. The foreign traders face a portfolio optimization problem between a safe asset in their domestic country and an asset in the small home country which has a risky return due to the unknown exchange rate change. Adjustments of the interest rate clear the market.

The optimal wealth allocation depends on the expected excess return of domestic bonds relative to foreign bonds, so that the investments depend on the expected exchange rate, the interest differential, and the risk of such investments. We extend the theoretical approach of Jeanne and Rose (2002) along two lines. Firstly, we introduce an explicit monetary and exchange rate policy by the central bank. Secondly, we specify technical trading as a source of noise in exchange markets.

Technical traders react to trend signals and create excess volatility through their actions. Strong signals, for example steep or rampant trends, induce technical traders to enter the market thereby increasing the exchange rate volatility. This yields a smile of the observed exchange rate volatility. Volatility increases if trends are strong and declines if trends fade, that is volatility smiles if plotted against the trend.

---

[9] Our approach can be generalized as a sticky-price economy. However, this approach would also have complicated the analysis without generating further insights in our context.

Technical trading: Trends and volatility

A central feature of our model is the technical traders' assessment of the excess return:

$$\rho_{t+1} = i_t - i_t^* + e_t - e_{t+1} \qquad (4)$$

of a foreign investment. Traders in the foreign exchange market face a portfolio allocation problem. They have to optimize the portfolio weights of the foreign asset position under uncertainty about the excess return of that asset. Based on public and individual information each trader chooses his optimal action, that is whether to enter the foreign exchange market at some cost and to determine the optimal size of the foreign position. The interest rates adjust to ensure money market equilibrium.

Heterogenity in the foreign exchange market is represented by two types of traders: fundamentalists and technical traders. These types of traders differ in their marginal costs of fundamental analysis. Fundamentalists use new information to update their fundamental analysis. In contrast, chartists use technical analysis to process the new information at time t and do not update the fundamental analysis.[10] Technical traders extract information f_t about the excess return from observed exchange rate trends.

$$E_t^{\text{fund}}(\rho_{t+1}) = E_t(\rho_{t+1}) \text{ and} \qquad (5)$$

$$E_t^{\text{chartist}}(\rho_{t+1}) = E_{t-1}(\rho_{t+1}) + (1-\mu)f_t + v_t. \qquad (6)$$

The technical traders' expectation of the excess return consists of the lagged expectation of the excess return ρ_{t+1} which includes the interest differential between foreign and home $i_t - i_t^*$, the trend expectation $(1-\mu)f_t$, and noise v_t. The term $(1-\mu)$ depicts the credibility of monetary policy as seen by the technical traders. If the monetary policy is credible, that is $\mu \approx 1$, the impact of trends on technical traders is negligible. The central bank is expected to break exchange rate trends. Only very large trends, $|(1-\mu)f_t| \approx 0$, can significantly influence the traders' decisions. If credibility is low, that is $\mu \approx 0$, even relatively small trends are expected to continue and to yield excess returns.[11]

The model solution for the conditional volatility v_e of the exchange rate is characterized by:

---

[10]   See De Grauwe and Grimaldi (2002).

[11]   A potential area for future research is the integration of a structural equation for the credibility parameter which may depend on other variables like the real exchange rate or the amount of reserves.

$$2ag - \ln(1+c) = \frac{\left(\frac{a\bar{B}}{N_i} v_e + (1-\mu)f\right)^2}{(1+c)v_e\left(1 + \frac{1+\beta}{\beta\sqrt{c}} \sqrt{1 - \frac{v_{fund}}{v_e}}\right)^2} \tag{7}$$

for $v_e \in (v_{e,\min}, v_{e,\max})$.[12] The equilibrium curve is also influenced by the fundamental variance v_{fund}, the number of fundamentalists N_i, the size of the noise c, the interest semi-elasticity of money demand β, the market size $\bar{B}$, the market entry costs g, and the risk aversion of the traders a.

The stylized volatility smile in Figure 6.2 shows the equilibrium solution. The smile is characterized by two levels of volatility. The low volatility equilibrium represents the fundamental volatility or base volatility of the exchange rate. It is located around the centre where trends are small. No chartists are in the market and excess volatility is zero. This volatility is caused by macroeconomic variables. In contrast, the high volatility equilibrium occurs at large trends when all technical traders are active. The difference in volatility between these two levels is the maximum excess volatility induced by technical trading. Since technical traders are most active when large trends occur the maximum level of volatility is reached at large trends.

---

[12] A full derivation of the equilibrium equation is left to the appendix available from the authors upon request (email Bernhard.Herz@uni-bayreuth.de). For a more detailed discussion of the theoretical model see Bauer and Herz (2005b). They also show that the comparison of a broad sample of countries allows the classification of the de facto exchange rate regimes and their credibility.

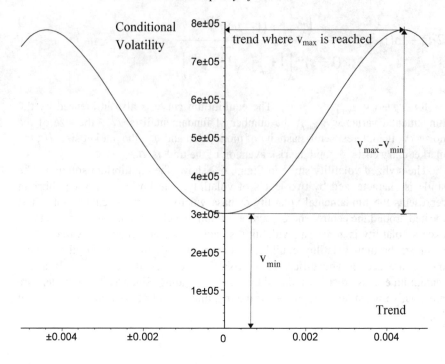

Figure 6.2   Stylized volatility smile with measure of fundamental and excess volatility

This brings us to the question, in which way do technical traders extract trend information from the data? Models of technical traders often use weighted averages of past returns r_t (for example, De Grauwe and Grimaldi, 2002)

$$f_t = \sum_{i=1}^{n} w_i r_{t-i} \qquad (8)$$

Positive weights w correspond to trend followers, negative weights to adverse trading strategies. Exponential trends are given by $w_i = w^i$, $0 < w < 1$. We use a simple moving average trend rule with $w_i = \frac{1}{n}$ and a window size of $n = 5$ trading days.

Implied volatility smiles are well known from empirical analysis of derivatives using various versions of the Black-Scholes pricing formula. Some explanations link these volatility smiles to technical trading due to portfolio insurance and hedging (for example, Frey and Stremme, 1997; and Sircar and Papanicolaou, 1998). Note that the smile of the *implied* volatility in this literature differs from the smile of the *measured* volatility discussed in this chapter. The implied volatility is the solution of the pricing formula of a derivative, where the derivation depends on certain assumptions on the underlying process of asset returns and market structure. In contrast, the measured volatility in our model is the empirical volatility of the asset itself.

Monetary policy: Fundamental and excess volatility

In our context, monetary policy influences the volatility of the exchange rate via two channels, fundamental exchange rate volatility and credibility. In the case of a managed exchange rate the conditional volatility of the exchange rate is low, while it is high in the case of a floating exchange rate. If monetary policy is focused on stabilizing the exchange rate, its goal is to reduce the expected difference between the exchange rate and the target rate $\bar{e}$:[13]

$$m_t = -\mu_{NB} E_{t-1}\left(e_t - \bar{e} - m_t\right) + \varepsilon_t. \tag{9}$$

The equilibrium exchange rate is given by equation (3) $e_t = m_t + \alpha i_t + q_t$. To stabilize the expected deviation of the exchange rate from its target value the money supply has to be adjusted according to the reaction function (9). The expected deviation must be calculated without the money supply itself in order to prevent circular calculation. Further we assume that the central bank is able to actually perform its policy.

Within this exchange rate policy the central bank reduces the fundamental or base volatility of the exchange rate. Monetary policy can also reduce the excess volatility. If the exchange rate management is credible ($\mu \approx 1$), excess volatility is reduced to a large degree, since technical traders have no incentive to enter the market. If the exchange rate is floating ($\mu_{NB} = 0$), the assumption of a trend breaking exchange rate policy would be unreasonable. Thus free floating exchange rates have ceteris paribus not only higher fundamental volatility, but also higher excess volatility.

An exchange rate regime is managed credibly if the market participants believe that the current de facto regime is continued within a short horizon. Therefore this type of credibility may not be confused with a predictor for exchange rate crises in a fixed exchange rate regime for example the interest differential, a black market rate exchange rate or the amount of reserves. Although not directly addressed in our the theoretical model, an irrevocably fixed exchange rate on the one and a currency crisis on the other side behave like border cases of the model. The fixed exchange rate results in very low fundamental and excess volatility and virtually no trends. An exchange rate crisis or a regime shift results in excessive market movements.

---

[13] The target value $\bar{e}$ may vary over time for example in the case of a crawling peg.

The amount of excess volatility depends on the activity of the technical traders and thus on the relative weight of fundamentalists and chartists in the market as well as the size of the noise. If there are only a few technical traders, the maximum excess volatility created by their activity is lower than in a market with a high share of technical traders. We assume that small currency markets like the euro-Romanian leu market are more likely to be influenced by technical trading than foreign exchange markets for the three major currencies US dollar, euro and Japanese yen.[14] Transactions between the large currencies are to a higher degree portfolio based or pure vehicle transactions for the exchange of less liquid currencies. Furthermore, the number of traders and trades in large markets is much higher than in small markets. Thus the individual weight of each trader is higher in small markets and information is more clumpy. The structure of private information in large foreign exchange markets should be closer to white noise than in small currencies markets.

Figure 6.3 plots the equilibrium volatility for various exchange rate regimes: the volatility smiles. Size and location of the smiles vary with the market structure and the exchange rate regime. The model can be solved for the conditional volatility of the exchange rate without specifying the type of trend used by the chartists. Figure 6.3 displays the impact of the type of the monetary regime and the credibility on the volatility smile derived in the theoretical model in equation (7).

Each of the smiles in Figure 6.3 can be characterized by its fundamental and excess volatility. Monetary policy can influence both base and excess volatility. The base volatility depends directly on the behaviour of macroeconomic variables like money. By managing the exchange rate the central bank (partially) offsets the fluctuations of fundamental variables and thus lowers the base volatility. The influence of the monetary policy on the excess volatility depends on its credibility. The chartists' activity and in turn the level of excess volatility is reduced only if the policy is credible, that is if the chartists believe in trend breaking interventions by the central bank.

---

[14] De Grauwe and Decupere (1992) find only very weak evidence for psychological barriers in dollar/yen and dollar/deutschmark exchange rates.

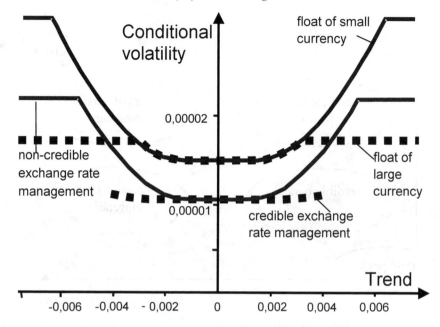

**Figure 6.3   Volatility smile for different market sizes and
exchange rate regimes**

Summarizing, we can combine our results to identify five sectors in the fundamental volatility-excess volatility plane:

1. Credibly managed exchange rate regimes with low base and low excess volatility
2. Non-credibly managed exchange rate regimes with low base and high excess volatility
3. Floats of large currencies with high base and low excess volatility
4. Floats of small currencies with high base and high excess volatility
5. Tight pegs with virtually no exchange rate volatility and currency crises with extremely high volatility are the border cases.

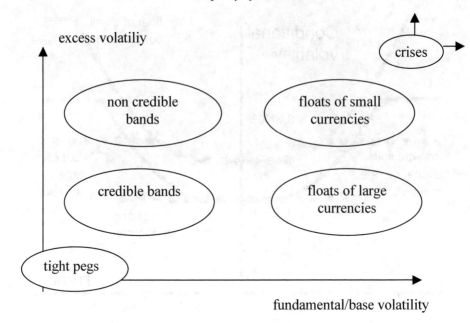

Figure 6.4 Classification scheme of exchange rate regimes based on market assessment

Empirical characteristics of the exchange rates

The theoretical model yields two main implications: (1) observed volatility smiles and (2) the size as well as the location of the smile, that is the base and the excess volatility, characterize the type of exchange rate policy and its credibility. In this empirical section we analyze the behaviour of exchange rates and test these hypotheses. After discussing descriptive statistics of the rates we analyze the smile of the measured volatility over the entire sample period. Afterwards we look into the development of the exchange rate regimes and their credibility over time.

Our data cover daily euro and US dollar exchange rates of Belarus, Kazakhstan, Russia and Ukraine as the four largest and economically stable CIS countries with the benchmark of three potential candidates for an EU accession, namely Bulgaria, Romania and Turkey. The data are from 10/05/1994 to 05/12/2004.[15]

---

[15] The Romanian leu series starts at 10/23/1995.

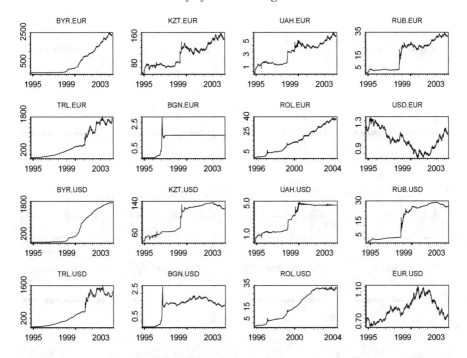

Figure 6.5   Euro and US dollar exchange rates: 1994-2004

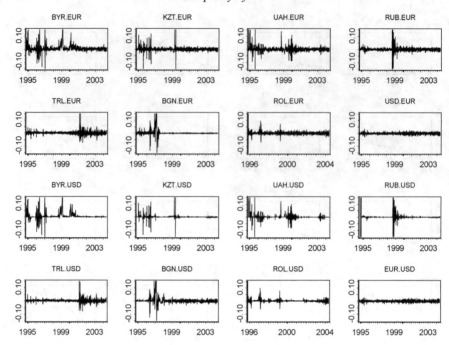

Figure 6.6   Daily returns of euro and US dollar exchange rates: 1994-2004

Looking at the euro and US dollar exchange rates and their logarithmic returns a number of characteristics are evident. Firstly, the exchange rates of the CIS countries have been relatively stable vis-à-vis the US dollar since approximately 1999. This is in line with the official objectives of monetary policy according to the legislation of the four CIS countries, that is price and exchange rate stability in Belarus, disinflation and the prevention of a real appreciation in Kazakhstan, price stability and limitation of real appreciation in Russia, and stability of the monetary unit (that is price level and exchange rate stability) in Ukraine.[16]

The Russian rouble (RUB) crisis from 1998 caused notable disturbances in the other exchange rate systems, too. This contagion was partially due to factors typically emphasized in the contagion literature such as strong trade links and investor behaviour. Contagion could have also been caused in some of the smaller CIS countries by their monetary policy focus on Russia. Belarus officially pegs his rouble (BYR) to the Russian rouble and the US dollar. Although since 2003 officially the Russian rouble is the main nominal anchor for the BYR and the US dollar conversion rate is only a side target, Belarus maintains a de facto crawling peg to the US dollar and tracks devaluation target against the US dollar more

---

[16]   See Keller and Richardson (2003).

closely than the rouble target. The greater smoothness of the BYR-USD exchange rate compared to the BYR-RUB rate indicates a greater de facto importance of the US dollar target. Also the Kazakhstan Tenge (KZT) closely tracks the Russian rouble mimicking the moderate re- and devaluations of the rouble to the dollar. The Ukraine Hryvna (UAH) is nearly stable vis-à-vis the US dollar since spring 2002 and faced minor disturbances in spring 2003. Before the 1998 crisis, only Russia and Kazakhstan smoothed their dollar exchange rates and in the first half of the 1990s all of the CIS countries had extremely volatile exchange rates with respect to the US dollar and the euro.

In contrast, the EU accession candidates Bulgaria and Romania stabilize their Deutschmark/euro exchange rates. Bulgaria installed a currency board system in 1997 and fixed the exchange rate of the lev (BGN) at a level which is equivalent to about 1.95 euros. The Romanian central bank has maintained a policy of constant leu (ROL) devaluation against the euro of approximately 30 per cent per annum for the last five years. Finally the Turkish lira (TRL) has obviously undergone a regime shift after the 2001 crisis from low to high volatility, that is from a managed to a floating regime.[17]

Volatility smiles

Figures 6.7 and 6.8 show OLS regressions of the volatility smile for the entire sample period and for the period after 2000, that is after the effects of the 1998 rouble crisis have bottomed out. We analyze the USD exchange rates of the CIS currencies and the euro exchange rates of the benchmark countries according to their nominal anchors. The first eight figures display the results on an individual scale, while the second half displays the same result on a common scale to allow for comparison. Each of the exchange rates can be classified according to the equilibrium patterns shown in Figure 6.3.

We estimate the observed trend and conditional variance in non-overlapping windows of about one week's length (five data points). In each window t the currently observed trend f_t is estimated by the mean of the returns (cf. equation 8). The conditional variance v_t is estimated by the empirical variance of returns. The model implies that technical traders react to the occurrence and strength of trends. Thus volatility increases after the appearance of trends. For all regressions we thus use data points (f_t, v_{t+1}). Bauer and Herz (2004) show that this separation of the windows from which trend and volatility are estimated ensures that typical time series processes like random walk, GARCH, GARCH-in-Mean or FIGARCH processes do not show the smile. They also prove that there is no endogenous bias which connects high volatility and large trends.

Using an OLS-regression we fit the even fourth order polynomial:

---

[17]   For the empirical analysis of the exchange rate behaviour we split the Turkish lira time series into two parts, one before the 2001 crisis (TRL1) and one afterwards (TRL2).

$$v_{t+1} = \gamma_0 + \gamma_2 f_t^2 + \gamma_4 f_t^4 \tag{10}$$

to the trend-volatility estimates (f_t, v_{t+1}). This type of regression is not robust. It reacts sensitively to credibility problems. Structural breaks like a change of the exchange rate regime or a currency crisis will bias the results towards a more pronounced U-shape and less credibility, that is if there is a sample period with low credibility within an otherwise credible sample, the credibility problem dominates the result. For example the regression on the USD rates for the entire sample period including the rouble crisis show distinct U-shapes while the regressions of the period after the crisis do not yield significant U-shapes.

The estimations are sensitive to the credibility problems. We track the development of each regimes' credibility throughout time in the next section.

Evidently, the euro and US dollar exchange rates of the small countries are characterized by a pronounced U shape in the analysis of the entire sample period. For the stable period, that is after 2001 in the case of Belarus and 2000 for the other countries, the typical characteristics of the exchange rate management are clearly visible. The crisis situations in the first years of the sample account for the limited credibility of the regimes and the high excess volatility during that period. The exchange rate management is responsible for the smaller short term trends and reduced exchange rate volatility in the case of the CIS countries as well as Romania and Bulgaria.[18]

Figure 6.8 helps to identify the de facto nominal anchors. Comparing the regressions of a currency against two possible anchors, the exchange rate to the de facto anchor shows smaller trends and a less pronounced U-shape than the other exchange rate.[19] In general the fundamental and the excess volatility of the CIS-US dollar exchange rates is significantly lower than the respective euro rates. In contrast the currencies of the potential EU members are characterized by lower fundamental and excess volatility in the case of the euro rates than the US dollar rates. Consequently, the CIS manage their exchange rates vis-à-vis the US dollar, Romania and Bulgaria vis-à-vis the euro. The BYR, the KZT and the RUB show very low volatility against the US dollar, and behave in a similar way as the US dollar against the euro. The BGN and to a lesser degree the ROL move more in line with the euro.[20]

The Bulgarian lev shows nearly no trend nor conditional volatility vis-à-vis the euro and mimics the euro very closely. The USD exchange rates of Belarus, Kazakhstan, and Russia show moderate volatility for intermediate positive trends

---

[18] For Belarus we observe excessive volatility and strong trends even in 2001.

[19] The regressions on the euro exchange rates of the CIS and the US dollar rates of the benchmark countries are available from the authors upon request.

[20] The regimes of Romania and Belarus are very similar: pre announced crawling pegs against the euro and the US dollar respectively. However, the fundamental short term volatility of the ROL/EUR exchange rate regime is significantly higher.

and nearly no volatility for low trends. Only the Ukrainian currency shows significant volatility and a U shape indicating technical trading and reduced credibility at least for part of the sample period.[21]

Obviously the exchange rates of the CIS as well as Romania and Bulgaria are relatively similar after the CIS recovered from the aftermaths of the Russian rouble crisis. The exchange rates are managed, that is there are no large trends visible and fundamental volatility is low. Markets also assess a relatively high credibility to the exchange rate policy since excess volatility is comparatively low. Figure 6.8 indicates the similarity of the exchange rate behaviour of these currencies when compared to the free float of the Turkish lira. Trends and volatility of the Turkish lira are up to 20 times larger than those of the other exchange rates.

One remarkable result of this first analysis is the conditional volatility of the Romanian leu and the Belarus rouble. Their excess volatilities are remarkably low implying that the pre-announced crawling pegs are credible. For the Leu the minimum of the volatility is at an average logarithmic trend of 0.0014 per cent per working day or 35 per cent per year, that is the smile is shifted to the right. The Romanian leu-euro rate has the lowest excess volatility of the euro exchange rate sample with the exception of the euro rates of the US dollar and the strictly pegged Bulgarian lev.

Finally the regime shift of the Turkish lira (TRL) after the 2001 crisis from a managed to a floating regime is clearly visible in Figure 6.8. The high base and excess volatility as well as the size of the occurring trends demonstrate that the actual exchange rate regime of Turkey is a free float and subject to a high degree of technical trading, that is market participants do not expect any sort of exchange rate management.

---

[21] The analysis in the next section highlights a credibility problem of the Ukrainian monetary policy in 2000 and in 2003.

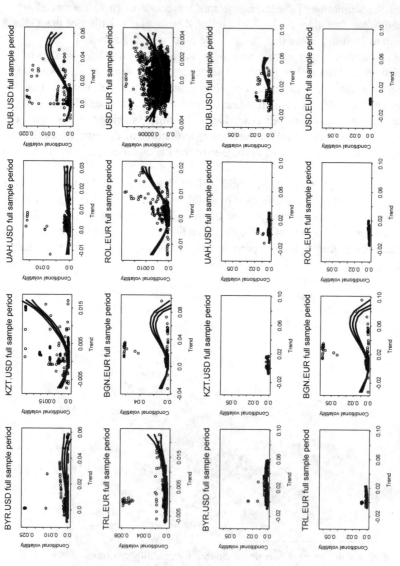

Figure 6.7 OLS regression of an even 4th order polynomial with five per cent confidence bands for the entire sample period, individual scaling (top), common scaling (bottom)

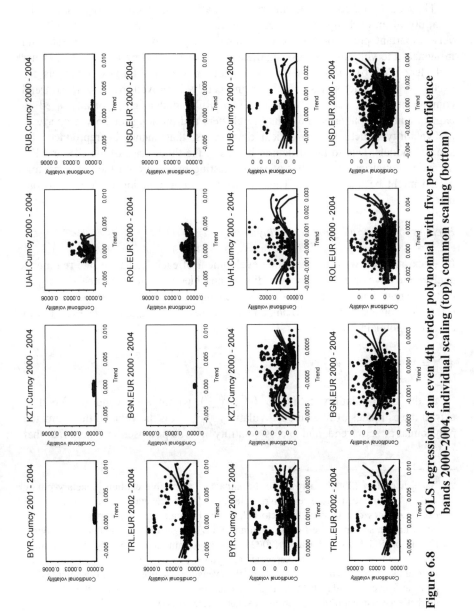

Figure 6.8 OLS regression of an even 4th order polynomial with five per cent confidence bands 2000-2004, individual scaling (top), common scaling (bottom)

Bauer and Herz (2004) show that the U shape of the conditional volatility is also evident in OECD exchange rates and is not replicated by simple benchmark models like a random walk. They further show that even sophisticated heteroskedastic time series models, namely GARCH (p,q) or FIGARCH ($1,d,1$), do not show a U shaped dependency between trend and volatility as is characteristic for the data.[22]

The model predicts and the empirical estimates from Figure 6.7 suggest that the volatility of an exchange rate is related to its trend. The actual trend is indeed a very important predictor for the conditional volatility of the exchange rate and influences the volatility process significantly. Bauer and Herz (2005a) and Bauer and Herz (2005b) show that the explanatory power of FIGARCH models for exchange rate time series can be significantly improved by adding a trend component to the variance equation. FIGARCH-models are typically used to explain complex patterns like volatility clusters and the long memory property in the volatility structure of empirical time series, that cannot be reproduced by simpler models. Due to the structural breaks in the time series of the CIS and EU accession countries the validity of such a testing procedure on the entire sample period might be questionable. Thus we forbear from applying these tests to our data.

Exchange rate regimes and credibility

In a next step we want to track the development of each exchange rate regime to analyze the development of their credibility and identify structural breaks. To gain better insight into the nature of the exchange rate regimes we perform our estimations on a yearly basis. Using an OLS-regression we again fit the even fourth order polynomial:

$$v_{t+1} = \gamma_0 + \gamma_2 f_t^2 + \gamma_4 f_t^4 \qquad (11)$$

to the trend-volatility estimates (f_t, v_{t+1}) within each window. We then extract the estimates of fundamental volatility γ_0 that is the value of the estimated polynomial at zero trend, and excess volatility $\frac{-\gamma_2^2}{4\gamma_4}$ as proposed in Figure 6.2, that

---

[22]   Bauer and Herz (2005b) investigate the impact of a credible explicit monetary policy within the microstructure exchange rate model and generate a classification for exchange rates due to their de facto behaviour. In contrast to other popular de facto classification schemes like Levy-Yeyati and Sturzenegger (2003), Reinhart and Rogoff (2004) or Reinhard and Calvo (2002), this algorithm does not rely on additional macroeconomic data like reserves, which are typically available only on a monthly base. Instead the classification is based only on the exchange rate itself which is available on a daily and even intraday base that is the exchange rate's behaviour that reflects the market's assessment of the underlying exchange rate regime.

is the difference between the fundamental volatility and the maximum of the estimated polynomial.

The visualization of the regression results in the following figures allows a more direct interpretation than the regressions illustrated in the Figures 6.7 and 6.8. The fundamental and the excess volatility are estimated from each volatility smile and both estimates for each country are displayed in a single graph. To analyze the development of the regimes and their credibility we carry out these estimations for each year separately. As shown above fundamental and excess volatility can be interpreted as measures for the type and the credibility of an exchange rate regime, if the degree of capital mobility is unaltered.[23] Indices of capital controls suggest that the degree of capital controls in the CIS has remained nearly unchanged since 1997 (see Table 6.2).

Table 6.2   Heritage fund: Index of economic freedom: Capital controls and foreign investment

	1995	1996	1997	1998	1999	2000	2001	2002	2003
Belarus	3	3	4	4	4	4	4	4	4
Bulgaria	2	2	3	3	2	2	2	2	3
Kazakstan	NA	NA	NA	4	4	4	4	4	4
Romania	2	2	2	2	2	2	3	3	3
Russia	2	2	3	3	3	3	3	3	3
Turkey	2	2	2	2	2	2	2	3	3
Ukraine	3	3	3	3	3	3	3	3	4

Figure 6.9 visualizes development of the fundamental and the excess volatility of the CIS-USD exchange rates and the benchmark euro exchange rates on a yearly basis. To allow a visual interpretation of the volatilities which vary over more than one order of magnitude, Figure 6.9 presents the square roots of the volatilities, that is, the standard deviations. The excess volatility is a measure of the credibility of the monetary policy. During a crisis, both fundamental and excess volatility increase as the credibility of monetary policy decreases. Clearly recognizable are the earlier problems of the Ukraine (1995) and Belarus (1996), the Russian rouble crisis (1998) and its aftermaths in Kazakhstan (1999) and Ukraine (1999-2000), as well as the problems in Belarus (1999-2001). Also the Turkish lira crisis in 2001 and the crisis of the Bulgarian lev triggered by the banking crisis in 1997 are clearly visible.

Figure 6.9 shows the fundamental and the excess volatility of the examined exchange rates on a yearly basis for each country, in greater detail and in equal scaling. We find that in the case of all four CIS countries the markets assigned a

---

[23]   The remaining parameters are also assumed to be stable.

relatively high credibility to the exchange rate management in recent years. The CIS-USD exchange rates after 2000 (Belarus after 2001) display low base and excess volatility indicating credible exchange rate management.[24] The paths to gaining this credibility, however, were quite different.

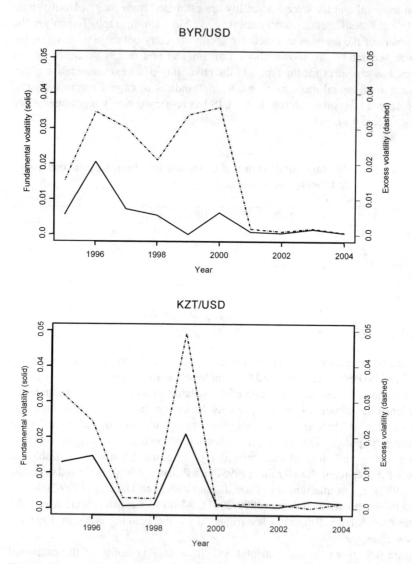

Figure 6.9   Markets' assessment of fundamental and excess volatility of the CIS-USD exchange rates and the benchmark euro exchange rates on yearly basis and common scaling

---

[24]   The Ukraine, however, encountered a credibility problem in 2003.

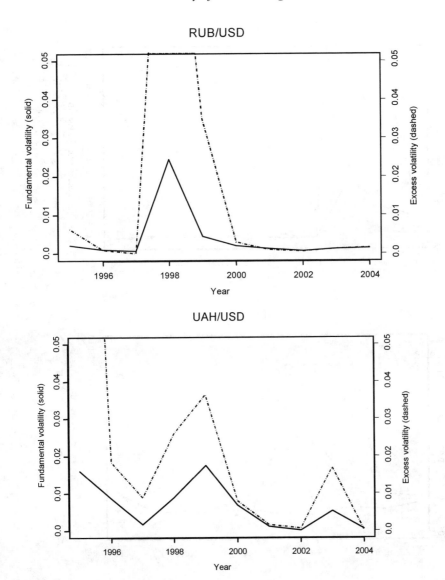

Figure 6.9 (cont.)

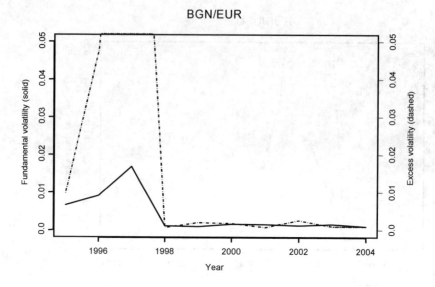

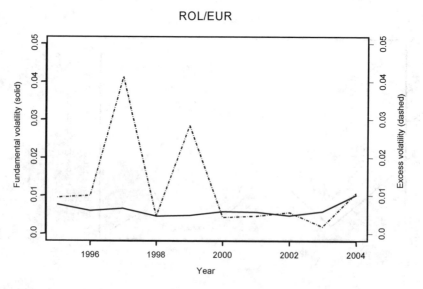

Figure 6.9 (cont.)

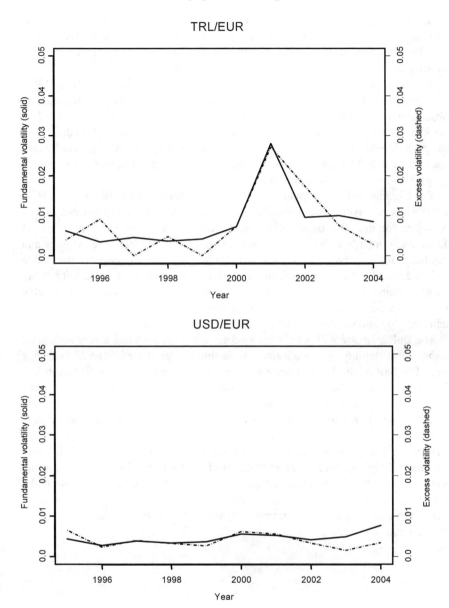

Figure 6.9 (cont.)

Belarus had a dramatic increase in fundamental volatility in 1996. In the following years fundamental volatility consolidated, but the Belarus rouble had considerable credibility problems until 2000. Beginning with 2001 markets assessed the Belarus rouble to be a more stable and credible exchange rate.

Russia reached some exchange rate stability and credibility as early as 1995. However, the 1998 rouble crisis disrupted exchange rate policy in Russia and subsequently in other CIS countries. The Russian rouble encountered a considerable increase in fundamental volatility and a marked loss of credibility in that year. Already in 1999, the rouble stabilized and regained a lot of credibility. Since the year 2000 market participants assess the Russian monetary and exchange rate policy to be relatively stable and credible.

The Ukraine and Kazakhstan gained relative stability for the first time in 1996 and 1997, respectively. The distortions of the Russian rouble crisis led to a loss of credibility for the Ukraine in 1998, which was followed up by a drastic rise in fundamental volatility and a further loss of credibility in 1999. The stability and credibility of the tenge suffered a large slump in 1999 as a side effect of the rouble crisis. Kazakhstan regained much of its credibility and fundamental stability rather quickly within a year. Since the year 2000 the tenge has been perceived as a stable and credible currency. The hryvna was assessed as less credible and behaved less stably in 2000 and seems to be subject to credibility problems in 2003.[25]

The Bulgarian lev with its currency board system is assigned a very high level of short term stability and credibility comparable to that of the USD-CIS exchange rates. The plot of the lev in Figure 6.9 shows that the crisis in 1997, which had already arisen in 1996, is completely surmounted with the introduction of the currency board. The overall assessment of the crawling peg regime of the Romanian leu is relatively credible, although in 2004 fundamental and excess volatility have increased. Fundamental and excess volatility remain at an intermediate level: far less than under a floating regime like the Turkish lira, but considerably higher than the currency board of the Bulgarian lev. The crisis of the Turkish lira in 2001 is characterized by a steep rise in fundamental volatility and a loss of credibility at the same time. While the extreme fundamental volatility declined to a level typical for a floating regime within a year, credibility remained low until 2003.

---

[25] The official exchange rate, as determined by the National Bank of Ukraine, does not show these fluctuations. Since we determine the market's assessment of the monetary policy we use market rates prepared by Bloomberg. Other sources for market determined rates like Oanda yield similar results. Since these fluctuations occur only in the hrynva exchange rate they seem to express the market sentiments indicating a lower degree of credibility.

Conclusions

Our empirical analysis indicates that in recent years the markets have assessed the exchange rate management of the four CIS countries Belarus, Kazakhstan, Russia and Ukraine as relatively credible. Both the de facto peg of the Ukraine and the crawling peg of Belarus as well as the management of Kazakhstan and Russia show low fundamental and low excess volatility. Only the Ukrainian peg faced minor credibility problems in 2003.

The paths to gaining this credibility, however, were quite different. Russia had reached some stability and credibility as early as 1995. The Ukraine and Kazakhstan gained stability for the first time in 1996 and 1997, respectively, while Belarus had considerable credibility problems until 2000. The 1998 Russian rouble crisis disrupted the exchange rate policies in all of these countries. While Russia suffered from credibility problems in 1999 and had recovered in 2000 the crisis reached other CIS countries in 1999. Kazakhstan had regained full credibility and fundamental stability as early as 2000, while the Ukraine remained with a high level of fundamental volatility in 2000 and Belarus struggled with credibility problems as long as until 2000.

Belarus like Romania manages the exchange rate as a crawling peg. Belarus has chosen the USD as nominal anchor, while Romania pegs its exchange rate to the euro. Markets assign a certain degree of credibility to both crawling pegs. The relatively constant rate of depreciation appears to have only nominal effects. Taken together all four CIS countries have reached relatively high levels of stability and credibility compared to the benchmark of the potential EU accession countries.

All four CIS countries have chosen the US dollar as their nominal anchor. The process of de-dollarization in Russia might offer the possibility of switching to a new policy target without risking losing credibility. The credibility gained through a policy of monetary stability over the past years might serve as the basis for a credible monetary policy focused on a different target. The growing importance of the euro area trade might provide an incentive to include the euro exchange rate as a policy target. When moving to an internal anchor, for example inflation targeting, maintaining credibility could be much more difficult, since monetary policy in the CIS does not have a positive record for this class of objectives.

References

Andersen, T.M. (1994), 'Shocks and the Viability of a Fixed Exchange Rate Commitment', *CEPR Discussion Paper*, 969.

Balduzzi, P., Foresi. S. and Hait, D.J. (1997), 'Price Barriers and the Dynamics for Asset Prices in Equilibrium', *Journal of Financial and Quantitative Analysis*, 32: 137-59.

Bauer, C. and Herz, B. (2004), 'Noise Traders and the Volatility of Exchange Rates', *Quantitative Finance*, 4, 4: 399-415.

Bauer, C. and Herz, B. (2005a), 'How Credible are the Exchange Rate Regimes of the New EU Countries? Empirical Evidence from Market Sentiments', *Eastern European Economics*, 43, 55-77.

Bauer, C. and Herz, B. (2005b), 'Technical Trading, Monetary Policy and Exchange Rate Regimes', *Global Finance Journal*, 15, 3: 281-302.

Bensaid, B. and Jeanne, O. (2000) 'Self-Fulfilling Currency Crises and Central Bank Independence', *Scandinavian Journal of Economics*, 102, 4: 605-20.

Bertola, G. and Caballero, R. (1992), 'Target Zones and Feedback Effects from Dynamic Hedging', *American Economic Review*, 82: 520-36.

De Grauwe, P. and Decupere, D. (1992), 'Psychological Barriers in the Foreign Exchange Markets', *Journal of International and Comparative Economics*, 1: 86-101.

De Grauwe, P., Dewachter, H. and Embrechts, M. (1993), *Exchange Rate Theory: Chaotic Models of Foreign Exchange Markets*, Oxford: Blackwell.

De Grauwe, P. and Grimaldi, M. (2002), 'The Exchange Rate and its Fundamentals: A Chaotic Perspective', *CESifo working paper*, 639, 6.

De Long, J.B., Shleifer, A., Summers, L.H. and Waldmann, R.J. (1990), 'Noise Trader Risk in Financial Markets', *Journal of Political Economy*, 98, 4: 703-38.

Frenkel, M. (1997), 'Exchange Rate Dynamics with Chartists, Fundamentalists, and Rational Speculators in the Foreign Exchange Market', *International Journal of Business*, 2, 1: 1-24.

Frey, R. and Stremme, A. (1997), 'Market Volatility and Feedback Effects from Dynamic Hedging', *Mathematical Finance*, 7: 351-74.

Hung, J.H. (1997), 'Intervention Strategies and Exchange Rate Volatility: A Noise Trading Perspective', *Journal of International Money and Finance*, 16, 5: 779-93.

Jeanne, O. (2000), *Currency Crises: A Perspective on Recent Theoretical Developments*, Volume 20 of Special Papers in International Economics, Princeton University.

Jeanne, O. and Rose, A.K. (2002), 'Noise Trading and Exchange Rate Regimes', *Quarterly Journal of Economics*, 117, 2: 537-69.

Keller, P.M. and Richardson, T. (2003), 'Nominal Anchors in the CIS', *IMF Working Paper*, WP/03/179.

Levy-Yeyati, E. and Sturzenegger, F. (2003) 'To Float or to Fix: Evidence on the Impact of Exchange Rate Regimes on Growth', *American Economic Review*, 93, 4: 1173-93.

Levy-Yeyati, E. and Sturzenegger, F. (2005), 'Classifying Exchange Rate Regimes: Deeds vs. Words', *European Economic Review*, 49, 6: 1603-35.

Melitz, J. (1988), 'Monetary Discipline and Cooperation in the European Monetary System: a Synthesis', in S. Micossi, F. Giavazzi and M. Miller (eds), *The European Monetary System*, Cambridge, Mass.: Cambridge University Press.

National Bank of the Republic of Belarus (2004), *Report on Implementation of the Republic of Belarus Monetary Policy Guidelines for 2003: Attaining Monetary Policy Objectives*, Technical report, National Bank of the Republic of Belarus.

Obstfeld, M. (1994), 'The Logic of Currency Crises', *Cahiers Economiques et Monétaires*, 43: 189-213.

Ohnsorge, F. and Oomes, N. (2004), 'The Case of the Missing Inflation: De-Dollarization in Russia', *IMF Working paper*.

Reinhard, C. and Rogoff, K. (2004) 'The Modern History of Exchange Rate Arrangements: A Reinterpretation', *Quarterly Journal of Economics*, 119, 1: 1-48.

Reinhart, C.M. and Calvo, G.A. (2002), 'Fear of Floating', *Quarterly Journal of Economics*, 117, 2: 379 -408.

Sircar, K.R. and Papanicolaou, G. (1998), 'General Black-Scholes Models Accounting for Increased Market Volatility from Hedging Strategies', *Applied Mathematical Finance*, 5: 45-82.

von Hagen, J. and Zhou, J. (2002), 'De Facto and Official Exchange Rate Regimes in Transition Economies', *ZEI - working paper*, B13.

Chapter 7

Monetary Policy Rules for Russia

Akram Esanov, Christian Merkel and Lúcio Vinhas de Souza[1]

Introduction

The last ten years have witnessed an upsurge in research on monetary policy rule evaluation motivated by the seminal paper of Taylor (1993). Following this study, a great number of researchers have investigated the Federal Reserve's (the US Central Bank) behaviour using either a simple Taylor rule or some simple variations thereof, like including lags of short-term interest rate or output deviations. Overall, for the US or other developed countries, the Taylor rule explains rather well the behaviour of central banks. Most of the time they stabilize deviations either from a target level inflation or output gap, using an interest rate instrument.

However, in the case of developing countries and emerging markets, such an outcome is not straightforward, as, given the specific nature of markets in emerging economies, the adequate policy instrument could not only be the short-term interest rate, but also the monetary base or the exchange rate. One must note that the inclusion of the exchange rate in the central bank's reaction function does not contradict the objectives of central banks, if exchange rate stabilization is a precondition for both output stabilization and bringing down inflation to a targeted level (Taylor, 2000).

Over the past few years a number of studies have investigated monetary policy rules in emerging markets, finding that even with some shortcomings, central banks in emerging markets also follow some rule-based monetary policy, and that an open-economy version of the Taylor rule can describe much of the variation in short-term interest rates (Calderon and Schmidt-Hebbel, 2003; Minella, et al., 2003; Mohanty and Klau, 2003; Taylor, 2001; and Torres Garcia, 2003).

[1]   Akram Esanov and Lúcio Vinhas de Souza were financed by the USAID/IRIS Project no. 220/001.0-03-337 'Analysis of Monetary and Trade Policy Questions for the Russian Federation', of which Lúcio Vinhas de Souza was the manager. We thank the comments of Felix Hammermann, Thomas Kick, Nienke Oomes (who also kindly supplied us with data), Franziska Schobert, Elena Rumyantseva, Rainer Schweickert and Oleg Zamulin, and of the participants of seminars held at the IFW, the Bank of Finland, the NES/CEFIR and the University of Lodz. All usual disclaimers apply.

It is, however, not clear whether this applies to transition economies, where financial markets are even less developed and where the implementation of a money-based monetary policy may face institutional problems. Because of even greater model specification difficulties and problems associated with collecting reliable data, very little research has been done on monetary policy rules in transitional economies. This study is one of the first attempts to fill this gap, as it examines the conduct of monetary policy in Russia during the period of 1993-2002. The empirical estimation of alternative rules for monetary policy allows a test of the statement that in financially less developed economies, monetary targeting rules can provide an effective description of the behaviour of the monetary authorities – and, in the case of Russia, of its stated objectives.

The rest of this chapter is organized as follows. Section two describes the evolution of the monetary policy instruments and the monetary regime followed by the Russian central bank in a chronological order. Section three specifies different empirical models to be used in evaluating monetary policy rules, while section four presents the results of our empirical estimations. Finally, section five draws some conclusions.

Development of monetary policy in Russia

The dissolution of the Soviet Union at the end of 1991 did not immediately lead to the establishment of a truly *Russian* monetary authority capable of conducting an independent and effective monetary policy,[2] as, until mid-1993, some of the former republics of the Soviet Union still used the rouble, the Russian national currency, and central banks of those republics conducted their own credit policy simultaneously with the Bank of Russia. Only after 1993 did the Bank of Russia start to conduct its own independent monetary policy, although the scope of the policy was limited by the need to finance a huge budget deficit, mainly caused by a dramatic decline in output (see Figure 7.1). This loose monetary stance continued until the middle of 1995, when the Russian economy started showing signs of stabilization and a new law on the Bank of Russia was passed, providing some degree of legal independence to the Bank of Russia in conducting monetary policy.[3]

---

[2] The Central Bank of the Russian Federation (Bank of Russia) was founded on 13 July 1990, based on the Russian Republic Bank of the State Bank of the Soviet Union. On 2 December 1990, the Supreme Soviet of the RSFSR passed the Law 'On the Central Bank of the RSFSR (Bank of Russia)', which declared the Bank of Russia a legal entity and the main bank of the Russian Federation.

[3] Nevertheless, today the Bank of Russia still maintains some functions not traditionally seen as belonging to a central bank: for instance, in spite of being a banking supervisor and regulator, the CBR has a majority stake in the largest Russian bank (and state owned bank), Sberbank Rossii, which has 23 per cent of all banking assets, 70 per cent of

These positive developments allowed the Bank of Russia to adopt a tighter monetary policy and to introduce a pegged exchange rate regime with a crawling band against the US dollar, from July 1995 onwards, replacing the previous 'dirty float'. As a result of these measures inflation slowed down (see Figure 7.2). Furthermore, because of favourable developments in the local securities market, direct credit to the government significantly decreased and the Bank of Russia started to conduct monetary policy through indirect instruments, such as interest rates and reserve requirements. However, the start of the Asian crisis of 1997 spread a negative shock throughout emerging markets. This external shock decreased investment confidence in Russia and caused capital outflows, forcing the Bank of Russia to defend the band. Although during the exchange market interventions in November 1997 the Bank of Russia lost over \$6 billion of its liquid reserves, which was equal to two thirds of total reserves at that time, the exchange band was successfully defended for a while.

Despite these efforts of the Bank of Russia, due to the severe financial crisis of August 1998, the government was forced to default on its domestic debt obligations. The rouble was devalued and the exchange rate band was abandoned, leading to the adoption of a 'dirty' floating regime (see Figure 7.3, where a de facto targeting of the nominal exchange rate also after 1998 seems apparent).[4] One consequence of the sharp depreciation was a rapid acceleration in inflation. Although rouble-denominated debt was restructured, investor confidence kept declining because of an increase in political uncertainty and private capital outflows. In such a situation, the Bank of Russia, fulfilling its role as a lender of last resort, attempted to preserve the financial system, by injecting liquidity into the banking system through a reduction of reserve requirements and extending large amounts of new credits. However, base money declined significantly in real terms, reflecting the sharp decline in output and increased use of non-monetary forms of payment.

---

household deposits, 20 per cent of corporate deposits and 21,000 branches across Russia, and, until late 2002, also had participation in the second largest state owned bank, the VTB. Further, acting as an agent for the Ministry of Finance, it set up and manages the government securities market, known as the GKO market.

[4] This may indicate that the choice of a more flexible exchange rate regime, contrary to earlier studies (see Dabrowski et al., 2002), could have been welfare improving for Russia, due to the shock-absorbing properties of such regimes – conditional on the quality of institutions and on the consistency of the policy mix (see Vinhas de Souza and Ledrut, 2003) – and given the higher propensity of commodity-based economies to be buffeted by external shocks, which are increased by having harder exchange rate regimes.

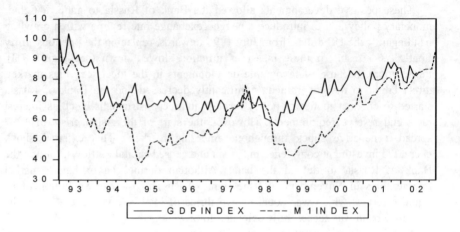

Figure 7.1   GDP index and M1, 1993-2003 (index 1993 = 100)

Source: IMF/IFS

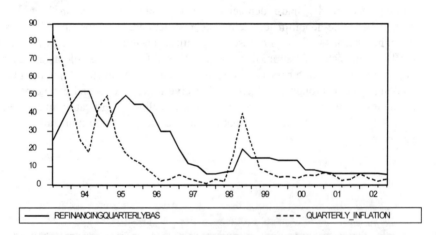

**Figure 7.2   Refinancing rate and inflation, 1993-2003 (quarterly based,
                     in per cent)**

Source: IMF/IFS

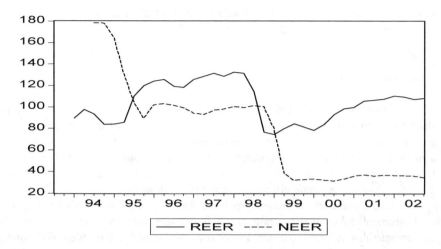

Figure 7.3   Real and nominal effective exchange rates, 1993-2003 (1995 = 100)

Source: IMF/IFS

As a consequence of the renewed inflationary pressures in 1999, one of the main objectives of the Bank of Russia was to bring inflation down, initially to 30 per cent and later to a 12-14 per cent range, while keeping output decline in the range of 1-3 per cent, within the framework of a 'dirty float' of the rouble. To achieve this objective, monetary policy was tightened by reducing net credit to the banking system. Because of this measure, inflation fell sharply and the exchange rate depreciation stopped. Furthermore, fiscal performance significantly improved, due to the approval of a new package of fiscal measures and improvements in revenue collection. As world energy prices increased (over 50 per cent of Russia's exports are of energy-related products – oil and gas), the results were trade surpluses, renewed capital inflows and a resumption of growth in Russia. The effects of these developments on the (real) exchange rate caused it to become one of the main targets of monetary policy (see Figure 7.3).

According to the Bank of Russia, the main objective of its monetary policy in 2000 was to reduce inflation to 18 per cent and to achieve an annual growth rate of GDP of 1.5 per cent. However, the continuing strength of the balance of payments and the Bank of Russia's reluctance to permit a real appreciation of the rouble has placed increasing pressure on monetary policy. Given this continued favourable economic situation in recent years, the Bank of Russia has placed more weight on the exchange rate stability, while accepting the inflationary consequences of such a decision. This policy of the Bank of Russia has slowed the real appreciation of the rouble and reduced inflation, even though the pace of disinflation has been slower than the one formally targeted by the authorities.[5]

Specification of the empirical model

As described above, since 1991 the Russian economy has experienced both sharp fluctuations in main macroeconomic variables and deep structural changes. Given this unstable nature of the economic environment in Russia, the task of estimating a monetary policy rule is complicated and no single policy rule equation might fully capture all aspects of the central bank behaviour during this period. Therefore, we will estimate different types of rules, described below.

The recent literature on monetary policy rules primarily distinguishes two types of instrument rules: interest rate based instrument rules and monetary based instrument rules, referred to as the Taylor rule and the McCallum rule (McCallum, 1988), respectively.[6] The key difference in these rules involves the choice of the instrument in the central bank's reaction function in response to changes in macroeconomic conditions. While the Taylor rule, which uses a short-term nominal interest rate as an instrument, is widely used in monetary policy estimations because of its simplicity, the McCallum rule uses the growth rate of the monetary base as an instrument, which figured prominently in monetary policy formulation before the 1990s.[7]

To address adequately the question of the adequacy of those rules for emerging markets, researchers use modified versions of them. One general consensus in this regard is that monetary policymakers in emerging economies are more concerned about exchange rate movements than those in mature economies (for instance, see Williamson, 2000), among other reasons due to the degree of exchange rate pass-through to prices. Hence, the exchange rate has been incorporated, resulting in the 'open economy' version of the central bank's reaction function. Moreover, some researchers, such as Ball (1998), even suggest that in a small open economy the central bank could use a weighted average of the nominal interest rate and the exchange rate as an instrument. However, this type of 'hybrid rule' has not been

---

[5] The policy relevance of such concerns with real appreciation are somewhat doubtful, as it is unclear if the real exchange rate of the Russian ruble is above its long run equilibrium value, or merely recovering from an undershooting (see IMF, 2003).

[6] Razzak (2001) shows that the McCallum and Taylor rules are, as one should expect, co-integrated.

[7] Perhaps the most traditional of those *quasi* 'monetary targeters' was the German central bank, the Deutsche Bundesbank (more precisely, the Bundesbank announced M3 as an intermediate target – 'Zwischenziel', it did not use it as an instrument or operational target). Some works (see, for instance, Clarida and Gertler, 1996) put into question the reliance of the Bundesbank on monetary aggregates.

popular among empirical researchers because of uncertainties involved in determining weights.[8]

Taylor rule

Following Taylor (2001), we estimate the modified open economy Taylor rule below:

$$i_t = \beta_0 + \beta_1 \pi + \beta_2 y_t + \beta_3 xr_t + \beta_4 xr_{t-1} + \beta_5 i_{t-1} + u_t \tag{1}$$

where xr_t is the growth of the real effective exchange rate, u_t is a white noise error term and t-1 indicates lagged values of the variables. The expected signs of the parameters are as follows: β_0, β_2, $\beta_5 > 0, \beta_1 /(1 - \beta_5) > 1$, $\beta_3 < 0$, and $\beta_4 < 0$.

Money based rules

As discussed in section two, the short-term interest rate has not been the most important instrument in conducting monetary policy in Russia.[9] Uncertainty in measuring real interest rates, shallow financial markets and big shocks to investment or net exports may make monetary aggregates a preferred instrument. This may be the case in Russia, especially during the 1990s.

The original McCallum rule can be expressed as follows:

$$\Delta b_t = \Delta x^* - \Delta v_t + 0.5(\Delta x^* - \Delta x_{t-1}) + u_t \tag{2}$$

where Δb_t is the rate of growth of the monetary base in per cent per year, Δx^* is the target rate of growth of nominal GDP, in per cent per year, Δv_t the rate of growth of base velocity, in per cent per year, and averaged over the previous four years in the original McCallum estimation, and Δx is the rate of growth of nominal GDP in per cent per year. In this rule the target value of nominal GDP growth is calculated as the sum of the target inflation rate and the long-run average rate of growth of real GDP.

---

[8] Ball-type rules are hybrid rules, related to the Monetary Conditions Index (MCI) literature (see Freedman, 1996). An MCI is an indicator of the stance of monetary policy, which does not only consider an output target but also the influence of the exchange rate on inflation.

[9] Currently the Bank of Russia officially adopts a money supply – aggregate M2 – as an intermediate anchor to policy.

We will initially use the M1 monetary aggregate as the policy instrument for monetary policy in Russia. We are aware that some studies attempt to explain inflation in Russia using monetary aggregates (see, for example, Pesonen and Korhonen, 1998, Dabrowski et al., 2002). However, our Granger causality tests indicate that at least in the short-run – up to seven months – there is only Granger causality from prices to monetary aggregates, and not the other way around.

It is widely accepted that this type of time series data usually suffer some level of autocorrelation, and if it is not corrected the estimation results cannot be treated as reliable. To correct for the autocorrelation problems, we will use differences rather than levels and add lags, according to information criteria and the statistical significances of the coefficients.

A hybrid rule

Ball (1998) argues that interest rate based Taylor rules are inefficient. He stresses that monetary policy affects the economy through exchange rate as well as interest rate channels. Ball sets up a simple model with an open economy IS curve, Phillips curve and a link between interest and exchange rate. Rearranging terms yields the following optimal policy rule:

$$wi_t + (1-w)xr_t = \alpha y_t + \beta(\pi_t + \delta xr_{t-1}) + u_t \qquad (3)$$

where w is a weight that depends on the calibration of the model and δ is the effect of a one per cent exchange rate appreciation on inflation, α and β also depend on calibrations of the model. The calibration parameters we use will be based on the work of Ball (1998). For a robustness test, we use different weights and check their effect on the estimated coefficients.

Finally, to address the econometric problem caused by several possible structural breaks in the Russian economy during the period 1993-2002, we use dummy variables.

Empirical results

Data and methodology

Data for Russia have to be treated cautiously. The availability is limited and phenomena such as dollarization and the barter economy may lead to a somewhat biased picture. Some authors (see, for example, Falcetti, et al., 2000) also believe that the 'transitional recession' decline in output was overestimated during the first years of the transformation period.[10] In our empirical estimations we use monthly data covering the time span 1993-2002. This period has been chosen for data availability reasons. Alternatively, on several occasions we use quarterly data to check the robustness of our results. The sources of the data are the International Monetary Fund's International Financial Statistics database, the website of the Bank of Russia, the monthly database of the Vienna Institute for International Economic Studies (WIIW), and the Russian European Centre for Economic Policy (RECEP). We use data on short-term interest rates (refinancing rates), consumer price inflation, monetary aggregates, the output gap, different exchange rate measures (dollar exchange rate, nominal effective exchange rate, and real effective exchange rate), the labour share as a proxy for the output gap, and the budget deficit. Our output numbers are from RECEP and WIIW (industrial production, as a proxy for GDP), deflated by the monthly consumer price inflation, due to the lack of a monthly GDP deflator.

Results for the Taylor rule

When we estimate an open economy version of the Taylor rule – in levels and in differences – the estimated coefficient of inflation is only significant in one specification (see Table 7.1 below). The estimated coefficient of the output gap does not show the expected sign and is insignificant for the estimations in levels (other proxies of the output gap, such as the real unit labour cost suggested by Gali and Gertler, 1999, also shows unsatisfactory results). The estimated coefficients of the exchange rate variables are insignificant. The estimated coefficient of the lagged interest rate is equal to 0.9 and remains relatively stable over the different model specifications, indicating that the interest rate in a new period is about 90 per cent of the old interest rate plus the effect of the other independent variables (in the levels estimations). The long-run response of the central bank can be calculated as follows:

$$\beta^{LR} = \frac{\beta_{\text{inf}}}{1 - \beta_5} \tag{4}$$

where β^{LR} is the long-run response on inflation and β_{inf} is the estimated coefficient for year-to-year inflation. We get a long-run response of about 0.3 and thus the Taylor principle ($\beta^{LR} > 1$) does not hold. This means that, according to our estimations, the central bank reacts to a 1 per cent increase of inflation with less

---

[10] For instance, Åslund (2001) estimates that, for an official figure of just 60.2 per cent of the Russian 1989 GDP in 1995, the actual figure, after taking into account, among other things, illegal and under-reported activities, was an amazing 94 per cent, showing, in other terms, a mere marginal GDP fall.

than a 1 per cent increase in the short-term nominal interest rate (leading, therefore, to a decrease in the real interest rate).

Table 7.1   Testing a Taylor rule for Russia, 1993-2002

Independent variable	Open economy rule – in levels (with annual inflation)	Open economy rule – in levels (with quarterly inflation)	Open economy rule – in differences (with annual inflation)[1]	Open economy rule – in differences (with quarterly inflation)[1]
Intercept	3.674 (2.626)	2.5922 (2.5667)	-2.3490 (1.7837)	-2.4329 (1.8413)
Year-to-year consumer price inflation[1]	0.0341 (0.0095) ***		0.0556 (0.0585)	
Quarter-to-quarter inflation[1]		0.3931 (0.3143)		0.0657 (0.2990)
Quarter-to-quarter inflation (-1)[1]		-0.0214 (0.2859)		-0.0345 (0.3193)
Output gap (ex-post data)	-0.1732 (0.5103)	0.0206 (0.4917)	1.011 (0.443) **	1.0133 (0.4611) **
Growth USD exchange rate	-10.9646 (21.2278)	-23.0876 (24.4396)	10.2635 (21.1343)	11.3104 (23.6234)
Growth in USD exchange rate (-1)	12.3213 (20.1511)	-6.3265 (22.4015)	32.4323 (20.2822)	33.3887 (22.6969)
Interest rate (-1)[1]	0.8823 (0.0342) ***	0.8902 (0.0341) ***	-0.2393 (0.0967) **	-0.2276 (0.0969) **
R square	0.94	0.94	0.10	0.10
Adjusted R square	0.94	0.94	0.06	0.04
Durbin Watson statistics	2.54	2.56	2.19	2.16

Breusch-Godfrey test	No rejection	No rejection	No rejection	No rejection

Notes:
1. The Breusch-Godfrey serial correlation LM-test (with no autocorrelation as a null hypothesis) was conducted for twelve lags.
2. (-1) indicates a first lag.
3. The effective sample period is 1993:3-2002:12 since we lose two months because of lags and differences.
4. [(1)] In this model the refinancing rate in differences is the dependent variable. Inflation rates and the lagged interest rate are used in differences too.
5. Standard errors are in parentheses. The asterisks indicate levels of significance at 10 (*), 5(**) or 1 (***) per cent level.

This unsatisfactory result of the output gap might be explained either if the objective of the Bank of Russia was limited to inflation and exchange rate stabilization or if the 'real time' output data significantly differed from the ex-post-data, so that we get a biased picture in our estimations (see for example Orphanides, 2001). Assuming that the Bank of Russia was indeed concerned with output stabilization during this period, we constructed a real-time series to correct the bias in data. We used the yearly output data published in the annual reports of the Bank of Russia,[11] and on the basis of them constructed a monthly series, interpolating and re-basing the available industrial production monthly series from the WIIW. When we run regressions using this 'real-time' output gap, its estimated coefficients are always non-significant and no substantial changes are observed in the regressions. Overall, the estimation results suggest that a simple Taylor rule and its modifications do not describe the interest rate setting behaviour of the Bank of Russia well.[12]

Results for the McCallum rule

Here, the expected signs of the estimated coefficients should be reversed, as a decrease in the monetary aggregate means a monetary contraction and a decrease in the interest rate, a monetary expansion.

The estimated coefficients are statistically insignificant, indicating a poor performance of the original McCallum rule as specified in equation (2). Moreover, this regression specification has another statistical disadvantage as it requires discarding a large number of observations in order to average the velocity of money over the four-year period. Because of this drawback, we decided to estimate

---

[11] For differences between the original WIIW series and the 'real-time' series, see figure A.7.1 in the appendix.
[12] We do not present those results, but they are available from the authors upon request (email Lucio-Mauro.VINHAS-DE-SOUZA@cec.eu.int).

a modified McCallum rule, where the interest rate instrument (of a Taylor type rule) is substituted by a real monetary aggregate. As the monetary aggregate series is non-stationary, we correct this statistical problem by differencing. In addition, we include seasonal dummies for December and January, as the Russian money supply shows seasonal spikes during these months. According to Dabrowski et al. (2002) this effect is probably attributable to technical and accounting measures. As the regression results indicate (see Table 7.2 below, second column), in general a modified McCallum rule performs much better in explaining the behaviour of the Bank of Russia than simple interest rate based rules. The estimated coefficients show the expected signs, but the measure of the output gap is still statistically insignificant[13] and/or show the wrong signs.[14]

Table 7.2   **Testing a McCallum rule for Russia, 1993-2002, using M1**

Independent variable	Difference model	Gap model[(1)]	Full Model
Intercept	0.0150	0.0108	0.0123
	(0.0042) ***	(0.0047) **	(0.0045) ***
Quarter-to-quarter inflation	-0.0028	-0.0026	
	(0.0006) ***	(0.0007) ***	
Quarter-to-quarter inflation (-1)	0.0022	0.0012	
	(0.0005) ***	(0.0008) *	
Monthly inflation			-0.0017
			(0.0015)
Dummy for period before 1995 * monthly inflation			-0.0050
			(0.0020) **
Monthly inflation (-1)			-0.0013
			(0.0007) *
Output gap (ex-post data)	-0.0001	-0.0013	0.0010
	(0.0497)	(0.0008)	(0.0009)
Growth in bilateral dollar exchange rate	-0.2319	-0.2566	-0.2920
	(0.0497) ***	(0.0529) ***	(0.0846) ***

---

[13] When we use nominal and real GDP as an alternative to the output gap, the estimated coefficients show no sign of improvement.

[14] As standard literature uses the gap as a measure of 'excess output' around a long run trend – a feature of a mature economy, and in which this excess output causes concerns about future inflation. The CBR may respond significantly positively to output growth, that is, increasing money after an output increase, if it *assumes it as the result of technological improvements*. That is, the interest rate should not change after a *permanent* output increase, but the money supply should increase to accommodate the shock.

Dummy for period before 1995* growth in USD exchange rate			0.2701 (0.1262) **
Growth in USD exchange rate (-1)	0.1330 (0.0483) ***	0.2955 (0.0533) ***	0.1107 (0.0480) **
Growth rate of M1 (-1)	0.2938 (0.0663) ***	0.1814 (0.0675) ***	0.2821 (0.0666) ***
Seasonal dummy for January	-0.1271 (0.0131) ***	-0.1123 (0.0137) ***	-0.1294 (0.0130) ***
Seasonal dummy for December	0.0807 (0.0111) ***	0.0845 (0.0112) ***	0.0885 (0.0107) ***
Dummy for before May 1998		-0.0159 (0.0065) **	
Dummy for the period before 1995			0.0431 (0.0231) *
R square	0.74	0.74	0.76
Adjusted R square	0.72	0.72	0.74
Durbin Watson statistics	2.02	1.70	1.97
Breusch-Godfrey test	No rejection	No rejection	No rejection

Notes:
1. The Breusch-Godfrey serial correlation LM-test (with no autocorrelation as a null hypothesis) was conducted for twelve lags.
2. (-1) indicates a first lag
3. The effective sample period is 1993:3- 2002:12 since we lose two months because of lags and differences.
4. [1] In this case we deduct the HP-trend from quarterly inflation and the growth in the dollar exchange rate.
5. Standard errors are in parentheses. The asterisks indicate levels of significance at 10 (*), 5 (**) or 1 (***) per cent level.

When we run regressions using the forward interpolated 'real-time' output gap, the estimated coefficients show always the expected signs and are statistically significant for the period from 1994-2002 (see Table 7.3 below).

Table 7.3   **Testing a McCallum rule for Russia, 1994-2002, using M1**

Independent variable	Difference model with 'real time' output gap	Difference model with ex-post output gap
Intercept	0.0164	0.0157
	(0.0040) ***	(0.0043) ***
Quarter-to-quarter inflation	-0.0025	-0.0026
	(0.0006) ***	(0.0006) ***
Quarter-to-quarter inflation (-1)	0.0016	0.0018
	(0.0006) ***	(0.0006) ***
Output gap (real time data – forward interpolation)	-0.0022	
	(0.0009) **	
Output gap (ex-post data)		-0.0006
		(0.0010)
Growth in real effective exchange rate	0.4311	0.4020
	(0.0671) ***	(0.0727) ***
Growth in real effective exchange rate (-1)	-0.2738	-0.2544
	(0.0642) ***	(0.0671) ***
Growth rate of M1(-1)	0.2700	0.2494
	(0.0659) ***	(0.0688) ***
Seasonal dummy for January	-0.1313	-0.1275
	(0.0125) ***	(0.0131) ***
Seasonal dummy for December	0.0861	0.0825
	(0.0107) ***	(0.0108) ***
R square	0.78	0.77
Adjusted R square	0.76	0.75
Durbin Watson statistics	2.03	1.98
Breusch-Godfrey test	No rejection	No rejection

Notes:
1. The Breusch-Godfrey serial correlation LM-test (with no autocorrelation as a null hypothesis) was conducted for twelve lags.
2. (-1) indicates a first lag
3. Standard errors are in parentheses. The asterisks indicate levels of significance at 10 (*), 5 (**) or 1 (***) per cent level.

The same results are obtained when we use a monetary base aggregate that is actually directly controlled by the monetary authority, namely M0, and M0 plus households holding (data kindly supplied by the IMF), to account for the degree of dollarization in the Russian economy (see Table 7.4).[15]

---

[15]   Because of the used approximation to real-time data, the results do not necessarily mean that the CBR was concerned with output stabilization, but they indicate that this *may have been the case*. Further evidence can only be obtained with actual real-time data, which was not available to us.

Table 7.4   **Testing a McCallum rule for Russia, 1994-2002, using M0 and M0 plus USD holdings**

Independent variable	Difference model with 'real time' output gap (M0)	Difference model with ex-post output gap (M0)	Difference model with 'real time' output gap (M0 plus USD)	Difference model with ex-post output gap (M0 plus USD)
Intercept	0.0176 (0.0049) ***	0.0182 (0.0050) ***	0.0088 (0.0043) **	0.0088 (0.0043) **
Quarter-to-quarter inflation	-0.0026 (0.0007) ***	-0.0029 (0.0007) ***	-0.0016 (0.0006) **	-0.0015 (0.0006) **
Quarter-to-quarter inflation (-1)	0.0022 (0.0006) ***	0.0024 (0.0006) ***	0.0014 (0.0006) **	0.0013 (0.0006) **
Output gap (real time data – forward interpolation)	-0.0015 (0.0009) *		0.0007 (0.0008)	
Output gap (ex-post data)		-0.0005 (0.0009)		-0.0007 (0.0008)
Growth in real effective exchange rate	-0.2545 (0.0532) ***	-0.2385 (0.0538) ***	0.0770 (0.0507)	0.0600 (0.0505)
Growth in real effective exchange rate (-1)	0.0917 (0.0537) *	0,0922 (0.0547) *	-0.1133 (0.0459) **	-0.1177 (0.0460) **
Growth rate of M0(-1)	0.1856 (0.0711) *	0.1799 (0.0719) **	0.5177 (0.1046) ***	0.4929 (0.1049) ***
Seasonal dummy for January	-0.1167 (0.0135) ***	-0.1201 (0.0137) ***	-0.0357 (0.0127) ***	-0.0371 (0.0129) ***
Seasonal dummy for December	0.0424 (0.0133) ***	0.0399 (0.0135) ***	0.0203 (0.0121) *	0.0232 (0.0120) *
R square	0.66	0.65	0.48	0.48
Adjusted R square	0.63	0.62	0.43	0.44
Durbin Watson statistics	2.10	2.10	2.38	2.39
Breusch-Godfrey test	No rejection	No rejection	No rejection	No rejection

Notes:
1. The Breusch-Godfrey serial correlation LM-test (with no autocorrelation as a null hypothesis) was conducted for twelve lags.
2. (-1) indicates a first lag.
3. Standard errors are in parentheses. The asterisks indicate levels of significance at 10 (*), 5 (**) or 1 (***) per cent level.

Overall, the estimation results allow us to conclude that the Bank of Russia has been targeting monetary aggregates in its policy decisions. At times of high inflation pressure, or a positive output gap calculated on the basis of the constructed real-time data, the Bank of Russia responded by reducing monetary aggregates in real terms, while at times of exchange rate appreciation the policy response was an expansionary monetary policy. Moreover, these results are not sensitive to the model specification and there are no major statistical problems.

Given the absence of explicit inflation targeting in Russia, we also estimate a 'gap model' as defined in Mohanty and Klau (2003), using a GMM estimator.[16] The advantage of this model, beyond correcting for endogeneity, is that it allows us to use an HP measure of trend inflation instead of a targeted level, as given by (5):

$$\Delta(\log(M1)) = \beta_0 + \beta_1(CPI - CPItrend) + \beta_2 y_t + \beta_3(xr_t - xrtrend) + \tag{5}$$
$$+\beta_4(xr_{t-1} - xrtrend_{t-1}) + \beta_5\Delta(\log(M1_{t-1})) + u_t$$

where M1 is the deflated monetary aggregate M1, CPItrend is the HP filter of the inflation rate and xrtrend is a log of the HP filter of the exchange rate change. We add another lag to inflation to control for autocorrelation. We again include seasonal dummies for December and January. Another dummy for the period before May 1998 is added, since the Chow test indicates a structural break at this point. The results are on Table 7.2 (third column).

The regression results indicate again that the Bank of Russia reacted to above trend inflation with a contraction in real monetary aggregates. If the dollar exchange rate in the current period was higher than the HP-trend, the Bank of Russia also responded with a reduction in monetary aggregates. All estimated coefficients are significant and exhibit the expected signs. Those results remain when using M0 and M0 plus dollar household holdings instead of M1.

Results for the Ball rule

The estimation results for the open economy Ball model are mixed and unstable (see table 7.5 below). It appears that the results suffer from a severe and persistent autocorrelation problem, unless we attach a 100 per cent weight to the real effective exchange rate and limit the sample period to 1996-2002. However, this last specification seems unrealistic given, among other reasons, central banks' limited foreign reserves (and the given that then equation (3) actually becomes an identity). Nevertheless, this outcome may be a reflection of an actual targeting of the exchange rate by the Bank of Russia from 1995 onwards.

---

[16]   The instruments list used included lagged values of the CPI, output gap and exchange rate.

Table 7.5   Testing a Ball rule for Russia, 1994-2002

Independent variable	Exchange rate weight = 1	Exchange rate weight = 0.5
Intercept	15,4424	29.5188
	(6.1673) **	(18.7053)
Output gap	0.8673	-1.2445
	(0.3644) **	(1.1052)
Output gap (-1)	0.9202	-0.2921
	(0.4386) **	(1.3301)
Output gap (-2)	0.5224	-1.0559
	(0.3628)	(1.1005)
Month-to-month inflation +	0.9126	0.8054
0.5 * (real effective	(0.1538) ***	(0.4665) *
exchange rate (-1))		
Month-to-month inflation (-	-0.7067	0.2628
1) + 0.5 * (real effective	(0.1518) ***	(0.4603)
exchange rate (-2))		
R square	0.75	0.20
Adjusted R square	0.73	0.16
Durbin Watson test statistics	0.97	0.16
Breusch-Godfrey test	Rejection	Rejection

Notes:

1. The Breusch-Godfrey serial correlation LM-test (with no autocorrelation as a null hypothesis) was conducted for twelve lags.
2. (-1) indicates a first lag.
3. Standard errors are in parentheses. The asterisks indicate levels of significance at 10 (*), 5 (**) or 1 (***) per cent level.

Testing responses during different time periods

The Russian economy has experienced different shocks during different time periods, and it would be insightful to see whether the Bank of Russia has responded differently in different periods. Since the 'money based' model performs best in the previous estimations, we will test it for different time periods.[17] First of all, we separate the period before and after 1995 (the time of the introduction of the exchange rate targeting regime), as Chow breakpoint tests

---

[17] Briefly, the results of estimating the interest rate rule varying the timeframe are similar to the ones obtained before: they suffer, again, from insignificance problems.

indicate a structural break at this point in time (and *not* in August 1998).[18] We use for this purpose the equation (6) below:

$$\Delta(\log(M1)) = \beta_0 + \beta_1 \inf_t + \beta_2 d \inf_t + \beta_3 \inf_{t-1} + \beta_4 y_t + \beta_5 dollarxr_t + \quad (6)$$
$$+ \beta_6 ddollarxr_t + \beta_7 dollarxr_{t-1} + \beta_8 \Delta(\log(M1_{t-1})) + \beta_9 d_1 + \beta_{10} d_2 + \beta_{11} d + u_t$$

where d is a dummy variable that is one for the period before 1995 and zero otherwise, and d_1 and d_2 are seasonal dummies for December and January over the sample period, respectively. The estimation results clearly suggest (see Table 7.2, column 4) that the Bank of Russia conducted different monetary policies before and after 1995. The estimated coefficients indicate that before 1995 the Bank of Russia was more concerned with reducing inflation,[19] while after 1995 priorities shifted towards exchange rate stabilization. These findings are consistent with the official announcements of the Bank of Russia, and are robust to the use of different monetary aggregates.

We obtain similar results when using a dummy variable for the period from October 1994 through August 1998. As one would expect, the commitment to react to changes in the exchange rate was greater during that period. During the high inflation period, the Bank of Russia attached a greater priority to inflation, while at times of relatively low inflation the main concern was exchange rate stabilization.

Concluding Remarks

This chapter examined the conduct of monetary policy in Russia during the period 1993-2002. We estimated three sets of monetary policy rules: the Taylor rule, the McCallum rule and the hybrid Ball rule, using both monthly and quarterly data. The regression results indicate that a simple Taylor rule and its different variations, where the short-term interest rate was used as a policy instrument, poorly describes the interest rate setting behaviour of the Bank of Russia.

The McCallum rule, where the policy instrument is a monetary aggregate, fits best the data. Again, given that the bank of Russia officially adopts a money supply as an intermediate anchor to policy and that, even today, its main actual instruments of monetary policy are deposit auctions, this is a consistent result.

Nevertheless, this is in sharp contrast with the recent experience of other advanced emerging markets, where interest rate rules produce a good description of the policy setting behaviour of the monetary authority (see, for instance,

---

[18] Detken and Gaspar (2003) show that a monetary authority that cares about price deviations will also care about exchange rate developments, even without formally targeting those. Therefore, exchange rate targeting may be *observationally equivalent* to inflation targeting.

[19] Of course, average inflation before 1995 was also substantially greater than afterwards.

Mohanty and Klau, 2003; Minella et al., 2003; Torres Garcia, 2003). The estimated coefficients are significant and remain unchanged across different equation specifications. The results indicate that during the period 1993-2002 the Bank of Russia has used monetary aggregates as a main policy instrument in conducting monetary policy. Furthermore, the results also suggest that the structural break in the series happened in 1995 (with the introduction of an exchange rate pegging regime) and not in 1998; before 1995 the Bank of Russia was more concerned with inflation reduction, and afterwards the primary objective was exchange rate stabilization. The estimation results of the hybrid, or Ball rule, where a weighted average of the interest rate and the exchange rate is used as a policy instrument, draw a mixed picture. Depending on the choice of the weights, results change and most of the time the estimated coefficients are insignificant.

The results of our estimations, of course, are backward looking, in the sense that they represent the relationships that exist so far in the data. As the experience of other advanced emerging markets shows, the promotion of forward looking behaviour among Russian economic agents, aided by the development of stronger institutions – especially by the strengthening of the credibility of the Bank of Russia and the development of its policy instruments, as indicated by the late 2002 reforms, plus the deepening of Russia's financial markets – shall, in time, enable the implementation of a successful interest rate policy rule, coupled with inflation targeting and a floating exchange rate regime, which shall also reduce the GDP costs of disinflation (as Minella et al., 2003, show for a similarly advanced emerging market, Brazil, which is also a large economy, with an important primary sector and a history of macroeconomic instability).[20]

---

[20] As a sign of this, Taylor rule regressions run only for the period after 2000 do show the expected signs for the variables, but most of them are non-significant (also, given the very short time period, the number of observations is very limited).

The Periphery of the Euro

Appendix

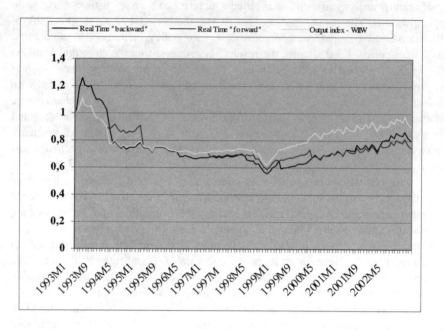

Figure A.7.1   Differences between ex-post and 'real time' data

References

Åslund, A. (2001), 'The Myth of Output Collapse after Communism', *Carnegie Endowment Working Papers Series*, 18.

Ball, L. (1998), 'Policy Rules for Open Economies', *NBER Working Paper*, 6760.

Calderon, C. and Schmidt-Hebbel, K. (2003), 'Macroeconomic Policies and Performance in Latin America', *Journal of International Money and Finance*, 27, 7: 895-924.

Clarida, R. and Gertler, M. (1996), 'How the Bundesbank Conducts Monetary Policy', *NBER Working Papers*, 5581.

Dabrowski, M., Paczynski, W. and Rawdanowicz, L. (2002), 'Inflation and Monetary Policy in Russia: Transition Experience and Future Recommendations', *CASE Studies and Analyses*, Warsaw, Poland.

Detken, C. and Gaspar, V. (2003), 'Maintaining Price Stability under Free-Floating: A Fearless Way Out of the Corner?', *ECB Working Papers Series*, 241.

Falcetti, E., Raiser, M. and Sanfey, P. (2000), 'Defying the Odds: Initial Conditions, Reforms and Growth in the First Decade of Transition', *EBRD Working Paper*, 55.

Freedman, C. (1996), 'The Use of Indicators and of the Monetary Conditions Index in Canada', in Bank of Canada, *The Transmission of Monetary Policy in Canada,* Ottawa, Canada, pp. 67-79.

Gali, J. and Gertler, M. (1999), 'Inflation Dynamics: A Structural Econometric Analysis', *Journal of Monetary Economics*, 44, 2: 195–222.

IMF (2003), *Russian Federation*: Selected issues, Country Report No. 03/146.

McCallum, B. (1988), 'Robustness Properties of a Rule for Monetary Policy', *Carnegie-Rochester Conference Series on Public Society*, 29 (North-Holland), pp. 173-204.

Minella, A., Springer de Freitas, P., Goldfajn, I., and Kfoury Muinhos, M. (2003), 'Inflation Targeting in Brazil: Constructing Credibility under Exchange Rate Volatility', *Journal of International Money and Finance*, 27, 7: 1015-40.

Mohanty, M. and Klau, M. (2003), 'Monetary Policy Rules in Emerging Market Economies, Issues and Evidence', *Working Paper* presented at the Kiel Workshop for Monetary Policy and Macroeconomic Stabilization in Latin America, Kiel Institute for World Economics.

Orphanides, A. (2001), 'Monetary Policy Rules based on Real-Time Data: Division of Monetary Affairs', *American Economic Review*, 91, 4: 964-85.

Pesonen, H. and Korhonen, I. (1998), 'The Short and Variable Lags of Russian Monetary Policy', *Review of Economies in Transition*, No. 4, Bank of Finland.

Razzak, W. (2001), 'Is the Taylor Rule Really Different from the McCallum Rule?', *Reserve Bank of New Zealand Discussion Paper* 2001/07.

Taylor, J. (1993), 'Discretion Versus Policy Rules in Practice', *Carnegie-Rochester Conference on Public Policy*, 39, 195-214 (North Holland).

Taylor, J. (2000), 'Using Monetary Policy Rules in Emerging Market Economies', *Revised paper* presented at the 75th anniversary conference at the Banco de Mexico.

Taylor, J. (2001), 'The Role of the Exchange Rate in Monetary Policy Rules', *American Economic Review Papers and Proceedings*, 91: 263-67.

Torres Garcia, A. (2003), 'Monetary Policy and Interest Rates: Evidence from Mexico', *Working Paper* presented at the Kiel Workshop for Monetary Policy and Macroeconomic Stabilization in Latin America, Kiel Institute for World Economics, 11-12.

Vinhas de Souza, L. and Ledrut, E. (2003). 'Modelling Alternative Paths to EMU for the Accession Countries', in L.M. Vinhas de Souza and B. van Aarle (eds), *The Euroarea and the New EU Member States*, United Kingdom: Palgrave-Macmillan Press, pp. 39-53.

Woodford, M. (1999), 'Pitfalls of Forward-Looking Monetary Policy', Mimeo, Stanford University.

PART 3
BELARUS

Chapter 8

Monetary Union between Belarus and Russia: Testing for Convergence of Monetary Policy

Igor Pelipas and Irina Tochitskaya

Introduction

After the break up of the Soviet Union, Belarusian officials frequently declared their readiness for economic and political integration with Russia up to creation of a common state. In April 1996, Belarus and Russia signed an agreement on the establishment of a Political and Economic Community; in April 1997, the Community was transformed into the Union. On 30 November 2000, in the context of economic integration between the two countries, state agreements 'On introduction of a common currency and creation of a common emission centre of the Union State' and 'On measures of creating conditions for the introduction of a common currency' were signed. However, attempts to implement the above-mentioned agreements in practice have shown that Belarus is not ready both politically and economically for a closer integration with Russia, in particular for introduction of the Russian rouble as a legal tender. Despite the political claims of Belarusian authorities on their adherence to the principles of economic integration, the issue of introduction of the Russian rouble as a common currency on Belarusian territory still remains open.

During the discussions on the creation of monetary union between Belarus and Russia either political issues of the economic integration or possible consequences (both positive and negative) of such integration for the two countries are usually considered. Although the literature on this issue is rather limited, usually it is stressed that these two countries have substantially different economic systems and economic policies. Gulde, et al. (2004) show that the long-run net economic impact of the proposed currency unification between Belarus and Russia is not clear. While common currency would bring substantial benefits for Belarus from reduced transaction costs and an improved macroeconomic environment, Belarus and Russia have different economic structures, and therefore are subject to asymmetric shocks.

A comparative analysis of macroeconomic indicators, economic legislation and the main futures of economic systems in Russia and Belarus reveal that these countries are not ready to form a monetary union *ad exemplum* of the EU. Russia and Belarus do not meet the criteria of the theory of optimal currency areas. The short-run effect of monetary union creation for Belarus, according to some estimates, could be the following: decrease of GDP by 7-9 per cent, increase of unemployment up to 11-16 per cent, and budget losses of 12-15 per cent (Klepach et al., 2004).

International experience and the European Union experience in particular, show that the success of economic integration and introduction of the common currency greatly depends on the degree of convergence of monetary policies among potential partner countries. Unfortunately, this aspect of economic integration between Belarus and Russia has not become an issue for empirical analysis. Thus, the chapter attempts to fill this gap by drawing attention to the degree of convergence in the variables, characterizing monetary policy within the context of economic integration between Belarus and Russia, and the possibility of forming a monetary union based on the Russian rouble as a common currency. The question, therefore, is to what extent the political claims of Belarus about the strengthening of the economic integration with Russia and the desire to introduce the Russian rouble are accompanied by appropriate economic policy due to which the convergence of major monetary policy indicators (for example, consumer price index, M0, M2, exchange rate, refinancing rate) between these countries should take place? From this point of view the study provides empirical evidence on whether Belarus and Russia are ready for a monetary union based on the assessment of the degree of convergence of major variables characterizing monetary policy, using both a traditional unit root test and a relatively new bound test for cointegration (Pesaran et al., 2001).

Although an insufficient convergence level of the monetary policies of two countries does not reject by itself the possibility of unification of two monetary systems, it makes the process quite difficult and adjustment rather painful. Taking into account constant discords between Belarus and Russia about the declared intentions and real economic policy, our analysis has clear policy implications. It contributes to a better understanding of the peculiarities of the integration process between Belarus and Russia and provides additional empirics concerning the degree of readiness of these two countries to create a monetary union. The theoretical aspects of the creation of currency unions, the debate about their desirability as well as political motives of the different political forces are within the scope of this chapter.[1]

The remainder of this chapter is organized as follows. Section two briefly discusses the relevant literature. Section three presents the estimation procedures. Section four describes the data used and provides the results of empirical analysis. Section five concludes.

---

[1] Gulde et al. (2004) discuss the theoretical consideration of currency unification, costs and benefits of a monetary union for Belarus and Russia and current operational environment in both countries in the context of the introduction of the Russian rouble as a common currency.

A brief overview of the relevant literature

A large body of papers provides different definitions of convergence, as well as attempts to settle the question empirically. These papers vary considerably in what concerns methodology, sample, and results. For a comprehensive survey of the literature on the convergence hypothesis see Rassekh (1998). However, for the purpose of our study, only the papers that deal with the tests of convergence in a time series framework are considered.

In econometrics, it is generally accepted that there is a distinction between stationary and non-stationary time series. If time series are non-stationary, cointegration between them is a necessary (but not sufficient) condition for convergence. When time series have the order of integration $I(1)$, they converge to each other, in case the differences between them are stationary (that is, have the order of integration $I(0)$). This definition is compatible with earlier concepts of convergence presented elsewhere, for example encompass the conditional and unconditional 'beta-convergence' put forward by Barro and Sala-i-Martin (1992, 1995). Bernard and Durlauf (1995) propose the following definition of long-run convergence: countries i and j converge in the long-run, if forecast of output for both countries are equal at a fixed time t, for example $\lim_{k \to \infty} E(y_{i,t+k} - y_{j,t+k} \mid I_t) = 0$, where I_t denotes information available at time t. This definition will be valid when the difference between series is a zero-mean stationary process and assumes that under convergence the variables must be cointegrated with cointegrating vector $[1, -1]$. If $\lim_{k \to \infty} E(y_{i,t+k} - \alpha y_{j,t+k} \mid I_t) = 0$, then countries i and j contain a common trend in the long run forecasts of the analyzed variables and relevant time series are cointegrated with cointegrating vector $[1, -\alpha]$. This bivariate approach can be generalized for a multivariate framework.

Based on definitions put forward by Bernard and Durlauf (1995, 1996), Oxley and Greasley (1995) and Greasley and Oxley (1997) consider the different types of convergence, namely: long-run convergence (time series are cointegrated with cointegrating vector $[1, -1]$ and the differences between them are a zero-mean stationary process), common trends (time series are cointegrated with cointegrating vector $[1, -\alpha]$, that is, differences between them are not equal in the long-run, but proportional at a fix time t), catching-up convergence (time series are cointegrated with cointegrating vector $[1, -1]$, and the differences between them are a stationary process with a non-zero mean). In this framework, it is naturally to employ systems-based cointegration techniques for testing of convergence.

It is worth mentioning that historically tests for convergence in a time series framework were formulated as univariate Dickey-Fuller unit root tests. Such an approach can sometimes be extended, using sequential unit root tests, which enable us to consider the structural breaks in the dynamics of the variables (Perron, 1989, 1990, 1997; Perron and Vogelsang, 1992). Ericsson and Halket (2002) discuss the shortcomings of the univariate technique, and indicate that implementation of convergence tests in a multivariate cointegration framework (Johansen, 1988, 1991, 1995; Johansen and Juselius, 1990) can yield more reliable results.

The bulk of the papers investigate the convergence of output per capita across different countries (Bernard and Durlauf, 1995; Li and Papell, 1999; Ericsson and Halket, 2002). But the same approaches have been widely employed for convergence analysis of the countries forming monetary unions. Most of the studies examine the monetary and, to some extent, fiscal policy coordination among the EU countries, and the European Monetary Union, with a special focus on four 'nominal convergence' criteria, which were laid down in the Maastricht Treaty. Haug et al. (2000) employ the Johansen cointegration approach to determine which of the European Union countries would form a successful Economic and Monetary Union. Karfakis and Moschos (1990) study the linkages of the interest rate between Germany and each of the following countries: Belgium, France, Ireland, Italy and the Netherlands. MacDonald and Taylor (1991) analyze the long-run relationships between real and nominal exchange rates and money supply. The evidence of partial convergence of short-run interest rates and money supply among Belgium, France, Germany, Italy and Netherlands is presented in Hafer and Kutan (1994).

Several studies provide empirical evidence of monetary convergence outside the EU. Implementing the cointegration technique, Haug (2001) assesses the readiness of New Zealand to form a currency union with either Australia, the 11 EU countries, or Japan and the USA. The test for convergence in key economic variables shows that New Zealand is not ready for currency union with any of the above-mentioned partners.

For the purpose of our analysis special attention has been paid to the papers that analyze the convergence of the monetary policy between transition-economy candidates for the EU membership and the EU members. Brada and Kutan (2001), using cointegration analysis, explore the possibility of the transition-economy candidates for EU membership, non-transition candidates and the countries which have recently joined the EU, to follow the common monetary policy. The results reveal the existence of a significant linkage only between German monetary policy and countries of the second and the third groups, while among transition countries the relations are rather weak or do not exist at all.

Among the studies that address the issue of convergence between transition economies, the following papers should be mentioned: Kočenda (2002) with an analysis of macroeconomic convergence between countries of Central and Eastern Europe; Kutan and Yigit (2004) who extended Kočenda's analysis; and Estrin et al. (2001) who discussed convergence between the former Soviet Union and Western countries.

Methodology

The definition of convergence

Let y_t^b and y_t^r denote the log of levels of variables in two countries (say, Belarus and Russia), b and r are country indices, t is the time index. It is assumed that the variables have the order of integration $I(1)$, and this assumption is the subject of empirical verification. Our study is based on the definitions of convergence in a time series framework that were summarized in Ericsson and Halket (2002):

1. Stochastic convergence (Carlino and Mills, 1993). The time series y_t^b and y_t^r exhibit stochastic convergence, if the differences $(y_t^b - y_t^r)$ are trend stationary. This is the weakest form of convergence.
2. Deterministic convergence (Li and Papell, 1996). The time series y_t^b and y_t^r exhibit deterministic convergence, if the differences $(y_t^b - y_t^r)$ are stationary and non-zero in the long-run. Deterministic convergence implies stochastic convergence, but not the opposite. This type of convergence means that two time series move in parallel, but their differences $(y_t^b - y_t^r)$ may be non-zero in the long-run.
3. Zero-mean convergence (Bernard and Durlauf, 1996). The series y_t^b and y_t^r exhibit zero-mean convergence, if their differences $(y_t^b - y_t^r)$ are stationary with zero-mean. Zero-mean convergence implies both stochastic and deterministic convergence, but not the opposite. This is the strongest form of convergence, when the time series move unidirectional in the long-run and the differences between them are zero-mean, hence the levels of variables tend to converge over time.

All these definitions of convergence can be incorporated both in univariate and bivariate tests for convergence.

Econometric techniques

In the univariate framework the convergence test can be presented as a standard Dickey-Fuller unit root test in the following form:

$$\Delta(y^b - y^r)_t = \mu + \delta t + \alpha(y^b - y^r)_{t-1} + \sum_{i=1}^{k} \gamma_i \Delta(y^b - y^r)_{t-i} + u_t \tag{1}$$

where Δ is the difference operator; μ, δ, α, γ are coefficients; u_t is the stochastic error term that follows the classical assumptions, namely, it has zero mean, constant variance, and is not autocorrelated. Based on this regression, the null hypothesis that the coefficient α is equal to zero is verified; t-statistics in this case have nonstandard distribution that assumed the use of special critical values. Stochastic convergence implies that $\alpha < 0$; deterministic convergence exists when $\alpha < 0$ and $\delta = 0$, while zero-mean convergence implies that $\alpha < 0$ and $\delta = \mu = 0$. The mentioned hypothesis can be tested using a 'general to specific' approach, assuming sequential reduction of the initial model based on the appropriate tests. The lag length in (1) is selected in order to avoid serial correlation of residuals.

It is known, however, that the univariate test has low power. Therefore, in order to increase the ability to uncover the convergence, in this chapter we implement bivariate tests for convergence. So far, testing for convergence in a multivariate framework has been performed with the Johansen procedure. Specifically, let x'_t be the vector of variables (y^b_t, y^r_t), then in a bivariate cointegration framework, the Johansen test is based on the following vector autoregression with equilibrium correction mechanism:

$$\Delta x_t = \pi x_{t-1} + \sum_{i=1}^{k} \Gamma_i \Delta x_{t-i} + \theta_0 + \theta_1 t + u_t \tag{2}$$

where π and Γ are 2 x 2 matrices of coefficients; θ_0 and θ_1 are 2 x 1 vectors of coefficients; u_t is the 2 x 1 vector error term, which is assumed to be normally and independently distributed with mean zero and variance matrix Ω. If two variables are cointegrated, then π has a reduced rank of one and can be written as $\pi = \alpha\beta'$, where α and β are 2 x 1 vectors of full rank. Under convergence, $\beta' = [1, -1]$ and this hypothesis is testable with the Johansen procedure. Under stochastic convergence, the null hypothesis is that $\beta' = [1, -1]$, and the trend is restricted in the cointegration space. Deterministic convergence and zero-mean convergence correspond to the additional null hypothesis concerning restrictions on θ_0 and θ_1.

However, the Johansen cointegration test, as a system procedure, requires all equations in the system to be well specified (Ericsson and Halket, 2002). In our study the entire sample consists of 144 monthly observations and the sub-sample includes less then 40 observations that may cause the misspecifications of the system of equations in the Johansen procedure. To avoid this problem while testing for convergence, we implement a relatively new bounds test for cointegration, proposed by Pesaran et al. (2001).

Like in the Johansen procedure, consider a vector of two variables $x'_t = (y^b_t, y^r_t)$, where y^b_t is the dependent variable and y^r_t is a regressor. The data generating process of x'_t is a p-order vector autoregression. The bounds test for long run relationships based on the following regression:

$$\Delta y^b_t = \mu_y + \beta_y t + \gamma_{1y} y^b_{t-1} + \gamma_{2y} x^r_{t-1} + \sum_{i=1}^{n} \psi_{iy} \Delta y^b_{t-i} + \sum_{i=1}^{n} \varphi_{iy} \Delta x^r_{t-i} + \varepsilon_{ty} \tag{3}$$

where γ_{1y} and x_{1y} are long-run multiples; μ_y is intercept, t is time trend. Lagged values of Δy^b_{t-i} and Δx^r_{t-i} are used for modelling the short-run dynamic structure. The bounds testing procedure for the absence of a long-run relationship between y^b_t and y^r_t is implemented through the exclusion of lagged levels variables y^b_{t-1} and y^r_{t-1} in equation (3). This hypothesis can be tested using a standard F test, for example we verify that the coefficients of variables y^b_{t-1} and y^r_{t-1} are jointly zero. If the intercept is restricted in the long-run relationship, this joint hypothesis is extended by imposing one more restriction, $t = 0$. F test has a non-standard distribution and special critical values are presented in Pesaran et al. (2001). Thus, the bounds test permits us to verify the hypotheses of different types of convergence like in the Johansen procedure, and obtain consistent estimates for relatively small samples.[2]

The data and empirical results

The data and their time series properties[3]

The following data are used in our study: 1) consumer price index (CPI); 2) monetary aggregate M0 (currency in circulation); 3) monetary aggregate M2 (M0 + demand deposits + time deposits, and securities (excludes stocks); 4) exchange rate (EXRATE); 5) refinancing rate (REF). The reason for selection of these variables is as follows: taking into account the availability of the data for both countries, these indicators are more or less relevant proxies, characterizing monetary policy and the results of its implementation. Thus, convergence between these variables means to some extent the convergence of monetary policies between the examined countries.

The sample covers the period 1992-2003 and is based on monthly data, that is 144 monthly observations. The data sources are the following: the National Bank of the Republic of Belarus, the Ministry of Statistics and Analysis of the Republic of Belarus, the Central Bank of the Russian Federation, and the State Committee of the Russian Federation on Statistics.

All time series are in natural logarithms, where cpi_by = lnCPI_BY, cpi_ru = lnCPI_RU, m0_by = lnM0_BY, m0_ru = lnM0_RU, m2_by = lnM2_BY, m2_ru = lnM2_RU, exrate_by = lnEXRATE_BY, exrate_ru = lnEXRATE_RU, ref_by =lnREF_BY and ref_ru = lnREF_RU. Indexes BY and RU denote the variables for Belarus and Russia respectively. Δ is a difference operator and denotes the first differences of the variables. The levels and first differences of the examined data are presented in Figure 8.1.

---

[2]   The Johansen test for cointegration is not robust for small sample sizes, but in the bounds test the OLS estimators of the short-run parameters are $\sqrt{T}$ consistent, and appropriate estimators of the long-run parameters are super-consistent in small samples.

[3]   All estimations in this chapter were made using econometric software PcGive Professional 9.3 (Doornik and Hendry, 1996) and Eviews 4.1.

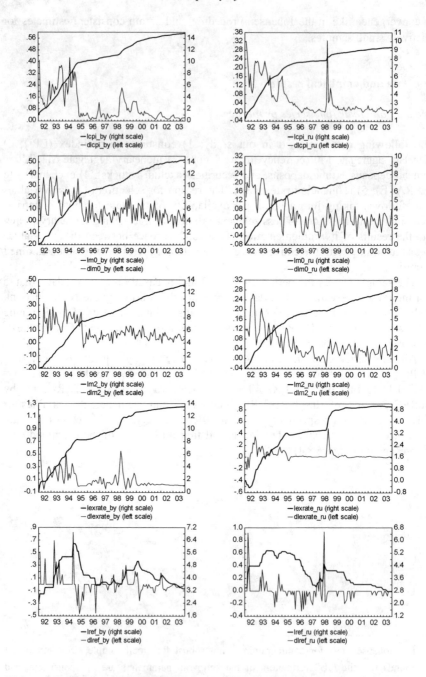

Figure 8.1 Levels and first differences of time series (log scale, d is a difference operator Δ)

The striking feature of the data examined (at least for the first four variables) is the structural breaks. Clearly, it is important to account for such structural breaks when analyzing the order of integration of the variables. Figure 8.1 shows that the level of variables is undoubtedly non-stationary, but the situation is not so clear-cut when we look at the first differences. Usually, for formal analysis of the order of integration, a traditional Dickey-Fuller unit root test is used. However, this test has low power, therefore, the probability of type II error, when false null hypothesis is accepted, is rather high. This is especially relevant for estimation of the order of integration of the first differences. There is a hazard that the null hypothesis of a unit root is not rejected, whereas in fact the first differences are stationary in the presence of structural breaks. There are several types of structural breaks, but as follows from Figure 8.1, one can see changes of the slope at least in four variables (breaking trend). A breaking trend supposes the change of the mean for the first differences of variables. Perron (1990, 1997), Perron and Vogelsang (1992) provide the appropriate unit root tests that enable us to take into account such a structural break. It should be noted that such tests are usually applied to the levels of variables. Since our main task is to examine the first differences of variables for a unit root, the technique put forward by Perron was slightly modified in accordance with this task.

The approach used in this chapter is as follows. First, the unit root test is employed for the levels of variables with break in the slope and the following regression is used:

$$y_t = \mu + \beta t + \gamma DT_t + \tilde{y}_t \qquad (4)$$

where y_t is level of variable; μ, β, γ are the parameters of the regression; $DT_t = 1(t > T_b)(t - T_b)$ is dummy that allows for breaking trend; t is time trend; $\tilde{y}_t$ is an error term. The point of structural break (change in slope) T_b is chosen endogenously to minimize the value of t-statistics for γ in (4). Equation (4) permits us to eliminate the trend from time-series, and obtain residuals that are used in the following unit root test:

$$\Delta \tilde{y}_t = \alpha \tilde{y}_{t-1} + \sum_{i=1}^{k} c_i \Delta \tilde{y}_{t-i} + \varepsilon_t \qquad (5)$$

where $\Delta \tilde{y}_t = \tilde{y}_t - \tilde{y}_{t-1}$; a, c_i are the parameters of the regression; k is the number of lags in regression; ε_t is an error term. Based on equation (5) the null hypothesis of the unit root is tested. If t-ADF for α coefficient is negative and exceeds in absolute values the appropriate critical value for a given level of significance, then the null hypothesis is rejected.

Since a change in the slope in the level of the variable corresponds to the change of a mean of its first difference, then the point of structural break T_b that is determined endogenously can be used exogenously in the unit root test for the first difference:

$$\Delta\Delta y_t = \mu + \gamma DU_t + \varphi D(TB)_t + \alpha\Delta y_{t-1} + \sum_{i=1}^{k} c_i \Delta\Delta y_{t-i} + \varepsilon_t \qquad (6)$$

where $\Delta\Delta y_t = \Delta y_t - \Delta y_{t-1}$; $\Delta y_t = y_t - y_{t-1}$; μ, γ, φ, α, c_i are the parameters of regressions; $DU_t = 1(t > T_b)$ and $D(TB)_t = 1(t = T_b + 1)$; k is the number of lags in regressions; T_b is the point of structural break; ε_t is an error term.

Such an approach seems to be logical while testing for unit root in the first differences with structural break, as the change in a mean is the consequence of structural break (change in the slope) in the level of the variables. In addition, the point of structural break defined endogenously at the first stage of analysis enables us to use the critical value for exogenously determined structural break at the second stage. Their absolute values are substantially lower than values for structural breaks determined endogenously; other things being equal, this reduces the probability of the acceptance of a false null hypothesis, and increases the power of the test. The robustness of the results has been verified using the technique proposed by Perron and Vogelsang (1992), where in equation (3) the point of structural break is determined endogenously (in our case T_b is chosen by minimizing the t-statistics for γ coefficient in equation (3)).

Unit root tests employed in this study are highly sensitive to the choice of the lag length in regressions (Weber, 2001). Usually the set of methods are employed in empirical research for choosing the lag length in the unit root tests, for example 'from general to specific', 'from specific to general', as well as informational criteria (Akaike and Schwarz). Different methods can lead to opposite results and cause uncertainty in testing for the unit root. It should be noted that the initial motivation for inclusion of the additional lags in the unit root test is the elimination of the residual autocorrelation in the regressions. In the given study we follow the above criteria and choose the lag length in the unit root tests to eliminate residual autocorrelation in the regressions. It can be expressed as follows: $k_{opt} \equiv \{k \in K: J_i > J^* \; \forall_i \in K, i < k$ and $J_k < J^*\}$, where k_{opt} is the optimal lag length in the unit root test that ensures the absence of the residual autocorrelation; k is selected from the set of integers K; J is the statistics for the null hypothesis of the absence of the residual autocorrelation; J^* are the critical values of these statistics for a given level of significance. As a result, the minimum lag length that eliminates the residual autocorrelation is selected.[4]

Table 8.1 reports the results of the unit root tests with structural breaks for the first four variables. For the last variables, where this kind of structural break is not observed, we implement a modification of Dickey-Fuller (ADFGLS test) where trend and constant are eliminated from analyzing time series using generalized least square method (GLS). Then new de-trended data are used in the traditional Dickey-Fuller test for verification of the null hypothesis of a unit root. If t-

---

[4] It should be noted that in our case the implementation of different criteria for lag selection in appropriate unit root tests leads to approximately the same results. Such estimations are available upon request (email pelipas@ipm.by).

ADFGLS is negative and exceeds the critical value for a given level of significance, then the null hypothesis is rejected (Elliot et al., 1996).

Table 8.1 Unit root tests

Variable	With structural break			
	T_b	Lag	*t*-ADF	AR 1-5
(A) T_b is chosen endogenously for the levels and exogenously for the first differences				
cpi_by	1995:04	4	-1.85	1.0286 [0.4036]
m0_by	1995:06	1	-1.86	2.2084 [0.0570]
m2_by	1995:06	3	-1.63	1.0891 [0.3695]
exrate_by	1995:01	5	-1.40	1.6837 [0.1432]
cpi_ru	1995:01	3	-3.29	2.2474 [0.0533]
m0_ru	1994:08	5	-3.46	1.0358 [0.3995]
m2_ru	1994:12	9	-4.01	0.8897 [0.4904]
exrate_ru	1994:12	9	-2.01	1.8455 [0.1091]
Δ*cpi_by*	1995:01	3	-4.44**	0.7275 [0.6041]
Δ*m0_by*	1995:06	0	-9.08**	0.9778 [0.4338]
Δ*m2_by*	1995:06	3	-8.33**	1.8261 [0.1123]
Δ*exrate_by*	1995:01	4	-4.54**	1.5705 [0.1732]
Δ*cpi_ru*	1995:01	0	-6.90**	1.6856 [0.1423]
Δ*m0_ru*	1994:08	4	-4.68**	2.0934 [0.0705]
Δ*m2_ru*	1994:12	8	-3.38*	1.7115 [0.1373]
Δ*exrate_ru*	1994:12	0	-5.76**	1.5871 [0.1680]
(B) T_b is chosen endogenously for the first differences				
Δ*cpi_by*	1994:12	3	-6.07**	1.1423 [0.3415]
Δ*m0_by*	1995:06	0	-9.08**	0.9778 [0.4338]
Δ*m2_by*	1995:06	3	-8.33**	1.8261 [0.1123]
Δ*exrate_by*	1995:01	4	-4.54*	1.5705 [0.1732]
Δ*cpi_ru*	1995:02	0	-6.88**	1.5129 [0.1900]
Δ*m0_ru*	1994:06	4	-5.06**	2.2589 [0.0526]
Δ*m2_ru*	1995:07	8	-4.21*	1.8458 [0.1092]
Δ*exrate_ru*	1995:03	0	-5.88**	1.2915 [0.2713]
Without structural break				
		Lag		*t*-ADFGLS
ref_by		2		-1.29
ref_ru		0		-0.89
Δ*ref_by*		1		-3.24*
Δ*ref_ru*		0		-9.70**

Notes: 1. T_b – point of structural break. 2. Critical values for the part A of the table: for the levels of the variables at the 5 per cent and 1 per cent level of confidence they are -4.44 and -5.26 respectively (Perron. 1997); for the differences of the variables when $\lambda = T_b/T = 0.3$ they are -3.33 and -4.05 at the 5 per cent and 1 per cent level of confidence respectively, when $\lambda = T_b/T = 0.2$ they are -3.22 and -3.86 at the 5 per cent and 1 per cent level of confidence respectively (Perron, 1990). Critical values for the part B of the table: at the 5 per cent and 1 per cent level of confidence they are -4.38 and -3.66 respectively (Perron and Vogelsang, 1992). 3. AR 1-5 is LM test for serial correlation of orders from 1 up to 5. 4. Critical valued for ADFGLS test are taken from Elliot, et al. (1996). 5. All computations were made using econometric packages PcGive Professional 9.3 and Eviews 4.1.
[*] Significant at the five per cent level.
[**] Idem., one per cent.

Part A of Table 8.1 presents the results of the tests based on the above-mentioned approach, when the point of structural break T_b is selected endogenously for the levels and exogenously for the first differences of the series. Apparently the null hypothesis of a unit root in the levels of variables cannot be rejected. At the same time, the null hypothesis of a unit root in the first differences of variables is rejected for all time series. Part B of Table 8.1 reports the results of the tests when the point of structural break is defined endogenously. Despite the slight discrepancy in the selection of T_b, the tests show analogous results. That offers evidence that the first differences of *cpi*, *m0*, *m2* and *exrate* are stationary with the changing means, and that they have the order of integration $I(0)$. Consequently, the levels of these variables have the order of integration $I(1)$. The same results provide on ADFGLS test for *ref* in the bottom part of Table 8.1.

Univariate test for convergence

Table 8.2 presents the univariate test for convergence for the full sample over the period 1992:01-2003:12. The coefficients of trend and constant of the relevant ADF regressions are tested sequentially, and in compliance with the results the hypothesis of the existence of stochastic, deterministic, or zero-mean convergence is verified. As is evident from Table 8.1, none of the variables examined converge with the full sample in accordance with univariate tests.

As the state agreements between Belarus and Russia 'On the introduction of a Common Currency and the Creation of the Common Emission Centre of the Union State' and 'On Measures for Preparing the Conditions for the Introduction of the Common Currency' were signed on 30 November 2000, the testing of the hypothesis of convergence after the above-mentioned agreements is of particular interest. Table 8.3 reports that according to the univariate test for convergence the null hypothesis is not rejected for all variables for the period after signing the agreements about the creation of monetary union between Belarus and Russia. Hence, the univariate tests detect no evidence of convergence among variables under investigation for the whole sample as well as for the period 2001:01-2003:12.

Table 8.2   Unit root tests for convergence (entire sample: 1992:01-2003:12)

Variable	*t*-ADF (constant and trend)	*t*-statistic for trend	*t*-ADF (constant)	*t*-statistic for constant	*t*-ADF (without constant and trend)
cpi_by-cpi_ru	-2.33(3)	1.96	-1.68(3)	2.46[*]	-
m0_by-m0_ru	-0.53(2)	0.05	-2.18(2)	3.84[**]	-
m2_by-m2_ru	-1.34(3)	1.04	-1.73(3)	3.21[**]	-
exrate_by-exrate_ru	-1.84(7)	1.21	-2.38(7)	2.95[**]	-
ref_by-ref_ru	-2.39(0)	1.54	-1.84(0)	0.84	-1.69(0)

Notes: 1. The numbers in parenthesis indicate an optimal lag length, selected so that ADF regressions error passes LM test for serial correlation of orders from 1 up to 5.
2. *t*-ADF and corresponding critical values (MacKinnon, 1996) were obtained using econometric package PcGive Professional 9.3.
[*] Significant at the 5 per cent level.
[**] Idem., 1 per cent.

Table 8.3   Unit root tests for convergence (sub-sample: 2001:01-2003:12)

Variable	*t*-ADF (constant and trend)	*t*-statistic for trend	*t*-ADF (constant)	*t*-statistic for constant	*t*-ADF (without constant and trend)
cpi_by-cpi_ru	-1.42(1)	1.29	-0.89(1)	1.00	2.23(1)
m0_by-m0_ru	-1.50(5)	-0.24	-2.71(5)	2.73[*]	-
m2_by-m2_ru	-0.84(0)	0.26	-2.63(0)	2.85[**]	-
exrate_by-exrate_ru	-2.31(3)	2.25[*]	-	-	-
ref_by-ref_ru	-2.85(1)	-1.82	-2.22(1)	1.93	-1.39(0)

Notes: 1. The numbers in parentheses indicate an optimal lag length, selected so that ADF regressions error passes LM test for serial correlation of orders from 1 up to 5.
2. *t*-ADF and corresponding critical values (MacKinnon, 1996) were obtained using econometric package PcGive Professional 9.3.
[*] Significant at the 5 per cent level.
[**] Idem., 1 per cent.

Bivariate test for convergence

Further, we proceed with the bivariate test for convergence using equation (3). Let y_t be *cpi_by, m0_by, m2_by, exrate_by, ref_by*, and x_t respectively *cpi_ru, m0_ru, m2_ru, exrate_ru, ref_ru*, then test $F_y(y|x)$ of no long-run relationship (cointegration) between variables under study, implies the verification of the following joint null hypothesis: $H_0: \gamma_{1y} = \gamma_{1y} = 0, \beta_y = 0$. If the coefficient of the trend is equal to zero, then the above hypothesis is reduced to $H_0: \gamma_{1y} = \gamma_{1y} = 0$. The long-run relationship (cointegration) between variables is the necessary condition for convergence among them.

The next tested hypothesis is homogeneity (that is $\beta' = [1,-1]$) of the parameters of long-run relationship. It means that $\gamma_{1y} = \gamma_{2y}$, or their difference is equal to zero. If the null hypothesis of the homogeneity of the parameters of the long-run relationship is not rejected both with trend and without trend in cointegrating vectors, then convergence will be observed between the pairs of examined variables. Stochastic convergence corresponds to $\beta_y \neq 0$, while deterministic convergence corresponds to $\beta_y = 0$, $\mu_y \neq 0$, and zero-mean convergence corresponds to $\beta_y = 0$.

The bounds tests suppose that the long-run relationships can be bi-directional. However, since the Belarusian monetary policy does not influence the Russian one, in our study we present only the results of regressions, where the Belarusian time series are the dependent variable.[5] Our analysis reveals the unidirectional linkage between Belarusian and Russian indicators, characterizing monetary policy, that is, if the relationship exists, Russian variables influence Belarusian, but not the opposite.

Initially, the models with six lags are estimated, and then it has been reduced, using 'general to specific' approach with testing for the absence of serial autocorrelation. Based on the obtained final regressions, the hypothesis of the long-run relationship between variables characterizing monetary policy and the hypothesis of homogeneity are tested. Tables 8.4 and 8.5 present the results.

---

[5]   Other regressions are not informative for the purpose of our study, but are available upon request (email pelipas@ipm.by).

Table 8.4 Bounds tests for convergence (entire sample: 1992:01-2003:12)

Regression	$H_0: \gamma_{1y} = \gamma_1 = 0$, $\beta_y = 0$	$H_0: \gamma_1 = \gamma_{1y} = 0$	Test for homogeneity, $\beta' = [1, -1]$	AR 1-5
cpi_ru→cpi_by	5.74(5)*	-	0.828 [0.365]	1.646 [0.153]
m0_ru→m0_by	9.23(4)**	-	1.541 [0.217]	1.267 [0.283]
m2_ru→m2_by	5.96(3)*	-	3.621 [0.059]	1.070 [0.380]
exrate_ru→exrate_by	-	2.95(5)	-	1.595 [0.167]
ref_ru→ref_by	-	6.89(5)*	4.102 [0.045]*	1.282 [0.276]
$F_c(0.01)$	6.10, 6.73	6.84, 7.84		
$F_c(0.05)$	4.68, 5.15	4.94, 5.73		
$F_c(0.10)$	4.05, 4.49	4.04, 4.78		

Notes: 1. Symbol → denotes the direction of relationships.
2. The numbers in parenthesis indicate an optimal lag length in regressions.
3. The numbers in square brackets are p-values of the appropriate tests.
4. AR 1-5 is LM test for serial correlation of orders from 1 up to 5.
5. Critical values (F_C) are taken from Pesaran et al. (2001).
6. Computations were made using econometric package PcGive Professional 9.3.
* Significant at the 5 per cent level.
** Idem., 1 per cent.

Table 8.5   Bounds tests for convergence (sub-sample: 2001:01-2003:12)

Regression	$H_0: \gamma_{1y} = \gamma_{1y} = 0,$ $\beta_y = 0$	$H_0: \gamma_{1y} = \gamma_{1y} = 0,$	Test for homogeneity, $\beta' = [1, -1]$	AR 1-5
cpi_ru→cpi_by	2.57(1)	-	-	0.545 [0.740]
m0_ru→m0_by	-	2.65(1)	-	1.375 [0.266]
m2_ru→m2_by	2.62(1)	-	-	1.692 [0.173]
exrate_ru→exrate_by	-	3.50(6)	-	1.662 [0.201]
ref_ru→ref_by	3.76(1)	-	-	2.516 [0.056]
$F_c(0.01)$	6.10, 6.73	6.84, 7.84		
$F_c(0.05)$	4.68, 5.15	4.94, 5.73		
$F_c(0.10)$	4.05, 4.49	4.04, 4.78		

Notes: 1. Symbol → denotes the direction of relationships.
2. The numbers in parenthesis indicate an optimal lag length in regressions.
3. The numbers in square brackets are p-values of the appropriate tests.
4. AR 1-5 is LM test for serial correlation of orders from 1 up to 5.
5. Critical values (F_C) are taken from Pesaran et al. (2001).
6. Computations were made using econometric package PcGive Professional 9.3.
* Significant at the 5 per cent level.
** Idem., 1 per cent.

It is evident that these results differ from those obtained by using the univariate tests for convergence. Thus, for the full sample both the hypothesis of the long-run relationship (cointegration) and of homogeneity, is not rejected for almost all variables, except exchange rate. For the entire sample, Belarus exhibits stochastic convergence to Russia *cpi, m0 and m2*, while in the case of *ref* the convergence is deterministic.

On the contrary, for the sub-sample 2001:01-2003:12, characterizing the joint dynamics of the variables after signing the state agreements between Belarus and Russia on creation of monetary union, the null hypothesis of no long-run relationship between variables is not rejected for all examined monetary indicators. As such relationship is the necessary condition for convergence, there is no evidence for convergence between these two countries over the period 2001:01-2003:12.

The results of the univariate and bivariate tests are summarized in Table 8.6. For the full sample the more powerful bivariate test detects the convergence at least for four variables of five. However, both univariate and bivariate tests do not confirm our initial hypothesis of the convergence of the variables, characterizing monetary policy for the sub-sample 2001:01-2003:12, after signing the agreement about the creation of monetary union between Belarus and Russia.

Table 8.6   Testing for convergence of monetary policy indicators: Summing up the results

Variable	Entire sample 1992:01-2003:12		Sub-sample 2001:01-2003:12	
	Univariate test	Bivariate test	Univariate test	Bivariate test
cpi	No convergence	Stochastic convergence	No convergence	No convergence
m0	No convergence	Stochastic convergence	No convergence	No convergence
m2	No convergence	Stochastic convergence or common trend	No convergence	No convergence
exrate	No convergence	No convergence	No convergence	No convergence
ref	No convergence	Deterministic convergence or common trend	No convergence	No convergence

186 *The Periphery of the Euro*

Probably, the revealed convergence is the consequence of the common trends in the dynamics of monetary variables in Belarus and Russia. However, since our tests do not detect convergence between variables under study after the signing of the agreements about the creation of a monetary union, evidently in the 2001:01-2003:12 period, coordination of monetary policy does not take place.

Concluding remarks

Using univariate unit root tests and bivariate bounds tests for cointegration we analyze the convergence of monetary policies between Belarus and Russia in a time series framework. Our conclusions are as follows.

First, the results obtained from univariate tests show no evidence of convergence between the Belarusian and Russian indicators of monetary policy (that is consumer price index, M0, M2, exchange rate, refinancing rate) for the period 1992-2003. Secondly, the implementation of the bivariate bounds tests for the long-run relationship for the entire sample reveals that Belarus and Russia consumer price index, M0 and M2 appear to converge stochastically; while in the case of the refinancing rate, convergence is deterministic. Thirdly, both univariate and bivariate tests do not confirm our initial hypothesis of the convergence of major monetary policy indicators between Belarus and Russia for the period after signing the agreement on the creation of a monetary union between the two countries (2001-2003). It is possible to draw the conclusion that the revealed convergence is the consequence of a common trend in the dynamics of monetary policy variables in Belarus and Russia for the period of 1992-2000. Therefore, our results indicate the lack of coordination of monetary policy between the two countries in 2001-2003 and raise additional doubts with respect to Belarus' readiness to introduce the Russian rouble as a legal tender.

References

Barro, R.J. and Sala-i-Martin, X. (1992), 'Convergence', *Journal of Political Economy*, 100: 223-51.
Bernard, A.B. and Durlauf, S.N. (1995), 'Convergence in International Output', *Journal of Applied Econometrics*, 10: 97-108.
Bernard, A.B. and Durlauf, S.N. (1996), 'Interpreting Tests of Convergence Hypothesis', *Journal of Econometrics*, 71: 161-73.
Brada, J.C. and Kutan, A.M. (2001), 'The Convergence of Monetary Policy between Candidate Countries and the European Union', *Economic Systems*, 25: 215-31.
Carlino, G.A. and Mills, L.O. (1993), 'Are US Regional Incomes Converging?', *Journal of Monetary Economics*, 32: 335-46.
Doornik, J.A. and Hendry, D.F. (1996), PcGive *Professional 9.0 for Windows*, London: International Thomson Business.

Elliott, G., Rothenberg, T.J. and Stock, J.H. (1996), 'Efficient Tests for an Autoregressive Unit Root', *Econometrica*, 64: 813-36.

Engle, R.F. and Granger, C.W.J. (1987), 'Cointegration and Error Correction: Representation, Estimation and Testing', *Econometrica*, 55: 251-76.

Ericsson, N.R. and Halket, J.R. (2002), 'Convergence of Output in the G7 Countries', Mimeo.

Estrin, S., Urga, G. and Lazarova, S. (2001), 'Testing for Ongoing Convergence in Transition Economies, 1970 to 1998', *Journal of Comparative Economics*, 29: 677-91.

Greasley, D. and Oxley, L. (1997), 'Time-Series Based Tests of the Convergence Hypothesis: Some Positive Results', *Economics Letters*, 56: 143-47.

Gulde, A.-M., Jafarov, E. and Prokopenko, V. (2004), 'A Common Currency for Belarus and Russia?', *Working paper*, Washington, DC: International Monetary Fund.

Hafer, R.W. and Kutan, A.M. (1994), 'A Long Run View of German Dominance and the Degree of Policy Convergence in the EMS', *Economic Inquiry*, 32: 684-95.

Haug, A.A. (2001), 'Co-Movement Towards a Currency or Monetary Union? An Empirical Study for New Zealand', *Australian Economic Papers*, 40, 3: 307-17.

Haug, A.A., MacKinnon, J.G. and Michelis, L. (2000), 'European Monetary Union: A Cointegration Analysis', *Journal of International Money and Finance*, 19: 419-32.

Johansen, S. (1988), 'Statistical Analysis of Cointegration Vectors', *Journal of Economic Dynamics and Control*, 12: 231-54.

Johansen, S. (1991), 'Estimation and Hypothesis Testing of Cointegration in Gaussian Vector Autoregressive Models', *Econometrica*, 59: 1551-80.

Johansen, S. and Juselius, K. (1990), 'Maximum Likelihood Estimation and Inference on Cointegration with Applications to the Demand for Money', *Oxford Bulletin of Economics and Statistics*, 52: 169-210.

Karfakis, C.J. and Moschos, D.M. (1990), 'Interest Rate Linkages within the European Monetary System: A Time Series Analysis', *Journal of Money Credit and Banking*, 22, 33: 388-94.

Klepach, A., Vardavanjan, G. and Osipova, O. (2004), 'Currency Union is Postponed but not Canceled', mimeo.

Kočenda, E. (2001), 'Macroeconomic Convergence in Transition Countries', *Journal of Comparative Economics*, 29: 1-23

Kutan, A.M. and Yigit, T.M. (2004), 'Nominal and Real Stochastic Convergence of Transition Economies', *Journal of Comparative Economics*, 32: 23-36.

Li, Q. and Papell, D. (1999), 'Convergence of International Output: Time Series Evidence for 16 OECD Countries', *International Review of Economics and Finance*, 8, 3: 267-80.

MacDonald, R. and Taylor, M.P. (1991), 'Exchange Rates, Policy Convergence, and the European Monetary System', *Review of Economics and Statistics*, 73, 3: 553-58.

The Periphery of the Euro

MacKinnon, J.G. (1996), 'Numerical Distribution Functions for Unit Root and Cointegration Tests', *Journal of Applied Econometrics*, 11: 601-18.

Oxley, L. and Greasley, D. (1995), 'A Time-Series Perspective on Convergence: Australia, UK and USA since 1870', *The Economic Record*, 71: 259-70.

Perron, P. (1990), 'Testing for a Unit Root in a Time Series with a Changing Mean', *Journal of Business and Economic Statistics*, 8: 153-62.

Perron, P. (1997), 'Further Evidence on Breaking Trend Functions in Macroeconomic Variables', *Journal of Econometrics*, 80: 355-85.

Perron, P. and Vogelsang, T.J. (1992), 'Nonstationarity and Level Shifts with an Application to Purchasing Power Parity', *Journal of Business and Economic Statistics*, 10: 301-20.

Perron, P. and Vogelsang, T.J. (1992), 'Testing for a Unit Root in a Time Series with a Changing Mean: Corrections and Extensions', *Journal of Business and Economic Statistics*, 10: 467-70.

Pesaran, M.H., Shin, Y. and Smith, R.J. (2001), 'Bounds Testing Approaches to the Analysis of Level Relationships', *Journal of Applied Econometrics*, 16: 289-326.

Rassekh, F. (1998), 'The Convergence Hypothesis: History, Theory, and Evidence', *Open Economies Review*, 9, 1: 85-105.

Sala-I-Martin, X. (1996), 'The Classical Approach to Convergence Analysis', *The Economic Journal*, 106: 1019-36.

Weber, C.E. (2001), 'Alternative Lag Length Selection Criteria and the Split-Trend Stationarity Hypothesis', *Applied Economics*, 33: 237-47.

Chapter 9

A Common Currency for
Belarus and Russia?

Anne-Marie Gulde, Etibar Jafarov and Vassili Prokopenko

Introduction

In recent years, a large number of countries have demonstrated strong interest in common currency arrangements.[1][2] The arrangements that have been contemplated ranged from the establishment of a completely new currency union by two or more independent countries to the incorporation of one or several individual countries into the existing union. In a number of cases, for example in the countries now forming the Economic and Monetary Union (EMU) and some Central American countries accepting the US dollar, monetary union was implemented.

This chapter discusses a proposed currency union for Belarus and Russia, with a focus mainly on the effects such union would have for Belarus. In evaluating the pros and cons, the chapter starts from the classical 'optimal currency area' criteria, but in addition highlights the importance of the economic structures and the institutional environment in both countries. Furthermore, given the disproportionate size of the economies of Belarus and Russia, the chapter also notes the specific challenges stemming from the establishment of an 'asymmetric' currency union between countries of different size and economic weight. The chapter concludes that the outcome of a cost-benefit calculation at this stage remains uncertain, but that the potential gains for Belarus would increase if the country were to create more favorable initial conditions through a faster liberalization of its economy.

---

[1] Common currency arrangements in this chapter refer to the use of a single currency in different countries. Hard pegs, such as currency boards that share many of the same costs and benefits, are not included in the definition of common currency for the purposes of this chapter.

[2] This wave of interest in common currency arrangements has probably been sparked by the successful launch of the European Monetary Union, as well as some more general globalization trends. With more or less strong political, popular, and economic backing, talks are currently underway on the design of a possible currency union for several Latin American countries, an extended currency union for the Caribbean countries, a second West African currency union, a currency union for the Gulf Cooperation Council countries, a currency union for several Asian countries, and so on.

The structure of the chapter is as follows. Section two briefly overviews the proposed currency union plan. Section three presents some theoretical considerations on the establishment of a currency union, with a special focus on issues involved in the creation of an 'asymmetrical' currency union.[3] Section four discusses the existing economic conditions for the currency unification for Belarus and Russia, while Section five focuses on the institutional environment of this union. Section six concludes.

The proposed currency union

Background

Discussions over monetary union between Belarus and Russia began in September 1993, only two months after the formal break-up of the rouble zone (Table 9.1 summarizes the chronology of these discussions).[4] The negotiations – which at least until the late 1990s were largely politically driven – subsequently stalled for several years, reflecting the different and sometimes diverging path of economic reforms in the two countries. Specifically, the Belarusian authorities have favoured a much more gradualistic approach to reforms than the Russian authorities, as a result of which the government in Belarus has remained heavily involved in many sectors of the economy. The Russian financial crisis of August 1998 further disrupted the integration process. Nevertheless, the idea of monetary and economic unification between the two countries has remained popular in both Russia and Belarus.[5] The improved macroeconomic conditions in both countries following the 1998 crisis have contributed to the intensification of the currency unification talks.

In December 1999, the authorities of Belarus and Russia signed the Union State Treaty. Under the terms of this Treaty, which was concluded without much public debate, Belarus and Russia agreed to proceed with a broad economic integration, including the establishment of a joint monetary system. In this connection, an agreement signed by Belarus and Russia in November 2000 stipulated introduction of a common currency for the Union State from January 1, 2008.[6]

---

[3] In this chapter, we define a currency union as 'asymmetric' when the relative sizes of the economies of member countries are of disproportionate dimensions and the members with small economies have a very limited influence over the common monetary and exchange rate policies.

[4] For the discussion of the dissolution of the rouble area, see Odling-Smee and Pastor (2001).

[5] See Colton (2002).

[6] This agreement was signed shortly after the long delayed unification of official and black market exchange rates in Belarus.

Table 9.1   **Belarus and Russia monetary integration: Chronology of developments, 1992-2002**

Date	Event
May 1992	Belarus introduces a national currency to replace roubles of the USSR.
September 1993	The Belarusian rouble becomes the sole legal tender in Belarus.
April 1996	Belarus and Russia sign an agreement on the establishment of a Political and Economic Community.
April 1997	The Community is transformed into a formal Union.
January 1999	The National Bank of Belarus (NBB) and the Central Bank of Russia (CBR) approve a schedule of actions in the area of monetary integration. It includes measures to unify monetary policy instruments, to coordinate steps in the exchange rate policy of national currencies, and to work out common principles for currency regulation, preparation for payment systems' unification, and creation of conditions for free circulation of securities.
November 1999	The Interbank Currency Council is established. It is an advisory body whose main objectives are to coordinate the work in the sphere of monetary systems' integration and to prepare for the introduction of a single currency.
December 1999	Belarus and Russia sign the Union State Treaty.
November 2000	Belarus and Russia sign an agreement that stipulates introduction of a common currency of the Union State from January 1, 2008.
June 2002	Belarus and Russia sign a Joint Action Plan for the introduction of a common monetary unit of the Union State.

Sources: various IMF Economic Reviews; and the authorities of Belarus (available from the Embassy of Belarus in Russia website <http://www.embassybel.ru/index.php?page=27>).

Recent developments

In June 2002, the authorities of Belarus and Russia signed a Joint Action Plan (JAP) for the introduction of a common monetary unit of the Union State, covering the period through 2005. The JAP established 40 tasks viewed by the authorities as appropriate and which should be completed in order to establish conditions for the introduction of a single currency. These tasks included a variety of measures aimed at the convergence of macroeconomic, fiscal, monetary, foreign exchange, financial, trade, and structural policies, as well as the harmonization of the relevant legislation. The JAP also specified the timing for the implementation of these tasks, and stipulated that the Russian rouble may take on the role of the common currency for the Union State starting January 1, 2005, provided that all tasks and measures under this plan are implemented in full during the years 2002-04.

Despite substantial preparatory work on the introduction of a common currency, some important procedural and institutional issues still remain subject to debate. These include the responsibility for the conduct of the common monetary policy, the availability of the LOLR facility in Belarus, the distribution of the central bank profits, and so on. Failure to agree on these issues is primarily caused by a difference of opinion between the Belarusian and Russian authorities on the planned design of the 'single emission centre', which will assume the responsibility for the conduct of common monetary policy (Box 9.1).

Theoretical considerations

Economic costs and benefits of a currency unification

There is a vast and growing body of literature on the implications of different exchange rate regimes for macroeconomic performance. Special attention is given to the analysis of costs and benefits of hard pegs and currency unions (Box 9.2 discusses different types of currency unions).[7] The analysis of common currencies generally starts from the original ideas of Robert Mundell on optimal currency areas (Mundell, 1961). The main advantages and disadvantages for any country willing to establish a currency union with another country (or a group of other countries) can be summarized as follows (Frankel, 1999):

1. The principal advantage of a currency unification is the reduction of transaction costs associated with the need to change currency to do business. Transaction costs from currency conversion are financial costs (commission fees and other administrative costs that economic agents have to pay to foreign currency dealers for foreign currency conversion) and in-house costs (costs associated with tying up resources to deal with foreign exchange management).[8] The more countries that are integrated, the greater will be the savings from setting up a currency union. Lower transaction costs, in turn, are likely to further increase trade, improve resource allocation, and contribute to higher growth.[9]

---

[7] An example is the emergence of the so-called 'bi-polar view' whose proponents believe that with increasing capital mobility intermediate exchange rate regimes between currency boards and free floating are unsustainable in the long term (Fischer, 2001). There is some empirical evidence of movements to either free floats or hard pegs (Ghosh, Gulde, and Wolf, 2003).

[8] Emerson, and others (1992) estimated that for the members of the European Monetary Union, total savings from abolishing conversion within Europe, including savings from 'reductions in inefficiencies inside firms', were at 0.4 per cent of GDP. For small open and less developed European economies, they estimated such savings at 1 per cent of GDP.

[9] Frankel and Rose (2000) estimated that a currency union more than triples trade among member countries without diverting trade away from other trading partners.

2. The principal disadvantage of a currency unification is the loss of the possibility of absorbing big shocks via a devaluation/revaluation or an adjustment in domestic monetary policy. If the shocks or transmission mechanisms in one country of the currency union differ from those in another country of the same union, these countries would be better off by using independent monetary or exchange rate policies. This would help stabilize output and avoid a painful adjustment through changes in wages, prices, and employment.

A currency union would, therefore, be desirable for countries with strong trade and financial integration and similar economic structures. Under such circumstances, shocks are likely to affect member countries similarly, making a single monetary policy desirable/effective. Where countries are dissimilar, a common monetary policy is unlikely to be optimal for all members. In this regard, Boone and Maurel (1999) showed that those prospective EMU members whose economic cycle is close to that of Germany (the largest European economy) would benefit from adopting the euro.

If countries are facing asymmetric shocks but are highly integrated, the loss of monetary and exchange rate policies as stabilization tools could theoretically be compensated by other mechanisms. These include flexibility in prices and wages, the mobility of labour and other factors of production, or fiscal transfers.[10]

It should be noted that most studies on optimal currency area properties are backward looking and do not reflect changes in policy preferences. But some authors argue that a currency union represents a structural break and optimal currency area criteria could be satisfied ex-post even if it is not fully satisfied ex-ante. They relate this in part to changes in monetary policy and in part to closer international trade with other members of the currency union[11] [12] (Frankel and Rose, 1996).

---

[10] Some economists argue that redistribution of income through the federal government is one of the key reasons why the currency union in the United States, which originally did not represent an optimal currency area, has survived without major problems (Sala-i-Martin and Sachs, 1991). Other reasons include labour and capital mobility.

[11] From a theoretical viewpoint, more international trade may result in either tighter or looser correlations of business cycles. For example, if countries become more specialized in the goods in which they have comparative advantage, as noted by Krugman (1993), more trade will cause the business cycles of countries to diverge. Alternatively, if demand shocks and intra-industry trade dominate, then more trade will cause the business cycles to become more similar.

[12] The short experiences of some countries of the EMU support this argument. For example, Italy, Spain, Portugal, Greece, Ireland – countries identified as 'in the periphery' (see Bayoumi and Eichengreen, 1992) – seem to have not suffered from the entrance into a currency union with Belgium, France, Germany, and the Netherlands – so-called 'EC core countries'.

Box 9.1 Belarusian and Russian views on the nature of currency union

The persistent failure in recent years of the Belarusian and Russian authorities to agree on some important procedural and institutional issues regarding the establishment of the currency union is primarily caused by a difference of opinion between the two countries on the planned design of the 'single emission centre', which will assume the responsibility for the conduct of common monetary policy.

The authorities of Russia favour a centralized approach, where the functions of the single emission centre would be performed exclusively by the Central Bank of Russia (CBR). Under this scenario, the National Bank of Belarus (NBB) would be able to operate with currencies and securities only with the permission of and in volumes determined by the CBR, though one or two representatives from the NBB may become members of the Board of Directors of the CBR. This model to a degree would mirror arrangements within the European Monetary Union (EMU) and the Eurosystem, where the decision-making of a single emission centre is performed by the European Central Bank (ECB) Governing Council and the implementation, that is the operation with foreign currencies, is carried out by the ECB and by national central banks on the basis of these decisions.

The authorities of Belarus have been opposing the idea of losing the right to control money supply. The Belarusian counterproposal is to set up the single emission centre with two central banks whose monetary policy would be coordinated by the Interbank Currency Council (ICC). As shown in table 9.1, the ICC is an advisory body whose main objective is to coordinate the convergence of monetary policies and to prepare for the introduction of a single currency. The NBB suggests that the ICC set monetary policy guidelines, which should then be approved by the Union State Council and become mandatory for both central banks. The ICC would set limits for central bank emissions of money (which would be proportional to the countries' GDP shares) and it would also coordinate the legal and regulatory activities of the two central banks. The CBR and NBB would each maintain a lender-of-last-resort (LOLR) facility for the banks on its territory. The NBB proposes that the ICC have six board members from each of the two central banks; in case of a split vote the chairman, who would be from the CBR, would have the decisive vote.

The Russian authorities have voiced concern about the effectiveness of the framework proposed by the NBB, and have also pointed out that this framework would not be consistent with the currently ensured CBR independence.

Box 9.2 A brief typology of currency unions

There are different types of currency unions with distinct features, and different implications for the role of the central bank. The distinctions relate to the degree to which member countries can participate in monetary policy making, the degree to which seignorage is shared, and the availability of the lender of last resort facility. The main types of currency unions are as follows:

1. *Dollarization:* A country adopts (either with the agreement of the issuing country or unilaterally) another country's currency as legal tender. In general there is no sharing of seignorage, no involvement of the adopting country in monetary policy decisions, and no lender of last resort support from the issuing country to the adopting country. In spite of these limitations countries have opted for (or contemplated) dollarization for stabilization purposes, to gain credibility, to lower borrowing costs, or to avoid the costs of operating a fully fledged central bank. Examples of dollarized countries or territories include Ecuador, El Salvador, Panama (all using the US dollar), Liechtenstein (using the Swiss franc), Andorra, Kosovo, Monaco, Montenegro, San Marino (using the euro), and Kiribati (using the Australian dollar).

2. *Creation of a new monetary area:* Two or more countries decide to replace their old currencies by a common new currency, issued by a joint institution and managed jointly by all countries involved in the union. Monetary policy is based on aggregate developments and may not be optimal for individual members, especially those with macroeconomic cycles differing from the average. There are generally some agreements on sharing of seignorage and lender of last resort facility. Examples include the European Monetary Union (EMU), the two CFA areas in Africa, and the Eastern Caribbean Currency Union (ECCU).*

3. *Joining an existing monetary area:* A country adopts another country's existing currency or joins an existing monetary union and obtains some representation in the monetary policy institutions, some seignorage, and, possibly, some or full lender of last resort protection. (Depending on the relative size of the entities involved, smaller members may, however, have little influence on the common policy.) An example would be the East German adoption of the Deutschmark in 1990. Another example is the currency union that existed between Belgium and Luxembourg from 1922 to 1999. This is also the case for the new member countries joining the EMU.

* The ECCU operates under currency board rules with the US dollar, and the two CFA areas operate under a fixed exchange rate regime with the euro. This limits the joint monetary management in these countries.

Preconditions on the operating environment

A successful monetary union must be supported by an adequate operating environment.[13] In ideal conditions, this environment should ensure that the common monetary policy is conducted by an independent and accountable central bank, which is not constrained by fiscal and quasi-fiscal activities or by the presence of weak financial institutions in member countries of the monetary union.[14]

Freedom from fiscal dominance The long-term sustainability of a monetary union requires the implementation of credible fiscal policies by all member countries of the union. Theoretically, a member country which is persistently unable to effectively manage public finances (that is to cover public expenditures by revenues) must either exit that monetary union and unilaterally monetize the budget deficit or remain in the union by persuading other members to inflate. Therefore, the fear of pressure to bail out governments with poor public finances requires the existence of ceilings on debt and deficits (the Maastricht Treaty conditions provided for such ceilings in the context of EMU).

Another key element of the institutional framework governing the relations between the monetary and the fiscal authorities is the independence of the central bank from the government. In particular, the opportunity of direct monetary financing of budget deficits should normally be eliminated in a monetary union. The relations between the common central bank and the national governments of member countries of the monetary union should be specified accordingly in the relevant legislation.[15] This should also include the distribution of central bank profits (seignorage) to governments (Box 9.3). Furthermore, freedom of the central bank from fiscal dominance implies that financial markets in countries of the monetary union have enough depth to absorb placements of public debt.

---

[13] The focus of this section is on a monetary union rather than a currency union. A currency union can also be 'dollarization' which in principle does not require any coordinated efforts by member countries to have an adequate operating environment.

[14] Another important precondition for a currency union is the support of a substantial fraction of the population.

[15] The lack of control by the central bank over its refinancing of commercial and developmental banks can also lead to excessive indirect central bank lending to governments. This was seen as one of the factors that led to a crisis in the West African Monetary Union and Central African Monetary Union in the late 1980s and a devaluation in 1994 (Medhora, 2000).

Box 9.3 Distribution of seignorage in a currency union

Seignorage revenue can be viewed as a continued flow of returns accrued to the central banks because of its unique function of issuing money. The revenue is called 'seignorage' because the central bank does not pay interest on the currency it issues while it collects interest on the assets obtained in exchange. Theoretically, seignorage revenue can be used by the central bank itself (to cover administrative expenses or adding to the reserves) or returned to the public. The transfer of seignorage revenue to the public can be achieved either via an explicit mechanism for transmitting central bank profits to the treasury, or using some less transparent quasi-fiscal activities.

In a currency union, the performance of the monetary policy function generates common seignorage revenue of the union. This seignorage normally accrues to the central bank of the union rather than to the central banks of the member countries. Therefore, member countries must decide how this revenue should be used (in case of 'dollarization', the seignorage accrues to the central bank of a 'dollarizing' country, and there is typically no sharing of seignorage with a 'dollarized' country). In this regard, the following three issues are of main concerned:

(i) Distribution of central bank dividends to member countries
In a currency union, the common central bank and the member countries must agree on the countries' shares in the flow of distributed dividends. It can be argued that the main principle governing the distribution of central bank dividends should be avoidance of a bias against any member countries. In practice, existing currency unions use different and sometimes complicated approaches for calculating the countries' shares (see table below).

(ii) The treatment of quasi-fiscal activities of the central bank
Quasi-fiscal activities of the central bank of a currency union can have a significant allocative impact. If quasi-fiscal activities can be quantified, they should be reflected in reduced transfers of dividends from the central bank of a currency union.

(iii) Accountability of the central bank
In addition to setting up clear rules for the transfer of seignorage revenue to the public, central bank of a currency union should be made accountable to the public for the use of seignorage revenue by the bank itself. Periodic disclosure of information on operating expenses and revenues pertaining to central bank operations would help to dispel public doubts about the openness of the central bank with regard to the use of seignorage revenue.

Currency Union	Formula for Distribution of Central Bank Profits
1. *Central African Monetary Union* (Six member states: Cameroon, Central African Republic, Chad, Congo, Equatorial Guinea, and Gabon)	15 per cent of the central bank profits are distributed in proportion to the respective amounts of currency in circulation in each member state; 15 per cent of profits are distributed in equal amounts to all member states; and 70 per cent of profits are distributed based on the percentage of each member state's relative contribution to the central bank's outturn.
2. *Eastern Caribbean Currency Union* (Eight member states: Anguilla, Antigua and Barbuda, Dominica, Grenada, Montserrat, St. Kitts and Nevis, St. Lucia, and St. Vincent and the Grenadines)	Returns on investment of central bank's external assets are distributed between the member states in proportion to the respective amount of currency in circulation in each member state. Other revenues of the central bank are distributed on the basis of the imputed equity interest of each member state in the central bank.
3. *European Monetary Union* (Twelve member states: Austria, Belgium, Finland, France, Germany, Greece, Ireland, Italy, Luxembourg, the Netherlands, Portugal, and Spain)	Monetary income is allocated to the national central banks in proportion to their paid-up shares in the capital of the European Central Bank. Under the transitional regime applicable until 2007, the amount of monetary income to be pooled is adjusted on the basis of compensating factors.
4. *West African Monetary Union* (Eight member states: Benin, Burkina Faso, Côte d'Ivoire, Guinea-Bissau, Mali, Niger, Senegal, and Togo)	After allocation to any optional reserve, be it general or special, the balance of central bank profits is allocated following a decision by the Council of Ministers of the Union.
5. *Officially 'Dollarized' Countries* (E.g., Andorra, Ecuador, El Salvador, Kiribati, Panama)	Central bank profits are not allocated to 'dollarized' countries.

Sources: the relevant Central Bank statutes; and ECB/2001/16.

Financial sector soundness   A strong and sound financial sector is another precondition for the long-term resilience of the monetary union. Financial instability can adversely affect the ability of the common central bank to exert monetary control. Furthermore, high cost of bailouts of financial institutions may produce substantial fiscal deficits in some member countries, which can weaken or even undermine the monetary union.

Sound functioning of the financial sectors, including those in monetary unions, requires an adequate regulation and supervision of financial institutions, and effective systemic liquidity support arrangements. These liquidity arrangements should in normal times prevent uncontrolled central bank liquidity support for financial institutions while establishing adequate liquidity crisis management procedures. In particular, the central bank should have the option to provide systemically important financial institutions under stress with a lender of last resort (LOLR) support. Despite the possibility of increasing moral hazard, the existence of such a facility has long been recognized as an important element in managing a liquidity crisis.[16]

Setting up an asymmetric currency union

Several specific issues should be taken into consideration in examining the asymmetric currency unions. In such unions, the assessment of costs and benefits of having a common currency should consider besides direct economic costs and benefits the following potentially important aspects.[17]

Disadvantages for a small member country   In an asymmetric currency union, the main disadvantage for a small member country arises from the fact that the conduct of monetary policy is essentially determined by the largest member country. When a small country decides to 'dollarize' itself, it normally obtains no involvement in the monetary policy decision making. When the common monetary policy is conducted with inputs from all member countries, the influence of small countries is typically minor.[18] Therefore, in the presence of asymmetric shocks small

---

[16]   Eichengreen (2000) showed that hard pegs (including currency boards and officially dollarized economies) are more often associated with banking crises than soft pegs. He suggested that the reduction of moral hazard associated with the removal of some of the LOLR function may not be enough to offset the increase in bank difficulties originating in the lack of an LOLR facility.

[17]   Dollarization or joining an existing monetary area on 'unequal rights' are the main examples of asymmetric currency unions. In practice, however, almost all currency unions can be viewed as more or less asymmetric: even a common central bank managed jointly by all member countries may be more likely to conduct monetary policy that would primarily reflect the needs of the largest member country(ies).

[18]   This can be illustrated by the arrangements within the European Monetary Union. In March 2003, the European Council decided to adapt the voting modalities in the ECB Governing Council to enlargement of EMU. As a result, national central bank governors

economies are most likely to bear brunt of costs that could arise from unfavourable exchange rate or interest rate movements, if there are no adequate mechanisms to deal with these shocks.

The costs for a small member country can increase when it agrees to lose (partly or completely) LOLR support and/or seignorage revenue. Regarding the LOLR facility, when a small country decides to 'dollarize' or join an existing monetary area on unequal rights, an alternative arrangement for the LOLR facility needs to be found in order to safeguard the financial system. The central bank of a small country can, for example, accumulate foreign exchange reserves in sufficient amounts and keep a limited LOLR function. Another alternative is to negotiate a credit arrangement between a consortium of foreign banks and the central bank, under the terms of which the central bank can get sizeable instant credit in the event of liquidity crisis. Besides, an efficient functioning of the interbank money market as well as the penetration of foreign banks (especially those from the large country of a currency union) can help prevent liquidity crisis and the need for a LOLR facility (see Broda and Levy Yeyati, 2003 for more details).[19]

Regarding the possible loss of seignorage revenue, several considerations need to be taken into account. A small country joining a currency union may obtain some representation in the common central bank and a share in the distribution of central bank profits (Box 9.3). If the small country joining a currency union does not obtain any representation in the common central bank, a special seignorage sharing arrangement can be negotiated. Such an arrangement can consist of either a constant flow of seignorage payments to the dollarized countries, calculated using a special formula, or a lump sum payment equal to the net present value of these flows (for more details, see Gruben, Wynne, and Zarazaga, 2003). A small country may decide to give up the seignorage if it believes that the benefits of the currency union are substantial enough to compensate for the loss of seignorage (see below).

Benefits for a small member country The above discussed disadvantages for small countries in joining an asymmetric currency union can be outweighed by benefits from such a union. Such benefits include a reduction in borrowing costs through the lower exchange rate risk premium and an avoidance of costs of running a fully-fledged central bank. Furthermore, small countries are typically more open to external trade than large countries, and therefore the benefits from savings on transaction costs are likely to be more important for small countries than for large countries.

---

who represent the biggest EU economies will be able to exert their voting rights in about 80 per cent of all ECB Governing Council meetings, while national central bank governors who represent the smallest EU economies, will only be able to vote in about 30 per cent of ECB Governing Council meetings.

[19] In a situation when the LOLR facility is capped for all member countries according to their relative shares in GDP, some member countries can be disproportionately affected if the size of their banking systems is out of line with the GDP share.

The benefits associated with a reduction of the potentially high exchange rate risk premium can be substantial for small countries. Many small countries have a history of currency crises resulting from monetary mismanagement. Under these conditions, these countries are likely to substantially benefit from a currency union with a large country whose monetary policy has a good reputation and whose currency is substantially more stable.[20] Such a union will reduce domestic currency risk for a smaller country, which will translate into the reduction of risk premium on interest rate thus stimulating investments and growth. Small countries also typically have less sophisticated and thin financial markets than large countries, which may contribute to high interest rate levels and/or high interest and exchange rate volatility. The more volatile and unpredictable is a country's exchange rate, the greater will be the benefits from the elimination of domestic currency risk.[21] This may also lead to a reduced need for foreign exchange reserves since small countries usually need more reserves than large countries to safeguard against excessive exchange rate volatilities.

Small countries may also opt for asymmetric currency unions to avoid the costs of running a fully-fledged central bank. These costs primarily include administrative expenses, costs of managing foreign exchange reserves, and costs of printing and maintaining national currency.

Economic costs and benefits of currency unification between Belarus and Russia

This section assesses the suitability of economic conditions in Belarus and Russia to the formation of a successful currency union. In particular, the gains from having a common currency – in terms of reduced transaction costs in bilateral trade and an improved macroeconomic environment in Belarus – are reviewed against the costs arising from possible asymmetries of shocks affecting the two economies (Table 9.2 compares several macroeconomic and structural indicators of Belarus and Russia). The section also reviews to what extent mitigating factors would help reduce some of the possible costs.

Trade patterns

Belarus was strongly integrated in the former USSR economy. More than a decade after the break up of the latter, the economy of Belarus remains closely connected

---

[20] Alesina and Barro (2000) argue that a small country with a history of high inflation that is close to a large and monetarily stable country has the strongest incentive to give its own currency, while Berg and Borensztein (2002) argue that official dollarization may offer more benefits than costs in highly dollarized economies.

[21] It should be noted that while a currency union may reduce the exchange rate risk premium on interest rates, the country-specific risk premium will remain.

to that of Russia.[22] This is reflected in exports to Russia of around one third of GDP (more than half of total exports), and in purchases from Russia of 40 per cent of GDP (around two-thirds of total imports; see Figures 9.1 and 9.2). Russia is by far the dominant trading partner of Belarus, since the second largest trading partner of Belarus (Germany) accounts for only around 10 per cent of her imports and 5 per cent of her exports. At the same time, Russia does less than 10 per cent of her total external trade with Belarus.[23]

Against this assessment of trade patterns and taking into account the fact that more than half of trade between Russia and Belarus is carried out in Russian roubles, currency unification would give rise to some savings from reduction in transaction costs for Belarus, while being relatively insignificant for Russia.[24] Even under assumption that the currency union will not substantially stimulate bilateral trade (because the existing volume of trade is already very high), currency unification will certainly bring savings, especially for Belarusian traders, from the elimination of transaction costs from currency conversion. The gains would be higher, of course, if trade between the two countries were to increase further.

Macroeconomic stability

Since the early 1990s, the macroeconomic performance of Belarus has been one of the weakest among its neighbors. This has primarily resulted from the inability of the authorities to implement a prudent fiscal policy and the reliance on inflationary (central bank) financing of budget deficits (Table 9.2).

---

[22] To some extent, this may be related to the slowness in reforming state owned enterprises in Belarus, which as a result continue to have difficulties in penetrating highly competitive Western markets.

[23] Nevertheless, Belarus is still one of the major trading partners of Russia (Figure 9.2).

[24] According to the NBB estimates, the Russian rouble and the Belarusian rouble are used in around 52 per cent and 8 per cent, accordingly, of trade transactions between Belarus and Russia. The remaining 40 per cent of bilateral trade is done in other currencies, mainly the US dollar.

Table 9.2   **Belarus and Russia: Basic data, 2000-2003 (in per cent; otherwise indicated)**

	2000	2001	2002	2003
GDP growth rates				
Belarus	5.8	4.7	5.0	6.8
Russia	10.0	5.1	4.7	7.3
CPI (e.o.p.)				
Belarus	107.5	46.1	34.8	25.4
Russia	20.1	18.6	15.1	12.0
Budget deficit (in per cent of GDP)				
Belarus	-0.2	-1.9	-1.8	-1.4
Russia	2.7	3.0	0.6	1.0
Net central bank lending to the government (in per cent of GDP)				
Belarus	1.3	1.2	-1.2	1.0
Russia	-1.2	-1.9	-0.6	-1.4
Current account balance as per cent of GDP				
Belarus	-2.6	-3.5	-2.6	-2.9
Russia	17.8	10.7	8.8	8.9
Gross official reserves in months of imports				
Belarus	0.5	0.5	0.6	0.5
Russia	5.5	5.7	6.9	9.1
Trade turnover (as per cent of GDP)				
Belarus	120.2	141.3	130.8	136.2
Russia	57.6	50.8	48.7	48.7
Population (in millions)				
Belarus	10.0	10.0	9.9	n.a.
Russia	145.4	144.8	144.2	n.a.
GDP per capita (in US$)				
Belarus	1,274	1,239	1,437	n.a.
Russia	1,785	2,137	2,400	n.a.
Enterprise reform (EBRD indicator 1/)				
Belarus	1	1	1	1
Russia	2	2.3	2.3	2.3
Banking system reform (EBRD indicator 1/)				
Belarus	1	1	1.7	1.7
Russia	1.7	1.7	2	2

Nonbank financial institutions reform (EBRD indicator 1/)				
Belarus	2	2	2	2
Russia	1.7	1.7	2.3	2.7
Belarusian GDP as per cent of Russian GDP	4.9	4.1	4.2	4.0
Belarusian reserve money as per cent of Russian reserve money	1.9	2.3	2.0	1.6
Belarusian (rouble) M2 as per cent of Russian (rouble) M2	1.3	1.5	1.6	1.4

Sources: Belarus and Russia authorities, EBRD, and authors' estimates.

1/ The EBRD indicators of small-scale and large-scale privatization, enterprise reform, banking system reform, and nonbank financial institutions reform have a range between 1 and 4+, where higher figure corresponds to a more advanced stage reached in privatization/reforms.

A. Exports

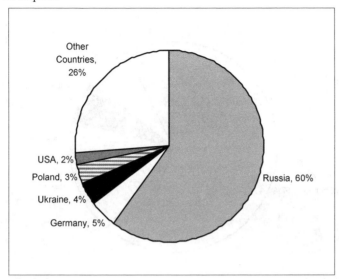

B. Imports

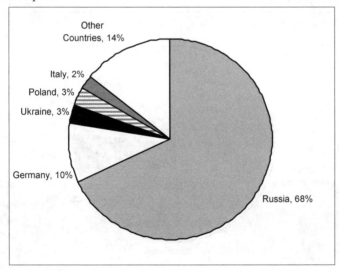

Figure 9.1 Belarus: External trade partners (in per cent of total; as of 2002)

Source: IMF, *Direction of Trade Statistics*, 2003.

A. Exports

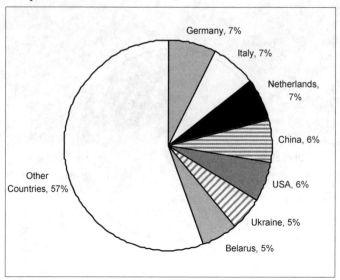

B. Imports

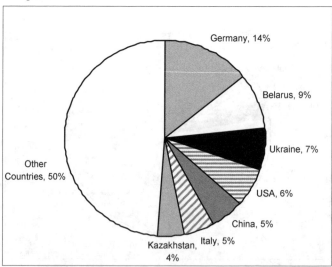

Figure 9.2   Russia: External trade partners (in per cent of total; as of 2002)

Source: IMF, *Direction of Trade Statistics*, 2003.

Despite the declining trend, the inflation rate in Belarus has been the highest among the CIS countries in the last five years. High inflation and depreciation of the currency, in turn, have contributed to dollarization of the economy and inability to attract sizeable foreign investments.

Therefore, a major benefit of a currency union with Russia for Belarus could be a relatively more stable macroeconomic environment. In fact, the currency union would allow Belarus to 'import' Russia's current macroeconomic stability. The union would likely contribute to a reduction in the inflation rate and the exchange rate risk in Belarus. Lower inflation would reduce distortions in the economy and uncertainty for investors, thus bringing down real interest rates. As to the exchange rate risk, a currency union would completely eliminate the RBL/RUB exchange rate risk, though the exchange rate risk with other currencies would remain.[25] The resulting improvement in macroeconomic performance would foster new investments and contribute to a closer integration of Belarus with Russia and the rest of the world.

The sustainability of macroeconomic stability in Belarus would, however, require the successful implementation of fiscal adjustment and structural reforms (section five). In particular, the fiscal policy should be adjusted in order not to create a background of uncertainty, which can result in a significant interest rate premium and weak demand for government securities. Similarly, the health of the banking system needs to be credible in the eyes of public.

Asymmetry of shocks

Regional shocks, especially the shocks to the terms of trade, are likely to have a highly asymmetric impact on Belarus and Russia, mainly due to the different production structures and degrees of openness of the two countries (Table 9.2, Figures 9.3 and 9.4).[26] Belarus has large foreign trade and agricultural sectors, while Russia has large energy and non-tradable goods sectors. Belarus exports mainly processed goods, while raw materials dominate Russia's exports. Accordingly, business cycles in the two countries are prone to different patterns, leading to rather weak estimates of the correlation between Russian and Belarusian GDP growth.[27]

---

[25] At the time of writing, Belarus maintains a crawling band foreign exchange regime against both the US dollar and Russian rouble. Such targeting of both the US dollar and the Russian rouble since end-2002 has been *de facto* consistent because the RUB/USD exchange rate has been relatively stable.

[26] It is interesting to note that the shocks are also likely to have a highly asymmetric impact on different regions of Russia itself.

[27] Using quarterly data for the period 1997–2002, and adjusting for seasonality, the correlation coefficient between real GDP growth rates in Belarus and Russia is estimated at only 0.14.

A. GDP

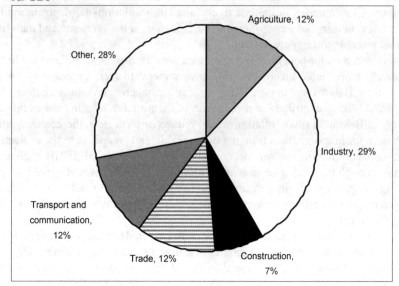

B. Employment

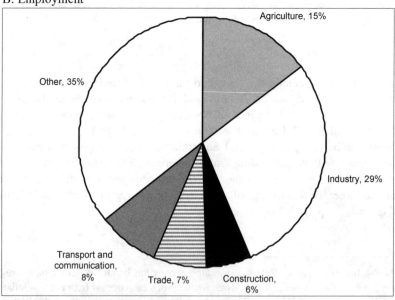

Figure 9.3   Belarus: GDP and employment by sectors (in per cent of total; as of 2002)

Source: IMF Statistical Appendices to the Country Reports.

A. GDP

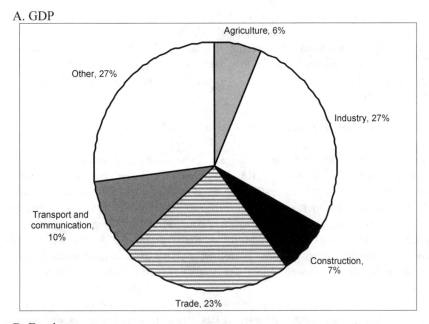

B. Employment

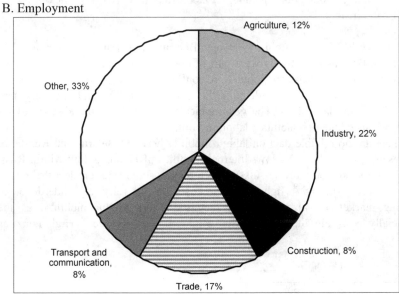

Figure 9.4   **Russia: GDP and employment by sectors (in per cent of total; as of 2002)**

Source: IMF Statistical Appendices to the Country Reports.

On this basis, a common currency with Russia is likely to make the economy of Belarus more vulnerable to external shocks. For example, a continued strengthening of the common currency due to a favourable external environment for Russia (for example in the case of persistently high world prices for oil and other major Russian exports) could potentially undermine competitiveness and growth in Belarus.[28]

Are there mechanisms to deal with the asymmetries?

One important factor that could mitigate some of the differences between the structures of the Belarusian and Russian economies is the character of bilateral trade between them. Belarusian-Russian trade rests to a large extent on processing of raw materials and energy into chemicals, refined oil products, and other finished manufactures – largely for export to third countries. For example, significant oil processing factories in Belarus – built essentially during the Soviet era – remain linked to Russian oil production. Therefore, a shock affecting the tradable goods sector of Russia may well affect the tradable goods sector of Belarus in a symmetric way.

Other more orthodox mechanisms to deal with the asymmetric responses to macroeconomic shocks may include: (i) labour mobility; (ii) wage flexibility; and (iii) fiscal transfers.

Labour mobility Labour mobility between Belarus and Russia could potentially be very high. Belarus and Russia were part of one country for a very long time, and the Belarusian and Russian population continue to have strong ties. Common marriages are widespread, reflecting the common culture and the very great similarity of the languages. The geographical proximity and the absence of visa requirements could also facilitate labour mobility.

There are no reliable data on labour mobility between Belarus and Russia, but at present it is likely to be low. Internal mobility of labour is low within Russia itself (Andrienko and Guriev, 2003), which may to some extent reflect the existing administrative barriers.[29] High relocation costs and the relatively underdeveloped housing market are also important factors limiting labour mobility, as they financially constrain the people who would like to migrate.[30] High non-wage

---

[28]   High productivity growth in Russia, resulting for example from vigorous enterprise restructuring or new investments, may cause a similar result.

[29]   Ekman (2000), for example, claims that the Soviet system of resident permits, *propiska*, has survived in Russia, even though this violates Russia's constitution.

[30]   Andrienko and Guriev (2003) claim that up to one third of Russian regions are locked in a poverty trap, where people do not have adequate resources to move to the prospering regions.

benefit spending and residual state provision of 'social services' in Belarus may also have discouraged people from moving out of Belarus (Sewell, 1997).[31]

Wage flexibility While there has been significant progress in liberalizing wages in Russia, wages in Belarus remain tightly controlled by the state.[32] By preventing real wages from adjusting to equate desired labour supply with enterprises' demand for labour, limited wage flexibility in Belarus has contributed to a weak financial situation of enterprises and an increase in fiscal imbalances.

Fiscal transfers Fiscal transfers could be an effective mechanism to deal with the asymmetries noted above. In this regard, it can be argued that the effects of external shocks on Belarus should not differ substantially from those on the neighbouring Briansk, Pskov, or Smolensk provinces of Russia, which have production structures that are broadly similar to Belarus (in particular, large agricultural sectors and almost no mineral resources). These provinces, however, may receive fiscal transfers from the federal government of Russia, which would help them absorb shocks.

However, there has been no agreement on creation of a similar fiscal federalism arrangement between Belarus and Russia to support the currency unification. Although Belarus has requested compensation from Russia in connection with losses due to continued use of the origin principle for assessing indirect tax liability in bilateral trade, there are no plans to create an explicit interstate fiscal transfer mechanism (like the 'Cohesion Fund' in the European Union, which is designed to subsidize poorer regions).[33]

---

[31] Following the Soviet tradition, Belarusian enterprises provide financing for housing for employees, kindergartens and summer camps for employee's children, as well as maintaining local infrastructure such as heating, electricity, water, and so on. In contrast, state-owned enterprises in Russia have been largely freed from such obligations.

[32] The Belarusian government carries out this control in the public sector through the *tarifnaya setka* (tariff system), based on tariff scales, the tariff rate of the first grade, and tariff qualification guide. Under this system, the government sets up the tariff rate of the first grade, which automatically affects other grades. This system tends to compress wage differences, even though bonuses and other payments that employees receive weaken this tendency (for details, see IMF, 2004b). The Russian government uses a similar system, but the share of the public sector in Russia is almost half as low as in Belarus. Another illustration of the wage control in Belarus is the instruction from the President of Belarus to increase monthly wages in Belarus to at least an equivalent of US$250 by end-2005 from below US$100 in 2001.

[33] Since mid-2000, Russia has moved to the origin principle of levying VAT. The estimates of 'losses' to the budget of Belarus caused by compensation of the VAT that Belarusian companies pay to the Russian budget ranges between US$150 million and US$200 million per year. The Russian authorities reportedly promised to reimburse Belarus for such losses starting from the time of establishing a currency union and for two years prior to the establishment of the currency union.

Until 2004, Belarus received large implicit import subsidies from Russia in the form of low prices for natural gas.[34] These subsidies allowed Belarusian households and enterprises to pay lower electricity and heating prices than would otherwise be possible. As such, they represented a sort of mechanism that helped to cushion asymmetric shock hitting gas producing and gas consuming regions. Since early 2004, however, Belarus had to import gas at much higher prices from other Russian suppliers as Gazprom stopped supplying Belarus with gas after the Belarusian authorities and Gazprom failed to reach an agreement on privatization of Beltransgaz (see IMF, 2004a). In June, 2004, Belarus and Russia agreed that Russia would sell gas to Belarus at the price that now applies to Ukraine while Belarus would charge higher tariffs for gas transit through its territory by Gazprom.

Is the operational environment supportive of a currency unification of Belarus and Russia?

Fiscal and Quasi-Fiscal Management

In recent years, the fiscal position of Belarus has been significantly worse than that of Russia. During 2000-2003, Belarus posted a budget deficit averaging 1.3 per cent of GDP, compared with an average budget surplus of 1.8 per cent of GDP in Russia (Table 9.2). Although the current level of the budget deficit in Belarus is not high, and the external debt of Belarus remains relatively small (partly because the foreign creditors have shied away from lending to Belarus), tighter fiscal policy is still needed in Belarus, for the following reasons:

1. First, the reported budget deficit data do not fully reflect the stance of fiscal policy in Belarus. This is because of the widespread use of quasi-fiscal activities, including energy cross-subsidies and directed credits from the state-owned commercial banks to specific classes of borrowers, often at below market rates.
2. Second, at least until 2004, a large share of the budget deficit in Belarus had been financed by direct lending from the NBB (Table 9.2). In contrast, the CBR has been prohibited from direct lending to the government in Russia since 1995.[35] Under the monetary union agreement, however, the Belarusian

---

[34] Under an agreement signed at the time the JAP was agreed, Belarus was to receive a quota according to which the Russian natural gas monopoly Gazprom would deliver gas at the same low price as that in border regions in Russia (this price is typically only about a third of the world market price), conditioned on the sale of a significant stake in the gas transport and distribution firm Beltransgaz.

[35] An easy access of the Belarusian government to the central bank resources had hindered the development of an active treasury bill and bond markets. An administratively

government's access to the central bank resources would either be prohibited or significantly limited.

3. Third, fiscal adjustment is needed owing to limited access by Belarus to international capital markets. During 2000-2003, for example, net foreign financing of the consolidated budget deficit amounted to -0.1 per cent of GDP, which means that Belarus was repaying foreign creditors despite financing needs. The currency union may, however, increase the Belarusian government's access to the financing from Russia's capital markets.

4. Finally, without necessary structural reforms (see below), Belarusian output growth is likely to stagnate or decline in the long term. This may increase the burden on fiscal management in the future.

The fiscal adjustment mostly needs to come from streamlining expenditures as Belarusian enterprises have a higher tax burden compared with their counterparts in Russia (the ratio of tax revenues to GDP in Belarus is one of the highest among transition countries). The state dominance of the economy largely contributed to this outcome in the past. But the experiences of the other CIS countries show that structural reforms may increase tax avoidance and reduce tax revenues.

Financial sector policies

In general, the financial sectors in both countries remain relatively underdeveloped and dominated by the state-owned commercial banks. However, privatization and corporate sector reforms in Russia have allowed it to develop a relatively more advanced banking system as well as a vigorous stock market (Table 9.2). All available indicators show that the level of financial intermediation in Belarus is considerably shallower than that in Russia (Table 9.3). Compared to Belarus, Russia has higher ratios of monetization and credit to economy (in terms of GDP), and a higher money multiplier. The largest Russian banks are also substantially bigger than the largest Belarusian banks in terms of capital or assets.[36] In 2003, the capitalization of the Russian stock market amounted to an equivalent of 37 per cent of GDP, compared with insignificant amounts in Belarus.[37]

---

imposed interest rate ceiling on government securities (equal to the refinance rate) and weak portfolio management in financial institutions have also contributed to this outcome.

[36] Using the data as of end-2003, the largest two Belarusian banks can be ranked among respectively the second and fourth dozen of the largest Russian banks in terms of assets.

[37] The Belarusian Currency and Stock Exchange reports only about US$0.5 million turnover in stock trading in 2001.

Table 9.3 Belarus and Russia: Selected financial intermediation indicators, 2000-2003

	2000	2001	2002	2003
Domestic currency broad money (in per cent of GDP)				
Belarus	7.0	7.3	7.6	9.5
Russia	15.7	17.9	19.6	24.2
Total broad money (in per cent of GDP)				
Belarus	17.4	15.2	15.0	17.1
Russia	21.4	23.7	26.2	29.8
Credit to the economy (in per cent of GDP)				
Belarus	16.5	14.9	15.4	17.8
Russia	13.1	16.7	18.7	22.4
Spread between 3-month deposit and lending rates (in per cent)				
Belarus	0.5	16.5	10.5	11.5
Russia	6.6	9.2	6.5	7.5
Dollarization ratio (FX deposits in per cent of total broad money)				
Belarus	59.8	52.1	49.2	44.4
Russia	26.9	24.5	25.4	18.9
Number of commercial banks				
Belarus	31	29	28	n.a.
Russia	1,311	1,319	1,329	n.a.
Stock market capitalization (in per cent of GDP)				
Belarus	4.1	2.9	n.a.	n.a.
Russia	15.3	25.7	36.5	n.a.

Sources: Belarus and Russia authorities, EBRD; and authors' estimates.

Reported financial soundness indicators are generally more favourable in Russia than in Belarus (Table 9.4).[38] While the Belarusian banks report relatively high levels of capital and declining levels of non-performing loans, official data indicate that almost half of the enterprise sector is loss-making, which raises

---

[38] Russian banks also have better ratings of international rating agencies than their Belarusian counterparts. For example, in 2003, Fitch rated many Russian banks 'B' while at the same time it rated only one bank in Belarus with the rating 'C.'

questions about the adequacy of accounting loan classification standards. In addition, there is a substantial exposure of Belarusian banks to the direct and indirect foreign exchange risks, given the high proportion of foreign exchange assets and liabilities – predominantly US$-denominated – on bank balance sheets. These foreign exchange risks are compounded by the very low level of international reserves at the NBB (Table 9.2).

Poor performance of the Belarusian banks is largely a result of state interventions in the operational management of banks. The Belarusian government owns directly or indirectly the four largest banks in the country which have a market share of around 70 per cent in terms of assets. The state uses these banks to make loans to 'priority' sectors or enterprises, sometimes at preferential terms. In turn, these banks are treated favourably in access to central bank and government resources. The state dominance of the banking system and the absence of a market environment have hindered incentives for banks to improve their credit assessment and risk management capacities, and these state-controlled Belarusian banks are periodically recapitalized by the Belarusian government. This situation will need to be addressed before the establishment of a currency union, because the possibility of recapitalizing Belarusian banks or even of providing LOLR support will be substantially reduced or completely eliminated.

Business environment

In contrast to Russia, the business environment in Belarus is characterized by government control of around 80 per cent of the economy. The Belarusian government assigns production targets for companies that it controls, does not allow them to lay off redundant labour, sets administrative wage targets, and forces enterprises to carry out quasi-fiscal activities, including cross-subsidizing other enterprises. Although these enterprises get support from the government by receiving directed credits and tariff and non-tariff protection, about half of them are loss making, and without changes in the institutional and regulatory environment, the proportion of these loss making companies may grow further.

The nascent Belarusian private sector, on the other hand, is suffering from 'red tape', including cumbersome licensing requirements, interventions of tax officials, and continuing changes in regulations. The state continues to maintain the right to introduce a 'golden share' in a private company, even if doing so was not foreseen at the time the companies were privatized (the President of Belarus may issue a decree giving the government effective control in any enterprise in which the state retains even one share). As a result, Belarus has not been able to attract sizeable FDI.[39]

---

[39] A large portion of current FDI to Belarus comes from a single project, Gazprom's Yamal-Europe pipeline.

Table 9.4 Belarus and Russia: Selected financial soundness indicators, 2000-2003

	2000	2001	2002	2003
Capital adequacy ratio				
Belarus	24.4	20.7	24.2	27.3
Russia	19.0	20.3	19.1	19.1
Nonperforming loans (in per cent of total loans)				
Belarus	15.2	14.4	8.3	3.7
Russia	7.7	6.2	5.6	5.0
Loan loss provisions (in per cent of nonperforming loans)				
Belarus	77.6	57.5	28.8	51.7
Russia	102.6	108.1	112.5	118.0
Return on assets				
Belarus	1.0	0.8	1.0	1.2
Russia	0.9	2.4	2.6	2.6
Return on equity				
Belarus	4.8	4.9	4.4	6.1
Russia	8.0	19.4	18.0	17.8

Sources: Belarus and Russia authorities, and authors' estimates.

The government's unwillingness to let state enterprises gain operational independence has undermined the privatization process. The high quasi-fiscal burden attached to the privatization terms, for example, led to the failure of the Belarusian government's efforts to divest parts of its shares in large petrochemical companies in 2002.

The currency union is expected to strengthen competition and limit quasi-fiscal support to public enterprises. Therefore, the Belarusian authorities need to take measures to increase viability of enterprises by levelling the playing field with Russia, including by harmonizing its tax and commercial laws, business codes and regulation with those of Russia. Privatization of state-owned enterprises by allowing enterprises to have operational independence and to abandon loss making activities would largely facilitate achieving these goals as well as attract foreign investments.

Conclusion

The long-run net economic effects of a proposed currency union between Belarus and Russia is not clear. On the one hand, strong trade integration between the two economies and the relatively weak macroeconomic performance of Belarus suggest that the currency union would bring substantial benefits for Belarus from reduced transaction costs and an improved macroeconomic environment. On the other hand, the macroeconomic symmetry condition is not satisfied: Belarus and Russia have different economic structures and therefore are subject to asymmetric shocks. Indeed, the correlation between real GDP growth in the two countries has been relatively small. The special character of trade between the two countries as well as the potential for growth in factor mobility may, however, at least partly offset the costs of asymmetric shocks.

A further critical challenge for a successful currency union of Belarus and Russia lies with the establishment of an adequate operating environment. Belarus needs to accelerate its institutional and structural reforms to catch up with Russia. These reforms should include a comprehensive fiscal adjustment aimed at the reduction of the budget deficit and the elimination of quasi-fiscal operations and heavy state control over the economy. The setting up of a currency union between Belarus and Russia may act as a catalyst to advance structural reforms in Belarus, but unless undertaken swiftly and in advance of the monetary unification, the currency union would be akin to 'shock therapy' with immediate full curtailment of fiscal subsidies and quasi-fiscal support for enterprises and banks in Belarus.

Finally, the currency union can only work if there is a centralized monetary policy and a strong central bank which can conduct this policy. The history of the monetary disintegration of Belarus and Russia in 1993 can be illustrative in this regard. Incentives for excessive monetary expansion by the central banks of Belarus, Russia, and all other countries that formed the Soviet Union, and lack of a centralized monetary policy due to the breakdown of the central planning led to uncontrolled inflation in 1991-1993, contributing to the dissolution of the 'rouble zone'. Therefore, the currently debated currency union between Belarus and Russia can work only if either (i) Belarus 'rouble-izes' its economy by accepting the use of the Russian rouble on the terms and conditions of the CBR, or (ii) both countries agree on a greater extent of economic and political integration – along with monetary unification – with the attendant willingness of Russia to engage in large scale fiscal transfers to facilitate the restructuring of the Belarusian economy. Anything in the middle is bound to fail.

References

Alesina, A. and Barro, R.J. (2000), 'Currency Unions', *NBER Working Paper*, 7927, Cambridge, Massachusetts: National Bureau of Economic Research.

Andrienko, Y. and Guriev, S. (2003), *Determinants of Interregional Mobility in Russia. Evidence from Panel Data*, Center for Economic and Financial Research, <http://www.cefir.org/Papers/cefwp25.pdf>.

Bayoumi, T. and Eichengreen, B. (1992), 'Is There a Conflict Between EC Enlargement and European Monetary Unification?', *NBER Working Paper*, 3950, Cambridge, Massachusetts: National Bureau of Economic Research.

Berg, A. and Borensztein, E. (2000), 'The Pros and Cons of Full Dollarization', *IMF Working Paper* 00/50, Washington, DC: International Monetary Fund.

Boone, L. and Maurel, M. (1999), 'An Optimal Currency Area Perspective of the EU Enlargement to the CEECs', *CEPR Discussion Paper*, 2119, London: Centre for Economic Policy Research.

Broda, C. and Yeyati, E.L. (2003), 'Dollarization and the Lender of Last Resort', in E.L. Yeyati and F. Sturzenegger (eds), *Dollarization*, Cambridge, Massachusetts: MIT Press.

Colton, T.J. (2002), 'Belarusian Public Opinion and the Union with Russia' in M.M. Balmaceda, J.I. Clem and L.L. Tarlow (eds), *Independent Belarus: Domestic Determinants, Regional Dynamics, and Implications for the West*, Cambridge, Massachusetts: Harvard University Press.

Eichengreen, B. (2000), 'When to Dollarize', Paper presented at the conference *Dollarization: A Common Currency for the Americas?*, organized by the Federal Reserve Bank of Dallas, <http://www.dallasfed.org/news/latin/00dollar_eichengr.pdf>.

Ekman, P. (2000), 'Two Kopek's Worth – Passports Are the Root of All Evil', *The Moscow Times*, 3 November, 2000.

Emerson, M., et al. (1992), *One Market One Money*, Oxford: Oxford University Press.

Fischer, S. (2001), 'Exchange Rate Regimes: Is the Bipolar View Correct?', Paper presented at the Meetings of the American Economic Association, New Orleans, <http://www.imf.org/external/np/speeches/2001/010601a.htm>.

Frankel, J.A. (1999), 'No Single Currency Regime is Right for All Countries or at All Times', *NBER Working Paper*, 7338, Cambridge, Massachusetts: National Bureau of Economic Research.

Frankel, J.A. and Rose, A.K. (1996), 'The Endogeneity of the Optimum Currency Area Criteria', *NBER Working Paper*, 5700, Cambridge, Massachusetts: National Bureau of Economic Research.

Frankel, J.A. and Rose, A.K. (2000), 'Estimating the Effect of Currency Unions on Trade and Output', *NBER Working Paper*, 7857, Cambridge, Massachusetts: National Bureau of Economic Research.

Ghosh, A.R., Gulde A.-M. and Wolf, H.C. (2003), *Exchange Rate Regimes: Choices and Consequences*, Cambridge, Massachusetts: MIT Press.

Gruben, W.C., Wynne, M.A. and Zarazaga, C.E.J.M. (2003), 'Implementation Guidelines for Dollarization and Monetary Unions', in E.L. Yeyati and F. Sturzenegger (eds), *Dollarization* (Cambridge, Massachusetts: MIT Press).

International Monetary Fund (2004a), 'Republic of Belarus – Staff Report for the 2004 Article IV Consultation', *IMF Country Report*, 04/141, Washington, DC: International Monetary Fund.

International Monetary Fund (2004b), 'Republic of Belarus – Selected Issues', *IMF Country Report*, 04/139, Washington, DC: International Monetary Fund.

Krugman, P. (1993), 'Lessons of Massachusetts for EMU', in F. Giavazzi and F. Torres (eds), *The Transition to Economic and Monetary Union in Europe*, New York: Cambridge University Press, pp. 241-61.

Medhora, R. (2000), 'Dollarization in the Americas: Lessons from the Franc Zone?', Paper prepared for the NSI conference on *Dollarization in the Western Hemisphere*, Ottawa.

Mundell, R.A. (1961), 'A Theory of Optimum Currency Areas', *The American Economic Review*, 51, 4.

Odling-Smee, J. and Pastor, G. (2001), 'The IMF and the Ruble Area, 1991–93', *IMF Working Paper*, 01/101, Washington, DC: International Monetary Fund.

Sala-i-Martin, X. and Sachs, J. (1991), 'Fiscal Federalism and Optimum Currency Areas: Evidence for Europe from the United States', *NBER Working Paper*, 3855, Cambridge, Massachusetts: National Bureau of Economic Research.

Sewell, D. (1997), 'Enterprises Divesting Social Assets – The Belarus Story', *World Bank Transition Newsletter*, 8, 3, <http://www.worldbank.org/html/prddr/trans/mayjun97/art5.htm>.

Chapter 10

Russian and Belarus Monetary Union: Problems and Perspectives of Creation

Vladimir Chaplygin

Introduction

This chapter discusses the probability of the creation of a credit and monetary union between Russia and Belarus. It concentrates on the issues where significant questions remain, starting with the applicability of the theory of optimum currency areas and the theory of currency substitution to events in the former Soviet Union. Information is also presented on the way in which the dialogue between the national central banks and the fiscal authorities takes place before monetary union in the member states is created. This information covers such areas as:

1. The monitoring of domestic economic and financial developments
2. Macroeconomic forecasts
3. The definition of macroeconomic objectives and information on macroeconomic policy changes.

Turning to the monetary issues we ask whether it is possible to launch the Russian rouble as a common currency for some of the regions and states in the former USSR and what are the ways to do so.

In recent years a great deal of attention has been directed to the issues of monetary integration between the leading European countries and the creation of a common currency area with the new members of the EU. However, the theory of optimum currency areas (OCA) (Mundell, 1961; McKinnon, 1963; Kenen, 1969) and the theory of currency substitution (Miles, 1978; Chrystal, 1977) focus their attention mainly upon well developed western market economies and are adjusted to their needs. They do not necessarily suit the needs of post-socialist (and especially post-soviet) economies. Economic science in the East is not always able to operate in the Western theoretical and practical manner, and the issue of monetary integration, whilst being a carefully studied problem in Western economic analysis, remains unknown in the post-soviet states, even in spite of the fact that the discussions about the probability of the reintegration of the former Soviet Union's republics have been ongoing for twelve years. The paths to economic and monetary integration in post-soviet states are extremely complicated as they also lie in the political sphere and, unfortunately, economic integration cannot be conducted without sufficient political will to cooperate, that is questions concerning the 'quality' and 'quantity' of political integration and mutual political relations in the states of the post-soviet era define the final goals of both economic and monetary cooperation.

National currencies and the independent states

A number of works have been published in Russian economic journals and literature about the problems of monetary union between Russia and Belarus, and issues relating to general integration. In particular, we would like to draw attention to the works of Alimova and Idrisov (1995), Evstigneev (1997), Valovaya and Konstantinov (1998) and Tereshenko (2002). Unfortunately, there is a lack of work with a sufficient econometric and statistical background and the studies mentioned are based mainly on theoretical assumptions. Alimova and Idrisov were the first to do research in the field of monetary integration with a special focus on interstate monetary relations in the Newly Independent States (NIS) and explored the application of standard OCA theory to post-soviet reality. V. Evstigneev focuses his attention mainly on the methodological issues of currency integration. T. Valovaya and Y. Konstantinov investigate the general questions of monetary and financial integration and cooperation in the NIS. But even before these works were published, the government of the Russian Federation announced its own plan for the preservation of a rouble area ('rouble zone of a new type') which aimed to keep all the republics within the single currency area and which stipulated the way to fast internal and external convertibility.

Nowadays the Russian and Belarus economies are ranked as one of the most developed integration groups within the former Soviet Union (excluding the Baltic republics) and convergence efforts by the national authorities include legislation, the economic and political environment, and the voting system. In a sense, the case of Russian-Belarus relations is an exception in the post-soviet context because the initial divergence between these states was not as great as in other cases. However, it is necessary to draw attention to the fact that the integration processes are still not far from their starting-point – not even a complete free trade area has been established as yet, but in 1992-1993 in several top level meetings both sides agreed to launch 'a new currency' as a common (or single) currency for the proposed Russian-Belarus monetary union.[1] Actually, even today, although they have declared the transition to economic and monetary union, both states have not quite decided what this involves: the launching of a new common currency or the

---

[1]   See, for instance, the agreement of 8 September 1993, 'On integration of the monetary systems of Belarus and the Russian Federation', and the agreement of 12 April 1994, 'On integration of the monetary systems of Belarus and the Russian Federation and the conditions of functioning the common monetary system', in the Garant law database.

declaration of the Russian rouble as the official means of payment in Belarus. At the same time it is not clear – neither at the academic nor at the political level – whether this means a common state, something like the former Soviet Union or an economic union with totally independent member states.

All the above-mentioned issues pose a number of important questions which need to be discussed before launching the single (or common) currency. First of all, what is the general economic reason for these countries to create a monetary union? What costs will each country bear and what are the economic benefits from creating a common currency area in this case? What will be the initial exchange rate between the national currencies and what will be its behaviour in the short, medium and long run? Is it better for both countries to remain individual monetary players? In the latter case the problem of independent monetary policies for each state has to be studied, as there is no evidence that a unified monetary policy will suit their needs better than two independent ones.[2]

Belarus, whose economy is relatively small, clearly cannot operate an independent economic policy as the optimal framework largely depends on the external environment, and on external shocks in particular. Unfortunately, neither Belarus nor Russia can find a 'reasonable' explanation for creating the union – grounds such as the reduction in the transaction costs of exchanging currency, the reduction of exchange risk (which leads to greater investment and trade and to lower risk premiums) are so negligible that they should not be considered very seriously. First of all, the exchange costs are not so important for the Russian side because Belarus is not its leading trade partner. Second, monetary substitution (which is the most probable path of future development) will not lead to greater investment and trade between the states unless Belarus becomes totally open to Russia and closed to the rest of the world. Third, Belarus has no opportunity to increase its trade with the rest of the world nowadays because of its very limited access to international markets. Fourth, the security and loan markets are almost closed for Belarus because of its unpredictable economic policy, but Russian investments are not a panacea which could resolve the problem.

Nowadays, neither the Russian nor the Belarus government are trying to promote nation-wide discussions about the costs and benefits of monetary unification and have largely neglected the huge structural disparities in the economic development of the two states. The problem is that Mundell's theory is just a 'core theory' which can be adopted to the contemporary situation, and it could be said that the proposed unification meets the OCA conditions.[3] The theory of currency substitution gives us the opportunity to look at the problem from an economic point of view: interstate monetary arrangements are widely explored in the literature and the only thing we need to do is to adapt such studies to the

---

[2]   That is what we can see in Minford and Rastogi (1990, pp. 47-81).

[3]   However the monetary union cannot be created if the countries only meet the standard criteria and that is why there are a lot of proposals to create a monetary union between different states but these studies cannot be put into practice for political reasons.

contemporary needs of both states. But as experience in Western Europe demonstrates, '... economic criteria [...] are secondary to political factors. Although the individual members of the EMU are separate political entities, monetary union is likely to be feasible only if part of a larger political calculus. History has shown that successful monetary unions have been successful political unions ...' (Tavlas, 2003).

Economic conditions before joining the monetary union

One of the issues is the problem of monetary coordination between the states which are about to create a monetary union, as the goal of monetary coordination is to harmonize the activity of the monetary authorities at the initial stages in order to accelerate and generate convergence in the future. There is nothing similar to the European Stability and Growth Pact between Russia and Belarus, and each republic is still trying to obtain the benefits from internal coordination between their monetary and their fiscal authorities but not from mutual cooperation at the interstate level. The problem is that it is difficult to find a balance of interests of all the parties involved, as each of them is used to applying its own methods and instruments, irrespective of their partner's goals. Generally speaking, coordination may be taken to mean any of the following situations:

1. Exchange of information between the policymakers
2. Mutual acknowledgement of the existence and probable behaviour of the other policymaker
3. Joint decision-making by the policymakers
4. Agreement between the authorities on a sequence of moves.

Furthermore, the governments of Russia and Belarus are in the process of negotiations on the interstate bank, which would be in charge of a common monetary policy for the union, but these negotiations are unsatisfactory because Belarus is simply unable to play an adequate role in the policy of the Central Bank of Russia. Nowadays Belarus is insisting on equal weights for both sides in the 'common central bank' (and even on its share of seignorage from money emission) but Russia is not ready to delegate part of its rights to the foreign party for free (some Russian regions are much larger than Belarus, but they have no rights in the voting process on the board of directors of the Central bank of Russia).[4]

---

[4] A lot of countries around the globe use the US dollar as an official (and unofficial) means of payment and a lot of international trade contracts are clinched in this currency, but neither the government nor the Federal Reserve Board of the USA are trying to sign an official agreement with any other country with the purpose of guaranteeing any losses which can occur in the case of devaluation of the dollar.

The problem is that there is no point in examining interstate coordination processes using the theory of optimal currency areas (with its special focus upon countries), but that it would be better to use classical OCA theory together with interregional analyses (89 Russian and six Belarus regions). In this case the average result would be more precise (nowadays Moscow produces approximately 21 per cent of Russian GDP, but its population is less than seven per cent of the total population of Russia). It can be suggested restructuring the Russian central bank system, which consisted of 89 local central bank branches, and creating eight to ten 'big banking regions' with the local central bank branch at the head. And after that the Russian and Belarus central bank system could create the Union reserve system, consisting not of the Central Bank of Russia and the National Bank of Belarus but of the local 'big regional central bank branches'. No one bank would be required to share its seignorage with the other central bank and the income from money emission would go directly to the state budget. Second, neither Russia nor Belarus would lose its central bank independence as the system would work on the principles of the reserve system. Third, this form of management would improve monetary and fiscal coordination as each member of the reserve system would become more sensitive to external and internal shocks. Fourthly, the factor markets (labour market, financial markets and so on) could improve their flexibility and this would lead to less inflation and more profits for both firms and the states. These features would mean that monetary and fiscal policy coordination would occur through the union reserve system taking fiscal policy into account as an element of the environment in which monetary policy operated. And finally, this scheme would be very open to other potential member states like Kazakhstan, Ukraine and Kyrgyzstan as it would not lead to huge structural disparities, neither in the fiscal nor in the monetary spheres, but would be very sensitive to market requirements (in terms of inflation targeting, money demand and supply and so on). Furthermore, the taxation systems of the member states could also be changed in the same way, as cooperation and coordination would be made possible in a better way and would lead to extra benefits.

Key features of the operational framework for the conducting of monetary and fiscal policy should include the following:

1. The Union reserve system, as the monetary authority, should have operational independence to pursue its statutorily imposed goal of price stability.
2. The system, therefore, would be required to respond to developments in the economy – including changes in fiscal policy – that have material implications for the achievement of the price stability target.
3. Most major discretionary changes in fiscal policy should be announced well in advance, which would generally provide enough time for the system to factor them into its macroeconomic assessments and monetary policy settings.

Leaving the formal analysis to be developed, we may say that in practice there is a natural solution to this question: the policy process underlying fiscal decisions is by its nature lengthy and complex and cannot be reverted once decisions reach the stage of implementation; on the contrary, the process underlying the monetary policy decisions can be implemented in a very short time. Hence, fiscal authorities will dominate as leaders in a Stackelberg equilibrium with the central bankers.

It has to be mentioned that despite the attempts by the National Bank of Belarus to run an inflation targeting policy (or something similar to inflation targeting) the latter seems to be very inefficient as it allows the authorities to stabilize only nominal output and nominal market flexibility while the real data remains unchanged or is even becoming worse. At the same time the justification for monetary targeting is that, if there is a stable relationship between the stock of money in the economy and the total value of money spending, then a choice of interest rate which keeps the stock of money growing at a particular rate will deliver the same rate of growth of money spending. If, furthermore, the volume of economic activity is reasonably stable, then the stable growth of money spending will deliver a reasonably stable rate of inflation. Furthermore, Belarus receives credits from Russia on a regular basis with the goal of stabilizing the monetary system of the country, and these quasi-credits will never return to Russia because they are used as a kind of financial support for the republican social system.

High price of monetary union

The discussion on the prospects of Russian-Belarus monetary union which began after the signing of the respective agreements raised the awareness of the fact that the price for economic and monetary unification will be rather high, will drag on for years and bring both new gains and losses:

1. First of all, it must be admitted that the governments' initial plans for the possibility of currency union without increasing the tax burden have turned out to be unrealizable. However, the tax increase can be justified because from the financial and economic points of view it must be admitted that attempting to solve the problems by increasing the state debt is fraught with considerable risk. The taxes which will be used for the implementation of important economic programmes will have an effect which will subsequently reduce the tax burden, but no one can disregard the fact that the tax increase may be fraught with the most dangerous method of covering the union budget deficit – the slowdown of the rate of economic growth. Therefore, the introduction of new taxes should be considered not only from the point of view of current needs but also from the perspective of future economic results.
2. Secondly, the possibilities of increasing the state debt of the union are not exhausted. Of course, covering expenses by state borrowing and thereby increasing the state debt is inevitable, but this strategy will not have any economic justification in the future perspective. The increase of the share of state debt in the all-union GNP will be economically defensible if the

borrowings are used for profitable 'future investments' and the growth in borrowing is compensated for by a reduction in other areas. The increase in state debt will entail the increase of interest payments that will probably be covered by tax increases and a reduction in social spending. In turn the increase in loan interest will cause a reduction in investment as it will make investment in state bonds more profitable. The central contention of supply-side economics is that a high level of taxation has a negative effect on economic performance. The so-called inverted Haavelmo effect can be seen as a theoretical and empirical foundation for the implementation of supply-side policies. The inverted Haavelmo effect refers to the occurrence of a negative balanced-budget multiplier instead of a positive one. The result of an expanding public sector, financed by extra taxes and/or social security contributions, will be a lower rate of economic growth and less employment than in the absence of such expansion.

Understanding the advantages and disadvantages of economic and monetary union requires the recalculation of costs – in the current, short-term and long-term dimensions. Thus, for example, the social costs in Belarus will burden the budget and, in spite of the financial support from Russia, such expenditures will not allow an improvement in the position of companies. On the contrary, the investment costs will promote the aligning of infrastructure development and should be financed from both states in different proportions. However, it seems that having chosen the easiest road to economic unification, neither Russia nor Belarus have estimated the real financial requirements of forming the monetary and economic union and solving any problems that may arise. One possible scenario is that the differences in economic structures (and as a result, their reaction to external shocks) will reverse convergence and even isolate the national economies from each other in spite of the declared aspiration of integration and cooperation.

Consequences of asymmetry

All the aforementioned, however, mostly concerns the financial needs of common economic integration, but not the creating of a monetary union. And the problem is not only that this requires the separation of the costs for economic and monetary integration but that the Russian and Belarus economies are asymmetric (or asymmetrically dependent), which means that even the states whose economic cycles are quite close to each other can face certain differences in the synchronization of their monetary or fiscal cycles. 'Asymmetrically dependent economies' can be defined as a certain economic entity in which each element behaves according to its own economic laws (asymmetry) but at the same time changes in one country have 'knock-on' effects inside the other, when according to the optimum currency area studies the member states of a common currency area should have symmetry. The forecasts of the evolution of monetary union and the determination of the economic effect are accomplished by the use of two-country econometric models, for example the model by Collard and Dellas (2002), who demonstrated the asymmetry of the state's economic development upon adoption of a common currency. Taylor (1993) and Mitchell (1998) determined the correlation between the supply of common currency and the wage level. These models allow the determination of the influence of 'residual' asymmetries on the whole process of economic integration and the choice of the types of asymmetry which have a major influence upon convergence (non-convergence) of the different economies.

The consequences of asymmetry may be found in different economic spheres of a monetary union:

1. They are found in the interest-rate elasticity of the demand/supply of the common currency in different countries. The determining points are the structure of the economy, the ratios of consumption and savings and so on.
2. Thus all the models consider the elasticity of money supply and money demand in the short run only for their influence on the exchange rate and neglect any other role they may have. It is obvious that the interest-rate elasticity of the money supply and demand affects the efficiency of implementation of monetary policy as a whole (because, for instance, of asymmetric responses to common monetary shocks). Some calculations show that initially, upon the introduction of the common currency, the integration group must not be regarded as an optimal currency area and that such costs of incompleteness are the price of the common monetary policy in a world of asymmetric economies.
3. If monetary policy is geared towards an exchange-rate goal when there are different elasticities of money supply and demand in the member states, this may result in a considerable destabilization of the business cycle. Thus, if there is asymmetry of the economic structures inside the union, the implementation of the common monetary policy may not always create a stable monetary zone.
4. The most economically powerful state of the union (anchor country) is always more prone to deflationary processes than to inflationary ones. This is an effect of the common monetary policy. And in this case the possibilities of overcoming the peculiarities of economic development by some form of monetary policy autonomy for member states' central banks are strictly limited.
5. Asymmetry has consequences for the labour markets when: wages rates and prices are slow to adjust; price inflexibility means the market does not clear; the goals of budgetary consolidation are in conflict with the wage policy; there is an asymmetry of efficiency of assets in the economy. The common market leads to the synchronization of the activity of different economic agents.

In the long run, if states at very different levels of economic development use a common currency there will be a need for convergence, and there will be inter-regional financial transfers: those are the reasons why the states must analyze pro and contra before launching a new common currency or joining the existing common currency area. Unfortunately, in the Russian-Belarus case the question to be discussed is not so obvious because neither the theory of general macroeconomic equilibrium nor Stackelberg studies say anything about multistage coordination, and it could be assumed that there is no sense in coordinating current activity between the states because of the countries' different economic weights. (Russian GDP is approximately 20 times as large as Belarus GDP). But coordination policy will let the authorities reduce unification costs and increase the benefits, without which the formation would simply collapse in the future.

Both economies can be described with certainty as 'open' but the different degrees of 'openness' are worth noting. And the big difference in openness is the value of the common 'residual' asymmetry that yields to quantitative and qualitative interpretation. One of the possible methods of calculation of the 'correction factors' is the determination of the different effects of the influence of the monetary policy instruments on the economies of the integrating countries. The minimization of the 'residual' asymmetries in the credit and monetary union depends on the choice of the economic procedure for integration (either by market conditions or by means of centralized planning). However, in the Russian-Belarus case a mixed approach may be applied. Nevertheless, the necessary condition for this to happen is that both states adopt a coordinated policy to substitute the Russian rouble for the Belarus rouble and the establishment of free market prices in most cases. This, coupled with other policies, will help to produce economic convergence throughout the entire territory. Nowadays there are different views on the question and different estimations of the economic starting positions – from the exaggeratedly negative to the extremely optimistic with the consensus on a 'middle way' point of view somewhere between the two extremes. However, all authors are confronted with the problem of asymmetry because there is a lack of evidence and research on the development of the most important economic indicators, such as economic growth, real productivity, unemployment rates and so on. Nevertheless, it may be suggested that the level of unemployment will rise in the transition period and, due to 'catching up', the Belarus average wage will rise to Russian levels and the attractiveness of investment in Belarus will be higher, and thus the interest rate will increase and the export of Belarus capital to Russia will be reduced, through a process of factor price equalization.

Even if the above-mentioned reconstruction of the integration processes as a regular evolution from the 'simple' forms to 'complex' ones is convincing, it is predominantly so by force of habit. One form of integration inevitably puts the whole system, including monetary, financial and other aspects, on the agenda: moreover, trade integration ('common market') logically demands the convergence of financial and other parameters of macroeconomic policy (in other words all that is usually considered to be a higher degree of integration) as its preliminary condition. Of course, many arguments can be developed in favour of the opposite point of view. If there is no market structure which can cause the convergence of factor prices and promote mutual intra-sector trade, and meanwhile the monetary system has been integrated to a considerable degree, any changes in the money supply in the joint monetary and financial market will cause asymmetric effects in the member countries. That means that the countries where the production of tradables is relatively capital-intensive will experience a more unfavourable effect than those where this is the case for non-tradables; therefore monetary integration seems to be impossible until trade integration is fully complete. In real life, these conditions for convergence are unlikely to be satisfied, but this discussion highlights the fact that in the extreme case the choice in favour of integration is made under conditions of uncertainty and, therefore, needs some additional information.

Entry exchange-rate mechanism

Models of purchasing power parity, or the Balassa-Samuelson hypothesis, naturally lend themselves to the exercise of determining whether a currency is 'overvalued' or 'undervalued' (furthermore, one implication of the Balassa-Samuelson hypothesis is that the standard practice of measuring misalignments as deviations from linear trends is likely to provide inappropriate conclusions). A long-run relationship between exchange rates and relative prices exists for all currencies with respect to at least one special reference currency or price deflator. A large number of works (see for example, Svensson, 2000, and McCallum and Nelson, 2000) have sought to characterize the adjustment of the real exchange rate towards its long-run value. Usually, the long-run real exchange rate is thought to be that which equates the prices of identical baskets of consumer goods in different countries, when these are expressed in terms of a common currency. The problem arises from the fact that the adjustment takes longer than can be rationalized by sticky prices. The econometric results reveal considerable evidence for the hypothesis that market imperfection is associated with the high persistence of deviations from purchasing power parity (such imperfections depend on a large number of factors, such as the development of market structures, fiscal and monetary restrictions, trade legislation and so on).

A critical element in creating a common currency area between different states is the defining of an appropriate exchange rate at which the states are ready to enter the monetary union. The problem is that no-one knows what the equilibrium exchange rate is and what the appropriate time to fix an exchange rate irrevocably against the neighbour currency will be – the band may be as wide as it can be narrow, so the decision to fix or peg it will influence the future economic development in each of the countries concerned. (In the case of Russia and Belarus one further problem is that Belarus has already fixed its exchange rate irrevocably against the rouble, but has not adjusted its financial and market structures to the Russian ones.) Meanwhile, some macroeconomic models (Minford and Rastogi, 1990) could be used to estimate the equilibrium exchange rate, but we should mention that these models are very sensitive to key assumptions, such as how large a current account deficit is or what the general economic expectancies are. The problem is that any junction of the monetary and credit systems could create monetary union but will not form the optimal currency area. The analysis found that adopting a fixed exchange-rate system does not necessarily lead to more trade. In a simple benchmark model with different preferences and only monetary shocks, trade is unaffected by the exchange-rate system, which is consistent with most of the evidence. Furthermore, for both trade and welfare a comparison across exchange-rate systems depends crucially on how each system is implemented, as the determinants of trade differ from the determinants of welfare:

1. More trade does not always correspond to higher welfare
2. Trade is higher under one exchange-rate system, while welfare is higher under the other.

Nowadays the disparities between the official and actual inflation rates in Belarus are quite high, and they also affect the divergence between the actual and official purchasing power parity of the Belarus rouble. It may seem very strange, but the aim of the republican authorities is to adjust (or to equalize) the official PPP of the Russian and Belarus currencies. This would be a solution which would allow them to define an exchange rate between the two currencies. But purchasing power parity is independent of the exchange rate. (There is no point in price comparing as the labour productivity, for instance, can differ from country to country just because of the difference in the technologies used. That is also the reason why the deviation between purchasing power parity and the exchange rate in less developed countries is usually higher than in well developed ones). It is worth considering this point as there is a large discrepancy to date between the PPP and the actual exchange rate of the Belarus rouble to the Russian rouble. The standard ratio 'exchange rate/PPP' for developing countries is usually within the range of 2.5-3, but in the case of Belarus we observe 5-7.5 (the higher figure is the production assets bound of PPP). Such a situation is unacceptable as this imbalance puts the brakes on economic development (the country cannot implement the investment programmes aimed at the establishment and development of its economy due to the exchange-rate disparities, which distort the price of imported capital goods and make it more profitable to invest in the old enterprises and build up production on their base than to start new ones with expensive foreign capital). Although the divergence 'exchange rate/PPP' is not an exclusive problem of the Belarus economy (in Russia such a problem is no less urgent) once the decision in favour of currency substitution has been taken, Belarus will become the centre of inflation for the common monetary area (in other words, the underestimation of productive assets in Belarus will require intensive investments so as to equalize the prices of productive assets in both countries, and there are no guarantees that these investments will stay in Belarus and not return to Russia).

Conclusion

There is a supposition that the development of the interstate integration processes both 'in breadth' and 'deep down' brings the participating countries to the same end-point. In practice, however, every stage of integration generates a threshold situation which is notable for its fundamental uncertainty and within the bounds of which the immediate economic incentives for further integration may stop operating or even become disincentives. These results are also observed during the transition from trade integration to monetary integration. Following this logic, after the integration of the commodity and financial markets, monetary union may turn out to be not closer but further away.

References

Alimova, T., and Idrisov, M. (1995), 'The Problems of Currency Relations in NIS', *The News of St. Petersburg State University*, Economic Series, 3.

Chrystal, K.A. (1977), 'Demand for International Media of Exchange', *American Economic Review*, 67, 5: 840-50.

Collard, F., and Dellas, H. (2002), 'Exchange Rate Systems and Macroeconomic Stability', *Journal of Monetary Economics*, 49, 3: 571-99.

Evstigneev, V. (1997), *Currency and Financial Integration in NIS and EU: The Semantic Comparison Analysis*, Moscow: Nauka Publishing.

Kenen, P.B. (1969), 'The Theory of Optimum Currency Areas: An Eclectic View', in R.A. Mundell and A.K. Swoboda (eds), *Monetary Problems of the International Economy*, Chicago: The University of Chicago Press, pp.41-60.

McCallum, B., and Nelson, E. (2000), 'Monetary Policy for an Open Economy: an Alternative Framework with Optimizing Agents and Sticky Prices', *Oxford Review of Economic Policy*, 16, 4: 74-91.

McKinnon, R.I. (1963), 'Optimum Currency Areas', *American Economic Review*, 53: 717-25.

Miles, M.A. (1978), 'Currency Substitution, Flexible Exchange Rates and Monetary Independence', *American Economic Review*, 68, 3: 428-36.

Minford, P., and Rastogi, A. (1990), 'The Price of EMU', in R. Dornbusch, R. Layard (eds), *Britain and EMU*, London: Centre for Economic Performance, LSE, pp. 47-81.

Mitchell, P., Sault, J., Smith, P. and Wallis, K (1998), 'Comparing Global Economic Models', *Economic Modelling*, 15: 1-48.

Mundell, R.A. (1961), 'A Theory of Optimum Currency Areas', *American Economic Review*, 51: 657-65.

Svensson, L.E.O. (2000), 'Open-Economy Inflation Targeting', *Journal of International Economics*, 50, 1: 155-83.

Tavlas, G.S. (2003), 'Monetary Union in Europe', *Submissions on EMU from Leading Economists*, London: <www.hm-treasury.gov.uk>.

Taylor, J. (1993) *Macroeconomic Policy and a World Economy*, New York: Norton and Co.

Tereshenko, A. (2002), 'Launching a Common Currency in the Union: The Assessment', *Bank Bulletin Magazine* (Belarus), 25, 210: 5-13.

Valovaya, T., and Konstantinov, Y. (1998), *The Conceptual Basis of Creating of the Payment Union in NIS and Ways to Currency Union*, Moscow: Russian Academy of Science.

Chapter 11

Money and Prices in Belarus: Information Content of Different Monetary Aggregates

Igor Pelipas

Introduction

Forty years have already passed since the famous statement of Milton Friedman that inflation is always and everywhere a monetary phenomenon (Friedman, 1963). However, the issue still generates controversy among economists. In applied analysis this issue is often reduced to an attempt to answer the question, 'Is inflation always and everywhere a monetary phenomenon?' There are two main groups of empirical research here: 1) use of cross-section data on a large number of countries over a long time span (usually, average data for the time period are taken); 2) use of time series for a single country. In the first case, commonly, the correlation coefficients between growth rates of money supply and inflation rates are calculated; in the second case, as a rule, the emphasis is laid on the analysis of the long-run relationship between money supply and price level. Among the voluminous research on the relationship between money supply growth and inflation one can find both papers supporting the viewpoint of the monetary nature of inflation and papers calling it into question.

For instance, some authors point out that close positive correlation between money supply growth and inflation is only taking place in countries with relatively high inflation, while in the countries with relatively low inflation (on average less than 10 per cent per year) such a correlation is practically non-existent (De Grauwe and Polan, 2001). Quite popular among applied researchers is the standpoint that inflation is a complex multifactor phenomenon. As a result, so-called eclectic models of inflation considering all possible factors are proposed (Hendry, 2001). In many instances, models of inflation are built in which money is not explicitly presented at all. This might support the illusion about the non-monetary nature of inflation (King, 2002).

Nelson (2003) presents an argumentation for a monetary treatment of inflation and shows that, first, the edicts about the non-existence of a relationship between money supply growth and inflation is a consequence of some methodological mistakes, especially, due to the use of averages for the whole period examined and ignoring the effect of lags in the relationship between monetary growth and inflation, or using incommensurable values of monetary growth and inflation for specific periods. Secondly, the inclusion of monetary aggregates into the models, where money has already been taken into account implicitly (for instance, through the output gap), is methodologically erroneous and this leads to the incorrect inference that the money supply does not influence inflation (see, for example, Estrella and Mishkin, 1997). The last remark, in our view, also concerns the eclectic models of inflation, where monetary factors, already implicitly taken into account, can appear insignificant when directly estimated (case of misspecification of the model).

Various authors often treat the notion of inflation in a diverse way ('wage-push inflation', 'cost-push inflation', and so on). This introduces confusion into empirical analysis, since not every price rise should be treated as inflation in the traditional meaning of this word. Therefore, it should be noted that inflation is the process of lasting rise of the general price level (or the process of reduction of the purchasing power of a monetary unit). One-time price increases for specific goods and services, or even one-time rise of the general price level, is not inflation in the classical definition of this term.

The relationship between money growth and inflation is shown, as a rule, in the long-run. In the short-run such a relationship may not be so evident or even be absent. This consideration logically leads to the use of cointegration analysis in empirical research on the issue (see Shirvani and Wilbratte, 1994; Hansen and Kim 1996; Masih and Masih, 1997, 1998; Crowder, 1998; Hasan, 1999; Baltensperger, Jordan and Savioz, 2000). During the last years, serious attention was given to the analysis of the relationship between monetary aggregates and inflation in the EU countries (Trecroci and Vega, 2000; Altimari, 2001). In some papers cointegration analysis has been used for the examination of the influence of money growth on inflation in transition economies (Kalra, 1998; Choudhry, 1998; Nikolić, 2000; Rother, 2002; Lissovolik, 2003).

The above-mentioned papers differ in their aims, tasks and methodology of analysis. Thus, a simple comparison of the obtained results to confirm the statement about the monetary nature of inflation is hardly possible. However, one important remark has to be made here: in empirical research we deal with more or less appropriate approximations. Consequently, we speak about specific monetary aggregates and price indexes, but not about an abstract relationship between money supply and inflation. Therefore, the lack of an empirical relationship between money and prices is not yet a reason for a theoretical inference about the disappearance of the monetary causes of inflation. Additionally, the lack of influence of the monetary aggregates on the price level dynamics in econometric analysis can mean in principle that these indicators have already been used by monetary authorities, more or less properly (Trecroci and Vega, 2000).

This chapter attempts to shed light on the relationship between different monetary aggregates and the consumer price index in the short-run and long-run to assess the information content of different monetary aggregates as well as the possibility of their implementation when forecasting inflation and conducting monetary policy in Belarus. The empirical analysis is based on the theoretical assumption that inflation has a monetary nature. In order to reveal the existence and the direction of a relationship between money and prices, the cointegration technique and the vector equilibrium correction model are used. Then, using the indicator model of inflation, the information content of different monetary aggregates is determined.

The remainder of the chapter is organized as follows. The second section provides the methodological framework for the analysis, and considers the basic model and econometric approaches to its estimation. The third section describes the data, and analyzes the dynamic properties of the time series used. The fourth section examines the relationship between different monetary aggregates and the consumer price index in the long-run. Special attention is given to the assessment of the stability of the obtained results, and the constancy of the parameters of the models. In the fifth section the causal relationships between the monetary aggregates and the consumer price index are investigated using Granger causality tests, an impulse response function, and a variance decomposition of the forecast error. The sixth section evaluates the forecast capacity of the indicator models of inflation, and assesses the informational content of the different monetary aggregates. The last section concludes.

Theoretical model, analytical framework and main hypotheses

The empirical analysis is based on the following assumption: there is an equilibrium price level where money supply is equal to money demand. Therefore, the price level is influenced by the money supply, and there exists an equilibrium correction mechanism of the price level.

This can be expressed by a simple graphic model (Figure 11.1). Let $1/P$ denote the relative price of money in terms of goods and services, where P is the price level. Then, $1/P$ is a monotonically decreasing function of the money supply M_s. The point $M_s = M_d$ corresponds to $1/P_0$, and equilibrium price level P_0. If the money supply expands, other things being equal, the price level also increases. Especially, the lower value of the relative price of the monetary unit ($1/P_1$), and respectively the higher price level P_1 correspond to point M_{s+} that denotes the increase of the money supply. If the demand for money changes, then the shift of the curve in Figure 11.1 occurs, which means a change in the equilibrium price level.

Suppose that the price level is lower than its equilibrium level, hence, the relative price of money is higher than its equilibrium level ($1/P_-$). In this case money supply exceeds money demand (point $M_s > M_d$), which leads to an increase in the demand for goods and services. As a result, the price level increases, and the equilibrium is restored. If the price level is higher than equilibrium ($1/P_+$), then the demand for money will exceed the supply (point $M_s < M_d$). Then, the demand for goods and services will shrink, the price level will go down, and as a result equilibrium will be restored. All this characterizes the changes of the price level in the short-run, while the long-run changes of the price level are determined by the dynamics of money supply.

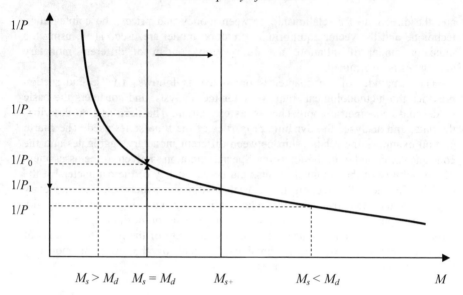

Figure 11.1   Equilibrium between price level and nominal money supply

An empirical verification of the hypothesis of the monetary nature of inflation means in our case testing for the existence and direction of a long-run relationship between the different monetary aggregates and consumer price index. If the price level (P_t) is a function of money supply (M_t), then it can be expressed as $P_t - f(M_t) = \varepsilon_t$. When P_t and M_t are nonstationary variables, while residuals ε_t are stationary, then these variables are cointegrated. In that case, cointegration is the statistical expression of the economic concept of long-run relationship between price level and money supply. The residuals ε_t are the deviations of the price level from the equilibrium path, and their stationarity denotes the existence of the equilibrium correction mechanism that restores the equilibrium price level.

Cointegration between P_t and M_t supposes causality at least in one direction, and the existence of the equilibrium correction model (Engle and Granger, 1987). Hence, the model presented above can be expressed by the cointegrated autoregression vector which allows us to take into account the long-run relationship between monetary aggregates and consumer price index, the short-run dynamics among variables and the equilibrium correction mechanism. It should be noted that initially P_t and M_t are considered as stochastic endogenous variables. Consequently, the theoretical arguments concerning the monetary nature of inflation can be verified empirically.

The cointegration analysis enables us to answer the main question of our research, namely whether there is a long-run relationship between prices and money in Belarus, and if it is the case, what is the direction of such a relationship. When conducting monetary policy, monetary aggregates will be useful if (i) monetary authorities are able to control their dynamics; and (ii) they contain useful information allowing us to explain price dynamics. In this context the concept of the exogeneity of money is of great importance. Let's consider the system for two variables P_t and M_t:

$$P_t = a_{11}M_t + a_{12}P_{t-1} + a_{13}M_{t-1} + \varepsilon_{1t},$$
$$M_t = a_{21}P_t + a_{22}M_{t-1} + a_{23}P_{t-1} + \varepsilon_{2t}.$$

If $a_{21} = 0$, and $a_{23} \neq 0$, then variable M_t is weakly exogenous with respect to P_t. In other words, money supply does not depend on the current values of the price level, but it can depend on their lag values. If $a_{21} = 0$, and $a_{23} = 0$, then variable M_t is strongly exogenous with respect to P_t. In that case money supply depends neither on current values of the price level nor on its lag values.

The definitions of exogeneity are important both for modelling inflation and for the use of monetary aggregates in monetary policy. In particular, the existence of weak exogeneity enables the modelling of the price dynamics and the verification of the appropriate hypothesis in the framework of single regression. Additionally, the existence of weak exogeneity is the necessary condition for the use of the monetary aggregate while conducting monetary policy. If the monetary aggregate really has an information content regarding price dynamics, it is necessary that $a_{11} \neq 0$, and $a_{13} \neq 0$. Strong exogeneity allows for forecasting the price dynamics within the framework of single regression. In the opposite case, a system of equations should be applied to obtain unbiased estimations of the regression coefficients. The absence of strong exogeneity of money (the influence of lag values of P_t on M_t) can be a consequence of accommodating monetary policy, when the money supply growth accompanies the increase of price level. If the monetary authorities, pursuing then monetary policy, do not take into account the dynamics of P_t, then money will be a strongly exogenous variable. Thus, the relationship between P_t and M_t is determined substantially by implemented monetary policy. The above-mentioned considerations are essential for the analysis of causality between P_t and M_t. If $a_{11} \neq 0$, $a_{21} = 0$, then money determines prices in the long-run (Granger long-run causality). Basically, the empirical verification of the hypothesis of the monetary nature of inflation can be reduced to testing the indicated restrictions. In the case when $a_{13} \neq 0$, Granger short-run causality takes place. If $a_{11} \neq 0$, and $a_{13} \neq 0$, then money has an influence on prices both in the long-run and short-run. Obviously, $a_{23} \neq 0$ shows the existence of the interrelationship between the money supply and the price level in the short-run. That fact does not prejudice the conclusion about the monetary nature of inflation, but can simply reflect the results of accommodating monetary policy.

Within the above-mentioned theoretical framework, the following hypotheses are tested in this chapter:

1. Natural logs of consumer price index and monetary aggregates are nonstationary variables with order of integration $I(1)$, therefore, their first difference characterizing inflation and the growth rate of different monetary aggregates are stationary variables.

2. Natural logs of consumer price index and different monetary aggregates are cointegrated, that is, the long-run relationship between prices and money exists. It is supposed that such a relationship is stable.
3. Monetary aggregates are weakly exogenous variables, and consequently, the change in the money supply influences the dynamics of prices in the long-run but not vice versa.
4. The change of monetary aggregates affects the dynamics of prices in the short-run. There is an interrelationship between prices and money in the short-run as a result of accommodating monetary policy.
5. All monetary aggregates contain useful information concerning price dynamics; yet, those characterizing the most liquid part of the money supply have the highest prospective properties.

The verification of the above hypotheses aims first of all to assess the informational content of monetary aggregates, while pursuing monetary policy and forecasting of inflation. At the same time this is, to some extent, the verification of the more general hypothesis of the monetary nature of inflation in Belarus on the basis of the available information.

Time series used and their dynamic characteristics

The data

The following time series have been used in our research (without seasonal adjustment):[1]

1. Consumer price index (CPI)
2. Monetary aggregate M0 (currency in circulation)
3. Monetary aggregate M1 (M0 + demand deposits in Belarusian roubles)
4. Monetary aggregate M2 (M1 + time deposits, and securities (excludes stocks) in Belarusian roubles).

The sample covers 1992-2002; both monthly (132 months) and quarterly (44 quarters) data are used. Following Golinelli and Pastorello (2001) the transformation of monthly data into quarterly is carried out using the averaging method implemented in Eviews 4.1. The reasons for the use of quarterly data are the following: 1) it is quite difficult to obtain well-specified models based on monthly data without a lot of dummies. This can introduce uncertainty in the obtained results. Quarterly data are smoother and, in our case, requires a minimum set of dummies; 2) one of the main objectives of the research is the analysis of the relationship between different monetary aggregates and the consumer price index in the long-run using cointegration

---

[1] The data of the Ministry of Statistics and Analysis and the National Bank of the Republic of Belarus has been used. Relevant time series can be found in the database of the IPM Research Centre: http://research.by.

techniques, and in this context the sample length is more important than the frequency of observations (Otero and Smith, 2000).

Short time series are widely used in cointegration analysis and they can be highly informative when substantial changes take place in the period under investigation. Moreover, the information content of the short time series can exceed the one of longer time series when in the last case the variation of variables is relatively small (Campos and Ericsson, 1999). This is the case for transition economies in general, and Belarus in particular, where time series are rather short, but the information content of each observation is relatively high.

All monthly time series characterizing the dynamics of monetary aggregates are period averages of relevant variables. The analysis of the order of integration of the variables is carried out using time series for the period from 1992 to 2003. In all other cases the analysis is conducted for the same period but the actual sample starts from 1991. This allows us to preserve the maximum number of degrees of freedom in the regressions with the limited number of observations.

The time series are in natural logarithms, where $cpi = \ln CPI$, $m0 = \ln M0$, $m1 = \ln M1$, $m2 = \ln M2$ denote logs of the levels of the variables, and $\Delta cpi_t = cpi_t - cpi_{t-1}$, $\Delta m0_t = m0_t - m0_{t-1}$, $\Delta m1_t = m1_t - m1_{t-1}$, $\Delta m2_t = m2_t - m2_{t-1}$ are the first differences of the logs of the variables, and approximations of the growth rates. Figures 11.2 and 11.3 present the time series used. Their striking feature is the structural break that occurred in the first half of 1995 (the grey shaded area indicates the supposed period of structural break). Clearly, it is important to take into account such structural breaks when analyzing the order of integration of the variables.

Order of integration of the variables

The estimation of the order of integration of the variables is one of the main stages of the analysis, as the examination of the long-run relationship in the framework of the cointegration technique supposes that the variables have the same order of integration. Figures 11.2 and 11.3 show that the level of variables is undoubtedly non-stationary, however, the situation is not so obvious if we look at the first differences.

If we assume that the first differences of the variables are stationary and have the order of integration $I(0)$, hence, the order of integration of the level of the variables will be $I(1)$.Often, for formal analysis of the order of integration, the traditional Dickey-Fuller unit root test is employed. However, this test has low power; the probability of a type II error, when a false null hypothesis is accepted, is rather high. This is especially relevant for the estimation of the order of integration of the first differences. There is the hazard that the null hypothesis of a unit root is not rejected, whereas in fact the first differences can be stationary.

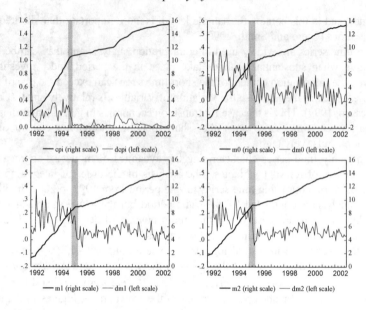

Figure 11.2   Dynamics of consumer price index and monetary aggregates: monthly data (log scale, d = difference operator Δ)

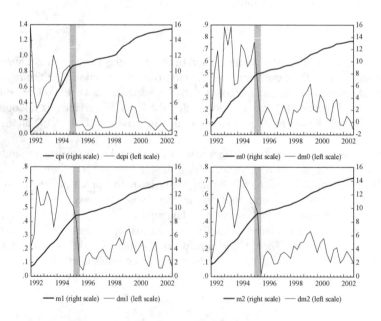

Figure 11.3   Dynamics of consumer price index and monetary aggregates: quarterly data (log scale, d = difference operator Δ)

Therefore, initially the more powerful ADF_{GLS}-test is applied, which is a modification of the Dickey-Fuller test where the trend (constant) is eliminated from time series using the generalized least squares method (GLS). Then, the new de-trended data are used in the traditional Dickey-Fuller test for the verification of the null hypothesis of a unit root. If t-ADF_{GLS} is a negative and exceeds the critical value for a given level of significance, then the null hypothesis is rejected (see Elliot, Rothenberg, and Stock, 1996). The results of the tests are reported in Table 11.1. The estimates lead to the conclusion that the first differences of the monetary aggregates are stationary, at least when monthly data are considered. With respect to quarterly data, the situation is more ambiguous, as for the first differences of several monetary aggregates the null hypothesis of a unit root is not rejected. ADF_{GLS}-tests indicate that the first differences of the consumer price index are non-stationary both with monthly and with quarterly series. However, this test, despite being more powerful in comparison with the standard Dickey-Fuller test, does not consider the possibility of structural breaks in the dynamics of variables.

There are several types of structural breaks, however, Figure 11.2 and 11.3 indicate that in any case, in the first half of 1995 we observe the change of the slope of the curves, which reflects the dynamics of the levels of variables (breaking trend). A breaking trend supposes a change of the mean for the first differences of the variables. It is possible that due to such structural break the null hypothesis of a unit root is accepted, whereas actually the first differences are stationary with changing mean.

Table 11.1   Unit root test without structural break

Variables	Monthly data		Quarterly data	
	t-ADF_{GLS}		t-ADF_{GLS}	
	constant and trend	constant	constant and trend	constant
cpi	-1.003(4)	0.197(4)	-1.781(1)	-0.504(1)
m0	-0.211(1)	0.663(3)	-1.103(1)	-0.138(2)
m1	-0.970(3)	0.186(3)	-1.727(1)	-0.633(1)
m2	-1.113(3)	0.055(3)	-1.791(1)	-0.631(1)
Δcpi	-2.180(3)	-0.185(3)	-2.731(0)	-1.248(0)
$\Delta m0$	-2.260(2)[*]	-2.505(2)[**]	-3.645(0)[**]	-2.611(0)[**]
$\Delta m1$	-2.961(2)[*]	-2.534(2)[**]	-2.734(0)	-1.505(2)
$\Delta m2$	-2.505(2)	-2.209(2)[**]	-2.647(0)	-1.937(0)[*]

Notes: * and ** denote rejection of the null hypothesis at the 10 per cent and 5 per cent significance level, respectively. ADF_{GLS}-tests and appropriate critical values are calculated using econometric software Eviews 4.1. Numbers in parentheses are optimal lag length chosen by Swartz information criteria. Maximal lag length for monthly data is six months, and for quarterly data is two quarters.

Perron (1990, 1992, and 1997) provided the appropriate unit root tests that enable us to take into account such structural breaks. It should be noted that such tests are usually applied to the levels of variables. Since our main task is to examine the first differences of variables for a unit root, the technique of the unit root test put forward by Perron was slightly modified in accordance with this task.

The approach used in this paper is as follows: the unit root test is employed for the levels of variables with breaking trend and the following regression is used:

$$y_t = \mu + \beta t + \gamma DT_t + \tilde{y}_t \tag{1}$$

where y_t denotes level (log) of variable; μ, β, γ are parameters of the regression; $DT_t = 1(t > T_b)(t - T_b)$ is dummy that allows for a breaking trend; t is a time trend; $\tilde{y}_t$ is an error term. The point of structural break (breaking trend) T_b is chosen *endogenously* so as to minimize the value of t-statistics for γ in (1). Regression (1) permits us to eliminate the trend from time series, and to obtain residuals that are used in the following unit root test:

$$\Delta \tilde{y}_t = \alpha \tilde{y}_{t-1} + \sum_{i=1}^{k} c_i \Delta \tilde{y}_{t-i} + \varepsilon_t \tag{2}$$

where $\Delta \tilde{y}_t = \tilde{y}_t - \tilde{y}_{t-1}$; a, c_i are parameters of the regression; k is a number of lags in regression; ε_t is an error term. Based on the regression (2), the null hypothesis of the unit root is tested. If t-ADF for α coefficient is negative and exceeds in absolute values the appropriate critical value for a given level of significance, then the null hypothesis is rejected.

Since a change in the slope of the level of the variable corresponds to the change of the mean of its first difference, then the point of structural break T_b that is defined endogenously can be used *exogenously* in the unit root test for the first difference:

$$\Delta \Delta y_t = \mu + \gamma DU_t + \varphi D(TB)_t + \alpha \Delta y_{t-1} + \sum_{i=1}^{k} c_i \Delta \Delta y_{t-i} + \varepsilon_t \tag{3}$$

where $\Delta \Delta y_t = \Delta y_t - \Delta y_{t-1}$; $\Delta y_t = y_t - y_{t-1}$; μ, γ, φ, α, c_i are the parameters of regressions; $DU_t = 1(t > T_b)$ and $D(TB)_t = 1(t = T_b + 1)$ are dummies; k is the number of lags in the regressions; T_b is the point of structural break; ε_t is an error term. The regression allows for the change of the mean, and represents the so-called innovation outlier model. This model is used when the structural break occurs gradually, as in our case.

This approach seems to be logical when testing for a unit root in the first differences with structural break, as the change in the mean is the consequence of the structural break (breaking trend) in the level of variables. In addition, the point of structural break defined endogenously at the first stage of analysis, enables us to use the critical value for the exogenously determined structural break at the second stage. The absolute value is substantially lower than the value when structural breaks one determined endogenously and, other things being equal, this reduces the probability of the acceptance of a false null hypothesis, and increases the power of the test. The robustness of the results is verified using the technique put forward by Perron (1992), where in regression (3) the point of structural break determined endogenously, that is T_b, is chosen by minimizing t-statistics for the α coefficient in (3).

The unit root tests are highly sensitive to the choice of the lag length in regressions (Weber, 2001). Different methods are employed in empirical research for choosing the lag length in the unit root tests, for example 'from general to specific', 'from specific to general', as well as informational criteria (Akaike and Schwarz). The different methods can lead to opposite results, and bring about uncertainty in testing for unit roots.

It should be noted that the initial motivation for the inclusion of additional lags in the unit root test is the elimination of the residual autocorrelation in the regressions. In our chapter we follow the above criteria, and choose the lag length in the unit root tests in order to eliminate residual autocorrelation in the regressions. It can be expressed as follows: $k_{opt} \equiv \{k \in K: J_i > J^* \ \forall_i \in K, i < k, J_k < J^*\}$, where k_{opt} is the optimal lag length in the unit root test that ensures the absence of the residual autocorrelation; k is selected from the set of integers K; J is the statistics for the null hypothesis in the absence of residual autocorrelation; J^* is the critical value of the statistic for a given level of significance. As a result, the minimum lag length that eliminates the residual autocorrelation is selected.

Table 11.2 reports the results of the unit root tests with structural breaks. The top half of the table presents the results of the tests based on the above-mentioned approach, when the point of structural break T_b is chosen endogenously for the levels and exogenously for the first differences. Apparently the null hypothesis of a unit root in the levels of variables cannot be rejected. At the same time the null hypothesis of a unit root in the first differences of variables is rejected at the one per cent level of significance both for monthly and quarterly data. The bottom half of Table 11.2 reports the results for the first differences when the point of structural break is chosen endogenously. Despite the slight discrepancy in the selection of T_b, the tests show analogous results. That shows the evidence that the first differences of the monetary aggregates $m0$, $m1$ and $m2$, as well as the consumer price index, which characterizes the inflation rate, are stationary with changing means, and have the order of integration $I(0)$. Consequently, the levels of all underlying variables have the order of integration $I(1)$ which enables us to apply the cointegration technique while analyzing the long-term relationship between different monetary aggregates and the consumer price index.

Table 11.2   Unit root test with structural breaks

Variables	Monthly data			Quarterly data		
	T_b	t-ADF	AR 1-7 (p-values)	T_b	t-ADF	AR 1-3 (p-values)
(1) T_b is chose endogenously for the levels and exogenously for the first differences						
cpi	1995:03	-2.327(4)	0.3016	1995:1	-3.329(1)	0.0739
m0	1995:05	-2.838(1)	0.3070	1995:2	-2.179(0)	0.7193
m1	1995:05	-1.920(3)	0.3025	1995:2	-1.703(0)	0.0557
m2	1995:05	-2.119(3)	0.3761	1995:2	-1.948(1)	0.5007
Δcpi	1995:03	-4.795(3)***	0.6441	1995:1	-4.341(1)***	0.1638
$\Delta m0$	1995:05	-8.897(0)***	0.5126	1995:2	-6.870(0)***	0.6636
$\Delta m1$	1995:05	-6.222(4)***	0.1112	1995:2	-5.523(0)***	0.3027
$\Delta m2$	1995:05	-6.480(4)***	0.2429	1995:2	-6.122(0)***	0.6573
(2) T_b is chose endogenously for the first differences						
Δcpi	1994:12	-5.717(3)***	0.2864	1994:4	-6.230(1)***	0.3312
$\Delta m0$	1995:02	-8.215(0)***	0.1002	1995:1	-7.099(0)***	0.3458
$\Delta m1$	1995:06	-6.254(1)***	0.1962	1995:2	-5.523(0)***	0.3027
$\Delta m2$	1995:06	-7.730(3)***	0.1231	1995:2	-6.122(0)***	0.6573

Notes: *** denotes rejection of the null hypothesis at the 1 per cent significance level. T_b is point of structural break. Critical values for top half of the table: for the levels of the variables they are -4.44 and -5.26 at 5 per cent and 1 per cent significance level, respectively (Perron, 1997), for the first differences of the variables in the case of monthly (quarterly) data when $\lambda = T_b/T = 0.3$ they are -3.33 (-3.39) and -4.05 (-4.14) at 5 per cent and 1 per cent significance level, respectively (Perron (1990)). Critical values for the bottom half of the table: in the case of monthly (quarterly) they are -5.33 (-5.51) and -4.58 (-4.76) at 5 per cent and 1 per cent significance level, respectively (Perron, 1992). Numbers in parentheses are optimal lag length, which was chosen as the minimum lag length necessary to yield uncorrelated residuals in the appropriate tests. AR 1-7 (1-3) is F-test for serial correlation of residuals of 1-n-order, H_0: serial correlation is not present (see Hendry and Doornik, 2001).

'Money-price' relationship in the long-run: co-integration analysis

Choice of the lag length

Different methods are used in empirical research for the selection of the lag length (for instance, informational criteria, or 'general to specific' approach). However, in our case, when accommodating monetary policy takes place it is difficult to analyze the direction of both the long-run and short-run relationship, based only on formal tests for choosing the lag length in the model. Let us assume the following situation: the expansion of the money supply leads to an increase of prices. Monetary authorities adjusting for the price increase expand the money supply. The result can be a vicious circle: the rise of prices follows the increase of money supply, then monetary expansion brings about an increase of prices and so forth. Evidently, this can be reflected in the dynamics of variables in appropriate regressions. It is quite possible to face a situation where the lag length, which has been chosen using, say, the 'general to specific' approach, exceeds the real lag of influence of one variable to another.

In our chapter, a different approach has been employed to select the lag length. As it was determined previously, inflation is the stationary variable with nonzero mean. This implies that after a certain shock (assume that it defines the impact of a money supply increase) inflation has to converge to the mean (equilibrium) level. The time of the return to that level could be treated as the time period over which the analysis of the long-run relationship among different monetary aggregates and the consumer price index should be conducted.

To determine the lag length, the regression (3) for Δcpi is used:

$$\Delta\Delta cpi_t = \mu + \gamma DU_t + \varphi D(TB)_t - \alpha\Delta cpi_{t-1} + \sum_{i=1}^{k} c_i \Delta\Delta cpi_{t-i} + \varepsilon_t. \qquad (4)$$

This regression is a model with an equilibrium correction mechanism for a single variable. Such correction will occur, if coefficient α is negative and statistically significant, as confirmed by testing for a unit root. In turn, the impulse response functions for monthly and quarterly data are estimated with equation (4). These functions characterize the time path of the variable to the equilibrium level after a unit shock. The model specifications correspond to those that were used in the unit root test. Figure 11.3 represents the impulse response functions with confidence intervals ±2 SE (standard errors).

As one can see, for monthly data the latest significant value of the impulse response function corresponds to the fifth month, while for quarterly data it is between second and third quarters. Thus the equilibrium is restored within two quarters. As far as inflation is concerned, one additional lag should be added while modelling the price level. Consequently, while modeling the long-run relationship between monetary aggregates and the consumer price index based on quarterly data, the lag length should be equal to three. Such a length is optimal for the aim of our study.

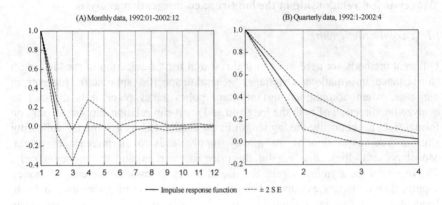

Figure 11.4   Time of adjustment to equilibrium level of inflation after unit shock

Johansen test

For the analysis of the long-run relationship between the consumer price index and monetary aggregates, the Johansen procedure is employed (Johansen, 1988, 1991, 1994; Johansen and Juselius, 1990). The appropriate vector model with an equilibrium correction mechanism can be written as:

$$\Delta X_t = \Phi D_t + \sum_{i=1}^{k-1} \Gamma_i \Delta X_{t-i} + \alpha\beta' X_{t-1} + \varepsilon_t, \quad t = 1,...,T \tag{5}$$

where X_t is a vector of endogenous variables; D_t is a deterministic vector (constant, trend, seasonable dummies and so on); Φ is a matrix of coefficients D_t; Δ is a difference operator; Γ_i is a matrix of coefficients characterizing the long-term dynamics of the variables; ε_t is a vector of serially uncorrelated stochastic errors. The number of cointegrating vectors is equal to the rank of matrix $\alpha\beta'$, where β' is the matrix of cointegrating vectors characterizing the long-term relationship between the variables, α is the matrix of the feedback coefficients characterizing the speed of the equilibrium correction of the system. The rank of the matrix and the number of cointegration vectors is determined by using trace statistics $LR(trace) = -T\sum_{i=r+1}^{k} \ln(1-\lambda_i)$, where λ_i are the eigen- values ($\lambda_1 \geq ... \geq \lambda_k$), T is the number of observations. The null hypothesis H_0 is that there are r cointegration vectors against the alternative H_1: $\geq r + 1$ that there are $r + 1$ cointegration vectors. If $LR(trace)$ is statistically significant, then the null hypothesis is rejected.

The model (5) is employed for all monetary aggregates ($m0$, $m1$, $m2$). As it has already been noted, the lag length k in the vector autoregressive model (VAR) is equal to 3. In the models for $m1$, and $m2$ the constant is included in VAR, while the trend is restricted in the cointegration space. This specification is determined by the presence of a trend in the time series, while the hypothesis of the equality to zero of the coefficients of the trend in the cointegration vectors is rejected at the 1 per cent level ($\chi^2(1) = 13.839[0.0002]$ for the model with $m1$, and $\chi^2(1) = 17.851[0.0000]$ for the model with $m2$). On the contrary, for the model with $m0$ we find the coefficient of the trend to be statistically insignificant at 5 per cent level of significance ($\chi^2(1) = 3.328[0.0681]$). As far as the bootstrap method gives a p-value equal to 0.162, the hypothesis that coefficients of the trend are equal to zero is not rejected. Taking into consideration that the variables have a trend, for the model for $m0$, the specification with a constant in VAR is selected.

The upper section of Table 11.3 presents the results of the cointegration test between the consumer price index and monetary aggregates. As we handle a small sample (44 observations), bootstrap p-values are used along with asymptotic p-values. For the simplicity in bootstrap analysis the number of pseudo-samples are restricted to 1000 (for details, see Bruggeman, Donati, and Warne, 2003). In addition, while computing trace statistics, the Bartlett correction for small samples is employed (Johansen, 2002).

As is evident from the results, the hypothesis of cointegration between the consumer price index and all monetary aggregates cannot be rejected. Moreover the utilization of the Bartlett correction, and bootstrap p-values provide analogous results. In accordance with Bartlett corrections, and bootstrap p-values $H_0: r = 0$, is rejected at the 1 per cent significance level for the models with $m1$, and $m2$, while for the model with $m0$ it is rejected at the 5 per cent significance level. Thus, there is a long-run relationship between the consumer price index and monetary aggregates $m0$, $m1$ and $m2$.

Tests for weak exogeneity presented at the bottom section of Table 11.3, indicates that in all models the monetary aggregates are weakly exogenous variables with a high degree of statistical significance. That indicates the direction of the linkage between the variables in the long-run, that is, the monetary aggregates influence the consumer price index. However, the hypothesis of the inverse direction of influence is rejected. The parameters of the long-run relationship are statistically significant for all cointegration vectors. Based on cointegration vectors presented in Table 11.3, the following equilibrium correction mechanisms are obtained:

$$EqCM0_t = cpi_t - 0.9335m0,$$
$$EqCM1_t = cpi_t - 1.34m1 + 0.0762trend,$$
$$EqCM2_t = cpi_t - 1.3991m2 + 0.0894trend.$$

These equilibrium correction mechanisms will be used in causal analysis, and in indicator models of inflation.

Table 11.3 Results of co-integration analysis

(1) Cointegration test

Null hypothesis, H_0	Eigenvalue	LR(trace)	Asymptotic p-value	Bootstrap p-value	LR(trace) Bartlett correction	Asymptotic p-value	Bootstrap p-value
cpi, m0 (lag = 3, constant in VAR)							
$r = 0$	0.4348	28.06	0.0004	0.0040	17.06	0.0289	0.0210
$r \leq 1$	0.0649	2.95	0.0859	0.3330	1.96	0.1616	0.3350
cpi, m1 (lag = 3, constant in VAR, trend in cointegration space)							
$r = 0$	0.6131	47.60	0.0000	0.0010	28.42	0.0236	0.0080
$r \leq 1$	0.1239	5.82	0.4833	0.7070	2.99	0.8780	0.7840
cpi, m2 (lag = 3, constant in VAR, trend in cointegration space)							
$r = 0$	0.6739	60.05	0.0000	0.0010	33.80	0.0042	0.0060
$r \leq 1$	0.2166	10.74	0.0974	0.2260	5.39	0.5415	0.3380

(2) Cointegration vectors, test for significance of β and α-parameters

Variables	Standardized cointegration vector, β	Test for significance of β-parameters, p-values in brackets	Feedback coefficients, α	Test for weak exogeneity, p-values in brackets
cpi	1.0000	10.502 [0.0012]	-0.358	21.781 [0.0000]
m0	-0.9335	8.665 [0.0032]	-0.035	0.481 [0.4880]
cpi	1.0000	23.161 [0.0000]	-0.949	35.799 [0.0000]
m1	-1.3400	20.474 [0.0000]	-0.070	1.173 [0.2788]
trend	0.0762	13.839 [0.0002]		
cpi	1.0000	26.889 [0.0000]	-0.991	30.740 [0.0000]
m2	-1.3991	24.114 [0.0000]	0.079	1.190 [0.2754]
trend	0.0894	17.851 [0.0000]		

Notes: in the upper section of the table computations are conducted using econometric software Structural VAR, version 0.20 (http://texlips.hypermart.net/warne/code.html), in the bottom section of the table computations are carried out by PcGive 10.3 (Doornik and Hendry, 2001).

The constancy of the long-run relationship for the whole sample is of great importance. Usually the constancy is estimated by the informal tests in the form of graphs of appropriate recursive tests. These graphs are important diagnostic tools; however, it should be stressed that they are only point estimations. In our chapter, the set of formal tests put forward by Hansen and Johansen (1999) are employed for the assessment of the constancy of the results of cointegration analysis, namely: 1) $\sup_{t \in T} \tau_{t|T}(\lambda_i)$ is a fluctuation test of the constancy of the non-zero eigenvalues;

2) $\sup_{t \in T} Q_T^t(i)$ and $\text{mean}_{t \in T} Q_T^t(i)$ are supremum and mean tests of the constancy of the parameters of the long-run relationship (β); 3) is a fluctuation test of the constancy of parameters Φ, Γ_1, α in the model (5) – S(6). The tests 1) and 2) are computed in two variants: for the fixed parameters Φ and Γ_1 in (5), and for recursive re-estimation of the parameters (see Bruggeman, Donati and Warne, 2003). While computing, 40 per cent of the initial sample is reserved. Table 11.4 presents the results of the testing with asymptotic and bootstrap p-values.

The hypothesis of the constancy of non-zero eigenvalues is not rejected for all models. Therefore cointegration between monetary aggregates and the consumer price index is not rejected for the whole sample. The parameters of the long-run relationship according to supremum and mean tests are stable as well. In addition, the hypothesis of the constancy of parameters Φ, Γ_1, and α in model (5) is not rejected. Hence, the obtained results concerning the long-run relationship between the consumer price index and monetary aggregates $m0$, $m1$ and $m2$, and the direction of this relationship from money supply to prices are stable over the sample.

Causality tests

Granger test

In this section the causal relationships between the variables are tested by the Granger causality test. Once we have obtained that the price index and different monetary aggregates are cointegrated, the causality test appears to be a VAR with equilibrium correction mechanism:

$$\begin{bmatrix} \Delta y_t \\ \Delta x_t \end{bmatrix} = \begin{bmatrix} \theta_1 \\ \theta_2 \end{bmatrix} + \begin{bmatrix} \omega_1' \\ \omega_2' \end{bmatrix} \mathbf{D}_t + \begin{bmatrix} \alpha_1 \\ \alpha_2 \end{bmatrix} (EqCM)_{t-1} + \begin{bmatrix} \sum_{j=1}^k \phi_{11j} & \sum_{j=1}^k \phi_{12j} \\ \sum_{j=1}^k \phi_{21j} & \sum_{j=1}^k \phi_{22j} \end{bmatrix} \begin{bmatrix} \Delta y_{t-j} \\ \Delta x_{t-j} \end{bmatrix} + \begin{bmatrix} \varepsilon_{1t} \\ \varepsilon_{2t} \end{bmatrix}. \tag{6}$$

In (6), in addition to a constant and lags of first differences of the variables, there is an equilibrium correction mechanism $EqCM$ with lag 1, and a vector of dummies $\mathbf{D}_t$.

Table 11.4 Tests for constancy of the results of cointegration analysis

(1) Fluctuation test of the constancy of the non-zero eigenvalues

Model (eigenvalue, λ)	Parameters Φ and Γ₁ are fixed for the whole sample			Parameters Φ and Γ₁ re-estimated recursively		
	$\sup_{t\in T}\tau_{t|T}(\lambda_i)$	Asymptotic p-value	Bootstrap p-value	$\sup_{t\in T}\tau_{t|T}(\lambda_i)$	Asymptotic p-value	Bootstrap p-value
Model 1 (λ_1)	0.0724	1.000	0.945	0.0811	1.000	0.947
Model 2 (λ_1)	0.1243	1.000	0.956	0.1859	1.000	0.910
Model 3 (λ_1)	0.1159	1.000	0.971	0.1096	1.000	0.981

(2a) Supremum test of the constancy of parameters of long-term relationship (β)

Model	Parameters Φ and Γ₁ are fixed for the whole sample			Parameters Φ and Γ₁ re-estimated recursively		
	$\sup_{t\in T}Q_T^t(i)$	Asymptotic p-value	Bootstrap p-value	$\sup_{t\in T}Q_T^t(i)$	Asymptotic p-value	Bootstrap p-value
Model 1	0.1427	0.991	0.777	0.3058	0.842	0.766
Model 2	0.3374	0.961	0.775	0.5488	0.821	0.712
Model 3	0.4714	0.878	0.593	0.7753	0.561	0.515

(2b) Mean test of the constancy of parameters of long-term relationship (β)

Model						
	$\text{mean}_{t\in T}Q_T^t(i)$	Asymptotic p-value	Bootstrap p-value	$\text{mean}_{t\in T}Q_T^t(i)$	Asymptotic p-value	Bootstrap p-value
Model 1	0.0425	0.893	0.659	0.0944	0.604	0.596
Model 2	0.1207	0.842	0.650	0.2172	0.559	0.450
Model 3	0.2049	0.596	0.325	0.2625	0.447	0.339

(3) Fluctuation test of constancy of parameters Φ, Γ₁, α

Model	Equation	S(6)	Asymptotic p-value	Bootstrap p-value
Model 1	cpi	0.4926	1.000	1.000
	m0	0.5247	1.000	0.996
Model 2	cpi	0.4641	1.000	1.000
	m1	0.6465	1.000	0.973
Model 3	cpi	0.3965	1.000	1.000
	m2	0.5877	1.000	0.980

Note: all computations are carried out using econometric software Structural VAR, version 0.20.

In this framework it is possible to test for Granger causality through two channels: first, the short-run causality; second, the long-run causality. Specifically, using standard F, or χ^2-tests the joint hypothesis: $H_0^1 : \phi_{12j} = 0, (j = 1,2,...,k)$, and $H_0^2 : \phi_{21j} = 0, (j = 1,2,...,k)$ are tested. If H_0^1 is rejected, then Δx_{t-y} is a causal variable with respect to Δy_t, that is there is a relationship $x \rightarrow y$ between x and y in the short-run. When H_0^2 is rejected, then there is a relationship $y \rightarrow x$ between x and y in the short-run. If both hypotheses cannot be rejected, then there is an interrelationship between variables in the short-run, that is $x \leftrightarrow y$. If there is no short-run causal relationship between variables, then the null hypothesis is not rejected. The long-run aspect of the relationship is analyzed by using standard t-statistics for α coefficient. The negative and significant coefficient of the variable, characterizing the equilibrium correction mechanism, indicates the presence of a long-run relationship between variables.

The equilibrium correction mechanisms, taken from the Johansen cointegration test, are used in Granger causality tests. We use a vector autoregression with asymmetric lags (the same approach is used, for example, in Masih, 1998). In the first stage in model (6) the following variables are included: the first differences of variables with lag 2, which corresponds to three lags for the levels of the variables; equilibrium correction mechanism *EqCM* with lag 1; a constant; one impulse dummy that reflects the impact of price liberalization in the first quarter of 1992. Then the initial model is reduced in order to minimize the Akaike final prediction error; the equilibrium correction mechanism remains in both equations of the system. As a next step, the system of obtained equations is used for testing Granger causality. The results are presented in Table 11.5.

Table 11.5   Granger causality test

Dependent variable	Short-run causality, Wald test $\chi^2(2)$		Long-run causality, t-statistics
	Δcpi	$\Delta m0$	$EqCM0_{t-1}$
Δcpi	-	17.201[0.000]	-2.720[0.010]
$\Delta m0$	32.577[0.000]	-	-0.592[0.557]
	Δcpi	$\Delta m1$	$EqCM1_{t-1}$
Δcpi	-	19.730[0.000]	-4.200[0.000]
$\Delta m1$	31.295[0.000]	-	-0.950[0.348]
	Δcpi	$\Delta m2$	$EqCM2_{t-1}$
Δcpi	-	25.489[0.000]	-3.280[0.002]
$\Delta m2$	11.530[0.000]	-	1.490[0.144]

Note: the numerals in brackets are the appropriate *p*-values.

Granger causality tests correspond to the results of the tests for weak exogeneity in the framework of cointegration analysis. The coefficients of the equilibrium correction mechanism are significant at the 1 per cent level in all equations for Δ*cpi*. As it has already been noted, that shows the influence of the money supply on the prices in the long-run, as well as the existence of the correction mechanism that brings back prices to their equilibrium path. In turn, the coefficients of the equilibrium correction mechanisms are statistically insignificant in the equations for the monetary aggregates. As far as the short-run is concerned, the relationship between the consumer price index and monetary aggregates is bi-directional, that is, the growth of the money supply determines the increase of the inflation rate and vice versa. Such interrelated dynamics may be the consequence of accommodating monetary policy and does not imply that the increase of the prices in itself is the cause of the money supply growth. Thus, the hypothesis of strong exogeneity of money is rejected. Consequently, it is quite possible that, while forecasting inflation, it will be necessary to use the system of equations that takes into account the interrelationship between prices and money in the short-run.

Impulse response function and variance decomposition

Granger causality tests are within-sample tests. Characterizing the relationships that have already existed between variables, they do not provide information about the behaviour of the variables out-of-sample. In order to get this information, the impulse response function and variance decomposition are employed. Both of these analytical tools are used in the framework of VAR with equilibrium correction mechanism (5). Let us assume that at time period $t = 0$ all variables are equal to 0, and that after that the monetary aggregate under investigation increases, say, by 1. The impulse response function shows the reaction of all variables in the system on this unit shock. The corresponding computations are carried out using econometric software JMulTi, 2.65 beta (Benkwitz and Kratzig, <www.jmulti.de>), and Gauss 3.2. Figure 11.5 presents the impulse response functions with 99 per cent confidence intervals obtained by using bootstrap methods (Holl's percentiles are used, the number of the pseudo-samples in bootstrapping are equal to 2000).

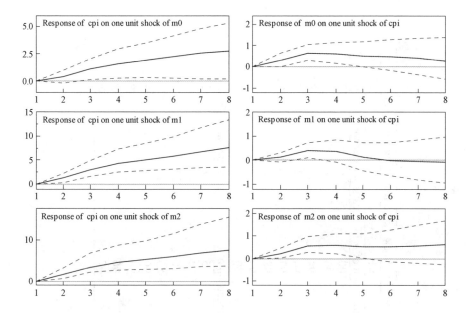

Figure 11.5   Impulse response functions

As is evident from Figure 11.5, a unit shock of all three monetary aggregates exerts a statistically significant long-run influence on the consumer price index. However, the unit shock of the consumer price index has a short-run effect on the dynamics of monetary aggregates, as a statistically significant influence is observed only between 2 and 4 quarters for different monetary aggregates, while for $m1$ practically none of the effect is revealed.

Variance decomposition of the forecast error provides analogous results (Table 11.6). Eight quarters after the unit shock of monetary aggregates 74.51 per cent of consumer price index forecast error variance is explained by $m0$, in turn, $m1$ and $m2$ explain 97 per cent, and 95 per cent of forecast error variance of the consumer price index. As far as the forecast error variance for monetary aggregates is concerned, it is mainly explained by the monetary aggregates themselves. The influence of the consumer price index is insignificant.

The results of the out-of-sample causality tests on the basis of the impulse response function and variance decomposition provide an even more precise picture than the in-sample Granger causality test. The out-of-sample dynamics of the consumer price index is determined by monetary shocks. The influence of prices on the dynamics of monetary aggregates is highly insignificant, and is observed only in the short-run. Thus, the causal tests confirm the hypothesis that monetary aggregates have an essential information content with respect to the dynamics of the consumer price index.

Table 11.6 Variance decomposition of the forecast error

% of variance of the forecast error, explained by shock of the following variables

Quarters	variance decomposition of m0		variance decomposition of m1		variance decomposition of m2	
	cpi	m0	cpi	m1	cpi	m2
1	0	100	0	100	0	100
2	6	94	1	99	4	96
3	16	84	6	94	11	89
4	16	84	6	94	11	89
5	14	86	6	97	8	92
6	11	89	2	98	6	94
7	9	91	1	99	5	95
8	7	93	1	99	5	95

Quarters	variance decomposition of cpi		variance decomposition of cpi		variance decomposition of cpi	
	cpi	m0	cpi	m1	cpi	m2
1	100	0	95	5	78	22
2	96	4	66	34	44	56
3	77	23	30	70	21	79
4	60	40	15	85	12	88
5	48	52	9	90	9	91
6	38	62	6	94	8	92
7	30	70	4	96	6	94
8	23	77	3	97	5	95

Prognostic possibilities of indicator models of inflation

In accordance with the above reasoning, all monetary aggregates influence the consumer price index both in the long-run and short-run. This section compares the informational content of different monetary aggregates, and evaluates their forecast potential considering the so-called indicator models of inflations for each of the monetary aggregates. It should be noted that in this case the indicator model of inflation is represented by a regression, of which the dynamics are explained by two variables: monetary aggregates (lags and equilibrium correction mechanism), and lags of the dependent variables that characterize inflation inertia (inflationary expectations). In addition, such a model, if necessary, can involve relevant dummies.

For the indicator model of inflation, the following specification is used: Δcpi with lags 1, and 2, $\Delta m0$ ($\Delta m1$ or $\Delta m2$), as well as their values with lags 1 and 2, $EqCM0$ ($EqCM1$ or $EqCM2$) with lag 1, constant and dummy $D921$ that enables us to consider the price liberalization at the beginning of 1992. The indicator models of inflation, obtained by using the 'general to specific' approach, and econometric software PcGets (Hendry and Krolzig, 2001), are presented in Table 11.7.

Table 11.7 Indicator models of inflation

(A)

$$\Delta cpi_t = \underset{(6.32)}{0.500}\Delta cpi_{t-1} + \underset{(3.65)}{0.388}\Delta m0_{t-2} - \underset{(-3.13)}{0.182} EqCM0_{t-1} + \underset{(5.30)}{0.915} D921 + \underset{(3.05)}{0.589}$$

Diagnostics:

AR1-3: $F(3, 36) = 2.0976[0.1177]$, ARCH1-3: $F(3, 33) = 0.6592[0.5830]$;
Normality: $\chi^2(2) = 5.9108[0.0521]$; Hetero: $F(7, 31) = 1.8580[0.1112]$;
Reset: $F(1, 38) = 2.6640[0.1109]$

(B)

$$\Delta cpi_t = \underset{\substack{(5.71)\\[3.88]}}{0.482}\Delta cpi_{t-1} + \underset{\substack{(3.36)\\[3.12]}}{0.434}\Delta m1 + \underset{\substack{(2.69)\\[2.03]}}{0.332}\Delta m1_{t-2} - \underset{\substack{(-5.12)\\[-3.28]}}{0.471} EqCM1_{t-1} + \underset{\substack{(5.83)\\[5.88]}}{0.805} D921 + \underset{\substack{(2.73)\\[1.94]}}{0.141}$$

Diagnostics:

AR1-3: $F(3, 35) = 2.1587[0.1104]$, ARCH1-3: $F(3, 32) = 3.7597[0.0203]$;
Normality: $\chi^2(2) = 0.9517[0.6214]$; Hetero: $F(9, 28) = 4.3749[0.0012]$;
Reset: $F(1, 37) = 0.5644[0.4572]$

(C)

$$\Delta cpi_t = \underset{\substack{(6.18)\\[4.21]}}{0.569}\Delta cpi_{t-1} + \underset{\substack{(4.47)\\[3.75]}}{0.751}\Delta m2 + \underset{\substack{(2.28)\\[1.91]}}{0.292}\Delta m2_{t-2} - \underset{\substack{(-4.61)\\[-3.07]}}{0.572} EqCM2_{t-1} + \underset{\substack{(4.48)\\[4.27]}}{0.727} D921 - \underset{\substack{(-4.58)\\[-3.91]}}{0.250}$$

Diagnostics:

AR1-3: $F(3, 35) = 1.7147[0.1818]$, ARCH1-3: $F(3, 32) = 2.2009[0.1071]$;
Normality: $\chi^2(2) = 4.3212[0.1153]$; Hetero: $F(9, 28) = 2.5807[0.0264]$;
Reset: $F(1, 37) = 0.0934[0.7616]$

Notes: AR denotes test for residual autocorrelation of 1-n orders, H_0: denotes the absence of residual autocorrelation; $ARCH$ denotes test for ARCH-effect, H_0: ARCH-effect is absent; Normality is a test for normality of the residuals, H_0: denotes that residuals are normally distributed; Hetero is a test for heteroskedastisity, H_0: heteroskedastisity is absent; Reset denotes the test for linearity, H_0: model has a linear specification (Hendry and Doornik, 2001). p-values are in parentheses. In the regressions in parentheses is standard t-statistics; in brackets is heteroskedasticity consistent t-statistics.

Despite their simplicity, the obtained models are well specified; the residual autocorrelation is absent. In the cases of residual heteroskedasticity, heteroskedasticity consistent *t*-statistics are used, and their utilization does not influence the results. All coefficients prove to be statistically significant (sometimes at 10 per cent level). The indicator models are used for defining the informational content of the different monetary aggregates and their prognostic possibilities. The informational content of monetary aggregates is estimated using the following equation (Atta-Mensah, 1995):

$$I(cpi \mid m) = -0.5 \ln[(1 - R_*^2)/(1 - R^2)] \qquad (7)$$

where $I(cpi|m)$ is the indicator of the informational content of a monetary aggregate; R_*^2 and R^2 are the coefficients of determination in regressions with monetary aggregates (including an equilibrium correction mechanism), and without them.

The monetary variable, that is the monetary aggregate and the equilibrium correction mechanism are excluded from the indicator model of inflation, and the coefficients of determination are used for the computations in equation (9). The results are presented in Table 11.8. As is evident, the highest informational content refers to the monetary aggregate $m1$, while $m0$ has the lowest.

Table 11.8   Informational content and forecast characteristics of different monetary aggregates

Monetary aggregates	Indicator of information content	Forecast constancy test	Forecast Chow test	Root-mean-square error
$m0$	0.253	0.702[0.9510]	0.144[0.9645]	0.0600
$m1$	0.518	0.450[0.9782]	0.094[0.9840]	0.0375
$m2$	0.430	1.350[0.8529]	0.293[0.8805]	0.0700

Notes: *p*-values are in the brackets.

For the assessment of the different monetary aggregates the out-of-sample forecast for 4 quarters is employed (see Table 11.8). All indicator models reveal themselves as plausible with respect to the forecast constancy test, and the forecast Chow test. However, in the model with monetary aggregate $m1$ the values of these tests are significantly lower than for $m0$ and $m2$. In addition, the root-mean-square error of forecast in the model with $m1$ is 42.5 per cent lower than in the model with $m0$, and 46.4 per cent lower than in the model with $m2$. Hence, based on the tests, the monetary aggregate $m1$ has the highest informational content, and the best forecast performance.

Encompassing tests, which permit to compare rival indicator models of inflation with respect to their informational content, can provide additional information. If one of the models comprises information that is contained in others, then it is considered as encompassing these models. Table 11.9 presents the results of the encompassing tests, which enable us to select the most informative model. The results testify that the indicator model of inflation with monetary aggregate $m1$, as provided by all tests, encompasses the model with $m0$, but not vice versa. Analogously, the model with $m1$ encompasses the model with $m2$. In accordance with the tests, the indicator model of inflation with $m2$ encompasses the model with $m1$ only in two cases at the 10 per cent significance level. Thus, it is possible to conclude that the model with $m1$ is not encompassed by the model with $m2$, whereas the model with $m2$ encompasses the model with $m0$, but not vice versa. Consequently, it is evident that the indicator model of inflation with monetary aggregate $m1$ and the corresponding equilibrium correction mechanism is the most informative. The model with $m2$ is on the second place, and the model with $m0$ closes this range.

Since the results of the Granger causality tests show that the monetary aggregates appear not to be strongly exogenous variables and that there is an interrelationship between them and the consumer price index in the short-run, the use of the indicator model of inflation on the basis of a single equation can lead to the wrong results in forecasting. In such a case, the system of equations should be used.

The system of equations is built for the most informative monetary aggregate $m1$. It allows for the relationship between money and prices in the short-run (Table 11.10). The initial model is reduced using the 'general-to-specific' approach. The obtained model takes both the influence of the lag and of the current values of the variables into account. The maximum likelihood test of overidentifying restrictions of the model (*LR*-test) does not reject the hypothesis of the acceptance of its reduction. The given model comprises the information of the basic model but is simpler. All the coefficients have the theoretically expected signs. Utilization of the appropriate *t*-statistics eliminates the presence of autocorrelation and heteroskedastisity and does not influence the results. There is no residual autocorrelation in the regression equations. All this is evidence of a well-specified model.

Table 11.9 Encompassing tests

	Null hypothesis			
Tests	Model with $\Delta m0$ encompasses model with $\Delta m1$		Model with $\Delta m1$ encompasses model with $\Delta m0$	
	distribution	test	distribution	test
Cox	$N(0,1)$	-7.859[0.0000]	$N(0,1)$	-0.118[0.9062]
Ericsson IV	$N(0,1)$	5.228[0.0000]	$N(0,1)$	0.109[0.9134]
Sargan	$\chi^2(3)$	16.056[0.0011]	$\chi^2(2)$	0.019[0.9907]
Joint model	$F(3,36)$	8.397[0.0002]	$F(3,36)$	0.009[0.9912]

Tests	Model with $\Delta m1$ encompasses model with $\Delta m2$		Model with $\Delta m2$ encompasses model with $\Delta m1$	
	distribution	test	distribution	test
Cox	$N(0,1)$	-0.130[0.8969]	$N(0,1)$	-3.337[0.0008]
Ericsson IV	$N(0,1)$	0.120[0.9048]	$N(0,1)$	2.660[0.0078]
Sargan	$\chi^2(3)$	0.323[0.9556]	$\chi^2(3)$	6.382[0.0944]
Joint model	$F(3,35)$	0.100[0.9595]	$F(3,35)$	2.355[0.0887]

Tests	Model with $\Delta m0$ encompasses model with $\Delta m2$		Model with $\Delta m2$ encompasses model with $\Delta m0$	
	distribution	test	distribution	test
Cox	$N(0,1)$	-6.536[0.0000]	$N(0,1)$	-1.501[0.1333]
Ericsson IV	$N(0,1)$	4.622[0.0000]	$N(0,1)$	1.297[0.1946]
Sargan	$\chi^2(3)$	12.988[0.0047]	$\chi^2(2)$	1.865[0.3936]
Joint model	$F(3,36)$	5.992[0.0020]	$F(3,36)$	0.929[0.4043]

Notes: Cox denotes Cox test for non-nested hypothesis estimates whether the adjusted likelihood of two rival models are compatible; Ericsson is the Ericsson instrumental variables test; Sargan is the Sargan restricted/unrestricted reduced form test, that checks if the restricted reduced form of a structural model encompasses the unrestricted reduced form from including exogenous regressors from rival model; Joint model is F-test checks each model parsimoniously encompasses the linear nesting model. This test in comparison with Cox and Ericsson tests is invariant to variables in common between the rival models (Hendry and Doornik, 2001). p-values are in the brackets.

Table 11.10 Vector model with equilibrium correction mechanism for M1

Variables	Δcpi_t			$\Delta m1_t$		
	coefficient	t-statistics	t-HACSE	coefficient	t-statistics	t-HACSE
Constant	0.141	2.77[0.009]	2.06[0.046]	0.058	2.56[0.015]	3.28[0.002]
Δcpi_{t-1}	0.484	5.59[0.000]	3.80[0.001]	0.178	3.36[0.002]	2.33[0.026]
Δcpi_{t-2}	-	-	-	0.2558	4.43[0.000]	4.19[0.000]
$\Delta m1$	0.426	2.65[0.012]	3.14[0.003]	-	-	-
$\Delta m1_{t-1}$	-	-	-	0.583	4.72[0.000]	9.75[0.000]
$\Delta m1_{t-2}$	0.335	2.63[0.012]	2.15[0.038]	-0.284	-2.50[0.017]	-1.92[0.063]
D921	0.806	5.90[0.000]	7.12[0.000]	-	-	-
$EqCM1_{t-1}$	-0.470	-5.05[0.000]	-3.83[0.000]	-	-	-

	Equation specification test					
AR 1-3 $F(3, 34)$	4.1103[0.0136]			2.6671[0.0633]		
ARCH 1-3 $F(3, 33)$	3.9439[0.0165]			0.4663[0.7077]		
Normality $\chi^2(2)$	2.6263[0.2690]			5.4028[0.06671]		
Hetero $F(11, 27)$	2.0676[0.0609]			1.9257[0.0809]		

System specification test

	Matrix of residual correlation (standard errors on diagonal)	
	Δcpi_t	$\Delta m1_t$
AR 1-3 $F(12, 64)$ 1.7752 [0.0716]		
Normality $\chi^2(4)$ 8.8363 [0.0653]	Δcpi_t 0.10490	0.01567
Hetero $F(33, 74)$ 2.1216 [0.0039]	$\Delta m1_t$ 0.01567	0.07824

LR is test of overidentifying restrictions: $\chi^2(3) = 1.3271$ [0.7227]

Notes: *p*-values are in brackets. *t*-HACSE is *t*-statistics, autocorrelation and heteroskedasticity consistent (Andrews, 1991).

Based on the system of equations the out-of-sample forecast for 4 quarters is estimated. Figure 11.6 depicts the result of the forecast, as well as an analogous forecast on the base of a single regression, with 95 per cent confidence intervals and root-mean-square errors. As is evident, the two models differ slightly in the forecast performance. The root-mean-square errors practically coincide. Moreover, the indicator model of inflation based both on a system of equations and on a single equation has coefficients with practically the same values and statistical significance. Hence, the absence of the strong exogeneity of money does not have a significant impact on the forecast performance of the indicator model of inflation on the basis of a single regression.

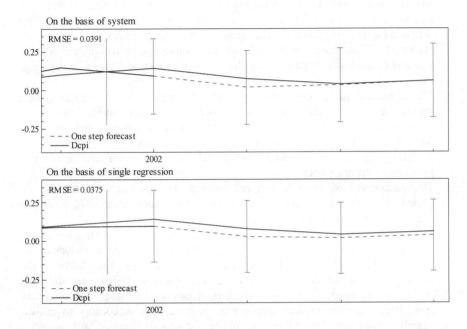

**Figure 11.6   Out of sample forecast with the indicator model of inflation with
            *m*1**

The model characterizes the influence of the monetary aggregate *m*1 on the price dynamics in the short-run and long-run. The statistically significant coefficient of the equilibrium correction mechanism indicates that the speed of the equilibrium correction is approximately 2 quarters (1/0.471). In addition, the model reveals that the inflation has a certain inertia caused by inflation expectations. The indicator model, despite its simplicity, has good prognostic characteristics and uses only one impulse dummy. It should be noted that the model corresponds to our theoretical considerations about the mechanism of influence of monetary aggregates on price dynamics.

Conclusions

The use of cointegration analysis and of a model with an equilibrium correction mechanism enables us to analyze the long-run and short-run relationship between different monetary aggregates and the consumer price index in Belarus over 1992-2002. This permits us to build an indicator model of inflation and assess the informational content of different monetary aggregates ($m0$, $m1$ and $m2$), as well as their forecast performance.

The main findings are:

1. The consumer price level and monetary aggregates $m0$, $m1$ and $m2$ are non-stationary variables, and have the order of integration $I(1)$. Hence, their first differences, that is, inflation and growth rates of monetary aggregates, are stationary. That makes it possible to use cointegration techniques for the analysis of the linkage between the dynamics of money and prices in the long-run.

2. The consumer price level and monetary aggregates are cointegrated. That means that long-run relationship exists between them. The monetary aggregates are weakly exogenous variables, and consequently, in the long-run there is a unidirectional relationship 'money – prices'. The weak exogeneity of the monetary aggregates is a necessary condition of their efficient use while pursuing monetary policy.

3. The parameters of the long-run relationship are constant over the sample period. This shows the constancy of the cointegration relationship and the equilibrium correction mechanism.

4. The causality test based on cointegrated VAR with an equilibrium correction mechanism reveals that the monetary aggregates influence the dynamics of the consumer price index in the short-run. Additionally, in the short-run the interrelationship between money and prices is observed. This interrelationship is the consequence of accommodating monetary policy, when the monetary authorities raise the money supply after a price rise. According to out-of-sample causal tests, based on the impulse response function and variance decomposition, the influence of the increase of prices on the dynamics of money does not exceed several quarters.

5. All monetary aggregates have the defined informational content and forecast possibilities with respect to the consumer price index. The formal tests reveal that the most appropriate variable is monetary aggregate $m1$, characterizing the most liquid part of money. The indicator model of inflation built on it has the lowest root-mean-square-error. Moreover, that model encompasses similar models with other monetary aggregates, and consequently, can be considered as the most informative while pursuing monetary policy.

6. The analysis shows that despite the fact of weak exogeneity of monetary aggregates, it is possible to use the indicator models of inflation based on a single regression, instead of the system of equations considering the relations between prices and money in the short-run. Specifically, the indicator model of inflation with $m1$ has the same forecast performance as the model that is built

in the framework of a system of equations. This fact substantially simplifies modelling and forecasting of inflation.

References

Altimari, S.N. (2001), 'Does Money Lead Inflation in the Euro Area?', *ECB Working Paper*, 63.
Andrews, D.W.K. (1991), 'Heteroskedasticity and Autocorrelation Consistent Covariance Matrix Estimation', *Econometrica*, 59: 817-58.
Atta-Mensah, J. (1995), 'The Empirical Performance of Alternative Monetary and Liquidity Aggregates', *Bank of Canada Working Paper*, 12.
Baltensperger, E., Jordan, T.J. and Savioz, M. (2000), 'The Demand for M3 and Inflation Forecasts: An Empirical Analysis for Switzerland', *University of St. Gallen Discussion Paper*, 7.
Bruggeman, A., Donati, P. and Warne, A. (2003), 'Is the Demand for Euro Area M3 Stable?', *ECB Working Paper*, 255.
Campos, J. and Ericsson, N. (1999), 'Constructive Data Mining: Modeling Consumers, Expenditure in Venezuela', *Econometrics Journal*, 2: 226-40.
Choudhry, T. (1998), 'Another Visit to the Cagan Model of Money Demand: The Latest Russian Experience', *Journal of International Money and Finance*, 17: 355-76.
Crowder, W. (1998), 'The Long-Run Link Between Money Growth and Inflation', *Economic Inquiry*, 36: 229-43.
De Grauwe, P. and Polan, M. (2001), 'Is Inflation Always and Everywhere a Monetary Phenomenon?', *CEPR Discussion Paper*, 2841.
Doornik, J.A. and Hendry, D.F. (2001), *GiveWin Version 2, An Interface to Empirical Modelling*, London: Timberlake Consultants.
Doornik, J.A. and Hendry, D.F. (2001), *Modelling Dynamic Systems Using PcGive 10, Vol. II*, London: Timberlake Consultants.
Elliot, G., Rothenberg, T.J. and Stock, J.H. (1996), 'Efficient Tests for an Autoregressive Unit Root', *Econometrica*, 64: 813-36.
Engle, R.F. and Granger, C.W.J. (1987), 'Co-Integration and Error Correction: Representation, Estimation, and Testing', *Econometrica*, 55: 251-76.
Estrella, A. and Mishkin, F.S. (1997), 'Is There a Role for Monetary Aggregates in the Conduct of Monetary Policy?', *Journal of Monetary Economics*, 40: 279-304.
Friedman, M. (1963), *Inflation: Causes and Consequences*, Asia Publishing House.
Golinelli, R. and Pastorello, S. (2001), 'Modeling the Demand for M3 in the Euro Area', Mimeo, <www.dse.unibo.it/golinelli/>.
Hansen, G. and Kim, J-R. (1996), 'Money and Inflation in Germany: A Cointegration Analysis', *Empirical Economics*, 21: 601-16.
Hansen, M. and Johansen, S. (1999), 'Some Tests for Parameter Constancy in Cointegrated VAR-models', *Econometrics Journal*, 2: 306-33.
Hasan, M.S. (1999), 'Monetary Growth and Inflation in China: A Reexamination', *Journal of Comparative Economics*, 27: 669-85.

Hendry, D.F. (2001), 'Modelling UK Inflation, 1875-1991', *Journal of Applied Econometrics*, 16: 255-75.

Hendry, D.F. and Doornik, J.A. (2001), *Empirical Econometric Modelling Using PcGive 10, Vol. I*, London: Timberlake Consultants.

Hendry, D.F. and Krolzig, H-M. (2001), *Automatic Econometric Model Selection Using PcGets 1.0*, London: Timberlake Consultants.

Johansen, S. (1988), 'Statistical Analysis of Cointegrating Vectors', *Journal of Economic Dynamics and Control*, 12: 231-54.

Johansen, S. (1991), 'Estimation and Hypothesis Testing of Cointegrating Vectors in Gaussian Vector Autoregressive Models', *Econometrica*, 59: 1551-80.

Johansen, S. (1994), 'The Role of the Constant and Linear Terms in Cointegration Analysis of Nonstationary Variables', *Econometric Reviews*, 13: 205-29.

Johansen, S. (2002), 'A Small Sample Correction of the Test for the Cointegration Rank in the Vector Autoregressive Model', *Econometrica*, 70: 1929-62.

Johansen, S. and Juselius, K. (1990), 'Maximum Likelihood Estimation and Inference on Cointegration With Applications to the Demand for Money', *Oxford Bulletin of Economics and Statistics*, 52: 169-210.

Kalra, S. (1998), 'Inflation and Money Demand in Albania', *IMF Working Paper*, WP/98/101.

King, M. (2002), 'No Money, No Inflation – The Role of Money in the Economy', *Bank of England Quarterly Bulletin*, 3: 162-75.

Lissovolik, B. (2003), 'Determinants of Inflation in a Transition Economy: The Case of Ukraine', *IMF Working Paper*, WP/03/126.

Masih, A.M.M. and Masih, R. (1997), 'Bivariate and Multivariate Tests of Money-Price Causality: Robust Evidence From a Small Developing Country', *Journal of International Development*, 9: 803-25.

Masih, A.M.M. and Masih, R. (1998), 'Does Money Cause Prices, or the Other Way Around?', *Journal of Economic Studies*, 25: 138-60.

Nelson, E. (2003), 'The Future of Monetary Aggregates in Monetary Policy Analysis', *Journal of Monetary Economics*, 50: 1029-59.

Nikolic, M. (2000), 'Money Growth-Inflation Relationship in Postcommunist Russia', *Journal of Comparative Economics*, 28: 108-33.

Otero, J. and Smith, J. (2000), 'Testing for Cointegration: Power vs. Frequency of Observation – Further Monte Carlo Results', *Economic Letters*, 67: 5-9.

Perron, P. (1990), 'Testing for a Unit Root in a Time Series With a Changing Mean', *Journal of Business and Economic Statistics*, 8: 153-62.

Perron, P. (1992), 'Nonstationarity and Level Shifts With an Application to Purchasing Power Parity', *Journal of Business and Economic Statistics*, 10: 301-20.

Perron, P. (1997), 'Further Evidence on Breaking Trend Function in Macroeconomic Variables', *Journal of Econometrics*, 80: 355-85.

Rother, P.C. (2002), 'Inflation in Albania', *Post-Communist Economies*, 14: 85-107.

Shirvani, H. and Wilbratte, B. (1994), 'Money and Inflation: International Evidence Based on Cointegration Theory', *International Economic Journal*, 8: 11-21.

Trecroci, C. and Vega, J.L. (2000), 'The Information Content of M3 for Future Inflation', *ECB Working Paper*, 33.

Weber, C.E. (2001), 'Alternative Lag Length Selection Criteria and the Split-Trend Stationarity Hypothesis', *Applied Economics*, 33: 237-47.

PART 4
UKRAINE

Chapter 12

Effects of the Shadow Economy in Ukraine: An Analysis Using a Macroeconomic Model

Bas van Aarle, Eelke de Jong and Robert Sosoian[1]

Introduction

Ukraine's transitional recession was among the deepest and most prolonged of the transition countries. It was characterized by a collapse of economic activity, hyperinflation and currency crises and a lack of coherent macroeconomic and structural policies. In contrast with the stagnation and decline of the formal economy, activity in the informal economy increased considerably. According to a number of studies, Ukraine has one of the largest shares of the unofficial economy among the CIS, Baltics, and CEE countries (only Azerbaijan and Georgia surpass the relative size of the Ukrainian shadow sector). During the last years macroeconomic stability was regained and economic growth and low inflation resumed, whereas fiscal and current account balance was restored. Since 2000 a policy of a fixed exchange rate against the US dollar has been successfully managed. Since 1999, the relative size of the unofficial economy has also started to decline from the high levels since transition was started.

The recent political overhaul (the 'Orange Revolution') has brought to power a new political elite. With the president Victor Yushchenko in charge many political and economic changes are hoped for and expected by the Ukrainians. It is clear though that all changes can not occur overnight and that the hoped for effects, in particular the positive effects on economic growth and stability, will take time to materialize. Complete institutional redesign and modernization of the public and business sector is even more a matter of long-term effort. In these changes also the adjustment of the large informal sector of the Ukrainian economy will play a decisive role.

This chapter tries to shed some light on these matters, focusing on the role of the shadow economy in Ukraine. We develop and estimate a dynamic open macroeconometric model of the Ukrainian economy, decomposing it into an

[1] The first author acknowledges the financial support from the Fonds voor Wetenschappelijk Onderzoek Vlaanderen (FWO).

official economy and its unofficial counterpart. The main goal is to gain more insight into the Ukrainian economy. There are already a few macroeconomic models of the Ukrainian economy. Gronicki and Pietka (1999) developed a quarterly model of Ukraine that contains a detailed analysis of the official and unofficial economy. ICPS (2003) runs a large scale annual model of the Ukrainian economy and is also providing macroeconomic forecasts at a quarterly rate using experts' evaluations and model-based projections. Kudina (2000) models the aggregate supply side of the Ukrainian economy and provides empirical estimates.

This study is built as follows: section one analyzes briefly the macro-economic adjustments in Ukraine during the period 1993-2004. Section two reviews two commonly applied methods to estimate the size of the shadow sector and suggests a few factors as the major determinants of Ukraine's informal economy. Section three develops a macroeconomic model of Ukraine. The model is used to analyze macroeconomic adjustment in the Ukraine and the role and workings of the shadow economy. After estimation of the model, we use it to simulate the effects of alternative scenarios of the relative size of the shadow economy.

Overview of the main features of the Ukrainian transition experience

Since its independence in 1991, Ukraine faced many difficulties connected with its transition from a planned economy to a market economy. Ukraine broke records in hyperinflation and deep economic decline, and its government was remarkably inert compared to its Central European colleagues. Since 2000 more positive developments are to be noted. Moreover, the recent political overhaul has brought prospects of increased reform, macroeconomic stability and economic growth. This section summarizes a set of stylized features on macroeconomic adjustment in Ukraine during the period 1993-2004 and which are already partly evident from Table 12.1.

Ukraine suffered one of the largest cumulative declines in output among the transition countries, only surpassed by Georgia, Moldova and Tajikistan. A number of structural and institutional factors made Ukraine's initial position less favourable than that of other CIS countries. At the start of the transition, Ukraine had the highest share of large-scale industrial enterprises heavily reliant on subsidies and excessively dependent on energy and was the second largest (after Russia) industrial producer in per capita terms among the CIS countries. The key consequence of over-industrialization in Ukraine was the creation of a powerful industrial lobby doing its best to retard any efforts at market-oriented reforms. As a result of the loss of traditional markets, manufacturing output fell sharply, declining by over 60 per cent in the first 5 years of transition (see Table 12.1).

Table 12.1   Summary of main macro-economic adjustments, Ukraine 1993-2003

	1993	1994	1995	1996	1997	1998	1999	2000	2001	2002	2003
Real GDP Growth (% yoy)	-14.2	-22.9	-12.2	-10.0	-2.9	-2.0	-0.3	5.9	9.4	5.3	8.4
CPI Inflation (% yoy)	4734.9	891.2	376.7	80.2	15.9	10.6	22.7	28.2	12.0	0.8	5.2
Employment Growth (% yoy)	-2.3	-3.8	3.0	-2.0	-2.7	-1.1	-2.3	-2.6	-1.2	1.7	1.9
Current Account (mln US$)	-765	-1163	-1152	-1185	-1335	-1296	1658	1481	1402	3173	2113
Exchange Rate (UKH/US$)	0.048	0.317	1.472	1.829	1.862	2.45	4.13	5.44	5.372	5.331	5.331
Real Exchange Rate (% yoy)	-72.1	27.4	-35.6	-18.9	-6.5	42.0	19.9	-2.6	-8.1	-3.5	-1.3
Fiscal Deficit (% GDP)	-6.3	-9.5	-7.4	-4.5	-6.7	-3.3	-2.4	-1.3	-1.6	0.5	-0.7
M0 (% yoy)		341.5	330.6	47.8	41.9	20.9	39.2	40.1	37.4	33.6	30.1
M2 (% yoy)	622.8	597.8	124.4	40.9	35.4	24.8	40.4	45.5	41.9	41.8	46.5
Foreign Reserves (mln US$)	120.7	506.7	863.8	1716	2170.5	765.1	1063.5	1440.8	2980.1	4242.6	6627.9

Source: IMF, own calculations.

Structural reforms indeed are likely to play a key role in determining growth outcomes.[2] The experience of CEE countries suggests that it is the success of implementation of structural reforms that largely determines the long-run economic performance, although initial reforms and conditions also matter a great deal.[3] In addition, the way the economy was privatized may matter: Ukraine's privatization, for example, was dominated by insiders who often had low incentives for undertaking serious enterprise restructuring.

The fact that the privatization in Ukraine was often non-transparent and led to the sales of attractive state assets for nothing is indicative of a more widespread problem of lack of good governance, institutional instability and corruption. In fact, the level of corruption in Ukraine is among the highest in the world. The 2002 Corruption Perception Index (CPI) ranks Ukraine 83rd among 91 countries. Despite a decade of transition, the institutional climate in Ukraine was largely unfavourable and worse than in the rest of the FSU on average. For example, the per capita cumulative FDI inflows into Ukraine during 1989-1999 were among the lowest in the region. And Ukraine's sovereign bonds were rated below junk bonds leading to high cost of borrowing. Also the growth of the shadow economy generally will be closely related to the lack of economic and institutional stability, an aspect that we will pick up in the next section. In Ukraine the size of the shadow economy reached a share of 68 per cent of the official economy by 1997 after which it gradually decreased but remained fairly high.

As a result of adverse demographic and labour market conditions, official employment in Ukraine dropped from 24.5 million people in 1990 to 21.8 million in 2002. Unemployment has been steadily increasing since the beginning of transition. As measured by the number of officially registered unemployed, the unemployment rate in Ukraine had reached 9 per cent by the end of 2002. The highest estimate of the unemployment rate was made by the Head of the Parliament's Committee on Social Policy and Labour issues, who announced at the end of 2000 that the actual unemployment rate in Ukraine reached 26.22 per cent.

Unlike Russia and other energy abundant countries, Ukraine lacked the resources to support its energy-inefficient economic structure and could not afford it any more. This fact became obvious after the 1998 crisis. Due to the non-payments and non-equivalent barter, the energy sector suffered from a fuel shortage and the energy system would crash unless some funds were granted for the purchase of fuels. The situation was particularly severe in 1999, when the external resources of financing were exhausted and Russia started to impose hard budget constraints.

Yushchenko was prime minister in a government first appointed in December 1999 and made crucial steps in the adaptation of a deficit-free budget and tightening of the financial discipline. The new government succeeded in

---

[2]   See Berg, et al. (1999), Christoffersen and Doyle (2000), Havrylyshyn (1999) and Fischer, et al. (1996).

[3]   See Coricelli (1998).

restructuring of the external debt, which gave it more room to manoeuvre and to discipline monetary and exchange rate policy. Mutual budget offsets were officially forbidden, as well as the barter in the energy sector. The non-monetary transactions fell drastically which further contributed to the increase in money demand. A new simplified system of taxation for small businesses was introduced. It has provided small private enterprises and the self-employed with the opportunity of considerable reduction of administrative burden in exchange for the higher payments to the budget.

The decline in GDP that started in 1991 finally became positive in 2000. After the dismissal of Yushchenko, the economy has continued its upward trend although the reform process was stalled. The successful macroeconomic stabilization is also evidenced by the evolution of the fiscal deficit, balance-of-payments and the exchange rate.

Inflation dynamics in Ukraine following its independence can be roughly divided into four periods. First, there was a period of gradual price liberalization and very high inflation, at times crossing the threshold of hyperinflation, from 1992 to late 1994. Then there was a process of stabilization from late 1994 to August 1998, and annual CPI growth eventually dipped below 10 per cent between late 1997 and mid-1998. Third, in the aftermath of the 1998 Russian financial crisis there was a moderate relapse of inflation, which hovered at a rate of 20-30 per cent per annum for a couple of years. Finally, inflation subsided rapidly and unexpectedly to just 6 per cent in 2001 and further into a small deflation in 2002.

The recent political turnaround leading to the new Yushchenko government is likely to imply further economic reform and economic stability. An interesting question is how the Ukrainian shadow economy may interfere and react to this process, a question that will be analyzed in the remainder of this study.

The shadow economy in Ukraine: Stylized facts and backgrounds

As noted above, the development of a large shadow economy has been a distinctive feature of Ukraine's economy. The development of a substantive shadow economy such as in Ukraine, clearly has a large number of consequences for the functioning of its economy, as we will explore later on. First we will discuss a number of aspects concerning measurement and determinants of the shadow economy.

In this study we interpret the shadow economy as encompassing all forms of economic activities that are not reflected in the official statistics.[4] This definition includes all activities which generate value added that are in the statistical underground (unresponding, unregistered or unsurveyed enterprises), the informal sector or the illegal sector. Some studies give a list of characteristics of shadow economy sector activities. These include activities that evade taxes and regulatory requirements (for example, licensing), ignore currency requirements (for example,

---

[4]   See Lacko (1998), Schneider (2000), Gregory and Mel'ota (2001).

local currency as the only legal tender) or other activities that fail to appear in statistical reporting mechanisms.

The shadow economy is often compared with the officially measured national income. It, therefore, comprises all presently unrecorded productive (that is value-adding) activities which should be in the national product (GNP). This definition allows us to compare and to add the shadow economy to GNP. This definition however excludes a major activity: private household activities (production that by convention is excluded from GNP).

The large size of Ukraine's shadow economy provides in a way both a comforting and a disturbing message. The comforting message is that Ukraine's national output is not as small and that its economic decline has not been as dramatic as official statistics suggest. In fact, the shadow economy has provided a buffer that has allowed ordinary citizens and small businesses to survive during hard times. The disturbing side is that such a large share of economic activity devoted to illegal or semi-legal activities cannot be efficient. Such an economy cannot collect taxes efficiently, is likely to further corruption and cannot make appropriate macroeconomic choices. Ukraine's private enterprise sector cannot develop efficiently because shadow economy enterprises cannot grow easily into larger enterprises as, for example, their access to outside capital is limited.

There are two commonly applied methods to estimate the size of the shadow sector: the monetary method and the electricity consumption method. There is a substantial literature dating back to Guttmann (1977), Feige (1979) and Tanzi (1983) that uses the demand for money to estimate the size and dynamics of the shadow economy. This methodology assumes that there exists an 'official' demand for money in the official economy and a 'shadow' demand for money in the underground economy. Guttmann (1977) and Feige (1979) assumed monetary ratios (either currency to demand deposits or M2 times velocity of transactions to GNP) that, except for the effect of the shadow economy, would have remained constant over time. Tanzi (1983) improved this approach through the use of an estimated demand for currency equation, where currency holdings (for official and unofficial purposes) relative to money (M2) is the dependent variable. In this equation, official currency demand depends upon the traditional money demand determinants such as real income, real interest rate and the ratio of wages and salaries to national income. He assumes wages are paid in cash and thus an increase in this ratio will require more currency. Tanzi (1983) captures unofficial currency demand by introducing 'tax variables'. Subsequent authors included additional variables, such as tax complexity or regulatory burden that were presumed to cause persons and businesses to operate in the shadow economy.[5] Another approach that is commonly used in estimating shadow economies in transition countries is based on comparisons of real GDP growth with electricity

---

[5]   See Scheider and Neck (1993), Shabsigh (1995), Hill and Kabir (1996).

consumption growth[6]: differences are then attributed to the growth of the shadow economy.

Mel'ota, Thiesen and Vakhnenko (2001) compare the two approaches in the case of Ukraine and conclude that the results of the monetary approach are more reliable than those of the electricity approach. The monetary approach is based on an empirical model that yields better results, while the electricity model seems primarily based on business cycle features. Moreover, they conclude that only the monetary method can estimate the causes of the shadow economy and identify the impact of individual policies.

Based on these methods of assessing a shadow economy share, the Ministry of Economy and European Integration of Ukraine independently calculates an integral coefficient of the shadow economy. Table 12.2 shows the development of the shadow economic sector as a share of official GDP and a share of total GDP, where total GDP includes both the legal economy and the shadow sector. The size of the unofficial economy in Ukraine in 2003 is of the order 36 per cent of official GDP and 31 per cent of total GDP and has come down from its peak around 1997.

Table 12.2   Dynamics of the shadow economy in Ukraine as a share of total GDP

	1991	1992	1993	1994	1995	1996	1997	1998
Shadow economy as a share of total GDP	18	23	26	30	36	42	43	42
Shadow economy in % to official GDP	22	30	35	40	50	65	68	62
	1999	2000	2001	2002	2003			
Shadow economy as a share of total GDP	40	38	35	33	31			
Shadow economy in % to official GDP	55	48	42	39	36			

Source: Ministry of Economy and European Integration, Ukraine.

According to a number of studies, Ukraine has one of the relatively largest shadow economies among the CIS, Baltics, and CEE countries. Johnson, Kaufmann and Zoido-Lobaton (1998) evaluate an average size of the shadow sector for transition economies for 1990-1997 and conclude that only Azerbaijan and Georgia surpass the significant size of the Ukrainian shadow sector (48.9 per cent to official GDP) with 60.6 per cent and 62.6 per cent respectively. In another cross-country study,

---

[6]   See Dobozi and Pohl (1996), Kaufman and Kaliberda (1996), Johnson, et al. (1997) and Lacko (2000).

Schneider (2003) finds that the share of Ukraine's informal economy reached 51 per cent of official GDP on average for 2000-2001. As shown in Table 12.3, this is well above the unweighted averages of the group of the CIS and Baltics (45 per cent), and the Central and Eastern European countries (29 per cent).

Table 12.3   **A comparison of the shadow economy relative to official GDP**

	1994-1995		1996	2000-2001
	Schneider (2003)	Johnson (1997)	Eilat and Zinnes (2002)	Schneider (2003)
Ukraine	47	90	115	51
Russia	41	69	54	45
FSU	40	67	71	45
CEEC	25	22	41	29
OECD	16	–	–	17

Source: Schneider (2003), Eilat and Zinnes (2002), Johnson, et al. (1997)

Kaufmann and Kaliberda (1996) calculate that Ukraine's GDP would be 40 per cent larger if the shadow economy were included and that the economic decline of 1990-1999 would be 41 per cent instead of the official 67 per cent if the shadow economy were included (Table 12.4).

Table 12.4   **Evolution of official GDP and total GDP**

	1990	1991	1992	1993	1994	1995	1996	1997	1998	1999
% change in official GDP	-4.0	-8.7	-9.8	-	-	-	-	-3.0	-2.0	-2.5
				14.2	22.9	12.1	10.0			
% change in total GDP	0.0	-7.5	-6.3	-7.8	-	-5.4	-5.2	-1.8	-3.2	-2.0
					11.7					
Official GDP index	100	91.3	82.3	68.2	45.3	39.8	35.8	34.7	34.0	33.2
Total GDP index	100	92.5	86.7	79.9	70.6	66.8	63.3	62.1	60.2	59.0

Source: Kaufmann and Kaliberda (1996)

What could be the reasons for the appearance of such a large shadow economy in Ukraine? Besides the fact of being present even in the times of the Soviet regime, a sudden transition to a market economy (along with a total restructuring of the economic, social and political structure) caused a hardship and lower living standards to the larger portion of the population. These changes and new challenges gave a start to the dynamic informal activities, mainly aimed at providing a living to those in need and those who were affected by the failure of the official 'formal' economy.

The research of Johnson, Kaufmann, McMillan and Woodruff (1999), Conway (2002) and a country study by the World Bank (2000) suggest that the following factors are the major determinants of Ukrainian businesses' hidden economic activities:

1. *Excessive taxation*: Ukrainian entrepreneurs report excessive taxation as one of the major impeding factors to business development and especially business start-up. According to the 1997 Global Competitiveness Report (World Bank, 2000), Ukraine is at the lowest score of 1.58 on a one-to-seven-scale basis, which evaluates country's taxation enhancing competitiveness. Very high taxes have driven many Ukrainian companies into the informal sector. Cost of production in Ukraine is very high due to the level of taxation. Personal income tax constitutes 35 per cent, VAT (value-added tax) is 20 per cent and payroll tax is as high as 50 per cent. As a result many employers elude the payroll taxes by signing two contracts with their workers. The first one is designed for the official Ukrainian tax authorities and only shows a small portion of the employee's actual salary. The second contract is retained for the company's internal use and indicates the employee's actual salary in full, expressed in US dollars.

2. *Burdensome regulation*: This factor can be measured in a number of different ways, while among the ones often cited are time required for managers to comply with the regulation and frequency of supervision visits by different state authorities. Such regulations include license requirements, labour market regulations, trade barriers, labour restrictions for foreigners and other forms of bureaucracy. The questioned sample of managers in Ukraine reports that a quarter of their working time is devoted to the state regulatory matters, which hints at the vagueness and intricateness of the regulatory system and explains businessmens' desire to escape numerous control procedures by moving into unofficialdom.

3. *Corruption and informal payments*: Almost 90 per cent of the firms declared extra payments for public services. Unequal distribution of public services, which is especially important for newly established firms, leads to deterring new businesses and increases the benefits of the shadow sector. Many obstacles that the growing number of emerging entrepreneurs face nowadays when dealing with corrupted authorities prevent them from going into business and reporting their economic activity legally. In order to launch an official business an entrepreneur requires more than 15 different permits from the state to make and/or sell his product or services. These 15 different bureaucratic agencies have the power to issue or to refuse the permits required to do business, and therefore each of these agencies behaves as a monopolist. Each of them sets the

quote (bribe) that the entrepreneurs have to pay in order to obtain the business license or permits.

4. *Street vendors and small manufacturing*: A result of non-payment of wages, salaries and pensions. The street vendors are most commonly 'babushkas'. The only income to supplement their minimal pensions is the profits from the sale of the sunflower seeds or field flower bouquets, which they trade in public spaces and on the corners of farmers' markets throughout Ukraine. Babushki pay 4 or 5 hryvnas to the police officers, who ignore the babushka's unlicensed activity in exchange for bribes. More sophisticated forms of street business in Ukraine concern different jobs ranging from transport services (private taxis), home delivery services, private laundry services, money changing booths, kiosks, street car-window washers, small local manufacturers offering hand-made sweets and snacks, watch and shoe repairs, and so on. The same force drives all of these entrepreneurs: their state's failure to provide an appropriate standard of living.

5. *Informal trade*: Informal workers are also largely involved in international trade. In some instances, informal trade takes the place of the customary forms of commerce in Ukraine. Most of the Ukraine's imports reach the destination consumer in the suitcases of the so-called 'shop-tourists' – the tourists visiting the foreign markets (Poland, Turkey, China) in search of inexpensive goods, which can be brought back to Ukraine duty-free and resold at the local markets for US dollars. An average shop-tourist can turn up to 50 per cent profit on a $3,000 investment in a month. When compared to the average wage in Ukraine such a profit explains the benefits of engagement in informal trade. These entrepreneurs are called 'chelnoky' and they make up to eight to ten shopping tours back and forth each year.

6. *Barter*: A part of Ukrainian enterprises are engaged in informal activities which involve non-monetary transactions where the goods are sold against promissory notes or exchanged for other goods or services (barter, see Guriev and Barry (2000) on a more detailed analysis of barter in transition). These transactions exist outside the formal monetary system and therefore are virtually invisible. Barter transactions in Ukraine are clearly a manifestation of the informal sector activities since they occur outside of the legal framework of the economy. They are normally not taxed or taxable and they remain unreported for the most part. Barter indicates that there is a lack of money in the budget – both in terms of lack of accepted currency and in terms of lack of cash income.

As noted in the introduction, there are likely to be many specific linkages between the existence of the shadow economy and economic performance and growth. The negative impacts can lead to macroeconomic, microeconomic and social problems:

1. *Macroeconomic problems*: According to the Laffer-curve argument, high tax rates push activities out of the official economy, they shrink the tax base and

thereby eventually reduce overall tax revenue. This revenue loss induces the government to increase taxes and decrease the quality of public goods and services. This drives firms further away from the official economy, resulting in a vicious circle. In addition, when tax revenues provide an insufficient source of budgetary financing, as was the case in Ukraine (and debt and domestic bond markets are unavailable) the government is often forced to resort to inflationary financing, which can destabilize the economy. The presence of a large informal economy in Ukraine made macroeconomic policy less effective. This, in turn, made it harder to attain and sustain macroeconomic stability. For example, the effectiveness of monetary policy is weaker than in other Eastern European countries since firms in the shadow economy use the banking system less. In Ukraine, which experienced hyperinflation, informal activities fled cash and transact in barter or in foreign currencies. In addition, official statistics tend to provide the wrong indicators for macroeconomic policy decisions in the presence of a large shadow economy.[7] For example, an increase in official unemployment may not signal as serious a need for a major fiscal stimulus, but rather a shift of economic activity into the shadow economy.

2. *Microeconomic problems*: There are many microeconomic efficiency problems created by the presence of a shadow economy. Firms in the informal sector have an unfair advantage in labour markets since they are not subject to labour regulations. On the other hand, firms in the informal sector may have trouble providing collateral, thus distorting their investment decisions. The inherent greater risk of doing business in the informal economy and the greater difficulty in raising funds from the capital markets, lead the informal economy to focus on the short-term and neglect large-scale and sophisticated investments. As a consequence, the shadow economy may operate more labour-intensively than would be optimal. Finally, operating in the shadow economy implies direct losses that raise the cost of production: these include time spent on bribing, avoiding licenses and taxes, and seeking private sector alternatives to public services.

3. *Social problems*: The presence of a large shadow economy in Ukraine where free-riding on public services is common, leads to a sense of unfairness and deepens the distrust of the ability of the political system to govern.[8] Moreover, it leads to an atmosphere in the Ukrainian society where avoiding state taxes appears morally just. Although it may seem from the term of '*shadow economy*' that this phenomenon is undesirable for a society, it has its own benefits. More than half of the income earned in the shadow economy is later on in some form spent in the official economy.[9] The shadow economy creates additional job placements, raises private consumption through enlarged family

---

[7] See Tanzi (1999).

[8] See Schneider and Enste (2000).

[9] See Schneider (1998).

earnings and greater variety of goods and services. Consequently, it may enhance the living standards of the country's population.

To have an analytical approach to analyzing the shadow economy in Ukraine, considering some of the aspects referred to above, we estimate a model of the size of the Ukrainian shadow economy. It relates the shadow economy as a percentage of total economy, *SHADOW* to its lagged value, a proxy for the complexity of the tax system, *COMPLEX*, a proxy of the effective regulatory burden, *EFFREG*, the rate of inflation, *INFLATION* and taxes as a fraction of GDP, *TAXES*.

The lagged value of the shadow economy captures the presence of inertial adjustment dynamics: for example Schneider (1997) documents that the shadow economy is highly persistent. Thus the level of the shadow economy in the year prior to the changes in the 'proxies' is likely to contain much information on the current and future level of the shadow economy. Figure 12.1 shows the estimated size of the shadow economy (as a per cent of the total economy), the degree of complexity of the tax system, the degree of effective regulation and the EBRD overall index of reforms during 1993-2003.

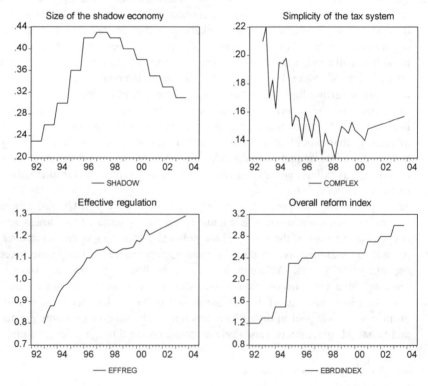

Figure 12.1   Proxys for tax complexity, effective regulatory burden and reforms 1993-2003

It finds there has been a declining trend of simplicity of the tax system during 1993-1997, that is increasing complexity, and since then it has decreased slightly.[10] Effective regulation has increased gradually; the reform process was halted basically between 1995 and 2000.

Tax complexity is measured by the index proposed by Wagner (1979), Clotfelter (1983) and Schneider and Neck (1993): this variable was constructed using a Herfindahl-Hirschman concentration measure:

$$COMPLEX_t = 1/HRF_t = 1/\sum_{i=1}^{n}(REV_{it})^2$$

where REV_{it} equals the *i-th* government revenue share of the total revenue among all *n* revenue items in a year *t*. Revenues from privatization and capital transactions of the government are excluded. *HRF* equals one if there is only one tax and thus the tax system is very simple. With increasing complexity (*COMPLEX*) the value of *HRF* decreases. The lower the index value, the more complex the tax system is.

Increasing complexity of the tax system may influence unofficial activity in either direction in an economy with unstable institutions. Scheider and Neck (1993) estimated a model for Austria and concluded that household labour supply in the official economy increases with the number of tax exemptions, suggesting that increasing complexity of the tax system dampens unofficial activity. Thus, a tax reform that broadens the tax base and reduces the number of taxes may contribute to more shadow economy activity. Clotfelter (1983), to the contrary, has argued that simplification of the tax system facilitates income reporting for taxpayers, increasing tax compliance and willingness to operate officially, thus dampening unofficial activity.

The specific institutions of a country can influence the tax complexity. In transition countries with uncertain rules and arbitrary official behaviour, simplification of the tax system may have a positive influence on the welfare of people: efforts and costs to legally avoid taxes are saved, which could be sizeable if the tax rules and exemptions change frequently and if taxpayers cannot be sure whether a legitimate tax exemption claimed would be accepted by arbitrary officials. If complexity of the tax system increases, the tax administration has more room for arbitrary actions. Hence, the taxpayer gains from simplification may well over-compensate the welfare loss incurred when tax exemptions are reduced. The effect of complexity of the tax system on the Ukrainian shadow economy is thus an empirical issue and the expected sign of tax complexity is indeterminate *a priori*.

When discussing the regulatory burden as a cause for unofficial activity, what should be considered is not only the quality and extent of formal regulations and rules per se, but rather the effective regulatory burden.[11] It also includes, for example, the freedom on the part of the state tax administration to interpret and

---

[10]   Data are obtained from Mel'ota, Thiesen and Vakhnenko (2001).
[11]   See Johnson et al. (1998).

implement tax rules. Since we cannot examine the effective regulatory burden in detail, a crude proxy is used for it. Following Mel'ota, Thiesen and Vakhnenko (2001) we use the number of government employees in the central and local governments who may be most relevant in determining the degree of effective regulation (*EFFREG*) and divide this number by the population. Government employees are defined as all employees in ministries, state committees, local administrations, and so on. Figure 12.1 shows that effective regulation has been increasing over time with the exception of a small period around 1998.[12] During 1998, the year when the government took additional steps to reduce the regulatory burden, improvements in registration procedures occurred and financial inspections decreased somewhat. In sum, the graph shows that contrary to the intentions and efforts of all governments since 1994, the effective regulatory burden did not decline.

Table 12.5 gives the estimation results of the model of the size of the Ukrainian shadow economy.

Table 12.5   An empirical model of the shadow economy in Ukraine

Dependent Variable: *SHADOW*
Method: Least Squares
Sample(adjusted): 1995:1-2003:4
Included observations: 36 after adjusting endpoints

Variable	Coefficient	Std. Error	t-Statistic	Prob.
SHADOW(-1)	0.82	0.10	7.96	0.00
COMPLEX	-0.02	0.01	-1.56	0.13
EFFREG	0.46	0.21	2.16	0.04
EBRDINDEX	-0.12	0.07	-1.66	0.10
TAXES	0.08	0.12	0.62	0.54
INFLATION	0.003	0.004	0.63	0.53
R-squared	0.95	Mean dependent var		0.53
Adjusted R-squared	0.94	S.D. dependent var		0.10
S.E. of regression	0.02	Akaike info criterion		-4.46
Sum squared resid	0.02	Schwarz criterion		-4.06
Log likelihood	89.28	Durbin-Watson stat		2.14

The explanatory power of the estimation is fairly high. Inertia in the shadow economy is a highly important factor. The proxy for the regulatory burden has the expected positive sign and is highly significant. The proxy for the complexity of the tax system is also positive (note that a negative number implies a positive effect

---

[12]   Data are obtained from Mel'ota, Thiesen and Vakhnenko (2001).

of complexity on the shadow economy) and is practically significant.[13] The positive sign indicates that rising complexity increases shadow economic activity in the long run. This suggests that tax complexity, be it the number of taxes or the number and extent of tax exemptions, all contribute to unofficial activity in Ukraine. The reform process may be seen as also reducing the shadow economy as its coefficient is substantial and significant at the 10 per cent level of confidence. Both taxes and inflation seem to exert some positive impact on the shadow economy although their coefficients lack some precision as the level of significance is not so high.

A number of conclusions therefore appear from the estimation of the shadow economy model that are also important from a policy perspective: (i) the Ukrainian shadow economy appears to be highly inertial, (ii) institutional factors such as the complexity of the tax system, effective regulation and the general reform and liberalization process have an important impact on the size of the shadow economy, (iii) macroeconomic variables as inflation and the overall burden of taxation may have had some positive effect.

A model of the formal, informal and total Ukrainian economy

This section develops a small macro-economic model of the Ukrainian economy that can be used for macroeconomic analysis. In particular we want to use the macroeconomic model to analyze the effect of alternative scenarios concerning the size of the shadow economy on economic variables in the current economic situation in Ukraine.

The base of the model that will be estimated in this section consists of a small dynamic open economy AD-AS-LM model with price and wage dynamics. It consists of 11 macroeconomic relations plus a set of additional definitions. Table 12.6 gives the structure of the model: the starting point is the notion that the total economy (part (c)) consists of the official economy (part (a)) and the shadow economy (part (b)). Data are of course only available on the official economy and there is the estimate of the size of the shadow economy. Together they enable us in this way to derive the variables of the shadow economy and the total economy which is defined as the sum of the formal and informal economies.

All variables are in domestic currency, unless otherwise indicated. (1) gives real private consumption (*RCON*) as a function of real disposable income (*RYDP*) and the real interest rate (*RSIN*). Real consumption is obtained by deflating private consumption by the domestic price level, which is approximated by the GDP deflator (*PGDP*). Disposable income (*YDP*) is defined in a relatively crude way in (12) – for reasons of data-availability using GDP and fiscal balances. The real interest rate is defined in (15) as the nominal short-term interest rate (*SIN*), minus

---

[13] The complexity variable attains values between 0 and 1 and measures the inverse of complexity. Multiplying it by –1 yields a (negative) variable that measures complexity.

286 *The Periphery of the Euro*

inflation. *GDP* is defined in (13) as the sum of consumption (*CON*), investment (*INV*), net exports (*EXP–IMP*), government consumption (*GCO*), and inventory accumulation (*CIN*). (14) defines real consumption, real investment, real exports, real imports, real disposable income and real GDP.

Real private investment (*RINV*), (2) is assumed to depend on the real interest rate (by a cost-of-capital argument) and real output (by an 'accelerator' argument) (*RGDP*). Real exports (*REXP*) in (3) depend on competitiveness vis-à-vis the EU (*REUR*) – defined in (14) as the nominal euro exchange rate (*EUR*) times the relative output price level – and competitiveness vis-à-vis Russia (*RRBL*), EU real output (*RGDPEU*) and Russian real output (*RGDPRUS*). Similarly, real imports (*RIMP*) in (4) depend on competitiveness vis-à-vis the EU and Russia, domestic real output and the oil price (*OIL*).

Money market equilibrium/the LM curve is given in (5) as a function of real output and the nominal interest rate. The demand for foreign currency deposits is assumed to depend on domestic inflation according to (6). The money supply (*M2*) is determined by the workings of the money multiplier (*MMP*) on the stock of base money (*M0*). Base money itself consists, according to (18), of a domestic component – credit of the Central Bank to the banking sector (*CBC*), and to the government, (*CLG–CGD*) – and a foreign component – the foreign exchange reserves (*RES$*). Velocity (*VEL*), the money multiplier and dollarization (*DOL*) are defined in (17). Government revenues (*REV*) are related to output according to (7), government spending (*GEX*) will be held exogenous. The fiscal deficit (*DEF*) is defined in (23) as the difference between total government revenue (*REV*) and total government spending (*GEX*). Labour demand (*EMP*) in (8) is a function of (i) real output and (ii) the real producer wage (*RWAG*) corrected for productivity (*PRO*) which serves as a proxy of (real unit) labour costs. In (19), the real wage equals the nominal wage (*WAG*) deflated by the price level and productivity is defined as real GDP per employee. The supply of labour (*LAB*) is defined in (20) as the sum of employed and unemployed persons (*UNE*).

Wage inflation according to (9) is driven by increases in output prices – reflecting wage indexation, the level of unemployment – reflecting a Phillips-curve element, and changes in productivity. The last effect could reflect the pressure on wages (and thereby on prices) from the Balassa-Samuelson effect that is often thought to have significant inflationary impacts in accession countries and an important factor behind the trend real appreciation noticed in many countries. Increases of domestic prices in (10) are the result of wage increases, increases of foreign prices and increases in oil prices (which are three cost-push arguments) and the level of output (a business-cycle/demand-pull argument). The effect of foreign prices proxies the amount of (exchange-rate) pass-through in the economy.

Table 12.6   A small macro-economic model of Ukraine

(a) OFFICIAL ECONOMY	
$\log(RCON) = \alpha_0 + \alpha_1(RSIN) + \alpha_2\log(RYDP)$	(1)
$\log(RINV) = \beta_0 + \beta_1(RSIN) + \beta_2\log(RGDP)$	(2)
$\log(REXP) = \gamma_0 + \gamma_1\log(REUR) + \gamma_2\log(RRBL) + \gamma_3\log(RGDPEU) + \gamma_4\log(RGDPRUS)$	(3)
$\log(RIMP) = \delta_0 + \delta_1\log(REUR) + \delta_2\log(RRBL) + \delta_3\log(RGDP) + \delta_4\log(OIL)$	(4)
$\log(M2/PGDP) = \varsigma_0 + \varsigma_1 + \varsigma_2 SIN + \varsigma_3\log(RGDP)$	(5)
$\log(FCD/PGDP) = \varsigma_0 + \varsigma_1 + \varsigma_2 d\log(PGDP)$	(6)
$\log(REV) = \chi_0 + \chi_1\log(GDP)$	(7)
$\log(EMP) = \lambda_0 + \lambda_1\log(RGDP) + \lambda_2\log(RWAG/PRO)$	(8)
$d\log(WAG) = \nu_0 + \nu_1 d\log(PGDP) + \nu_2\log(UNE) + \nu_3 d\log(PRO)$	(9)
$d\log(PGDP) = \eta_0 + \eta_1 d\log(WAG) + \eta_2 d\log(EUR * PPIEU) + \eta_3 d\log(OIL) + \eta_4 d\log(RGDP)$	(10)
$SIN \equiv SINUSA + d\log(EXR) + RP$	(11)
$YDP \equiv GDP - REV + GEX - GCO$	(12)
$GDP \equiv CON + INV + EXP - IMP + GCO + CIN$	(13)
$RCON = \dfrac{CON}{PGDP}, RINV = \dfrac{INV}{PGDP}, REXP = \dfrac{EXP}{PGDP}, RIMP = \dfrac{IMP}{PGDP}, RYDP = \dfrac{YDP}{PGDP}, RGDP = \dfrac{GDP}{PGDP}$	(14)
$RSIN \equiv SIN - d\log(PGDP)$	(15)

$$EUR = EXR * EXREUR, RBL = EXR * EXRRUS, REUR = \frac{EUR * PPIEU}{PGDP}, RRBL = \frac{RBL * PPIRUS}{PGDP} \quad (16)$$

$$MMP = M2 / M0, VEL = GDP / M2, DOL = FCD / M2 \quad (17)$$

$$M0 \equiv CBC + CLG - CGD + RES\$ * EXR \quad (18)$$

$$BOP\$ \equiv CUA\$ + CAA\$ + FIA\$ + ERR\$ = d(RES\$) \quad (19)$$

$$CUA\$ \equiv (EXP - IMP) / EXR, FIA\$ \equiv FDI\$ - FDO\$ + OCF\$ \quad (20)$$

$$PRO = RGDP / EMP, RWAG = WAG / PGDP \quad (21)$$

$$LAB \equiv EMP + UNE \quad (22)$$

$$DEF \equiv REV - GEX \quad (23)$$

(b) SHADOW ECONOMY

$CONSH = CONTO - CON$	$RCONSH = CONSH / PGDP$
$INVSH = INVTO - INV$	$RINVSH = INVSH / PGDP$
$EXPSH = EXPTO - EXP$	$REXPSH = EXPSH / PGDP$
$IMPSH = IMPTO - IMP$	$RIMPSH = IMPSH / PGDP$
$WAGSH = WAGTO - WAG$	$RWAGSH = WAGSH / PGDP$
$GDPSH = GDPTO - GDP$	$RGDPSH = GDPSH / PGDP$
$YDPSH = YDPTO - YDP$	$RYDPSH = YDPSH / PGDP$
$LABSH = LABTO - LAB$	$EMPSH = EMPTO - EMP$
$UNESH = LABSH - EMPSH$	$PROSH = (GDPSH / PGDP) / EMPSH$

(24)

(c) TOTAL ECONOMY

$CONTO = 1/(1 - SHADOW) * CON$	$RCONTO = CONTO / PGDP$
$INVTO = 1/(1 - SHADOW) * INV$	$RINVTO = INVTO / PGDP$

$EXPTO = 1/(1 - SHADOW) * EXP$ $REXPTO = EXPTO / PGDP$

$IMPTO = 1/(1 - SHADOW) * IMP$ $RIMPTO = IMPTO / PGDP$

$WAGTO = 1/(1 - SHADOW) * WAG$ $RWAGTO = WAGTO / PGDP$

$GDPTO = 1/ (1 - SHADOW) * GDP$ $RGDPTO = GDPTO / PGDP$

$YDPTO = 1/ (1 - SHADOW) * YDP$ $RYDPTO = YDPTO / PGDP$

$LABTO = 1/(1 - SHADOW) * LAB$ $EMPTO = 1/(1 - SHADOW) * EMP$

$UNETO = LABTO - EMPTO$ $PROTO = (GDPTO / PGDP) / EMPTO$ (25)

$\log(RCONTO) = \alpha_0 ' + \alpha_1 (RSIN) + \alpha_2 \log(RYDPTO)$ (1')

$\log(RINVTO) = \beta_0 ' + \beta_1 (RSIN) + \beta_2 \log(RGDPTO)$ (2')

$\log(REXPTO) = \gamma_0 ' + \gamma_1 \log(REUR) + \gamma_2 \log(RRBL) + \gamma_3 \log(RGDP^{EU}) + \gamma_4 \log(RGDP^{RUS})$ (3')

$\log(RIMPTO) = \delta_0 ' + \delta_1 \log(REUR) + \delta_2 \log(RRBL) + \delta_3 \log(RGDPTO) + \delta_4 \log(OIL)$ (4')

$\log(M2 / PGDP) = \zeta_0 ' + \zeta_1 + \zeta_2 SIN + \zeta_3 \log(RGDPTO)$ (5')

$\log(EMPTO) = \lambda_0 ' + \lambda_1 \log(RGDPTO) + \lambda_2 \log(RWAGTO / PROTO)$ (8')

$d\log(WAGTO) = \nu_0 ' + \nu_1 d\log(PGDP) + \nu_2 \log(UNETO) + \nu_3 d\log(PROTO)$ (9')

$d\log(PGDP) = \eta_0 ' + \eta_1 d\log(WAGTO) + \eta_2 d\log(EUR * PPI^{EU}) + \eta_3 d\log(OIL) + \eta_4 d\log(RGDPTO)$ (10')

Interest rates and exchange rates are linked through the uncovered interest rate parity cum risk premium (*RP*) assumption (11). The balance of payments (*BOP*$, defined in bln US$) is defined in (19) as the sum of the current account (*CUA*$), capital account (*CAA*$), financial account (*FIA*$) and net errors and omissions (*ERR*$), matching the change in foreign exchange reserves. In (20), the current account equals exports of goods and services minus imports and the capital account equals net foreign direct investment (*FDI*$-*FDO*$) and other capital flows (*OCF*$), which in accession countries consists to a large extent of short-run portfolio capital flows. Both foreign direct investment and other capital flows remain exogenous in the model, for simplicity.

The variables in the shadow economy (extension *SH*) and total economy (extension *TO*) are calculated in (24) and (25) using the data of the official economy and the estimate of the size of the shadow economy. The variable *SHADOW* measures the size of the shadow economy as a fraction of total economy activity as explained in the previous section. Equations (1')–(5'), (8')-(10') of the total economy are estimated here rather than their equivalents of the official economy. Together with (6)-(7), these relations constitute the estimated part of the model. In this way we avoid the problem that when estimating (1)-(10) and using those relations in the model for simulation, the formal economy will not be interrelated with the shadow economy when simulating with the model. In that case a growth of the shadow economy keeps the formal sector constant and raises total output proportionally. In contrast, in the form of the model used here, changes in the shadow economy will lead to changes in the formal economy, but leave the total economy unaffected. This direct linking of the formal and informal economy is clearly a much more realistic setup of the model. Moreover, the model implicitly assumes in this way that the parameters (except for the constants $\alpha_0 - \eta_0$) in these relations will not differ between the official, shadow and total economy. This is done for simplicity and to keep the model tractable.

In Appendix A the definitions of the variables and the data sources are provided. Before performing the estimations the raw data were seasonally adjusted using the Census X12-method and tested on stationarity properties. Practically all variables appeared to be non-stationary. To take into consideration that variables are non-stationary, the structural equations of the model are estimated in the form of a vector error correction model (VECM) to distinguish short-term and long-term effects.[14] The estimation results are provided in Appendix B. Most estimations are

---

[14]   The VECM has the co-integration relations built into the specifications so that it restricts the long-run behaviour of the endogenous variables to converge to their co-integrating relationship while considering at the same time the short-run adjustment dynamics towards the long-run equilibrium. The co-integration term is known as the error-correction term since the deviation from long-run equilibrium is corrected gradually through a series of partial short-run adjustments. A VECM of a vector of endogenous variables *y* and exogenous variables *x* and of lag length 1 is written as:

quite satisfactory: most relations give some support for the theoretical notions underlying the model either in short-run or long-run or both, and the fit of most relations is acceptable.

The estimated structural relations yield – together with the set of definitions in the model – a small but concise macroeconomic model that provides an account of the goods, labour and money market. In most cases the structural relations could be estimated with some degree of acceptability and accuracy. Model simulation is now needed to assess the tracking ability of the estimated models. In its standard form, the model contains 26 exogenous variables (*CAA\$, CGD, CIN, CLB, CLG, ERR\$, EXREU, EXRRUS, FDI\$, FDO\$, FIA\$, GCO, GDPEU, GDPRUS, GEX, LAB, OCF\$, OIL, PPIEU, PPIRUS, RGDPEU, RGDPRUS, RP, SINUS, COMPLEX, EFFREGULATION*) and 68 endogenous variables (*BOP\$, CON, CONSH, CONTO, CUA\$, DEF, EMP, EMPSH, EMPTO, EXP, EXPSH, EXPTO, GDP, GDPSH, GDPTO, IMP, IMPSH, IMPTO, INV, INVSH, INVTO, M0, M2, MMP, PGDP, PRO, PROSH, PROTO, RCIN, RCON, RCONSH, RCONTO, RES\$, REUR, REV, REXP, REXPSH, REXPTO, RGCO, RGDP, RGDPSH, RGDPTO, RIMP, RIMPSH, RIMPTO, RINV, RINVSH, RINVTO, RRBL, RREV, RWAG, RWAGSH, RWAGTO, RYDP, RYDPSH, RYDPTO, SIN, UNE, UNETO, UNESH, VEL, WAG, WAGSH, WAGTO, YDP, YDPSH, YDPTO, SHADOW*).

Figure 12.2 provides a dynamic in-sample simulation of the model. The solid lines indicate the actual data, the dotted lines the simulated adjustment according to the model. The model is simulated for the three-year period 2000:IV-2003:IV. Dynamic simulation implies that the simulation model is provided the adjustment path of the exogenous variables plus the initial value of the endogenous variables in the model. It answers the question whether or not the model – given the adjustment of the exogenous variables – would predict comparable adjustment dynamics as those that have actually resulted. Dynamic simulations are an appropriate (and demanding) manner to assess the tracking ability of models.

In many cases the model tracks the main macroeconomic trends fairly well, in particular in the light of the still rather volatile macroeconomic adjustments in the Ukrainian economy during this period, as suggested by the actual data. There is some tendency to underestimate actual inflation and overestimate actual wage growth. This in its turn has some impact on the simulated (un)employment and other real variables. The simulation of the monetary side – apart from the underestimated dollarization, fiscal balance and the balance-of-payments adjustments seems adequate in particular. In frame (b) and (c) also the shadow

---

$$\Delta y_t = \alpha_0 + \alpha_1 y_{t-1} + \sum_{k=1}^{K} \beta_k x_{k,t-1} + \sum_{k=1}^{K} \delta_k \Delta x_{t-1} + \alpha_2 \Delta y_{t-1} + e_t$$

where e_t is a white noise error term. Coefficients from the long-term relationship can be calculated as $-\beta_k / \alpha_1$, the short-run effects are given by δ_k. Note that the estimation results in Appendix B, give β_k in the long-run estimation so that one has to multiply by $-1/\alpha_1$ to obtain long-run elasticities.

economy and total economy dynamics are shown. Overall, we see similar trends in the formal, informal and total economy, reflecting the observed slowly adjustment of the size of the shadow economy (see again Figure 12.1). Moreover, the model has some ability to track these patterns.

Next, we would like to carry out out-of-sample experiments using the model. In particular, we like to compare a s.c. 'pessimistic' scenario where the shadow economy increases again: during the period 2004-2008 it is assumed to increase its share of the total eonomy by 1 per cent each year. From the initial level of 32 per cent it thus reaches a value 37 per cent of total GDP by the end of 2008. In the 'optimistic' scenario, on the other hand, the shadow economy continues to decline. During the period 2004-2008 it is assumed to decrease its share of the total eonomy by 1 per cent each year. It reaches a value of 27 per cent of total GDP in 2008. A baseline scenario considers the case where the size of the shadow economy remains throughout the same period at its initial level of 32 per cent.

In the pessimistic scenario the following conditions, for example, could be expected to prevail: (i) no change in elite and resource-oriented policy (supply of inputs and protectionism), (ii) widespread rents and non-market incentives, (iii) external soft budget constraints: (a) soft fiscal policy (increase of budget and enterprise arrears, reliance on Treasury bills, writing-off debts, numerous regional and sector privileges), (b) soft monetary policy (the high level of growth of money supply), (c) soft political constraints (multi-vector orientation toward the West and Russia simultaneously).

The pessimistic view of development of Ukraine's economy means that piecemeal reforms will be conducted only under external pressure, and by the minimal possible extent necessary to escape an immediate crash. Having these rents the authorities will avoid structural changes in the economy. The selective approach for certain groups of taxpayers will not stimulate other enterprises to demonstrate profitability. The real budget revenues will go down, and authorities will rely on the old methods of covering budget deficit through the domestic Treasury bills, new arrears, external borrowing at high rates and so on. The business circles will not welcome such a policy. Evolution of the administrative control system will lead to the powering of executive branch, especially of its most bribe-intensive divisions. The high level of government interference in the economy will preserve high risks for doing business in Ukraine. Without sound improvements in the social and wage policy, rule of law, human rights, and so on, many dynamic and educated people will emigrate.

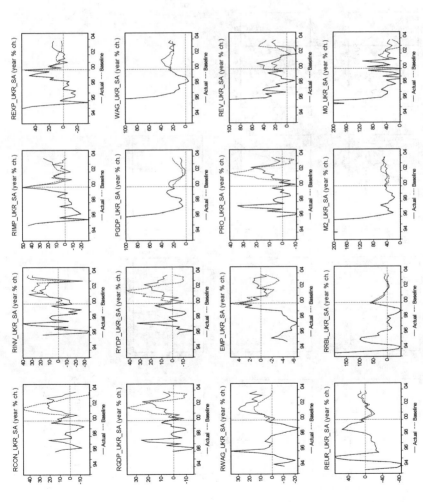

Figure 12.2 Adjustment in the Ukrainian economy: Actual (solid lines) vs simulation (dashed lines)

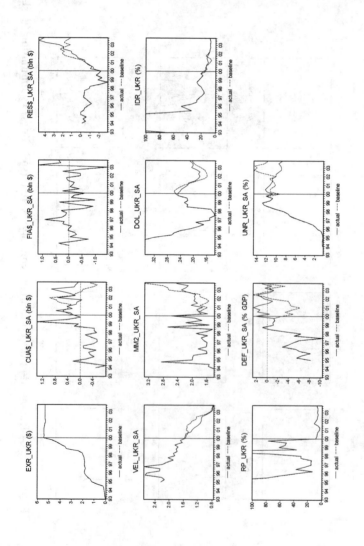

(a) Formal Economy

Figure 12.2 (cont.)

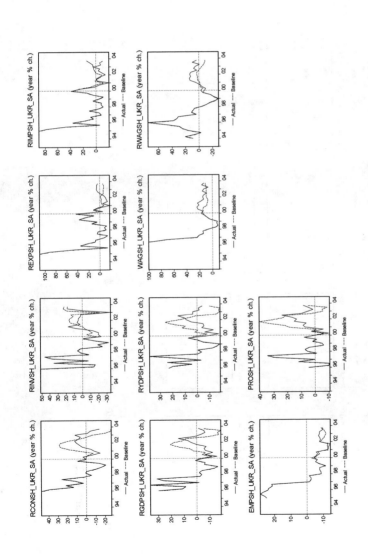

(b) Shadow Economy

Figure 12.2 (cont.)

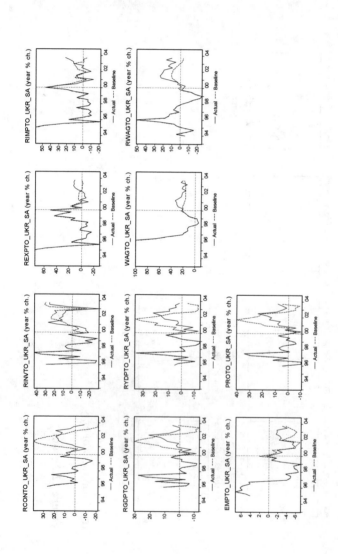

(c)   Total Economy

Figure 12.2 (cont.)

In the baseline scenario (the size of the shadow economy remains constant at 32 per cent) the following conditions are expected to dominate: (i) slow replacement of the old elite by more competent professionals, (ii) limited, slowly shrinking rents concentrated in a few sectors with restricted access, (iii) shrinking external soft budget constraints, (iv) domination of the market-oriented policy, (v) slow improvement in taxation and legislation business framework. The baseline scenario is based on somewhat stricter monetary and fiscal policy. Discretionary resource-oriented policy will continue, although at a lesser magnitude. Slowly shrinking sources of rents, particularly non-monetary payments and mutual offsets, will be limited. The ruling circles will somewhat harden the budget constraints, hence allowing market forces to operate more freely. However, protection of domestic producers will remain a priority and will be conducted through the case-by-case considerations (the personal meetings between producers and the Prime Minister). Government will still continue to interfere in the economy in favour of certain regions, sectors or specific enterprises (tax loopholes or free economic zones). The new market-oriented sectors will somewhat strengthen their positions due to better management and attraction of the more qualified Western-trained specialists.

The optimistic scenario could reflect the following conditions: (i) quick changes in elite, arrival of market-oriented professionals, (ii) tough restrictions on and elimination of the rent sources, (iii) fiscal, monetary and institutional policies with the emphasis on the right market incentives, as well as social safety development. The optimistic nature of this scenario could be based on a further expanding of policy reforms and structural changes in the economy. In addition, a policy of enhancement of the fiscal discipline will lead to a further increase of the budget revenues, successful fulfillment of the government obligations (first of all, elimination of wage, pension and other arrears) and consequently further improvement of the living standards of the population. At the same time, it will restrict rent seeking. The number of Western-educated and market-trained Ukrainians returning back to Ukraine will steadily grow, which will significantly improve the quality of management of government services and reduce the bureaucracy and bribery.

The following additional assumptions are used regarding the other exogenous variables:

Table 12.7   Baseline and alternative scenarios, 2004-2008

Baseline scenario 2004:1 2008:4	
CAA$: constant	*GCO* : 6% growth p.a.
CGD : constant	*GEX* : 6% growth p.a.
CIN : 0	*GDPEU* : 4% growth p.a.
CLB : constant	*PPIEU* : 2% growth p.a.
CLG : constant	*GDPRUS* : 8% growth p.a.
ERR$: 0	*PPIRUS* : 4% growth p.a.
EXREUR : constant	*LAB* : constant
EXRRUS : constant	*RP* : constant
EXR : constant	*SINUSA* : 2% p.a.
FDI$: 0.300	*OIL*: 33$
FDO$: 0	*WTR* : 6% growth p.a.
OCF$: 0	*SHADOW* : constant
Alternative scenarios 2004:1 2008:4	
Optimistic scenario: decrease *SHADOW* to 27%	
Pessimistic scenario: increase *SHADOW* to 37%	

The effects of the two different scenarios on the variables in the official, shadow and total economies are presented in figure 12.3. We present again the results for the formal, informal and total economy. The picture of the total economy reflects the underlying baseline scenario and is not affected by changes in the relative of shadow economy; by definition, the relative shadow economy affects the division of economic activity between the formal and informal sectors.

A number of interesting conclusions can be drawn from this exercise: (i) different scenarios of the relative size of the shadow economy have a significant influence on outputs in the goods markets, wages and employment in the labour markets, exports and imports as such changes in the relative size of the shadow economy basically imply a reallocation of activity between official and shadow economies. (ii) Government revenues have output in the formal economy as tax base in the model (and reality), as a result government revenues are higher in the optimistic scenario than in the pessimistic scenario as in the latter the tax bases slowly erode. (iii) The implications for monetary policy of such changes in the relative size of the shadow economy: inflation and monetary aggregates appear to be little effected by the different scenarios.

From a policy point of view, we conclude that the development of the shadow economy is of major importance for Ukraine's economy in the near future. Especially the reallocation effects between the formal and informal sector and the fiscal effects can be quite significant. Given its intertial nature found earlier, a large effort will be needed to reduce further its size.

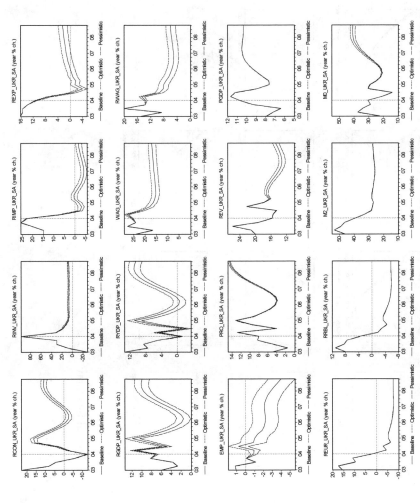

Figure 12.3 Adjustment in the baseline (solid), 'optimistic' (dotted) and 'pessimistic' (dashed) scenarios

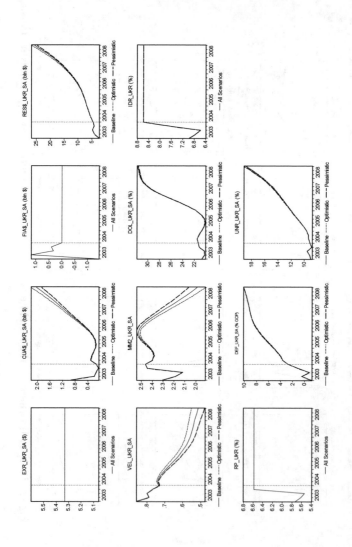

(a) Formal Economy

Figure 12.3 (cont.)

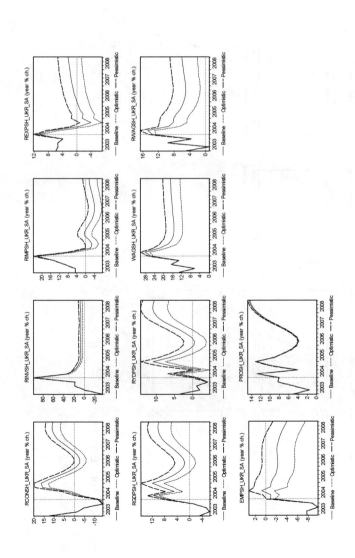

(b) Shadow Economy

Figure 12.3 (cont.)

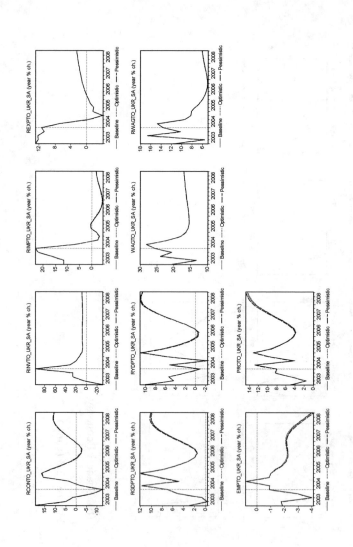

(c) Total Economy

Figure 12.3 (cont.)

Conclusion

During the period 1993-2004 Ukraine faced many difficulties and challenges connected with its transition from a planned economy to a market economy. Ukraine's transitional recession was among the deepest and most prolonged of the transition countries. Lack of coherent macroeconomic policies resulted in hyperinflation and currency crises. In contrast with the stagnation and decline of the official economy, activity in the unofficial economy increased considerably. The share of Ukraine's unofficial economy reached 67 per cent of official GDP on average for the 1997-1998 period. Since then unofficial economy has declined, parallel with the process of more economic stability and economic growth.

In a number of studies, Ukraine still has one of the largest shares of unofficial economy among the CIS, Baltics, and CEE countries. It appears that an excessive taxation and burdensome regulation are the main sources of the Ukrainian high shadow sector and have a significant influence on the size of unofficial economy.

This study developed a small dynamic open economy AD-AS-LM model of the official and unofficial sector of the Ukrainian economy. We investigated the effects of the two different scenarios of the size of unofficial activity on the variables in the official, shadow and total economies.

A number of conclusions were drawn from this analysis: (i) both the official economy and the shadow economy have the same general trends, (ii) in case the relative size of the shadow economy changes, the relocation of employment and activity between the formal and informal economies takes place, (iii) different scenarios have a significant influence on the labour market, export and import in both official and shadow economies.

The shadow economy and its effects will necessarily play an important role in the many challenges and high expectations that the new Yushchenko government is facing after its election victory.

Appendix A: Data sources and definitions

The following data have been used in the analysis:

Table A.12.1   Variables and data sources

Variable	Name	Units	Source
CON	Private consumption	bln n.c., quarterly	IMF IFS line 96F..ZF and nat.stat.off.
RCON	Real consumption	bln n.c., quarterly	calculated as $RCON \equiv CON/PGDP$
PPI	Producer price index	1995=100	IMF IFS line 63...ZF
SIN	Money market interest rate	%	IMF IFS line 60B..ZF
YDP	Disposable income	bln n.c., quarterly	calculated as $YDP \equiv GDP-REV+GEX-GCO$
RYDP	Real disposable income	bln n.c., quarterly	calculated as $RYDP \equiv YDP/PPI$
INV	Gross fixed capital formation	bln n.c., quarterly	IMF IFS line 93E..ZF and nat.stat.off.
GDP	Gross domestic product	bln n.c., quarterly	calculated as $GDP \equiv CON+INV+EXP-IMP+CIN+GCO$
PGDP	GDP deflator	1995=100	
RGDP	Real gross domestic product	bln n.c., quarterly	calculated as $RGDP \equiv GDP/PPI$
EXP	Exports of goods and services	bln n.c., quarterly	IMF IFS line 90C..ZF and nat.stat.off.
REXP	Real exports	bln n.c., quarterly	calculated as $REXP \equiv EXP/PPI$
EUR	Exchange rate vs euro	per.avg	calculated from IMF IFS line ..RF.ZF
REUR	Real exchange rate vs euro	per.avg	calculated as $REUR \equiv EUR*PPIEU/PGDP$
WTR	World trade	bln US$	calculated from IMF IFS
IMP	Imports of goods and services	bln n.c., quarterly	IMF IFS line 98C..ZF and nat.stat.off.
RIMP	Real imports	bln n.c., quarterly	calculated as $RIMP \equiv IMP/PPI$
OIL	Oil price	$ per barrel	IMF IFS line
M2	Money, M2	bln n.c	IMF IFS line 35...ZF and nat.stat.off.

EMP	Employment	1000	IMF IFS line 67E..ZF and nat.stat.off.
WAG	Wages	n.c., quarterly	IMF IFS line 65...ZF and nat.stat.off.
UNE	Unemployment	1000	IMF IFS line 67C..ZF and nat.stat.off.
REV	Government revenue	bln n.c., quarterly	IMF IFS line 81...ZF and nat.stat.off.
GEX	Government expenditure	bln n.c., quarterly	IMF IFS line 82...ZF and nat.stat.off.
GCO	Government consumption	bln n.c., quarterly	IMF IFS line 91F..ZF and nat.stat.off.
CIN	Change in inventories	bln n.c., quarterly	IMF IFS line 93L..ZF and nat.stat.off.
RES$	Foreign exchange reserves	bln $	calculated from IMF IFS line .1L.DZF
CUA$	Trade balance	bln $, quarterly	calculated as $CUA \equiv (EXP-IMP)/EUR$
CAA$	Capital account	bln $, quarterly	calculated from IMF IFS line 78BJDZF
FDI$	Foreign direct investment	bln $, quarterly	calculated from IMF IFS line 78BEDZF
OCF$	Other capital flows	bln $, quarterly	calculated as $OCF \equiv CAA-FDI$
M0	Base money, M0	bln n.c., quarterly	IMF IFS line 14..ZF and nat.stat.off.
CBC	Central Bank credit to banks	bln n.c., quarterly	IMF IFS line 12E..ZF
CLG	Central Bank lending to govt.	bln n.c., quarterly	IMF IFS line 12A..ZF
CGD	Deposits govt. at CB	bln n.c., quarterly	IMF IFS line 16D..ZF
LAB	Labour force	1000	calculated as $LAB \equiv EMP + UNE$
SHADOW	Shadow economy	% total economy	Dherzhkomstat and Ministery of Economic Affairs
EBRDIN DEX	Overall Index of reforms	index	EBRD
COMPLE X	Complexity of tax system		Mel'ota, Thiesen and Vakhnenko (2001)
EFFREG ULATION	Effective regulatory burden		Mel'ota, Thiesen and Vakhnenko (2001)

Appendix B: Estimation results

Vector Error Correction Estimates
Sample(adjusted): 1995:3-2003:4
Included observations: 34 after adjusting endpoints, t-statistics in [ ]

Cointegrating Eq:	CointEq1
LOG(RCONTO(-1))	1.00
SIN(-1)/100-DLOG(PGDP(-1))	0.89
	[7.72]
LOG(RYDPTO(-1))	-0.92
	[-126.72]
Error Correction:	D(LOG(RCONTO))
CointEq1	-0.48
	[-3.12]
D(LOG(RCONTO(-1)))	0.75
	[3.59]
D(SIN(-1)/100-DLOG(PGDP(-1)))	-0.07
	[-0.70]
D(LOG(RYDPTO(-1)))	-0.22
	[-1.51]
R-squared	0.66
Adj. R-squared	0.57
Sum sq. resides	0.06
S.E. equation	0.05
F-statistic	7.13
Mean dependent	0.01
S.D. dependent	0.07

(a) Real consumption (1')

Vector Error Correction Estimates
Sample(adjusted): 1995:3-2003:4
Included observations: 34 after adjusting endpoints, t-statistics in [ ]

Cointegrating Eq:	CointEq1
LOG(RINVTO(-1))	1.00
SIN(-1)/100-DLOG(PGDP(-1))	10.64
	[7.90]
LOG(RGDPTO(-1))	-1.09
	[-10.16]
Error Correction:	D(LOG(RINVTO))
CointEq1	-0.11
	[-5.08]
D(LOG(RINVTO(-1)))	0.06
	[0.45]
D(SIN(-1)/100-DLOG(PGDP(-1)))	-0.01
	[-0.03]
D(LOG(RGDPTO(-1)))	0.01
	[0.04]
R-squared	0.85
Adj. R-squared	0.79
Sum sq. resides	0.17
S.E. equation	0.08
F-statistic	14.99
Mean dependent	0.01
S.D. dependent	0.18

(b) Real investment (2')

Vector Error Correction Estimates
Sample(adjusted): 1995:1-2003:4
Included observations: 36 after adjusting endpoints, t-statistics in [ ]

Cointegrating Eq:	CointEq1
LOG(REXPTO(-1))	1.00
LOG(REUR(-1))	-0.38
	[-1.80]
LOG(RRBL(-1))	-0.17
	[-1.13]
LOG(GDPEU(-1)/PPIEU(-1))	-8.78
	[-9.07]
LOG(GDPRUS(-1)/PPI_RUS(-1))	2.37
	[5.12]

Error Correction:	D(LOG(REXPTO))
CointEq1	-0.11
	[-1.82]
D(LOG(REXPTO(-1)))	-0.35
	[-2.92]
D(LOG(REUR(-1)))	-0.22
	[-2.08]
D(LOG(RRBL(-1)))	0.10
	[0.85]
D(LOG(GDPEU(-1)/PPIEU(-1)))	-0.60
	[-0.41]
D(LOG(GDPRUS(-1)/PPIRUS(-1)))	0.06
	[0.18]

R-squared	0.81
Adj. R-squared	0.75
Sum sq. resides	0.10
S.E. equation	0.06
F-statistic	13.99
Mean dependent	0.02
S.D. dependent	0.12

(c) Real exports (3')

Vector Error Correction Estimates
Sample(adjusted): 1995:3-2003:4
Included observations: 34 after adjusting endpoints, t-statistics in [ ]

Cointegrating Eq:	CointEq1
LOG(RIMPTO(-1))	1.00
LOG(REUR(-1))	-0.69
	[-8.87]
LOG(RRBL(-1))	0.09
	[1.66]
LOG(RGDPTO(-1))	-0.34
	[-6.66]
LOG(OIL(-1))	-0.31
	[-8.11]

Error Correction:	D(LOG(RIMPTO))
CointEq1	-0.39
	[-3.43]
D(LOG(RIMPTO(-1)))	0.18
	[1.49]
D(LOG(REUR(-1)))	0.11
	[1.01]
D(LOG(RRBL(-1)))	0.38
	[3.84]
D(LOG(RGDPTO(-1)))	-0.06
	[-0.62]
D(LOG(OIL(-1)))	-0.08
	[-0.83]

R-squared	0.75
Adj. R-squared	0.66
Sum sq. resides	0.05
S.E. equation	0.04
F-statistic	8.03
Mean dependent	0.01
S.D. dependent	0.08

(d) Real imports (4')

Vector Error Correction Estimates
Sample(adjusted): 1995:3-2003:4
Included observations: 34 after adjusting endpoints, t-statistics in []

Cointegrating Eq:	CointEq1
LOG($M2$(-1)/$PGDP$(-1))	1.00
SIN(-1)/100	9.76
	[6.32]
LOG($RGDPTO$(-1))	-1.59
	[-12.99]

Error Correction:	D(LOG($M2$*100/$PGDP$))
CointEq1	-0.03
	[-3.85]
D(LOG($M2$(-1)/$PGDP$(-1)))	0.25
	[1.94]
D(SIN(-1)/100)	-0.05
	[-0.98]
D(LOG($RGDPTO$(-1)))	0.17
	[2.43]
R-squared	0.83
Adj. R-squared	0.78
Sum sq. resides	0.02
S.E. equation	0.03
F-statistic	15.21
Mean dependent	0.04
S.D. dependent	0.06

(e) Money demand (5')

Vector Error Correction Estimates
Sample(adjusted): 1995:3-2003:4
Included observations: 34 after adjusting endpoints, t-statistics in []

Cointegrating Eq:	CointEq1
LOG(FCD(-1)/$PGDP$(-1))	1.00
DLOG($PGDP$(-1))	-3.33
	[-9.90]
@TREND(92:1)	-0.06
	[-23.13]
C	1.87

Error Correction:	D(LOG(FCD/$PGDP$))
CointEq1	-0.26
	[-4.16]
D(LOG(FCD(-1)/$PGDP$(-1)))	0.53
	[6.60]
D(LOG(FCD(-2)/$PGDP$(-2)))	0.41
	[6.37]
D(DLOG($PGDP$(-1)))	-0.69
	[-4.72]
D(DLOG($PGDP$(-2)))	-0.13
	[-0.92]
R-squared	0.94
Adj. R-squared	0.91
Sum sq. resids	0.03
S.E. equation	0.04
F-statistic	31.30
Mean dependent	0.03
S.D. dependent	0.12

(f) Foreign currency demand (6')

Vector Error Correction Estimates
Sample(adjusted): 1995:3-2003:4
Included observations: 34 after adjusting endpoints, t-statistics in [ ]

Cointegrating Eq:	CointEq1
LOG(REV(-1)/$PGDP$(-1))	1.00
LOG(GDP(-1)/$PGDP$(-1))	-0.56
	[-29.17]

Error Correction:	D(LOG(REV//$PGDP$))
CointEq1	-0.23
	[-2.39]
D(LOG(REV(-1)/$PGDP$(-1)))	-0.01
	[-0.07]
D(LOG(GDP(-1)/$PGDP$(-1)))	0.25
	[2.11]
R-squared	0.75
Adj. R-squared	0.68
Sum sq. resids	0.07
S.E. equation	0.05
F-statistic	11.04
Mean dependent	-0.002
S.D. dependent	0.10

(g) Government revenue (7')

Vector Error Correction Estimates
Sample(adjusted): 1995:3-2003:4
Included observations: 34 after adjusting endpoints, t-statistics in [ ]

Cointegrating Eq:	CointEq1
LOG($EMPTO$(-1))	1.00
LOG($RGDPTO$(-1))	1.04
	[5.99]
LOG($RWAGTO$(-1)/$PROTO$(-1))	-0.38
	[-4.14]

Error Correction:	D(LOG($EMPTO$))
CointEq1	-0.04
	[-1.37]
D(LOG($EMPTO$(-1)))	0.10
	[0.75]
D(LOG($RGDPTO$(-1)))	-0.01
	[-0.16]
D(LOG($RWAGTO$(-1)/$PROTO$(-1)))	-0.076
	[-1.55]
R-squared	0.71
Adj. R-squared	0.65
Sum sq. resids	0.01
S.E. equation	0.01
F-statistic	11.03
Mean dependent	-0.01
S.D. dependent	0.02

(h) labour demand (8')

Vector Error Correction Estimates
Sample(adjusted): 1995:4-2003:4
Included observations: 33 after adjusting endpoints, t-statistics in [ ]

Cointegrating Eq:	CointEq1
DLOG(WAGTO(-1))	1.00
DLOG(PGDP(-1))	-3.15
	[-2.06]
LOG(UNETO(-1))	0.03
	[2.62]
DLOG(PROTO(-1))	-11.00
	[-8.77]

Error Correction:	D(DLOG(WAGTO))
CointEq1	-0.05
	[-2.54]
D(DLOG(WAGTO(-1)))	-0.25
	[-1.48]
D(DLOG(PGDP(-1)))	0.19
	[0.71]
D(LOG(UNETO(-1)))	-0.12
	[-2.24]
D(DLOG(PROTO(-1)))	-0.22
	[-1.78]

R-squared	0.24
Adj. R-squared	0.17
Sum sq. resids	0.11
S.E. equation	0.06
F-statistic	2.64
Mean dependent	-0.01
S.D. dependent	0.07

(i) Wages (9')

Vector Error Correction Estimates
Sample(adjusted): 1995:3-2003:4
Included observations: 34 after adjusting endpoints, t-statistics in [ ]

Cointegrating Eq:	CointEq1
DLOG(PGDP(-1))	1.00
DLOG(WAGTO(-1))	0.54
	[5.32]
DLOG(EUR(-1))+DLOG(PPIEU(-1))	-0.73
	[-5.60]
DLOG(OIL(-1))	0.04
	[0.58]
LOG(RGDPTO(-1))	-0.02
	[-4.22]

Error Correction:	D(DLOG(PGDP))
CointEq1	-0.41
	[-10.05]
D(DLOG(PGDP(-1)))	-0.22
	[-3.01]
D(DLOG(WAGTO(-1)))	0.32
	[6.45]
D(DLOG(EUR(-1))+DLOG(PPIEU(-1)))	-0.02
	[-0.48]
D(DLOG(OIL(-1)))	0.02
	[1.10]
D(LOG(RGDPTO(-1)))	-0.01
	[-0.30]

R-squared	0.93
Adj. R-squared	0.90
Sum sq. resids	0.01
S.E. equation	0.02
F-statistic	35.74
Mean dependent	0.01
S.D. dependent	0.05

(j) Prices (10')

References

Berg, A., Borenztein, E., Sahay, R., and Zettelmeyer, J. (1999), 'The Evolution of Output in Transition Economies: Explaining the Differences', *IMF Working Paper* WP/99/73.

Christoffersen, P., and Doyle, P. (2000), 'From Inflation to Growth. Eight Years of Transition', *Economics of Transition*, 8, 2: 421-51.

Clotfelter, C.T. (1983), 'Tax Evasion and Tax Rates: An Analysis of Individual Returns', *The Review of Economics and Statistics*, LXV, 3: 362-73.

Coricelli, F. (1998), *Macroeconomic Policies and Development of Markets in Economies in Transition*, Central European University Press/Oxford University Press.

Dobozi, I. and Pohl, G. (1996), 'Real Output Decline in Transition Economies – Forget GDP, Try Power Consumption Data', *Transition Newsletter*, 6, 1-2: 17-18, World Bank: Washington, DC.

Eilat, Y. and Zinnes, C. (2002), 'The Evolution of the Shadow Economy in Transition Countries: Consequences for Economic Growth and Donor Assistance', *CAER II Discussion Paper* no. 83.

Feige, E.L. (1979), *How Big is the Irregular Economy?*, *Challenge*, 22: 5-13.

Fischer. S., Sahay, R., and Vegh, C. (1996), 'Stabilization and Growth in Transition Economies: The Early Experience', *Journal of Economic Perspectives*, 10, 2: 45-66.

Gregory, P. and Mel'ota, I. (2001), 'New Insights into Ukraine's Shadow Economy: Has it Already Been Counted?', *Working Paper*, Institute of Economic Research and Policy Consulting, Kiev.

Gronicki, M. and Pietka, K. (1999), 'Macroeconomic Model for Ukraine', *Working Paper* (No. 190), Center for Social and Economic Research, Warsaw.

Guriev, S. and Barry, I. (2000), 'Barter in Russian Firms', in P. Seabright (ed.), *The Vanishing Ruble: Barter and Currency Substitution in Postcommunist Economie*, Cambridge: Cambridge University Press.

Guttmann, P.M. (1997), 'Subterranean Economy', *Financial Analysts Journal*, 33 (1997): 26-7.

Havrylyshyn, O. (1999), 'The State of the State: A Fiscal Perspective on State Formation and Transformation in Ukraine and Other Countries of the Former Soviet Union', *Working Paper*, European University Institute, Florence, <www.lse.ac.uk/collections/EPIC/>

Hill, R. and Kabir, M. (1996), 'Tax Rates, the Tax Mix, and the Growth of the Underground Economy in Canada: What Can We Infer?', *Canadian Tax Journal*, 44, 6: 1552-83.

ICPS (2003), 'Economic Modelling and Forecasting Project in Ukraine',

Johnson, S., Kaufmann, D. and Shleifer, A. (1997), 'The Unofficial Economy in Transition,' *Brookings Papers on Economic Activity*, 2: 159-239.

Johnson, S., Kaufmann, D. and Zoido-Lobodan, P. (1998), 'Regulatory Discretion and the Unofficial Economy', *American Economic Review*, Papers and Proceedings, 88: 387-92.

Johnson, S., Kaufmann, D., McMillan, J. and Woodruff, C. (1999), 'Why Do Firms Hide? Bribes and Unofficial Activity after Communism', *Programme of Policy Studies for Project Preparation and Appraisal, Working Paper 42*, European Bank for Reconstruction and Development.

Kaufmann, D. and Kaliberda, A. (1996), 'Integrating the Unofficial Economy into the Dynamics of post-Socialist Economies: A Framework of Analysis and Evidence,' *Policy Research Working Paper* no. 1691, World Bank.

Kudina, A. (2000), 'An Approach to Forecasting Ukrainian GDP from the Supply Side', *CASE Working Paper* no.196.

Lacko, M. (1998), 'The Hidden Economies of Visegrad Countries in International Comparison: A Household Electricity Approach', in L. Halpern and Ch. Wyplosz (eds), *Hungary: Towards a Market Economy*, Cambridge, Mass.: Cambridge University Press, pp.128-52.

Lacko, M. (2000), 'Hidden Economy – An Unknown Quantity? Comparative Analysis of Hidden Economies in Transition Countries, 1989-95', *Economics of Transition*, 8, 1.

Mel'ota I., Thiesen, U. and Vakhnenko, T. (2001), Fiscal and Regulatory Causes of the Shadow Economy in Transition Countries: The Case of Ukraine, *Institute for Economic Research Policy Consulting*, <www.ierpc.kiev.ua/>.

Schneider, F. (1997), 'The Shadow Economies of Western Europe', *Journal of the Institute of Economic Affairs*, 17, 3: 42-8.

Schneider, F. (2000), 'The Increase of the Size of the Shadow Economy of 18 OECD-Countries: Some Preliminary Explanations', *Paper presented at the Annual Public Choice Meeting*, 10-12 March 2000, Charleston, S.C.

Schneider, F. (2003), 'The Development of the Shadow Economies and Shadow Labour Force of 21 OECD and 22 Transition Countries', *CESifo Dice Report* 1/2003.

Schneider, F. and Dominik, E. (2000), 'Shadow Economies: Size, Causes, and Consequences', *The Journal of Economic Literature*, 38, 1: 77-114.

Schneider, F. and Neck, R. (1993), 'Shadow Economy under Changing Tax Systems and Structures', *Finanzarchiv*, Band 50, pp. 344-68.

State Committee of Statistics of Ukraine (2003), *Quarterly National Account of Ukraine in 1994-2002*, Kiev.

Tanzi, V. (1983), 'The Underground Economy in the United States: Annual Estimates, 1930-80', *International Monetary Fund Staff Papers*, 30: 283-305.

Wagner, R.E. (1976), 'Revenue Structure, Fiscal Illusion and Budgetary Choice', *Public Choice*, 25: 45-61.

Chapter 13

Determinants of Inflation in Ukraine: A Cointegration Approach

Nina Leheyda

Introduction

The transition from a centrally planned to a market economy in the countries of the former Soviet Union and transition economies of Central and Eastern Europe has been characterized by the movement from the periods of high inflation and real output decline towards macroeconomic stabilization. The transition process foresees a full rearrangement of the economic relationships, in particular, requires a new structure of the relative prices. Therefore, monetary overhang and urgent need for price liberalization were characteristic for most transition economies in the early 1990s. Ukraine witnessed one of the highest rates of inflation in the early 1990s – about 10,000 per cent in 1993. By 2001, the single digit inflation rates were recorded in most of the transition economies (Fisher, Sahay, 2001).

Ten stylized facts about prices in transition are being discussed in Koen and de Masi (1997). In particular, the price liberalization led to the initial sharp price growth, which was followed by a long period of relatively high inflation. The 'core' inflation was influenced by seasonality and administrative interference. The prices of tradable goods moved rapidly towards the world levels. The prices for services did not grow as fast as many of them were kept under administrative control because of social considerations. The relative prices across transition economies have been converging gradually. By the later stages of the transition process, the inflation rates subsided and inflation stabilization is considered one of the major achievements of the transition period.

In this chapter, the focus is on the inflationary processes in Ukraine during the last few years. Ukraine does not have a formal inflation-targeting framework for monetary policy. However, in the 'Main Guidelines on Monetary Policy for 2004' (National Bank of Ukraine, 2003), it is spelled out that conditions will be created for the gradual movement to targeting inflation. Currently, exchange rate stability is considered to be the goal of monetary policy by the National Bank of Ukraine (NBU). However, the control of monetary factors over the inflationary processes is also mentioned among the key current priorities of monetary policy.

Although in mature economies the interest rate is a major instrument of monetary policy, in Ukraine, as in other transition economies, this instrument has been argued to be weak, and the monetary policy is rather focused on controlling monetary aggregates. The intermediate targets of monetary policy in Ukraine are money supply (level and growth rate), monetary base (level and growth rate) and the amount of loans to the real sector. However, there should be a well-specified and stable relationship between money and prices in order to achieve price stability through controlling monetary aggregates.

The existence of the homogenous relationship has become questionable in recent years as there has been a considerable gap between the growth rates of money supply and inflation, which even widened during 2001-2003. For instance, in 2003 the consumer prices grew by 8.2 per cent year-on-year (yoy) end-of-period (eop), while the monetary base and money supply increased by 31.9 per cent and 46.9 per cent yoy eop, respectively, and the real output went up by 9.4 per cent.

The closer relationship between prices and money can be broken under the circumstances of the rapid demand growth for real cash balances and remonetization of the economy, as a result of which the simple quantity theory of money will not hold. Of course, the latter theory tells us predictions only about the long-run, and nothing about the short-run effects. Besides, in reality, there could be a lag between money and prices, which should be taken into account while setting up a policy to control inflation.

On this background and in the light of the positive macroeconomic changes in the country, I pose the following questions. Is there any stable relationship between money and prices? Which factors (monetary or non-monetary) could explain more precisely the movements in prices? What are the short-term and long-term effects on prices? Could any implications be drawn for the monetary transmission mechanisms and conducting monetary policy in Ukraine?

To answer the above questions, the cointegration approach following Juselius (1992) and Metin (1995) is applied. The authors used cointegration techniques to trace the sectoral sources of inflation: monetary, labour and foreign and then use the short-run equation with the error-correction terms from the different sectors to evaluate the sources of Danish and Turkish inflation, respectively. Under this approach, inflation is viewed as a result of the excess demand in the different markets.

The long-run money demand, purchasing power parity and mark-up relationships were found to govern prices in the long-run. In the short-run, inflation inertia, money supply, wages, exchange rate and real output as well as some exogenous shocks influence inflation dynamics.

The structure of the chapter is as follows. After a brief description of monetary policy and price developments in Ukraine, I review some empirical evidence for transition economies and previous research for Ukraine in this field. Further, I develop a simple theoretical framework of inflation, discuss the estimation procedure and present the estimation results. The chapter concludes with policy implications.

Monetary policy and price developments in Ukraine

Inflation and exchange rate developments

Through 1991-2003 Ukraine has moved from the extremely high inflation rates at the start of the transition process to the moderate inflation rates starting in 2001. The history of Ukrainian inflation can be roughly divided into the following four periods:[1]

1. *1991-1994*: This is a period of hyperinflation following the price liberalization. The inflation rate reached its peak of more than 10,000 per cent in 1993. High budget deficits were recorded that were almost fully monetized.
2. *1995-first half of 1998*: During this period, the inflation rate was gradually reduced to 10 per cent in 1997 notwithstanding the significant rise in the administered prices for services in 1995-1996. The fiscal adjustment allowed reducing the budget deficit to 5 per cent of GDP in 1995. In September 1996, a new national currency, hryvnia, was introduced. This, together with the other factors, contributed to the exchange rate stabilization and price stability. The fixed exchange rate, however, resulted in the hryvnia appreciation and, finally, in the worsening of the external current account. This led to a loss in the international reserves, which caused the monetary expansion and inflation. The fiscal position became unsustainable, as the Government borrowed heavily in the domestic debt market through selling t-bills and at the international capital markets under short maturity and high interest rates. The sharp depreciation followed Russia's August 1998 default with a consequent upsurge in inflation.
3. *End of 1998-first half of 2000*: Following the crises, the strict regulations on the foreign exchange market were introduced from September 1998 to March 1999. In the middle of 1999, the increase in the international oil and gasoline prices led to the hryvnia devaluation that evoked inflation. There was also another depreciation spike at the end of 1999, which could be attributed to the loose macroeconomic policies. The nominal exchange rate stabilized only in early 2000. In February 2000, a floating exchange rate regime was announced. However, to keep the nominal exchange rate stable, the NBU has intervened in the interbank foreign exchange market.

   Rather high inflation in 2000 can be explained by the rise towards the cost-recovery levels in the administered prices for municipal services and staples in the first half of 2000. The substantial increases in food prices, especially bread, were caused by the poor harvests in 1999-2000.
4. *Second half of 2000-present*: There has been a stable exchange rate that contributed to the increased trust of the population towards the national currency. Lower expectations about the future exchange rate may have led to

---

[1] A detailed overview of Ukraine's inflation performance can be found in Lissovolik (2003).

lower expectations towards future prices, which could have contributed to inflation stabilization. Some inflation inertia could be attributed to the backward-looking expectations and price controls. Notwithstanding the expansionary monetary policy, single-digit inflation rates were recorded in 2001-2003. The inflation rate went down to only 6 per cent in 2001, while in 2002 a decrease of 0.6 per cent in the consumer prices was recorded. Good 2001-2002 harvests led to low food prices. In 2003, consumer prices grew by 8.2 per cent yoy, which, to a large extent, can be attributed to the poor harvest and the associated panic and speculation in the grain and bread products market. The prices for bread and flour were first administered and then liberalized.

Wage growth should be viewed as a potential determinant of inflation in Ukraine, when it is not backed by productivity growth. Recently, there have been several upward adjustments in the minimum wages, which are an indicative salary floor for many employers and sectors.

During the last few years the positive trade balance fostered the inflow of foreign currency and allowed the NBU to accumulate high foreign exchange reserves. A strong increase in the money demand did not require the full sterilization of the increased money supply and prevented fuelling inflation. The velocity of money has reduced in Ukraine, which may be attributed to different factors. These are, first of all, the factors that influence the liquidity preferences for the transactions and precautionary demand for money: declining opportunity cost of money, de-dollarization, remonetization; financial instruments changes (increased trust in the banking sector, new financial instruments – for example, ATM cards); better predictions concerning future money value; macrostabilization, improved financial discipline and corporate governance, and so on.

Price statistics in Ukraine

The price statistics for Ukraine include the calculation of CPI, producer price index (PPI) and GDP deflator by the State Statistics Committee of Ukraine.[2]

CPI is the most important index used for policy-making and business decisions. It comprises the three major components: the prices for food products, non-food products and services. Their weights are chosen based on the results of the households survey (IER, 2001) and vary from time to time. The weight for food products is 50-70 per cent, the shares of non-food products and services range between 15 and 30 per cent. Thus, the volatility in the CPI index can be to a large degree attributed to the volatility and seasonality in the food prices (in particular,

---

[2]   In this section I just give a brief overview of the price indexes in Ukraine and point out those features that could be important for further estimation. A good description of the price indexes and measurement problems can be found in Revenko (2002) and Lissovolik (2003).

summer deflation). Food prices are influenced mostly by the agroclimatic conditions, domestic inputs and import prices.

The price changes of both domestically produced and imported goods are reflected in the CPI. The prices for domestically produced goods constitute 92 per cent and 62 per cent of the food and non-food prices, respectively.

The prices for the non-food products are the most stable, with the exception of a few outliers. The rise in the prices in September-October 1998 reflects the consequences of the Russian August 1998 financial crisis. The spike in July 1999 mirrors the rise in the international oil and gasoline prices. In fact, the most volatile component of the non-food products are the prices for gasoline but this is true only for 1998-1999, which may be explained by the pass-through from the external shocks.

The prices for services have been also rather stable during the last several years. The services prices are mostly not market-determined, and are subject to the administrative decisions. In 1999-2000, there have been several upward adjustments in the prices for the municipal services towards the cost-recovery levels. The prices for services still remain a potential threat for future inflation as they have not been raised fully to the cost-recovery levels.

PPI includes the export goods as well as the goods sold in domestic markets. The monthly changes in the PPI do not follow any clear pattern, which is why the dynamics of the PPI are very difficult to predict. The weight of the major industries such as energy, ferrous metals, chemical, machine-building and food industries is about 80 per cent in the PPI. The shares of the prices for the ferrous metals, food industry and light industry products in the PPI are 24 per cent, 15 per cent and 1 per cent, respectively (IER, 2001).

The GDP deflator is calculated in Ukraine using 80 per cent of the CPI and 20 per cent of the PPI as weights. It could probably be the best inflation indicator, however, it is difficult to estimate it correctly.

Empirical evidence

Macroeconomic models for transition countries

The empirical literature on inflation is really vast: a large number of studies can be found for advanced economies as well as for transition and developing economies.

Given the large number of empirical studies on the inflation and econometric techniques being used, this literature review focuses only on those papers related to transition economies, which use the cointegration approach in studying the inflation determinants (anyway, this is actually the mainstream of all recent inflation studies), which allows us to study several sources of inflation simultaneously.[3]

There exists a number of inflation studies for Russia. In one of the earlier works (Korhonen, 1998), the author has studied the relationship between inflation and money supply growth. The effect of the monetary expansion was felt within three months. In the later studies on Russia, it was also found that inflation is caused by money growth (for example, Ohnsorge and Oomes, 2004).

The empirical studies on the advanced transition economies show that the impact of monetary policy upon inflation is rather restricted from either monetary aggregates or interest rates (for example, Kim, 2001; Kuijs, 2002). On the other hand, there is a significant effect of foreign prices, exchange rate and wages, sometimes that of the aggregate demand.

The impact of the monetary, labour and foreign sectors on Polish inflation was analyzed in Kim (2001). The labour and external sectors had a large impact on inflation, while the monetary sector appeared not to have any significant effect.

In the study on the monetary transmission mechanisms and inflation in the Slovak Republic (Kuijs, 2002), the author estimated the long-run cointegrating relationships for the goods, labour, money and foreign exchange markets. It was found that the inflation was influenced through foreign prices, exchange rate and wages, and, insignificantly, through the aggregate demand. The money supply had a slight but rapid effect on the prices.

Another study on the determinants of inflation in the Czech Republic, Hungary and Poland reports that the exchange rate and output gap are especially important in explaining inflation in those countries (Golinelli and Orsi, 2002).

The author of the study on modelling inflation in Georgia (Maliszewski, 2003) derived a theoretical model considering the three markets: goods, money and exchange rate. The long-term price level is determined by the balance between the aggregate supply and aggregate demand. The exchange rate plays a major role in explaining the inflation behaviour, and there is a low persistence of inflation. A similar approach was applied in the case of Uzbekistan, where a large influence of the goods and money market disequilibria was found (Ranaweera, 2003).

Ukraine's evidence

There are several studies devoted to investigating the inflation determinants in Ukraine. The purpose of this research is to take a different theoretical set-up, test the model empirically and check the robustness of the results obtained in the other studies. Since the number of these studies for Ukraine is not extensive, I choose to report all relevant inflation studies that have been encountered, with different econometric approaches.

---

[3]   Empirical inflation studies can concentrate on one particular source of inflation (these are the so-called structural models, for example, Phillips curve, mark-up model, and so on).

In one of the earliest studies, based on the VECM technique, inflation was found to be an essentially monetary phenomenon during 1993-1996 (Banaian, Bolgarin and de Menil, 1998).

There have also been several studies done by the NBU experts (for example, Bolgarin, Mahadeva and Stern, 2000). The authors of this particular study have developed a monetary multi-equation transmission model. A 1 per cent shock to the interest rates reduces the values of all model variables, except for the world prices. The same shock in the world export prices has only a temporary impact on all variables, a shock to the exchange rate (depreciation) has a positive effect on all variables.

In another econometric study (Schevchuk, 2001), the author applied VECM for January 1994-March 2000 to investigate the relationship between M2, industrial production, inflation and real exchange rate. The Johansen cointegration test testified the cointegration of the above variables. The evidence from the impulse response functions is that the money supply influences inflation, and inflation, in its turn, influences the real exchange rate and industrial production. According to the forecast error variance decomposition results, the inflation in Ukraine is a monetary phenomenon. It has a non-monetary component in the short-run but in the long-run the price level is 70 per cent determined by the money supply.

Piontkivsky, et al. (2001) investigated the impact of the fiscal deficit on inflation within the VAR framework for 1995-first half of 2000. The fiscal imbalance was found to be an important determinant of inflation. The exchange rate and monetary base have little effect upon the prices.

A mark-up and a money market model have been estimated in the most recent paper on the determinants of inflation in Ukraine (Lissovolik, 2003). The cointegration between broad money and CPI was found to be statistically significant for 1993-2002, and for the early sub-samples, but not for 1996-2002, which the author explained by the strong remonetization. The mark-up model for 1996-2002 showed a greater role of administered prices in the CPI. In the long-run, the prices are influenced by the exchange rate and wages. Nevertheless, broad money is one of the short-term inflation determinants. The author attributes the weak link between money and inflation to the poor availability or quality of the data, the strong remonetization in 1996-2002, (which is 'long-term' within the model, but is rather medium-term in reality, and, thus, the link between money and prices could be re-established), and the impossibility of finding a consistent long-term framework within the given data.

As can be seen, the link between money and prices, the exchange rate and prices is not clear in Ukraine's case. There is little evidence about the impact of the foreign prices. Therefore, further studies, generating new evidence, could only be encouraged.

Theoretical framework and estimation procedure

Theoretical framework

The framework for analyzing inflation is summarized below. The price formation is influenced by shocks from (following Hendry, 2000):

1. Excess demand for goods and services from the private sector
2. Excess demand for the factors of production
3. Excess money holdings that stimulate excess demand (many variants of the quantity theory of money)
4. Excess fiscal deficits
5. External shocks, affecting exchange rate, imports and exports
6. Supply-side factors: cost-push and mark-up relationships
7. Other factors: for example, wars, world wide commodity shocks, price controls, and so on. These factors could be included in any other theory.

The new political macroeconomics of inflation take into account the role of the non-economic factors in explaining inflation, that is, the role of institutions, political processes and culture.

To sum up, four major blocks of factors determining inflation may be pointed out: demand-side (that is, persistent increases due to the continued excess demand); real or supply shocks (or cost-push inflation; primarily, the negative productivity shocks, domestic currency depreciation, rising wages, interest rates, taxes, price shocks from inputs markets); inertial (expectations, sticky wages and prices) and institutional factors. In reality, it is a mixture of all factors that appears to cause the inflationary or disinflationary processes.

In this section a simple theoretical model of inflation for Ukraine is being derived following the general approach being used in the other inflation studies on transition economies (for example, Kim, 2001; Lissovolik, 2003). The starting point is an IS-LM model framework for a small open economy. All variables in this section are expressed as natural logarithms.

According to economic theory, the general price level is a weighted average of the price of tradable (p_t^t) and non-tradable goods (p_t^n):

$$p_t = \lambda p_t^t + (1 - \lambda) p_t^n \tag{1}$$

where λ is the share of the tradable goods in the consumption basket.

Assuming the purchasing power parity (PPP), the price of the tradable goods is determined in the world market (small open economy assumption), and is a function of the foreign prices (p_t^f) and exchange rate (e_t):

$$p_t^t = e_t + p_t^f \tag{2}$$

The price of the non-tradable goods can be determined in two ways, which leads further to distinguishing between model 1 and model 2.

Model 1 The demand for non-tradable goods follows the overall demand in the economy, and the price of non-tradable goods is determined by the internal money market equilibrium, under which the real money supply ($m_t - p_t$) is equal to the real money demand ($m_t^d - p_t$):

$$p_t^n = v\left(m_t - \left(m_t^d - p_t\right)\right) \tag{3}$$

where V represents the relationship between the aggregate demand and the demand for non-tradable goods (scale factor).

The demand for the real money balances can be expressed as a function of the scale variable (income, wealth or expenditure, in real terms) and a vector of the expected rates of return (the own rate of return on money and the opportunity cost of holding money):

$$m_t^d - p_t = \gamma + \delta\left(y_t - p_t\right) + \mu r_t \tag{4}$$

A long-run unitary elasticity of the nominal cash balances with respect to the price level is being assumed.

Substitute (4) into (3) to get equation (5):

$$p_t^n = v\left(m_t - \left(\gamma + \delta\left(y_t - p_t\right) + \mu r_t\right)\right) \tag{5}$$

Finally, substituting (2) and (5) into (1), I get the following price equation:

$$p_t = f\left(e_t, p_t^f, m_t, y_t - p_t, r_t\right) \tag{6}$$

Model 2 One can also assume that the price of the non-tradable goods is determined as a mark-up over the unit costs of production: domestic and import inputs costs. The mark-up is equal to one in the perfectly competitive markets ($P = MC$), and is greater than one in the imperfectly competitive markets ($P > MC$). Under the constant mark-up, a cost change will result in a price change. This approach is discussed, in particular, in de Brouwer and Ericsson (1995) for the Australian case.

The price mark-up behaviour can be expressed as:

$$P_t^n = \theta \left(ULC_t \right)^l \left(P_t^{in} \right)^k \tag{7}$$

where ULC_t is unit labour cost, P_t^{in} is price of other inputs (domestic and import); or in the log-linear form:

$$p_t^n = \ln \theta + l \left(ulc \right)_t + k \left(p^{in} \right)_t \tag{8}$$

Eventually, substituting (2) and (8) into (1), I get the following price equation:

$$p_t = f \left(e_t, p_t^f, \left(ulc \right)_t, \left(p^{in} \right)_t \right) \tag{9}$$

Estimation procedure

Equations (6) and (9) are the systems, where the variables are contemporaneously set. One could actually estimate a complete VAR model for both systems and test for the cointegrating vectors, and, if there are any, estimate the VECM. But, in reality, it may be quite difficult to deal with such a model. The application of the Johansen procedure to the whole system may not discover the existing cointegrating relationships due to the small sample, possible structural breaks, a large variety of the potential inflation determinants, and difficulties in interpreting the cointegration space, and getting the coefficients close to the theoretical priors. Segmenting the variables a priori based on the economic theory, I focus my analysis on three dominant theories of price formation in a small open economy: monetary inflation and imported inflation in model one, and monetary inflation and cost-push inflation in model 2[4], and, as a first step, look for the long-run relationships as suggested by economic theory, based on the sectoral VARs. The idea is that the balance or imbalance of each sector can be measured by the deviation from the steady-state position. These deviations represent the disequilibria that influence inflation, and, thus, should be included into the short-run model, which I estimate as a second step.

Note that in the further discussion and estimation, I do not differentiate between the prices of tradables and non-tradables but rather consider the general price level since I look at equations (6) and (9) from now on.

---

[4] In some studies on transition economies, the goods market is being modelled to represent the demand side, often based on the estimation of the potential output. I choose not to model the output gap and demand side explicitly, as it may be very difficult to estimate in such a transition economy, like Ukraine, that undergoes significant structural changes.

Long-run model: Foreign exchange market According to the PPP, the parity in the national price levels is enforced by the goods market arbitrage. In terms of the overall price level, the following relationship should hold (note that I allow for the coefficients α and β in our estimations):

$$p_t = \alpha p_t^f + \beta e_t \tag{10}$$

Usually, the PPP is being viewed as determining the exchange rate in the long-run. If it holds, the short-run deviations:

$$ecm_{foreign} = \alpha p_t^f + \beta e_t - p_t \tag{11}$$

that is, the real exchange rate, should be stationary. A deviation in the long-run PPP can be due to the shock to the nominal exchange rate, domestic and foreign prices. The positive PPP gaps lead to higher domestic prices (for example, through imported inflation or devaluations).

Long-run model: Money market In the conventional LM curve, the real money demand depends positively on the aggregate real output[5] and negatively on the nominal interest rate. Assume that the money supply is set exogenously. In the equilibrium, the real money supply should be equal to the real money demand, therefore, the monetary condition equilibrium will be:

$$m_t - p_t = \gamma + \delta(y_t - p_t) + \mu r_t \tag{12}$$

The above equation envisages that the actual stock of money adjusts to its desired level instantaneously. But this may not be the case, first of all, due to the transaction costs and uncertainty. Besides, the desired level is not observable. Thus, one should take into account the short-term disequilibrium between the actual cash balances and their desired (long-term) level (which will drive the price level) and distinguish between the short-run and long-run behaviour.

Consequently, the error-correction term will be:

$$ecm_{money} = (m_t - p_t) - \gamma - \delta(y_t - p_t) - \mu r_t \tag{13}$$

---

[5] According to the quantity theory hypothesis, there should be a unitary income elasticity $\delta = 1$, or it should be $\delta = 0.5$ for the Baumol-Tobin model of the economies of scale. In the empirical money demand studies, the coefficients may be quite different and often much greater than 1.

Long-run model: Mark-up relationship Inflation may be attributed to the supply-side factors, which have an impact on the unit cost and profit mark-up. When the firms' costs go up, they have to raise their prices to maintain the profit margins:

$$p_t = \ln\theta + l\left(ulc\right)_t + k\left(p^{in}\right)_t \tag{14}$$

The short-term disequilibrium from the long-run mark-up relationship may be expressed as:

$$ecm_{markup} = p_t - \ln\theta - l\left(ulc\right)_t - k\left(p^{in}\right)_t \tag{15}$$

It should be noted that (10), (12) and (14) are just long-run relationships, or equilibrium conditions, for the particular sectors of the economy, without any implications about causality. The obtained cointegrating vectors cannot be interpreted as the structural equations. However, one may think about them as a consequence of the constraints imposed by the economic structure on the long-run relationships among the jointly endogenous variables (Harris, 1995), and, thus, think about them as long-run relationships that may govern prices in the long run.

Short-run model Having estimated the long-run relationships, a single-equation error correction model, which would represent the short-run inflation, can be obtained on the basis of all variables, used in the cointegration relationships in the first differences, and the sectoral error-correction terms. Then, the overparameterized model should be 'tested down' through applying a general-to-specific approach to obtain a parsimonious representation.

Short-run model: Model 1

$$\Delta p_t = \beta_0 + \sum_{i=1}^{k-1}\beta_{1i}\Delta p_{t-i} + \sum_{i=1}^{k-1}\beta_{2i}\Delta m_{t-i} + \sum_{i=1}^{k-1}\beta_{3i}\Delta\left(y-p\right)_{t-i} + \sum_{i=1}^{k-1}\beta_{4i}\Delta\left(neer\right)_{t-i} \tag{16}$$

$$+ \sum_{i=1}^{k-1}\beta_{5i}\Delta p_{t-i}^f + \gamma_1\left(ecm_{money}\right)_{t-1} + \gamma_2\left(ecm_{foreign}\right)_{t-1} + \beta_6 D_t + u_t$$

where all variables are, as defined before, in the first differences, *neer* is the nominal effective exchange rate, D_t is a vector of variables: centred seasonal dummies and specific dummies to capture the short-term effects, and u_t is an error term with the usual properties.

The positive γ_1 implies the excess money supply (in excess of the steady-state demand for money) and, consequently, an increase in the next period's inflation rate. γ_2 represents the impact of the deviation of the external sector from its long-run equilibrium (how the domestic prices compare to the international prices), the low value shows the slow adjustment process.

Short-run model: Model 2

$$\Delta p_t = \alpha_0 + \sum_{i=1}^{k-1} \alpha_{1i} \Delta p_{t-i} + \sum_{i=1}^{k-1} \alpha_{2i} \Delta \left(ulc\right)_{t-i} + \sum_{i=1}^{k-1} \alpha_{3i} \Delta \left(p^{in}\right)_{t-i} + \sum_{i=1}^{k-1} \alpha_{4i} \Delta \left(neer\right)_{t-i} \tag{17}$$

$$+ \sum_{i=1}^{k-1} \alpha_{5i} \Delta p_{t-i}^{f} + \lambda_1 \left(ecm_{markup}\right)_{t-1} + \lambda_2 \left(ecm_{foreign}\right)_{t-1} + \alpha_6 D_t + \varepsilon_t$$

where all variables are as defined above, and ε_t is an error term with the usual properties. The mark-up error-correction term measures the deviation of the prices from the long-run value, positive λ_1 implies the higher prices.

The significance of the error-correction terms in the short-run models would demonstrate that the long-run equilibrium conditions hold, and that the adjustment is made to get back to the equilibrium, in case of the short-run disturbances to these long-run relationships.

Model estimation for Ukraine

Data description and tests for stationarity

Data description Monthly data for January 1997-December 2003 were used in order to have a sufficient number of observations. For the early 1990s the data are rather unreliable. Nevertheless, quarterly or yearly data would be much more appropriate for testing the above hypothesis.

As a measure of the general price level, the CPI was constructed (January 1997 = 100) on the basis of the data of the State Statistics Committee.[6]

As a scale variable, I use the industrial production (calculated by the State Statistics Committee) deflated by PPI (expressed in January 1997 prices) since the monthly data for GDP is very unreliable in Ukraine.

To express the money stock, broad monetary aggregate M2[7] (available at the Website of the NBU) was considered. To calculate it in real terms, a special price index was constructed: 0.5 per cent of the CPI plus 0.5 per cent of the PPI.

---

[6]   It would be more correct to use a 'core' inflation indicator in such a study. The two most conventional measures are the core inflation index with the prices of food and energy excluded and the core inflation index with the administratively controlled prices excluded (Ganev, et al. 2002). Such indices are not calculated in Ukraine, and I also choose not to calculate these indices on my own due to certain difficulties (for example, non-availability of the detailed break-down of prices) and the possibility of getting rough final estimates and, thus, measurement errors. Furthermore, such indices are also difficult to calculate due to a very high share of food products in the CPI, much higher than in the developed countries, as a result of which one may end up with the price index for a very narrow group of products.

[7]   Some economists consider that the narrow money (the reserve money according to the IMF's IFS) should be used for the money demand studies as it may better reflect the

As a proxy for the unit labour costs, I take the average nominal wages for the whole economy, published by the State Statistics Committee.

To calculate the real effective exchange rate index, I have followed the methodologies described in Betliy (2002) and calculated several real effective exchange rate (REER) indices based on contracts currency (imports), trade (imports) and equal weights.[8]

To calculate the REER on the basis of trade (import) weights, three currencies were included: USD, EUR, Russian rouble (RR). Russia and European Union are the major trading partners and the average shares of the imports from the FSU countries and Europe are 55 per cent and 32 per cent, respectively. The share of imports from European countries was increasing during the last years at the expense of the declining share of imports from FSU countries. The share of imports from America remained relatively stable, at about 5 per cent. I assume that the other remaining partners from Asia and Africa are also likely to conduct their trade transactions dollar-denominated.

To calculate the REER on the basis of contracts currency weights, the following average currency structure of Ukrainian imports during 2001-2002 was used: 78 per cent of USD-, 12 per cent of euro- and 8 per cent of RR-denominated transactions.

As for the foreign price levels, I have taken for the USA: PPI for all commodities and CPI for all urban consumers from the US Department of Labour, Bureau of Labour Statistics; for the EU: Harmonized Index of Consumer Prices (HICP) and PPI for total industry (excluding construction) from the European Central Bank; and for Russia: PPI and CPI from the Central Bank of Russia. The general foreign price level was calculated as a weighted average of the producer price indices for the countries whose currency constitutes the major currency of the trade contracts (geometric average, 1997 = 100).

The nominal effective exchange rate was estimated as a weighted average of the bilateral exchange rates for the countries whose currency constitutes the major currency of the trade contracts (geometric average, 1997 = 100).

The data are not seasonally adjusted, and, to account for the seasonal effects, I prefer to use the centred seasonal dummies.[9]

---

policy stance of the monetary authorities. However, many researchers prefer using broader monetary aggregates to avoid the impact of the portfolio reallocation as a result of financial innovations (Golinelli and Orsi, 2002). In general, the economic concept of the money demand function could be more applicable to broad money (with or without foreign currency deposits) (Ghosh, 1997). It has also been argued that in most transition economies the broader monetary aggregates are more closely linked to inflation than the narrow aggregates (Lissovolik, 2003).

[8] The contracts currency weights reflect the structure of the currencies in the trade transactions. The import weights represent the shares of foreign trading partners in imports.

[9] There exist different methods of seasonal adjustment, and, probably, different variables will require different methods of adjustment (for example, additive, multiplicative,

To account for the effect of the administrative decisions and other exogenous shocks, the step dummies are used: August98, October98, April99, July99, September99, January00, April00, June00, June02, November03.

Tests for stationarity   To test the time series for stationarity, the Augmented Dickey-Fuller (ADF) test was applied. The test has failed to reject the hypothesis of the presence of a unit root. All considered variables were found to be stationary in the first differences, that is, integrated of order one (I(1)) (see the ADF results in Table 13.1). The graphs of all variables in levels and differences are presented in Figures 13.1, 13.2 and 13.3.[10]

The lag structure in the ADF test was chosen on the basis of the Akaike information criterion (AIC), and, further, the residuals were tested for the higher-order serial correlation using the Breusch-Godfrey test.

The trend for lforppi, lnwage, lm2 turned out to be significant at 5 per cent significance level, which means that there is a linear deterministic trend in these time series. The trend term for lcpi, lry, lrm2, lneer and reer was not significant.

Census X-11, and so on). In this case the dynamic models might react sensitively (<www.vwl.uni-freiburg.de/fakultaet/fiwiII/econometricssieben.pdf>) and preference could be given to the unadjusted time series plus the seasonal dummies.

[10] The previous studies on Ukraine also found the stationarity of the above variables in the first differences (as well as in the majority of the similar studies on the transition economies, these variables are treated as I(1) variables). The graphical inspection for lforppi and lneer, however, shows that the variance has changed in the middle of the sample.

Table 13.1   Unit root test results (Augmented Dickey–Fuller test)

Variable	n	Model	ADF test statistics	k
lcpi	81	c	-1.47	2
lcpi	80	c,t	-1.15	3
dlcpi	80	c	-3.37*	2
lneer	81	c	-1.86	2
lneer	81	c,t	-0.72	2
dlneer	81	c	-5.90**	1
reer	81	c	-1.60	2
reer	81	c,t	-0.79	2
dreer	80	c	-5.53**	2
lforppi	79	c	-0.72	4
lforppi	79	c,t	-2.45	4
dlforppi	79	c	-2.81*	3
lnwage	81	c	0.90	2
lnwage	81	c,t	-1.66	2
dlnwage	80	c	-6.66**	2
lry	79	c	0.91	4
lry	79	c,t	-0.75	4
dlry	80	c	-8.21**	2
lm2	81	c	1.42	2
lm2	78	c,t	-1.84	5
dlm2	81	c	-8.33**	1
lrm2	82	c	1.67	1
lrm2	78	c,t	-0.74	5
dlrm2	80	c	-4.17**	2

Note: n is the number of observations, c is a model with constant only, c,t is a model with both constant and trend included, and k is the order of test augmentation. * and ** means rejection of the null hypothesis at 5 per cent and 1 per cent significance level, respectively. The order of the test augmentation was chosen on the basis of AIC and residual diagnostics for serial correlation.

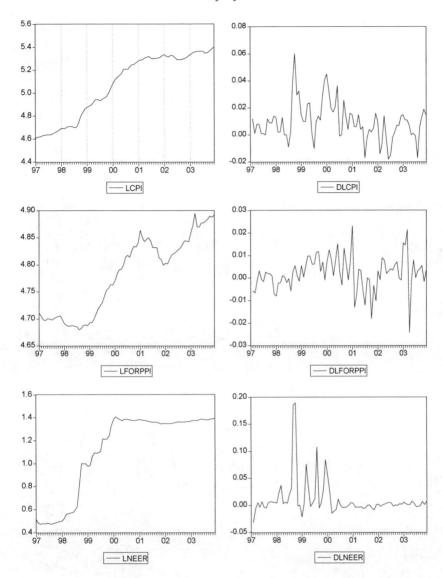

Figure 13.1 **Foreign exchange market: Data in levels and first differences**

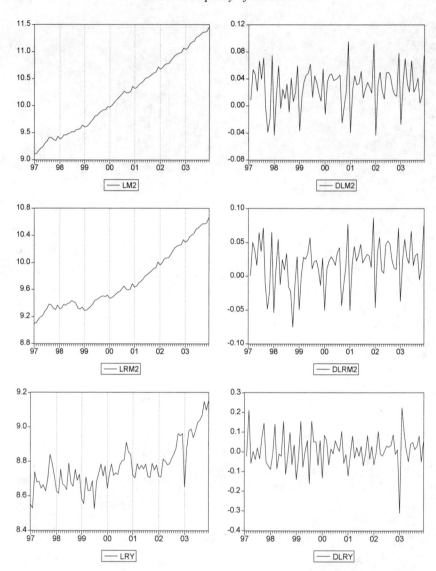

Figure 13.2   Money market: Data in levels and first differences

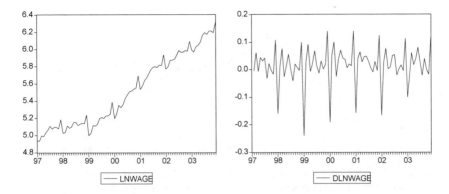

Figure 13.3   Mark-up model: Data in levels and first differences

Model estimation

Estimation of long-run relationships   In this section, I present the results of the estimated cointegrating vectors, based on the sectoral analysis using Johansen maximum likelihood procedure for finite order autoregressions.[11]

It should be noted that the Johansen procedure can be severely biased in the small samples (Phillips, 1994), not with respect to the estimated coefficients but to the size of the trace statistic, which is over-sized (as a result, fewer cointegration vectors are found). It is also sensitive to the number of variables and the number of lags included. The Johansen VAR procedure allows the simultaneous evaluation of the multiple relationships and imposes no prior restrictions on the cointegration space. However, it requires the good knowledge of the identification schemes at a later stage, and the cointegration space may be difficult to interpret. Nevertheless, the Johansen procedure is being argued to be more efficient (than, for example, the Engle and Granger static procedure), and especially should be preferred in the multivariate context.

Foreign exchange market   In this part the results of the real effective exchange rate (reer) estimation are presented. In Figure 13.4, the reer index (January 1997=100), based on the contracts currency weights, is depicted.

---

[11]   The difference of the cointegration approach used in this chapter to that by Lissovolik (2003) is that the author applies the Johansen procedure to the whole VAR system and I rather concentrate on the sectoral VARs, thus trying to distinguish between the different theories of the inflation determination apriori.

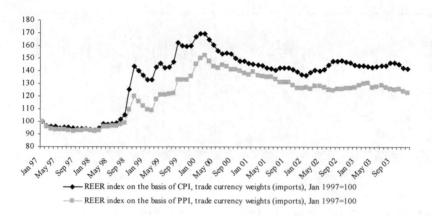

- ◆— REER index on the basis of CPI, trade currency weights (imports), Jan 1997=100
- ■— REER index on the basis of PPI, trade currency weights (imports), Jan 1997=100

Figure 13.4   Ukraine: Real effective exchange rate dynamics, 1997-2003

Source: own calculations.

The indices based on the equal weights and import trade weights have shown the index depreciation starting 2002. The index, calculated on the basis of the trade currency weights (trade contracts currency), which shows the currency appreciation trend, seems to be the most reliable and appropriate, and the trend coincides with the trend of the reer index, calculated by the Institute for Economic Forecasting (Kryuchkova, 2003), which calculation relies on a larger number of the currencies and, which, thus, may be more accurate. Furthermore, the trend is more in line with the empirical evidence from other transition economies, where the reer trend appreciation is observed (which is usually interpreted as some evidence for the Balassa-Samuelson effect).

The ADF tests for reer (presented in Table 13.1) and the graphical inspection show that the reer index is not stationary and is not even trend-stationary for the whole sample, so that this error-correction term should not be included into the short-run inflation function.

Notwithstanding this, I have also performed separately the Johansen cointegration test on the external sector variables and found the existence of the long-run relationship between domestic and foreign prices and exchange rate, which can be interpreted as the PPP relationship.

The Johansen cointegration test was conducted for $lcpi, lforppi, lneer$ under the assumption of no deterministic trend in the data[12] and with including the

---

[12] It is usually assumed that the time series contain deterministic trends. However, the trend components of some of the series may contain some stochastic elements. A misspecification of the trend components may result in the incorrect statistical inference (Mehra, 1991).

centred dummies to reflect the seasonality of the time series[13] (the results of the Johansen LR test can be found in Table 13.2). The LR trace test indicates one cointegrating equation at 1 per cent significance level (normalized cointegrating coefficients).

Table 13.2   **Cointegration test results, foreign exchange market: Johansen LR test**

Hypothesis	Eigenvalue	LR	Critical value (5%)	Critical value (1%)
$H_0 : r = 0$	0.27	32.36	24.31	29.75
$H_0 : r \leq 1$	0.09	7.63	12.53	16.31
$H_0 : r \leq 2$	0.00	0.28	3.84	6.51

Note: Sample: 1997:01-2003:12. Included observations: 80. Critical values were derived assuming no exogenous series. Lags interval: one to three (found on the basis of AIC and residual diagnostics). Centred seasonal dummies were included. Assumption: no linear deterministic trend in the data.

Foreign exchange market: Cointegrating vector at 1 per cent level.

lcpi	lforppi	lneer
1.00	-0.94	-0.60
	(0.01)	(0.03)

Note: Standard errors are given in the parenthesis.

    There is also no intercept in the cointegrating vector. Based on the Pantula principle described in Harris (1995), which was suggested by Johansen, one should choose a model with the intercept if to say that the model with no deterministic components in the data is not realistic. The intercept may be necessary in general to account for the units of measurement of the variables. On the other hand, according to the theory, there should be no intercept in the PPP relationship and the cointegration tests, based on the other assumptions, produced rather implausible results.

[13]   The centred seasonal dummies sum up to zero over time. The inclusion of the step or impulse dummies or other exogenous series will influence the critical values for the cointegration tests (the critical values will be different depending on the number of the dummies being used). In this case, the theoretical values provided by Johansen and others will be only indicative (Harris, 1995). That is why I have decided to include only the centred seasonal dummies in the Johansen test, which will not have any effect on the underlying distribution of the test statistics. In the specification with the first differences, the usual dummies will cause a drift, which is why the use of the centred seasonal dummies is usually recommended.

Table 13.3   Cointegration test results, money market: Johansen LR test

Hypothesis	Eigenvalue	LR	Critical value (5%)	Critical value (1%)
$H_0: r = 0$	0.34	42.88	24.31	29.75
$H_0: r \leq 1$	0.11	10.53	12.53	16.31
$H_0: r \leq 2$	0.02	1.41	3.84	6.51

Note: Sample: 1997:01-2003:12. Included observations: 79. Critical values were derived assuming no exogenous series. Lags interval: one to four (found on the basis of AIC and residual diagnostics). Centred seasonal dummies were included. Assumption: no linear deterministic trend in the data.

Money market: Cointegrating vector at 1 per cent level

lrm2	lry	lneer
1.00	-0.94	0.11
	(0.06)	(0.44)

Note: Standard errors are given in the parenthesis.

Table 13.4   Cointegration test results, mark-up model: Johansen LR test

Hypothesis	Eigenvalue	LR	Critical value (5%)	Critical value (1%)
$H_0: r = 0$	0.41	78.08	34.91	41.07
$H_0: r \leq 1$	0.32	35.38	19.96	24.60
$H_0: r \leq 2$	0.05	4.17	9.24	12.97

Note: Sample: 1997:01-2003:12. Included observations: 81. Critical values were derived assuming no exogenous series. Lags interval: one to two (found on the basis of AIC and residual diagnostics). Centred seasonal dummies were included. Assumption: no linear deterministic trend in the data.

Mark-up model: Cointegrating vector at 1 per cent level

lcpi	lnwage	lneer	c
1.00	-0.28	-0.41	-3.06
	(0.04)	(0.04)	(0.18)
0.00	1.00	-1.46	-4.80
		(0.48)	(0.34)

Note: Standard errors are given in the parenthesis.

Money market: Money demand For the money market specification, the real industrial output was chosen as a scale variable. To represent the opportunity cost of holding money, several options were considered: nominal effective exchange rate, general price level, inflation rate, expected inflation and both price level and exchange rate. I choose to present the results on the money market specification with the nominal effective exchange rate, since these have been the most plausible results in terms of the magnitude and sign of the coefficients in the long-run relationship. Besides, under Ukrainian circumstances, the exchange rate could be really the most appropriate variable to reflect the prevailing money market conditions during recent years and to represent the opportunity cost of holding foreign exchange assets.

In particular, the choice of the nominal effective exchange rate to represent the opportunity cost of holding foreign exchange balances was motivated by the fact that in the past for the majority of the Ukrainian population, US dollar cash holdings have been a major alternative asset to the domestic money; the foreign assets have represented a significant part of the public's portfolio, and there has been a limited choice of the financial instruments outside money. Thus, because of the under-developed financial markets in Ukraine and rather non-market determined interest rates, there has been the substitution between the domestic money and US dollar cash holdings (currency substitution) rather than the substitution between the different financial assets. The nominal effective exchange rate rather than its depreciation is taken in the estimations as the depreciation rate does not show much volatility and has been rather stable during recent years (actually almost zero).

The Johansen cointegration test based on the assumption of no linear deterministic trend in the data yielded the existence of one cointegrating relationship at 1 per cent significance level (the results of the Johansen LR trace test can be found in Table 13.3). The obtained cointegrating vector can be interpreted as the long-run money demand equation.

Mark-up model The major problem that I have encountered in the estimation of the mark-up model is the choice of the measure for the unit labour costs and the prices for the other inputs.

The nominal wages are used as a proxy for the unit labour costs. In general, the wage growth could be an important cost-driven factor of the inflation dynamics. During the last years, on the background of the strong economic growth, de-shadowing of the economy and low inflation rates, there has been significant nominal and real wages growth. A more appropriate measure to look at the contribution of wages to inflation would be, however, to consider the productivity-adjusted labour costs, since the wage growth leads to the inflation growth only if the wages growth exceeds the labour productivity growth. However, due to the absence of trustworthy data on the unit labour costs on the monthly basis, it could be still reasonable to test empirically the contribution of the wages growth to the inflation dynamics using the nominal wages as a proxy.

As for the prices of the other inputs, the exchange rate has been chosen as a proxy for the import costs.

The Johansen LR trace test was conducted for *lcpi,lnwage,lneer* under the assumption of no linear deterministic trend in the data (the results can be found in Table 13.4), and two cointegrating equations at 1 per cent significance level (normalized cointegrating coefficients) were found, one of which is similar to the long-run mark-up relationship, being searched.

Since the causality between prices and wages is important and, usually, the direction of the causality is not clear, I have also performed the Granger causality test between the wages and prices and found that the prices do not Granger cause the wages, but rather the causality runs from the wages to the prices.

Estimation of inflation function The error-correction terms from the estimated above long-run relationships are included into a general error correction inflation model as well as the short-run dynamics, that is, the variables in the first differences, and some auxiliary explanatory variables.

Short-run model 1 In inflation model 1 (Table 13.5), the error-correction terms for the money market and for the foreign exchange market are included. The reduction of the general model was carried out by sequentially removing the longest lag of each variable with the lowest t values. The model seems to satisfy the diagnostic tests, the results of which are presented in Table 13.6.[14] The test for the parameter stability is required due to the volatility of the economic variables in the transition period and the possibility of the structural break. The recursive estimates of the coefficients which are depicted in Figure 13.5 show the robustness of the results (the parameters do not move outside the initial error bands), notwithstanding some initial volatility. For some variables, the error bands converge relatively fast. The recursive residuals are also within a two standard deviations band (with the exception of a few points outside the region, which may be either outliers or possibly points associated with the coefficients changes), indicating that the estimated parameters are rather stable (Figure 13.6). The actual and fitted values of the residuals are depicted in Figure 13.7.

The feedback from the short-run exchange rate movements to inflation is rather rapid. It seems as if the inflation history affects the degree of the inflation persistence, which is reflected by the high coefficient near the lagged prices. The effect is strong and felt within a lag of one month. Inflation is also influenced by the lagged money supply and real output. Seasonality and some exogenous shocks play a role in inflation determination. The error-correction term for the external sector was found to be significant, and the adjustment back to the steady state is rather slow.

---

[14] Although there is some evidence for serial correlation and autoregressive conditional heteroscedasticity at 10 per cent significance level. Nevertheless, correcting for serial correlation usually has a relatively minor impact on the results.

Table 13.5   Estimation of inflation function (model 1)

dlcpi	*c*	*dlcpi (-1)*	*dlneer*	*dlrm2 (-1)*	*dlry*	*dq3*	*dq4*	*June02*	*July99*	*June00*	*Ecmforeign (-1)*
	0.004	0.23	0.19	0.08	-0.02	-0.006	0.006	-0.02	-0.02	0.02	-0.08
	(2.90)	(2.39)	(7.56)	(2.44)	(-2.00)	(-3.76)	(4.30)	(-2.39)	(-3.06)	(2.36)	(-4.33)

Note: The initial model included 4 lags of each variable, centred seasonal dummies, step dummies: June02, August98, July99, September99, June00, April99, October98, January00, April00, November03 and error-correction terms for the money market and foreign exchange market. dq3 and dq4 are centred seasonal dummy variables for 3d and 4th quarters. Ecmforeign(-1) is an error-correction term for the foreign exchange market lagged by one period. T-statistics are given in parenthesis.

Table 13.6   Inflation model 1: Diagnostic statistics

Test	*Test statistics*	*P-value*
R-squared	0.76	
Jarque-Bera test	2.83	(0.24)
Ramsey RESET test	1.15	(0.32)
Breusch-Godfrey LM test	2.35	(0.10)
ARCH test	2.86	(0.09)
White-heteroscedasticity test	0.66	(0.82)

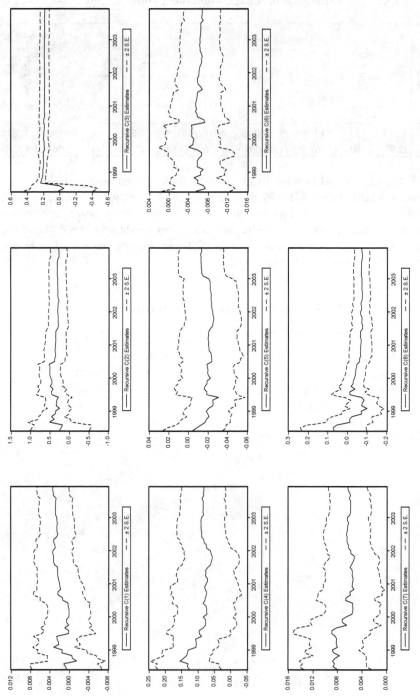

Figure 13.5   Parameter stability (without step dummies)

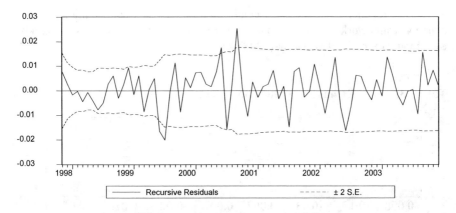

Figure 13.6 **Recursive residuals (without step dummies)**

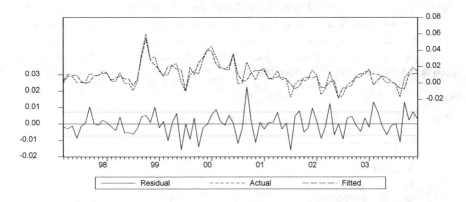

Figure 13.7 **Actual and fitted values (with step dummies)**

Short-run model 2 The estimation results, diagnostic statistics and tests for parameter stability for inflation model 2 are presented in Tables 13.7, 13.8 and Figures 13.8, 13.9 and 13.10. As well as in inflation model 1, the error-correction term for the foreign exchange market turned out to be significant and of similar magnitude. The same seasonality impact and the effect of dummy variables are observed. The inflation is influenced by the exchange rate and wages. One should note, however, the negative sign near the wages variable, which is rather difficult to explain. In the future studies, however, the estimation of the mark-up relationship should certainly deserve more attention: one should try to estimate the unit labour costs and find some better measures to represent the other inputs costs.

Weak exogeneity is a necessary condition for an appropriate conditional single-equation framework. In my estimations I treat all the other variables as weakly-exogenous, following Lissovolik (2003).[15]

Table 13.7   Estimation of inflation function (model 2)

dlcpi	*c*	*dlneer*	*dlmwage*	*dq3*	*dq4*	*June02*	*July99*	*June00*	*Ecmforeign (-1)*
0.008	0.17	-0.03	-0.007	0.007	-0.02	-0.02	0.02	-0.10
(9.10)	(6.56)	(-2.27)	(-5.27)	(4.68)	(-2.42)	(-2.49)	(2.65)	(-7.03)

Note: The initial model included 4 lags of each variable, centred seasonal dummies, step dummies: June02, August98, July99, September99, June00, April99, October98, January00, April00, November03 and error-correction terms for the foreign exchange market and mark-up model. dq3 and dq4 are centred seasonal dummy variables for 3rd and 4th quarters. Ecmforeign(-1) is an error-correction term for the foreign exchange market lagged by one period. T-statistics are given in parenthesis.

Table 13.8   Inflation model 2: Diagnostic statistics

Test	Test statistics	P-value
R-squared	0.72	
Jarque-Bera test	0.12	0.94
Ramsey RESET test	2.08	0.13
Breusch-Godfrey LM test	0.99	0.37
ARCH test	5.46	0.02
White-heteroscedasticity test	0.82	0.63

---

[15] An interested reader may look into the paper for Lissovolik's argumentation. A single-equation inflation model was also estimated in Ohnsorge and Oomes (2004) and in some other studies. A proper approach, however, would be to do the short-run dynamics within the VECM framework if the variables turn out to be endogenous.

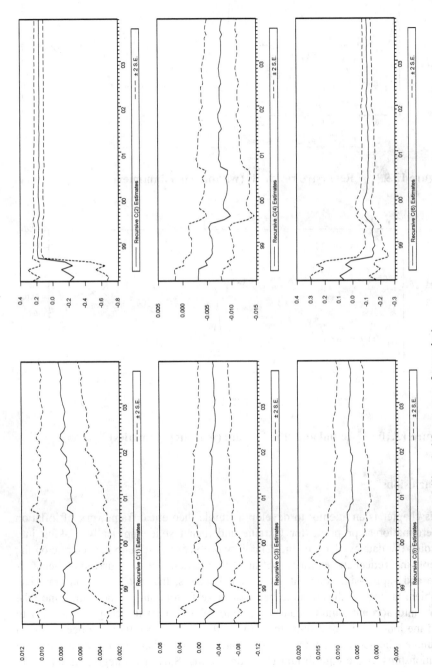

Figure 13.8   Parameter stability (without step dummies)

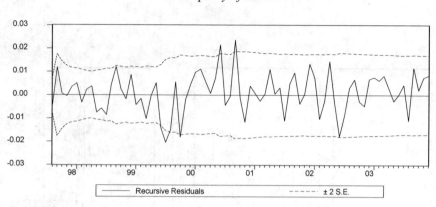

Figure 13.9   Recursive residuals (without step dummies)

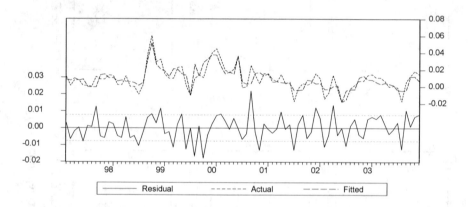

Figure 13.10   Actual and fitted values (with step dummies)

Conclusions

This chapter is an attempt to develop a simple theoretical framework of inflation determination appropriate for Ukraine and then test it empirically. Taking into account the data availability and reliability problems, I chose to concentrate on the simple theoretical and empirical set-up. The inflation is usually driven by demand-side and supply-side, internal and external factors, the theoretical and empirical problem is how to differentiate between these factors and at the same time take them into account simultaneously. A major objective of the chapter has been to find the long-run relationships that govern the Ukrainian inflation process, and to examine whether one can derive a reasonable inflation function by imposing those relationships as the equilibrium correction terms. Such a cointegration approach, thus allows distinguishing between short-term and long-term effects, and develop a general model that embeds several hypotheses of inflation.

The long-run equilibrium relationships for the foreign exchange market, money market and mark-up model were found (discovered also in a number of the other studies on the transition economies). Thus, it may be argued, that the foreign prices, exchange rate and wages have long-run effects on the prices.

The equilibrium error-correction models of inflation were estimated. The most important determinants of inflation seem to be exchange rate, inflation inertia and lagged money supply. The feedback from the short-run exchange rate movements to inflation is rather rapid. The statistically significant effect of the external sector disequilibrium in both specifications (of similar magnitude) was found. No evidence was found that the excess money supply affects inflation in the way implied by the monetarists models. The money market disequilibrium term does not enter the short-run inflation function. That may also mean that the money shocks do not have any impact on price stability, but are rather related to the velocity shifts that require simply a more accommodative stance. No impact of the mark-up disequilibrium term on inflation was found.

A significant impact of the exchange rate upon inflation in the short run, the existence of the long-run relationship between the exchange rate and prices and the significance of the external sector disequilibrium term in the inflation function may imply that the exchange rate is an important transmission channel of monetary policy to inflation. Consequently, the moderate inflation in recent years may be attributed to exchange rate stability (and positive expectations towards future exchange rates, and, eventually, prices) and lower foreign inflation. This finding is important in the view of another not well-functioning major transmission mechanism such as the interest rate. The significant effect of the foreign prices and exchange rate on the price level was found in the advanced transition economies as it has been mentioned above.

The slight impact of the monetary policy upon the inflation from the monetary aggregates as implied by the lagged money supply term directly, and by the insignificance of the money market disequilibrium term, on the one hand, and the existence of the long-run relationship between money, prices, exchange rate and real output, on the other hand, raises the question about the possible implications for the use of the monetary aggregates as a good intermediate target to achieve price stability. To derive some more precise conclusions about the link between money and prices, one should try to incorporate the money velocity changes into the model. Furthermore, at present, there seems to be no independent monetary policy in Ukraine as the money supply depends on the foreign currency inflow, which leads to the very limited control over inflation.

The major drawbacks of the applied cointegration technique are that, first of all, it has been applied in the presence of a rather short time span, data reliability problem and possible instability in the long-run relationships. The small sample does not allow considering a larger number of variables and lags in the short-run model. The major challenge was to model inflation dynamics in the midst of the structural changes in the economy and high administrative interference in the prices. The cointegration technique may be quite difficult to apply in economies that undergo structural changes (also dedollarization, demonetization, and so on), and in some years there could be some completely different long-run equilibrium. The break-down into the sub-samples is not quite appropriate for the meaningful analysis, since afterwards one ends up with the small sub-samples.

Second, each sector was estimated separately, thus, the biased estimators could be obtained. Potential alternatives could be estimating the long-run relationships based on a complete VAR model and the multi-equation short-run model afterwards, if the variables turn out to be endogenous, or focusing on one particular source of inflation. At the same time, the estimated macroeconomic model has been a step away from atheoretical VAR models.

This study has also been another attempt to estimate the demand for real cash balances, studies that are not so extensive for Ukraine, and the mark-up model. More research in this direction would be desirable. In general, I have modelled the demand factors only through the monetary side. The other demand-driven forces could come from the labour market (for example, estimation of the Phillips curve) or from the aggregate demand side. It could also be interesting to try to take explicitly into account the impact of the dedollarization effect through adding the amount of the foreign currency in circulation to the monetary aggregates (see, for example, Ohnsorge and Oomes, 2004, for the case of Russia), as well as to study the role of inflation and exchange rate expectations in the current inflation dynamics. Cointegration tests could be performed that account for the existence of a structural break (unknown vs. known), as, for example, the Gregory-Hansen (1996) test.

References

Banaian, K., Bolgarin, I.V. and de Menil, G. (1998), 'Inflation and Money in Ukraine', *Working Paper* No. 98-06, Paris: DELTA.
Betliy, O. (2002), *Measurement of the Real Effective Exchange Rate and the Observed J-curve: Case of Ukraine*, Master's thesis, unpublished, Kiev: EERC.
Bolgarin, I., Mahadeva, L. and Stern, G. (2000), 'Some Methodological Aspects of Developing and Applying the Model of Monetary Transmission Mechanism in Ukraine', *Visnyk NBU*, 11, 57:4-7.
De Brouwer, G. and Ericsson, N.R. (1995), 'Modeling Inflation in Australia', *Research Discussion Paper* No. 9510, Sydney: Economic Analysis and Economic Research Departments, Reserve Bank of Australia.
Fischer, S. and Sahay, R. (2000), 'The Transition Economies after Ten Years', *Working Paper* No. 00/30, Washington, DC: IMF.
Ganev, G., Molnar, K., Rybinski, K. and Wozniak, P. (2002), 'Transmission Mechanism of Monetary Policy in Central and Eastern Europe', *Reports* No. 52, Warsaw: CASE.

Ghosh, A.R. (1997), 'Inflation in Transition Economies: How Much? And Why?', *Working Paper* No. 97/80, Washington, DC: IMF.

Golinelli, R. and Orsi, R. (2002), 'Modeling Inflation in EU Accession Countries: The Case of the Czech Republic, Hungary and Poland', *Working Paper* No. 9, Berlin: Ezoneplus.

Gregory, A.W. and Hansen, B.E. (1996), 'Residual-based Tests for Cointegration in the Models with Regime Shifts', *Journal of Econometrics*, 70, 1: 99-126.

Harris, R.I.D. (1995), *Using Cointegration Analysis in Econometric Modelling*, Prentice Hall/Harvester Wheatsheaf.

Hendry, D.F. (2000), 'Does Money Determine UK Inflation over the Long Run?', in R. Backhouse and A. Salanti. (eds), *Macroeconomics and the Real World*, Oxford: Oxford University Press.

Institute for Economic Research and Policy Consulting (IER) (2001), *Summary of Presentation and Discussion During the Round Table 'Macroeconomic Indicators in Ukraine: Methodological Aspects'*, Kiev: IER.

Juselius, K. (1992), 'Domestic and Foreign Effects on Prices in an Open Economy: The Case of Denmark', *Journal of Policy Modelling*, 14, 4: 401-28.

Kim, B.-Y. (2001), 'Determinants of Inflation in Poland: A Structural Cointegration Approach', *Discussion Papers* No. 16, Helsinki: Bank of Finland, Institute for Economies in Transition, BOFIT.

Koen, V., and De Masi, P. (1997), 'Prices in the Transition: Ten Stylized Facts', *Working Paper* No. 97/158, Washington, DC: IMF.

Korhonen, I. (1998), 'A Vector Error Correction Model for Prices, Money, Output, and Interest Rate in Russia', *Review of Economies in Transition*, 5.

Kryuchkova, I. (2003), 'Price Competitiveness of Ukraine's Economy: Convergence of External and Internal Prices: Trends and Perspectives', *Visnyk NBU*, 9 (September): 6-9.

Kuijs, L. (2002), 'Monetary Policy Transmission Mechanisms and Inflation in the Slovak Republic', *Working Paper* No. 02/80, Washington, DC: IMF.

Lissovolik, B. (2003), 'Determinants of Inflation in a Transition Economy: The Case of Ukraine', *Working Paper* No. 03/126, Washington, DC: IMF.

Maliszewski, W. (2003), 'Modelling Inflation in Georgia', *Working Paper* No. 03/212, Washington, DC: IMF.

Mehra, J.P. (1991), 'Wage Growth and Inflation Process: An Empirical Note', *American Economic Review*, 81, 4: 931-37.

Metin, K. (1995), 'An Integrated Analysis of Turkish Inflation', *Oxford Bulletin of Economics and Statistics*, 57, 4: 513-31.

National Bank of Ukraine (2003), *Main Guidelines for Monetary Policy for 2004*, Kiev: NBU.

Ohnsorge, F., and Oomes, N. (2004), 'Inflation, Money Demand and De-Dollarization in Russia', in *IMF Country Report* No. 04/316, 'Russian Federation: Selected Issues', Washington, DC: IMF.

Phillips, P.C.B. (1994), 'Some Exact Distribution Theory for Maximum Likelihood Estimators of Cointegrating Coefficients in Error-Correction Models', *Econometrica*, 62, 1: 73-93.

Piontkivsky, R., Bakun, A., Kryshko, M. and Sytnyk, T. (2001), 'The Impact of the Budget Deficit in Ukraine', *Research report* commissioned by INTAS, Kiev: International Center for Policy Studies (ICPS).

Ranaweera, T. (2003), 'Market Disequilibria and Inflation in Uzbekistan, 1994-2000', *Policy Research Working Paper* No. 3144, Washington, DC: World Bank.

Revenko, A. (2002), 'About National Peculiarities of Inflation and CPI', *Financial Risks*, 4, 31: 20-25.

Schevchuk, V. (2001), 'The Influence of Monetary Policy on Industrial Production, Inflation and Real Exchange Rate in Ukraine in 1994-2000', *Visnyk NBU*, 1 (January): 12-15.

Chapter 14

Monetary and Exchange Rate Developments in Ukraine: Present and Future

Olena Bilan

Introduction

Over the recent decade inflation targeting regimes have become very popular in many countries. The success these regimes have had and the benefits they bring to the economy persuade more and more central bankers to shift from their current policies to inflation targeting. This concerns both relatively advanced countries and transition economies, such as Ukraine's. Adopting inflation targeting in Ukraine has been discussed by experts and policy makers for several years now. The local monetary authorities consider this option to be feasible over the medium-term. However, for this regime to be successful in a transition economy, it is very important that a set of preconditions be fulfilled. Among these are nominal exchange rate flexibility, absence of monetization of budget deficit, central bank independence and the ability of the central bank to control money supply, a clear understanding of monetary transmission mechanism, a sound and well-developed financial sector, accurate inflation forecasts, and so on (Mishkin, 2000; Carare, et al., 2002). In this chapter we discuss the past approach to monetary and exchange rate policies in Ukraine in order to assess the viability of an inflation targeting regime. We purposefully pay much attention to 'negative' aspects, that is, those that could create obstacles to a successful adoption of inflation targeting and hence require changes or improvements.

The chapter is organized as follows. Section one gives an historical overview of the exchange rate arrangements in Ukraine, discusses the major benefits that this regime has achieved, and describes the possible dangers that a quick change of the institutional environment may entail. Section two provides a description of the monetary policy framework, namely, the monetary policy goals and instruments at the disposal of the central bank. Section three addresses the mechanism of monetary transmission. The several econometric studies cited here shed light on the issue and contribute to a better understanding of the monetary policy framework in Ukraine. Section four summarizes the above and concludes with an evaluation of the feasibility of adopting an inflation targeting regime in Ukraine.

Exchange rate arrangements: An historical overview

When talking about the history of monetary and exchange rate developments in Ukraine it is useful to divide the duration into several periods. A convenient starting point for the first period would be October 1996 – the month when the new currency, the hryvnia, was introduced. Shortly after its introduction, the hryvnia was tied to the US dollar (first unofficially and then officially) using an exchange rate band (see Figure 14.1). Adoption of this regime contributed to stabilization of people's expectations and helped the Ukrainian government to progressively reduce turbulent inflation. However, in late 1997/early 1998 the Ukrainian government started to borrow actively at the domestic and foreign markets in order to finance the budget deficit. These borrowings were conducted in an unsustainable manner and were among the main causes for the financial crisis that Ukraine experienced in August 1998.

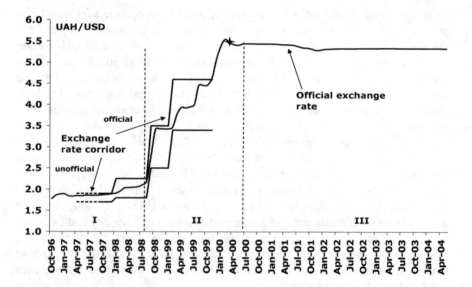

Figure 14.1   UAH/USD exchange rate (monthly average)

Source: NBU.

Note: Vertical dashed lines separate periods; star denotes de-jure adoption of a free floating exchange rate regime.

The second period (from late 1998 to mid 2000) started with the reaction to the 1998 crisis. The hryvnia was devalued sharply (by 60 per cent over two months) causing a considerable loss of confidence by the population in its national currency and further progress in the dollarization process. The growth rate of prices accelerated substantially as well (see Figure 14.2).

Only during the second half of 2000 did the foreign exchange market stabilize. At that point the Ukrainian economy entered the third period (mid 2000 to 2003) with a stable exchange rate vis-à-vis the US dollar. At the same time Ukraine officially announced it would switch from the managed peg to a free floating exchange rate regime. However, de facto the National Bank of Ukraine (NBU) has been keeping the exchange rate at an almost constant level with respect to the US dollar, which can be considered as an implicit exchange rate peg.

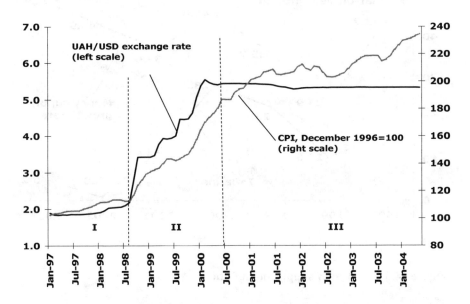

Figure 14.2   Exchange rate and consumer prices

Source: NBU, State Statistics Committee of Ukraine, own calculations.
Note: Vertical dashed lines separate periods.

Thus, even after the official regime shift the monetary policy remained almost fully subordinated to the exchange rate policy, and the growth rate of money supply was determined by current account and capital account balances. Thus, the large current account surplus in the year 2000 and thereafter promoted a considerable monetary expansion. Notwithstanding the sizeable growth rates of money supply of 40-45 per cent per year, inflation has remained at a one-digit rate (see Figure 14.3).

The adoption of an implicit exchange rate peg regime right after the sharp devaluation period was undoubtedly beneficial for the economy, and that for several reasons. First, it helped to stabilize the people's expectations regarding the exchange rate and in this way promoted the de-dollarization process. As Figure 14.4 demonstrates, dollarization of the banking sector did indeed start to decrease in 2000. The increase in net sales of foreign cash by the population indicates that the same trend took place in the non-banking sector. Second, it helped to reduce inflation (i) through stabilization of the inflation expectation, which are closely linked to expectations regarding future exchange rates, and (ii) by lowering the prices of imported goods.

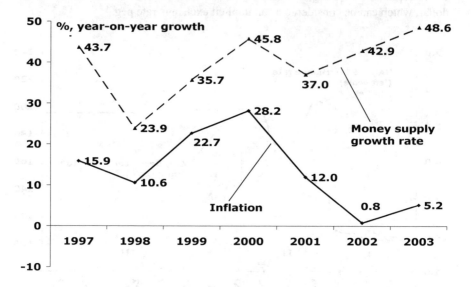

Figure 14.3   Money supply and inflation

Source: NBU, State Statistics Committee of Ukraine, own calculations.
Note: Average year-on-year figures are shown.

While keeping the exchange rate constant was certainly a necessary and a wise step right after the crisis, the disadvantages of such an exchange rate regime outweigh the benefits more and more as the economy develops. Continuing this policy into the future may even lead to a dangerous situation for the following reasons.

First, and most importantly, the growth rate of the money supply depends to a large extend on the inflow of foreign currency. Supporting the exchange rate at a certain level requires the NBU to promote the inflow of foreign currency, thus fuelling the economy with additional amounts of money. Taking into account that Ukraine has a large current account surplus, there is a danger of monetary overhang. As will be shown in the next section, the sterilization abilities of the central bank remain quite limited, implying that monetary effect on inflation is almost completely out of the hands of the NBU.

Second, this policy introduces distortions on the credit market. In particular, when taking decisions about borrowing, economic agents do not take the exchange rate risk into account and tend to borrow in foreign currency, while receiving profits/incomes in national currency.

Third, the longer such policy is continued, the more it is perceived as a commitment. As a result, each minor fluctuation of the exchange rate will tend to generate panic.

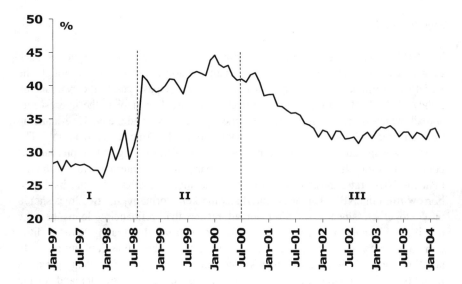

Figure 14.4   Dollarization of the Ukrainian banking sector

Source: NBU, own calculations.
Note: measured as the ratio of foreign currency deposits to total deposits.

Monetary policy framework

The official goal of monetary policy as stated in the Constitution of Ukraine and in the Law on the Central Bank is to provide 'stability for the national currency'. In practice, the NBU Council adopts a document each year, called 'Main Guidelines of Monetary Policy', which sets out a list of projected monetary policy indicators for the coming year. These indicators concern inflation, growth rates of the money supply and the monetary base, and the exchange rate level. However, there is no commitment to achieve any of the projected indicators. Thus, the projected indicators are usually revised and adjusted to reflect the actual situation towards the end of the year. In other words, there is no clearly defined monetary policy goal that the central bank is trying to achieve. The same concerns the intermediate targets (or so called 'operating guide'). The NBU officials do not define what indicators they use as intermediate targets.

When conducting monetary policy the NBU uses a standard set of instruments: (i) standing facilities, (ii) open-market-type operations, and (iii) reserve requirements. While the list of available instruments is quite impressive on paper, in practice the NBU has a limited ability to conduct a flexible monetary policy in practice. To understand why this is so, let us consider each instrument separately.

Standing facilities

The NBU provides the banking sector with several types of refinancing loans, such as a constantly operating credit line, credit auctions, and so on. Although the variety of refinancing loans has increased over the past years, the refinancing policy of the NBU remains quite ineffective. Figure 14.5 depicts the interest rate spread, which is the difference between the interbank rate and the NBU refinancing rate, and the volume of refinancing loans provided during a given month. The interest rate spread shows the relative bank costs of borrowing at the interbank as compared to the NBU. A positive spread means that the interbank rate is higher than the NBU rate, thus, it is less costly (and more beneficial for the banks) to borrow from the NBU than at the interbank market. Normally, the two lines should move together, since a growing spread means that refinancing loans become relatively cheaper. However, as can be seen from the graph there is little correlation between the two lines except for the November 2003 liquidity crisis. In addition, most of the time the interest rate spread was negative, indicating excess liquidity in the banking sector and, as a consequence, a very low demand for the NBU's standing facilities. In such circumstances the NBU is practically deprived of the possibility to use this instrument of monetary policy.

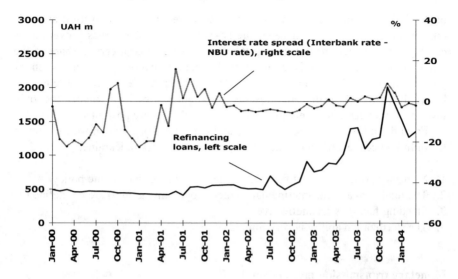

Figure 14.5   Interest rate spread and volume of refinancing loans

Source: NBU, own calculations.

Open-market-type operations

The NBU was able to use traditional government bonds for open market purchases and sales only before the August 1998 crisis. After the collapse of the government bonds market, the banks' demand for them died out and has not revived until today. Consequently, government bonds are no longer used for monetary policy purposes.

To improve the situation in 1999 the NBU introduced an alternative instrument, the so-called certificates of deposit (Grebenyk, 1999) and used them quite actively throughout 2000. The certificates of deposit (CDs) are short-term securities issued by the central bank and distributed only among banks for sterilization purposes. The CDs pay interest to the holder and hence a net increase in the money supply is created whenever a security is due. This feature and the short-term nature of the CDs represent a major disadvantage as compared to government bonds. Thus, CDs do not greatly improve the sterilization capacity of the NBU.

Reserves requirement

Before 2002 the reserves requirement ratio (RRR) in Ukraine was unified for all deposit types and actively used for monetary policy purposes (especially in post-crisis periods of 1998-1999). In 2002 it became differentiated, depending on the type of deposits; but the unified RRR was reintroduced again in late 2004. Now the monetary authorities recognize that the instrument is very powerful and costly for banks, hence, at this time changes in the reserve requirement ratio itself are used only in exceptional cases. Instead, the so-called required reserves 'covering' is employed for money market tuning. 'Covering' means that a certain share of the required reserves, which is allowed to be held ('covered') in vault cash or government bonds (for example, 20 per cent of required reserves can be 'covered' by vault cash). Basically, the reserve requirements policy remains the only instrument that can effectively influence the banks' liquidity positions.

From the information discussed here and in the previous section we can draw a list of inferences regarding the monetary policy framework in Ukraine:

1. Monetary policy is almost fully subordinated to the exchange rate policy
2. The final goal and the intermediate targets ('operating guide') are not defined
3. Standing facilities are ineffective
4. The sterilization ability is very limited.

Monetary transmission mechanism

It is commonly held that the monetary transmission mechanism (MTM) – the way through which money propagates into the real economy – is quite poorly understood in Ukraine. As a result, when conducting monetary policy, that is, when choosing when to expand or when to contract the money supply, and by how much, monetary authorities usually rely upon gut feelings or rules of thumb, rather than upon a clear understanding of the likely consequences of their actions. To successfully conduct monetary policy it is crucial to know how and through which mechanisms policy actions will affect the real economy.

The economic literature proposes quite a long list of channels through which monetary expansion may transform the real sector. They can be conveniently grouped as follows (Mishkin, 1996):

1. The traditional interest rate channel
2. Other asset price channels
   a. The exchange rate channel
   b. The equity price channel (Tobin's Q theory, wealth effect)
3. Credit channels
   a. The bank lending channel
   b. The balance sheet channel
   c. The cash flow channel
   d. The unanticipated price level channel
   e. The household liquidity channel.

However, most of these channels cannot operate in Ukraine because of specific institutional arrangements. All of the listed channels, except three (interest rate, bank lending, and exchange rate), presuppose well-developed stock markets. Since the stock market in Ukraine is very shallow (with a capitalization of about ten per cent of GDP), channels that rely on stock prices are implausible. Of the three remaining channels, the exchange rate channel, which presupposes flexible exchange rates, can also not work in Ukraine since there have been no exchange rate fluctuations since 2000. Hence, we are left with the traditional interest rate channel and bank lending channel.[1] There is a possibility that both of them may operate in Ukraine; yet a formal investigation would be needed to confirm that they do indeed work in practice.

There is very little empirical evidence on MTM in Ukraine; however, several studies shed some light on the two above-mentioned channels. Bilan (2002) made an attempt to investigate the first part of the interest rate channel, the so-called liquidity effect hypothesis, which stipulates that exogenous monetary expansion leads to a reduction of nominal interest rate. The evidence is based on the semi-structural VAR model, which incorporates specific features of monetary policy in Ukraine. The results strongly support the hypothesis that an exogenous monetary policy shock reduces the short-term interest rate, giving grounds to believe that the interest rate channel may operate in Ukraine. The bank lending channel was explored in depth by Kryshko (2001). His macro-evidence based on a vector error correction model supported the existence of the bank lending channel, while the micro-evidence based on a panel-data model appeared to be rather inconclusive.

As we can see, although there is some empirical evidence in favour of both channels, the issue still requires more research in order to reveal the complete picture of the ways through which money affects real variables.

Inflation targeting: Is it plausible in Ukraine?

Now we can summarize all the information above to ask whether Ukraine is ready to adopt inflation targeting. Table 14.1 lists the preconditions stated in Carare, et al. (2002)[2], which are required to successfully adopt an inflation targeting framework. It should be noted that switching to inflation targeting might be quite successful even if some of the conditions are not fulfilled.[3] However, it is not likely

---

[1] The interest rate channel emanates from the traditional Keynesian IS-LM model. Here monetary expansion leads to a fall in real interest rates, which in turn lowers the cost of capital, causing a rise in investment spending, thereby leading to an increase in output. The bank lending channel works as follows: an expansionary monetary policy, which increases bank reserves and bank deposits, increases the quantity of bank loans available; more loans stimulate investment activity and, consequently, real output.

[2] We omit the first group of conditions that concern the mandate to pursue the inflation objective and the accountability of the central bank, since they can be fulfilled later when designing the strategies for adopting inflation targeting.

[3] Russia is one of the examples where inflation targeting has been quite successful in spite of a not fully independent central bank and a vulnerable financial system, among others.

that the benefits of inflation targeting will outweigh the costs if a substantial number of the prerequisites is not in place.

Table 14.1   Prerequisites for adoption of inflation targeting

	Fulfilled (+)/ Not (-)	Comment
Macroeconomic stability		
No fiscal dominance	+	Purchases of government bonds by the NBU at the primary market was prohibited by Law in 1999. Since then monetization of budget deficit has not taken place, although there is some pressure from the fiscal authorities.
Strong external position	+	The NBU has accumulated a sufficient amount of foreign exchange reserves (3.4 months of import as of April 2004). The regulation of foreign exchange transactions is very strict and almost fully excludes speculative operations.
Low inflation rate	+	As shown in Figure 14.3, inflation in 2002-2003 has reduced to a modest level.
Financial system development and stability	-	Although some development of corporate bonds market was observed in 2003, the stock market as well as the market for government bonds remain very shallow and illiquid.
Conduct of monetary policy		
Monetary goal and instruments	-	In section two we concluded that the monetary goal and the intermediate targets are not defined. In addition, the NBU has a limited ability to affect the money market situation because of a lack of efficient instruments for monetary policy. Given the instability and the unpredictability of money demand this may contribute to excess monetary pressure on prices to which the central bank will not be able to respond.

Transmission of monetary policy	-	The stronger the transmission links and the better they are understood, the easier it will be for the central bank to steer inflation to the desirable level. As we saw in section three, the understanding of the MTM in Ukraine is very poor.
Exchange rate policy	-	It was demonstrated in section one that since 2000 the NBU has pursued a policy of targeting the nominal exchange rate (implicit peg). This is absolutely incompatible with an inflation targeting regime that presupposes that the inflation target has precedence over any other objective.
Inflation forecasting	-	There are at least two major problems that make inflation forecasts in Ukraine very imprecise. First, there is no core inflation index or some alternative, which would help tracking the effect of monetary policy on the price level. Second, the Ukrainian economy is characterized by a high degree of state interventions in price formation mechanisms.
Coordination issues	-	The coordination between the fiscal and monetary authorities is very weak. The most frequently debated issue is the unpredictable management of the state treasury account within the central bank, which strongly and unexpectedly affects liquidity positions of the banking sector.

From the information provided in Table 14.1 we can conclude that the adoption of inflation targeting is hardly feasible for Ukraine in the short-run. Although Ukraine has reached macroeconomic stability in terms of a low inflation rate, the absence of fiscal dominance and a strong external position, the underdevelopment of its financial markets and, more importantly, the inability of the central bank to conduct monetary policy effectively, the subordination of the monetary policy to an exchange rate anchor, and the limited knowledge about monetary transmission mechanism make it doubtful that adoption of an inflation targeting regime could be successful in the near future. However, should the monetary authorities and the government undertake serious steps towards satisfying the listed conditions the

Ukrainian economy might, in the medium-term, gain all the benefits an inflation targeting regime can offer.

References

Bilan, O. (2002), 'Is There a Liquidity Eeffect in the Ukrainian Interbank Market?', *EERC MA Thesis Paper*, NaUKMA.

Carare, A., Schaechter, A., Stone, M., and Zelmer, M. (2002), 'Establishing Initial Conditions in Support of Inflation Targeting', *IMF Working Paper*, 02/102.

Grebenyk, N. (1999), 'The Certificate of Deposit of the National Bank of Ukraine', *Visnyk NBU*, 12, 7 (Депозитний сертифікат Національного банку України, Вісник НБУ, No. 12).

Kryshko, M. (2001), 'Bank Lending Channels and Monetary Transmission Mechanism in Ukraine', *EERC MA Thesis Paper*, NaUKMA.

Mishkin, F.S. (1996), 'The Channels of Monetary Transmission: Lessons for Monetary Policy', *NBER Working Paper*, 5464.

Mishkin, F.S. (2000), 'Inflation Targeting in Emerging-Market Countries', *American Economic Review*, 105-9.

Index

University of Plymouth Library

Subject to status this item may be renewed
via your Voyager account
http://voyager.plymouth.ac.uk
Tel: (01752) 232323